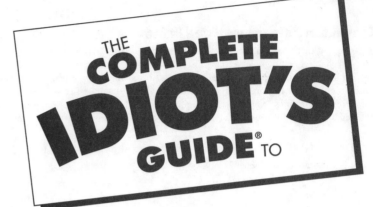

THE
COMPLETE
IDIOT'S
GUIDE® TO

Submarines

by Michael DiMercurio
and Michael Benson

ALPHA
A Pearson Education Company

International Standard Book Number: 0-02-864471-9
Library of Congress Catalog Card Number: 2002115729

04 03 02   8 7 6 5 4 3 2 1

Interpretation of the printing code: The rightmost number of the first series of numbers is the year of the book's printing; the rightmost number of the second series of numbers is the number of the book's printing. For example, a printing code of 02-1 shows that the first printing occurred in 2002.

Printed in the United States of America

For marketing and publicity, please call: 317-581-3722

The publisher offers discounts on this book when ordered in quantity for bulk purchases and special sales.

For sales within the United States, please contact: Corporate and Government Sales, 1-800-382-3419 or corpsales@pearsontechgroup.com.

Outside the United States, please contact: International Sales, 317-581-3793 or international@pearsontechgroup.com.

Publisher: *Marie Butler-Knight*
Product Manager: *Phil Kitchel*
Managing Editor: *Jennifer Chisholm*
Acquisitions Editor: *Gary Goldstein*
Development Editor: *Joan D. Paterson*
Production Editor: *Katherin Bidwell*
Copy Editor: *Krista Hansing*
Illustrator: *Barbara Field*
Cartoonist: *Chris Eliopoulos*
Cover/Book Designer: *Trina Wurst*
Indexer: *Brad Herriman*
Layout/Proofreading: *John Etchison, Becky Harmon*

Contents at a Glance

.

Contents

Foreword

Submarines and the men who operate them are enigmas. Like the multimasted men-of-war that ruled the age of sail, these complex and expensive machines embody all of mankind's technical achievements up to the date of their design. Crammed into compact, self-sufficient vessels are the latest developments in sensors, weapons, communications, navigation, propulsion, and life support, along with highly trained crews. The ships and their men leave port, disappear from view, and go on their own to any place on the world's oceans. Once there, they remain for long periods while charting the unexplored, gathering intelligence, or attacking enemy ships and shore points. Inside their hulls, sailors work, eat, and sleep, then work again, confined to small spaces while roaming a vast expanse. And each man knows that in time of peril he must calmly face whatever the challenge, relying solely on his abilities and those of his crewmates, for it is unlikely that anyone else could reach the ship quickly enough to save it.

The same laws of nature govern the operation of all submarines—from the smallest research submersible to the largest ballistic missile boat. However, the ability to work under the sea did not come about overnight. The required technology evolved slowly. Even as Archimedes was quantifying the fundamental principles used in submarine design—buoyancy, displacement, and moving fluids about—ancient Greek sponge divers had dreams of walking on the ocean's floor and traveling in undersea ships. But it was not until 1776, during the American Revolutionary War, that the *Turtle*, a small human-propelled wooden egg, traveled hidden across a harbor, allowing the one man inside the boat to plant an explosive charge on the hull of an enemy ship. Only during the last 150 years did the submarine become a true warship. European and U.S. navies began their current fleets in the early 1900s, and the world watched in awe as rapid advances in hull materials, mechanical and electrical equipment, and undersea warfare transformed the submarine from a curiosity into a steely killer from the deep.

The basic tenets of submarine warfare are also simple. They are little changed from the days of the *Turtle*, and combine the human element with the technology of the machine. To be an effective weapon, a submarine and its crew must:

- Remain undetected—stealth is the submarine's major advantage.

- Get close and shoot first—long shots have low odds of success.

- Maintain propulsion—without motion, a submarine is a sitting duck, and it will eventually sink to the bottom.

- Be highly trained—things happen fast underwater; everyone must know what to do in any situation and be willing to do it without hesitation.

- Fix everything that breaks—otherwise, it won't be ready when needed.

What puzzles us is how these mysterious ships are designed, built, and operated, and why someone would voluntarily spend a part of his life aboard one. *The Complete Idiot's Guide to Submarines* answers those riddles and more in terms that are easy to understand. This is a unique and fascinating look at these undersea vessels and their invaluable role in defending the United States.

—Lee Vyborny, co-author of *Dark Waters: An Insider's Account of the NR-1, the Cold War's Undercover Nuclear Sub,* and one of the original 12 crew members on the NR-1

Introduction

When I reported to Navy Nuclear Power School and later to Submarine School, I had hoped that someone would give me a book that started from the beginning. Instead, both courses of study ripped right in, assuming that the student had been sailing on a naval vessel since birth. I hungered for something that would be able to explain something as complicated and wonderful as a nuclear submarine to someone who is interested but who is not a nuclear engineer, and who would find engineering boring.

I tested all the explanations in this book on my model for the interested but nontechnical reader, my beloved son, Matthew DiMercurio. While Matt is talented in science and math, he—at the time—was 13 but so full of questions he could keep me talking for hours. My challenge was to describe these cool machines to someone who didn't know what differential equations were. As my novels gained popularity, I continued to hear from readers by e-mail, many of them asking technical questions about the submarine (what is an anechoic coating and why is it used?). I spent many hours patiently and—I hope—humorously explaining the boat to the interested but nontechnical reader. When I was asked if I was interested in a project like this, I jumped on it. The result is this book—a look at how to operate a nuclear submarine, starting from the very beginning. I hope that someday this becomes required reading at U.S. Navy Submarine School.

The Complete Idiot's Guide to Submarines is a comprehensive initiation into the world of the modern nuclear submarine. It takes a detailed look at modern submarines and contains an exhaustively researched history, from the first submersibles to today's nuclear subs. An extensive look at submarines in battle and tips for future submariners also is included.

Don't worry—while submarines are some of the most complex machines on the planet, you won't find yourself out of your depth. Even an admiral will be able to understand these explanations.

What You'll Find in This Book

Following a quick room-by-room tour of a modern state-of-the-art U.S. Navy submarine, you'll learn the fundamentals of how a submarine works (why does it sometimes float and sometimes sink?). We'll talk about how submarine emergencies (including fire, flood, and nuclear reactor accidents) are handled.

You'll learn about how submarines and nuclear power became a match, and we'll take a detailed look at the sensor systems and weapons systems in today's subs. I'll explain how you would operate a nuclear submarine, and finally we'll take a look at the history of subs, dating all the way back to the American Revolution.

Part 1, "To Swim Like a Fish: Touring a Submarine," is where you'll learn your way around. We start with a guided tour of a modern nuclear submarine.

Part 2, "The Atomic Age," explains how the splitting of the atom led to a most efficient powerplant for the modern submarine.

Part 3, "How Nuclear Subs Work," teaches you about a submarine's eyes and ears, as well as how it attacks and defends itself.

Part 4, "Operating a Nuclear Submarine," puts you in charge. There are a lot of rules that need to be learned and skills to be developed, but we think you're ready. It's much more fun than driving a car.

Part 5, "Subs at War," offers a strategic guide to both the U.S. "fast-attack" subs and submarine missile systems.

Part 6, "The History of Submarines," takes you from the first submersibles of the nineteenth century to the beginning of the nuclear era.

Extras

Along the way, you'll see boxes containing information designed to aid your learning experience.

Mike's Corner

You'll find some of my own personal observations and stories under this heading.

Beneath the Surface

Here you will find observations that lend a perhaps unexpected insight into the subject matter.

Subtalk

This sidebar helps define inside submarine terminology.

Secrets of the Deep

This sidebar explains unexpected facts.

Trademarks

All terms mentioned in this book that are known to be or are suspected of being trademarks or service marks have been appropriately capitalized. Alpha Books and Pearson Education, Inc., cannot attest to the accuracy of this information. Use of a term in this book should not be regarded as affecting the validity of any trademark or service mark.

Part 1

To Swim Like a Fish: Touring a Submarine

The very word "submarine" evokes dark, smoky combat scenes, sonar pings, bearded haggard men fighting far at sea in desperate battles. Or modern nuclear sailors, surrounded by nuclear tipped missiles, guardians of the peace and waiting for battle. Today will be a great adventure, because today you will park the car in the visitor lot at Submarine Squadron Eight and walk down the pier to take a nuclear submarine to sea. During your voyage, you'll wonder which is more fascinating—the greatest war-fighting machine on the planet, the men who take her to sea, or the procedures for winning in combat far beneath the waves.

Take your last deep breath of fresh air and prepare to "take her down" to where the enemy and the sea conspire to make sure you won't come back, but where the skills of the crew and the designers who crafted this magnificent ship even the odds.

See you at test depth!

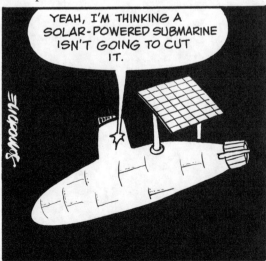

A Tour Before Diving

In This Chapter

- Greetings from Pier 22
- Getting oriented—shape, size, and smell
- How a submarine works
- Meeting the crew

Welcome to your tour of a state-of-the-art U.S. Navy nuclear submarine. You are standing on Pier 22 of Norfolk Naval Station in the Tidewater section of the state of Virginia. The pier is a long jetty of concrete, stretching westward into the Elizabeth River from the high-security checkpoint next to the towering structure of the haze-gray tender ship. (The tender ship is a gray-painted old-fashioned cruise ship, but instead of deck chairs and parlors, there are parts bins and machine shops; instead of dining halls, there are offices and conference rooms. This is where the squadron organization lives and works, and every year or so it will go to sea, just to prove the screw still rotates.)

Your destination is the end of the pier, where the sole in-port submarine of Submarine Squadron 8 is tied up—all the other units of the squadron are already deployed at sea. The USS *Hampton*, SSN-767, is preparing to get underway for a rapid-deployment exercise, and you are lucky enough to be sailing with the crew. (SSN means Submersible Ship Nuclear, a fast-attack (hunter killer) submarine, although the Submarine Force insists this stands for Saturdays, Sundays and Nights.)

Sleek, Black, and Dangerous in the Water

The *Hampton* is in the Los Angeles class of submarine. The class of submarine is always named after the first ship to be built in this style. The lead ship of the class, in other words, was the USS *Los Angeles*.

The first thing you notice about the Los Angeles–class submarine is her sleek shape as she lies tied up to the pier. The hull (the outer shell of the submarine) is long and cylindrical and black, with only the top few feet protruding above the dark water of the slip.

Subtalk

Sound-absorbing coating is called **anechoic,** which would seem to mean "no echo." The foam lessens, or attenuates, inside noises from getting out and absorbs incoming sonar pings from active sonars. We stole this technology from the Russians, who invented it first.

The skin of the ship is made of a slippery *anechoic* foam, a sound-absorbing coating. When you step off the gangway onto the deck, it feels like you are stepping onto the back of a whale.

Above the hull is the sail—formerly called the conning tower on this submarine's ancestors—a 20-foot-tall fin housing the masts and antennae and periscopes. As you look forward, the hull sinks into the water at the elliptical curve of the bullet-nosed bow.

Aft (the back of the sub) behind the sail, the hull continues for half a football field before sloping gradually into the water. Fifteen feet from where the hull vanishes, the rudder sticks up from the waves like a disembodied airplane tail, its black paint and draft markings the only clue that it belongs to the ship.

The topside watch—called a watchstander (a sailor in a crackerjack uniform)—welcomes you to the ship and calls below to the duty officer, a young man in his mid-20s in a khaki uniform, who steps out of a hatch aft of (that is, behind) the sail.

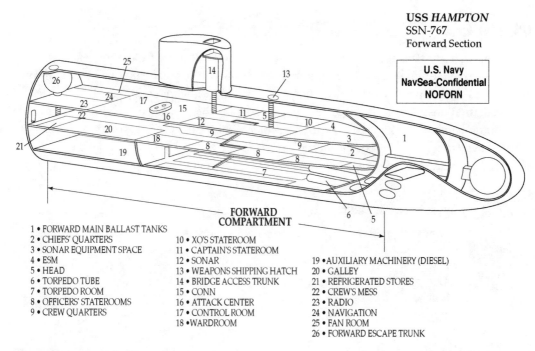

USS *HAMPTON*
SSN-767
Forward Section

U.S. Navy
NavSea-Confidential
NOFORN

FORWARD
COMPARTMENT

1 • FORWARD MAIN BALLAST TANKS
2 • CHIEFS' QUARTERS
3 • SONAR EQUIPMENT SPACE
4 • ESM
5 • HEAD
6 • TORPEDO TUBE
7 • TORPEDO ROOM
8 • OFFICERS' STATEROOMS
9 • CREW QUARTERS

10 • XO'S STATEROOM
11 • CAPTAIN'S STATEROOM
12 • SONAR
13 • WEAPONS SHIPPING HATCH
14 • BRIDGE ACCESS TRUNK
15 • CONN
16 • ATTACK CENTER
17 • CONTROL ROOM
18 • WARDROOM

19 • AUXILIARY MACHINERY (DIESEL)
20 • GALLEY
21 • REFRIGERATED STORES
22 • CREW'S MESS
23 • RADIO
24 • NAVIGATION
25 • FAN ROOM
26 • FORWARD ESCAPE TRUNK

Forward section of the Hampton.

Duties of the Duty Officer

The duty officer is a dolphin-wearing, qualified-in-submarines commissioned officer who is in command of the submarine when the ship is in port. (Dolphin-wearing because all sailors qualified in submarines wear a patch or pin resembling pilot's wings, except the design is two scaly fish facing a diesel sub plowing through the waves.) The duty officer acts on behalf of the commanding officer (the CO, or captain), even when the captain is onboard. Although the captain remains in command of the ship, the duty officer takes care of the details. His main duty: knowing where his authority ends and the captain's begins. It is a sad day when the duty officer exceeds that authority and fails to call the captain. Not even the second-in-command, the executive officer (XO), can tell the duty officer what to do. Reporting to the duty officer are the duty chief, the engineering duty officer, and other inport watchstanders.

The biggest job of a duty officer is preparing the submarine to get underway. Even if the ship departs at 1:00 in the afternoon (1300 hours), the duty officer has an all-nighter because launching a space shuttle has a simpler countdown checklist than launching a nuclear sub.

Down Ladder—Entering Feet First

The watchstander introduces himself as Lieutenant Phillips and hands you a plastic device resembling a cigarette lighter that he asks you to wear on your belt at all times. He explains that it is a thermoluminescent dosimeter, which will record your total radiation dose during the journey. The lieutenant then leads you to the 25-inch-wide upper hatch, a thick metal lid with a thinner steel fairing, and instructs you to shout "down ladder" before you proceed down into the hull. (A "fairing" is a skin of metal or fiberglass over an object to streamline it to the hull.)

> **Secrets of the Deep** _____
>
> Perhaps the most striking sensation when you first enter a submarine is the smell! It is a strange brew of diesel fuel, diesel exhaust ("on a nuclear submarine?" you ask yourself), cooking oil, lubrication oil, and two other smells that the duty officer explains to be ozone from the high-voltage electrical systems and amines from the atmospheric control systems. All in all, it is a pleasant smell, an immediate reminder that you are standing on the deckplates of a combat fast-attack nuclear submarine.

You tentatively step down into the dark maw of the opening, your feet feeling for the rungs of the ladder leading you into the beast, the oily steel of the hatch ring cool and smooth. You step down into a 10-foot-tall airlock, called the forward escape trunk, a deck-tall cylinder with a hatch at the bottom.

You lower yourself through the opening of the lower hatch. Your first sensations are the sounds of the ship, a high-pitched, 400-cycle whine of the forward electronic systems and the baritone growl of the air handlers. The harsh sunshine pier-side is gone, replaced by the relative dimness of fluorescent lighting.

At the base of the ladder, you look around at what appears to be a cozy restaurant, which the duty officer explains is the crew's mess. A dozen booths are arranged on one side of the room, with the food service area on the other.

The ceiling is low, a perforated beige metal. The walls—the bulkheads—are a wood-grain laminate trimmed in stainless steel, much like a cross-continental train compartment.

The crew is cleaning up from breakfast and manning their stations—maneuvering watches—for the *ship*'s departure in one hour. You catch a glimpse of the crowded galley and then are hustled down a narrow corridor that leads forward—that is, toward the front of the sub.

Subtalk

The **ship** is a boat, and the boat is a ship. Submarines are quite properly called ships because they are vessels that displace more than a thousand tons. But the tradition of the old days is never forgotten, from when submarines were tiny and were *not* ships. Back in World Wars I and II, submarines were correctly called *boats*. The terms are almost interchangeable, but not quite. You "surface the ship," "submerge the ship," and "rig ship for dive," but the leading chief is the "chief of the boat" and training for the unqualified is the "school of the boat." By the way, never ever call a Navy destroyer, frigate, cruiser, or, God help you, aircraft carrier a "boat"—you'll be laughed off the ... *ship*.

The Reactor Is Critical

You duck your head into the wardroom, a combination officers' mess, conference room, and briefing room, and then go past the officers' staterooms, which are small cubbyholes with three coffinlike bunks stacked on top of each other, fold-down desks, and a fold-down sink. On the other side of the passageway is the empty crew quarters, with four bunks closed off by privacy curtains stacked up on either side of a central passage.

Suddenly a speaker in the ceiling—the "overhead"—crackles and a booming voice reverberates throughout the compartment: "The reactor is critical!"

The duty officer explains that the reactor is being started and that at this point the bomb-grade, uranium-fueled core is splitting atoms of uranium fast enough to generate a steady high level of neutrons—subatomic particles ejected during the splitting of an atom.

Visiting the Torpedo Room

Soon the engineroom will be started up and the ship will "divorce from shorepower," which means it will soon be on its way. The duty officer tells you to hold any further questions for the tour of the engineering spaces, and he leads you further down the passageway to the "goat locker," the chief petty officers' quarters, a suite that includes a crowded sleeping area and a small lounge. The duty officer leads you back down the passageway to the ladder to the lower level, where you emerge into the torpedo room.

The room is quiet, cool, and cavelike, the dim lighting illuminating the shiny green all-business bodies of the Mark 48 ADCAP torpedoes and the encapsulated Tomahawk cruise missiles.

Forward in the compartment are the four torpedo tubes, nestled in a tangle of piping, valves, and cables. The torpedo control console and the vertical launch panels seem to have more controls than a fighter jet cockpit.

You are led back between the racks stacked full of deadly-looking weapons to peek into the oily-smelling auxiliary machinery compartment where a hulking gigantic engine fills the room, tucked in a cocoon of piping, valves, cables, and electrical panels.

The duty officer explains that this is the emergency diesel engine—the source of much of the air's aroma—which will save the ship in the event of reactor trouble.

Sounding Out the Sonar and Control Rooms

Back up the stairs to the middle level and up the next steep flight to the upper level, you emerge into a narrow laminate-walled passageway. At the passageway's end forward is the sonar equipment space, a humming set of tall cabinets in an otherwise deserted room. The adjoining space is a cubbyhole called the ESM, the *electronic countermeasures* cubicle.

You are shown the executive officer's stateroom and the captain's stateroom, two tiny sea cabins each about 10 feet square. Then you are ushered into the darkened and hushed sonar room. It reminds you of pictures of an air traffic control center, with four consoles featuring multiple video screens.

You meet the sonar chief, who tells you briefly about the screens above the background whine of the 400-cycle power. From here you are led to the heart of the submarine—the control room.

The room is smaller than the kitchen in your house, a cramped space filled with piping, cables, valves, and consoles. The center of the room is taken up by the elevated periscope stand, where two side-by-side periscopes are manned by navigation technicians taking visual measurements of landmarks to establish a navigation position, called a "fix." A fix is established using visual landmarks when near land, or from the GPS navigation satellites. The large unit on the port side is the SINS, or Ship's Inertial Navigation System. This equipment doesn't get a fix, but it does a decent job of guessing where the ship is based on the last fix.

Aft of the railed periscope stand are two *plotting tables*, each with a chart of the seaway leading out of Norfolk. The duty officer shows the track leading to the Atlantic through the two bridge-tunnel channels while he scans the weather report and the current and tide listing.

On the port side of the room—on the left as you face forward, or the bow—is a cluster of chairs at a console that reminds you of the cockpit of a 747. Two pilot seats are set behind a tall, sloping console, with airplane-style control yokes. Be-tween the seats is another low console, and behind that is a third seat.

"The watchstander who will sit on the port side is the sternplanesman," the duty officer says. "He will control the horizontal fins back aft at the screw, called the sternplanes, sort of like the elevator controls on an airplane. We won't need him until we're submerging. The watchstander on the inboard side is the helmsman, controlling the rudder and the ship's course on orders from the officer of the deck and, once we dive, the bowplanes."

Further to the left is a seat at a wraparound L-shape console, which, like the other panels, is choked with instrumentation, buttons, levers, and toggle switches. Further aft, in the middle of the room's port-side consoles are the navigation equipment stations.

The duty officer leads you to the starboard (right) side of the room, where a long console of control stations and seats is laid out. This is the attack center, a cluster of fire-control computer stations used for targeting enemy submarines and surface ships, and the weapon control panel used to line up and program torpedo tubes, torpedoes, and cruise missiles.

Subtalk

The **plotting tables** are maps by which the conning officer and the navigator plot the ship's position and **PIM (point of intended motion)**. Surface ship sailors (**skimmer pukes**) don't call the ship's intended motion PIM; they call it the ship's **track**.

Secrets of the Deep

The U.S. fleet has almost 70 submarines. Russia has approximately the same number.

Meeting the (Annoyingly Youthful) Captain

As you are looking at a display screen, the duty officer comes to attention and greets the ship's commanding officer, the captain. The captain shakes your hand, and you notice that he seems young to be in command of one of the Navy's frontline submarines. But though he is not yet 40, he carries himself with a quiet authority that seems to fill the room.

Secrets of the Deep

Onboard a submarine, it is vital that there is never a misunderstanding during the exchange of permission requests and orders: A botched order could be fatal at depth. Certain words are not used aboard the ship, such as the word *close*. You never "close" a door on a submarine—you "shut" the door. *Close* sounds too much like the word *blow* on an internal communication circuit in a high-noise environment, and *blow* means that the ship is flooding and needs to do an immediate emergency main ballast tank blow to the surface.

The duty officer speaks to the captain in a quiet, respectful voice. "Captain, request permission to raise and lower masts as necessary and rotate and radiate on the radar in preparation for getting underway." (Does a submarine have masts, which you would think of as posts holding up sails? Yes they do. A mast is an equipment package that is raised by a structural spar lifted from the sail by hydraulics, with the purpose of sampling some element of the atmosphere while maintaining submerged stealth. Examples: ESM antenna, periscope, and BRA-34 radio antenna.)

The captain nods. "Very well, raise and lower masts as necessary and rotate and radiate on the radar."

"Aye, sir," the duty officer says, and then acknowledges the captain formally. "Raise and lower masts as necessary and rotate and radiate."

This Mission Is Classified

You have time to go on a tour of the engineering spaces before it is time to go to the top of the sail, when the ship departs Port Norfolk for the operation area in the Atlantic. The duty officer explains that this will be a classified tour and that he may not be able to answer all your questions.

He cautions that the aft compartment is a high-noise area in addition to being a controlled radiation area, and he tells you to follow all instructions. You swallow and follow him back down the steep stairs to the middle level and aft through the passageway to the crew's mess.

In the aft starboard corner of the room, tucked behind the galley, are narrow steps leading down to a heavy hatch. The duty officer opens it and waves you through. You find yourself standing in a long, brightly lit, featureless corridor.

"This is the reactor compartment shielded tunnel. With the reactor operating critical, the compartment is a high-radiation area. Inside the compartment itself, you wouldn't survive a half hour, but this passageway is lined with lead and polyethylene. The lead shields the gamma radiation, and the poly shields the neutron flux."

The overhead PA system clicks again, and the voice announces, "The reactor is in the power range!"

"That means the system is ready to supply steam to the secondary loop," the duty officer explains. "Let's take a look inside the reactor compartment while we're here."

Secrets of the Deep

You notice how quiet and cool and bright the reactor compartment shielded tunnel is, as if you'd stepped into the scrubbed operating room of a new hospital. This is the first space that isn't filled to bursting with piping and cables and odd equipment.

USS HAMPTON
SSN-767
Aft Section

**U.S. Navy
NavSea-Confidential
NOFORN**

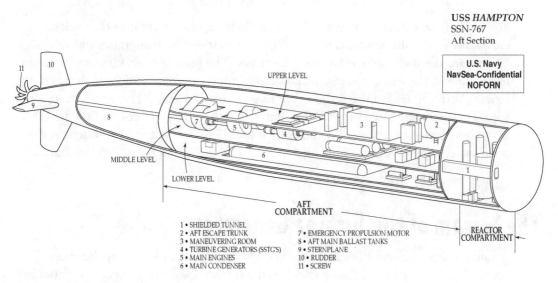

UPPER LEVEL

MIDDLE LEVEL

LOWER LEVEL

AFT COMPARTMENT

REACTOR COMPARTMENT

1 • SHIELDED TUNNEL
2 • AFT ESCAPE TRUNK
3 • MANEUVERING ROOM
4 • TURBINE GENERATORS (SSTG'S)
5 • MAIN ENGINES
6 • MAIN CONDENSER
7 • EMERGENCY PROPULSION MOTOR
8 • AFT MAIN BALLAST TANKS
9 • STERNPLANE
10 • RUDDER
11 • SCREW

Aft section of the Hampton.

The duty officer stops at a chained and padlocked hatch, where he points out a thick window and mirror. You look into the reactor compartment, a space crowded with huge machinery. The duty officer points out the reactor shield tank, the pressurizer, the steam generators—the boilers—and the reactor recirculation pumps, and then he waves you farther aft down the tunnel to another hatch.

A Steamy Time in the Engineroom

You step from this hatch, moving from the brightness of the reactor tunnel to the dimness of another space. You stare around you, again finding yourself surrounded by piping and cables and electrical panels and control handles.

"This is the aft compartment—also called the engineroom," the duty officer explains. "It's hot because we're bringing steam into the engineroom to start the steam turbines. Come on."

At the hatch is an area of tall consoles. The duty officer continues: "This is the motor control center, which has a number of breakers that control the electrical load centers, or buses, and the reactor inverters, which are devices that allow the reactor control rods to go up or down to control reactor power level. Come around this way."

You pass the entrance to a control room, and you stare inside at the four watchstanders and their consoles. "This is maneuvering, the engineering spaces' control room. We'll come back in a moment," the duty officer says.

You walk aft on catwalks toward two huge cylindrical objects set into the deck on either side of the ship's centerline, the objects penetrated by huge pipes and valves. "These are the ship's service turbine generators. The reactor heats up water to steam in the boilers, the steam generators, and the steam comes here and spins these turbines." At the aft end of the turbines are large boxes of metal. "These are the generators. They generate electricity for the ship. Ironically, a large fraction of the power from these generators is used by the reactor itself." As you watch, two watchstanders open some large valves, and immediately a frightening sound roars into the space.

"They're starting the port turbine generator now. Let's watch."

The Scream of the Turbine Generator

A sound like a plaintive scream rises in the space, soon shaking you by the chest. The scream rises to a howl and then a shriek as the turbine spins up, and you are reminded of a jet engine starting. Soon the noise steadies to a loud, high-pitched hum, and the watchstanders are busy around the machine. One of them trots to the door of the maneuvering room and shouts, "Port TG on the governor and ready for loading!" A boom sounds near the generator, startling you.

"Don't worry—when the breaker shuts, the turbine jumps as it is paralleled in. The turbine just came online and is picking up the load that was carried by shorepower. Soon we'll divorce from shorepower and be on our own."

The PA's booming voice sounds again throughout the engineroom: "The electric plant is in a half-power lineup on the port turbine generator!" Suddenly the room becomes broiling hot and humid. Sweat breaks out on your forehead.

"Steam leaks!" the duty officer shouts over the roar of the turbine. "We have a huge refrigeration plant onboard, but whenever you put a steam plant insidea big pipe like a submarine, it's hot."

"The reactor," the PA system announces, "is self-sustaining!"

The turbine on the starboard side suddenly begins to scream as the watchstanders start it up. You watch in fascination as that turbine comes up to speed, a second jet engine in your ear. Another thump sounds, this one from the starboard side.

> **Secrets of the Deep**
>
> You had heard that submarines were supposed to be quiet. But nothing could be further from the truth. Subs are noisy—on the inside, anyway.

"The electric plant is in a normal full-power lineup," the overhead speaker rasps. "Engineering watch supervisor, report to maneuvering."

The duty officer explains: "The engineering officer of the watch—the officer in charge back aft—is about to have the shorepower cables removed. We need to hurry up and finish this tour."

The duty officer leads the way farther aft between the turbine generators to two more steam turbines. "These are the main engines. As soon as shorepower is removed, the crew will warm these up." Aft of the main engines is a huge steel structure.

A Sub's Transmission: The Reduction Gear

"This is the reduction gear," says the duty officer. "It's sort of like the transmission on a car. It changes the high RPM (revolutions per minute) of the main engines, which are efficient at high speeds, to the low RPM of the shaft for the screw, since the screw is efficient at low speeds." The duty officer squints at you a second. "You do know what a screw is, right? The bladed device at the stern that rotates to push the ship forward? Each blade acts like an airplane wing, creating low pressure on the forward surface and high pressure on the aft surface to thrust the ship forward. Its true name is the 'propulsor' but everyone just calls it the screw."

"Since the main engines rotate at thousands of RPM and the shaft rotates at a few tens of RPM, the gear ratio is huge, which is why the reduction gear is also big."

He continues, "These are being changed out to electrical motors because the reduction gear is one of the biggest noise sources. By the way, all the mechanical rotating equipment you'll see back here is mounted on highly engineered sound mounts to avoid making noise into the water. It may be loud in here, but out there …," the duty officer shakes his head. "Nothing—quiet as a hole in the ocean."

He steps down a few steps on a narrow catwalk to another machine. "This is the clutch, which will disconnect the drive train so this motor can turn the shaft. This is the emergency propulsion motor, or EPM. Farther down the shaft line is the thrust bearing, which takes the pushing force from the screw and shaft and transmits the force to the hull. Then there's the *shaft seals*, which keep the water out of the 'people tank.' Now follow me."

> **Subtalk**
>
> The **shaft seals** are a mechanism that allows the rotating shaft to penetrate the pressure vessel of the hull without seawater leaking in. They use auxiliary seawater, which is at a higher pressure than the water outside, to flush the shaft penetration bearing. The high-pressure water keeps the outside water out. The trouble is, this unavoidably puts a small amount of water into the bilges, which is collected and occasionally pumped overboard by the drain pump. One popular drill involves flooding from the shaft seals, simulating a shaft seal failure with thousands of gallons of the deep blue sea pouring into the people tank. Sometimes we play practical jokes with newcomers to the ship—we tell them to "go feed the shaft seals." You'd be surprised how many people fall for that one.

The Least You Need to Know

- Because modern submarines run on nuclear power, the quantity of radioactivity absorbed by the crew is constantly monitored.

- The control room might be smaller than the kitchen in your house, but from here all tactical control of the ship takes place.

- The reduction gear on a submarine functions like the transmission on a car.

- The ship is a boat and the boat is a ship, but this is only true for submarines.

Chapter 2

Finishing the Tour

In This Chapter

- When maneuvering is a location
- Standing on the bridge
- The mission—the "op"—begins
- Learning to dive

"This is engineroom middle level," your guide continues. "A lot of auxiliary equipment is here: the refrigeration plants, engineroom freshwater cooling system, hydraulic equipment, and some other pumps. Let's go below." The duty officer disappears down another hatch and ladder to yet another lower deck.

"Engineroom lower level. Home of the main seawater system, which brings seawater into those large heat exchangers there—the condensers. The condensers change the steam exhaust from the turbines to liquid water so it can be pumped back to the boilers to make more steam."

The duty officer walks forward past a maze of piping and equipment. The noise level here is not as loud as in the top deck, but it's still nearly deafening.

Meandering to Maneuvering

"Let's go up to maneuvering," he says over the din, glancing at his watch. "We need to hurry—the captain will be looking for me."

Up another ladder to the middle level, another jungle of pipes and equipment, and back to the upper level, where the shrieking noise of steam turbines seems much louder. The duty officer walks to the side door of the nuclear control room.

"Request permission to enter maneuvering with a guest," he asks.

"Enter maneuvering," the engineering officer calls.

We walk into the small room. On the forward wall are three consoles with sloping lap sections, a vertical readout section, and a sloping overhead section. Behind each console is an operator in a seat. The engineering officer of the watch stands behind the three operators. The console on the left has two large stainless-steel rings resembling steering wheels.

"That's the steam plant control panel," the duty officer explains. "The wheels are the throttles to the main engines. The outer bigger one is the ahead throttle. The inner one is the astern."

Subtalk

Recirc is short for "recirculation." In the reactor, the recirc pumps force the coolant water through the reactor core and to the boilers and back to the pumps, through a continuing loop. When speaking of ventilation modes, the word recirculate is not shortened, and means the air in the ship is not refreshed by outside air but simply flows in a loop from the fan room to the spaces, through the atmospheric control equipment and back to the fan room.

He points to the middle panel. "Reactor plant control panel. The reactor operator controls the control rods and the reactor *recirc* pumps—which pump water through the reactor and transfers its heat to the boilers—to produce heat for the secondary steam loop." He points to the last panel, the one on the right. "Electric plant control panel, which controls the breakers, the electrical buses, the motor generators, the turbine generators, and the battery."

After a hushed conversation with the engineering officer and a phone call, the duty officer points to a panel over the engineering officer's seat. "That's the chicken switch panel. Each one of those levers does an emergency shutting of hull and backup valves to a seawater system in case of flooding."

The engineering officer of the watch smirks. "But if I shut the wrong one, we lose propulsion and go down faster," he says.

The aft wall is a dizzying array of panels, gauges, and switches. As you look at it, an odd whooping noise sounds in the room coming from one of the phones. The engineering officer picks up the phone, his eyes on the duty officer.

Moving Forward

"Cap'n wants you forward," the engineering officer says. "Time to drive us out."

The duty officer nods and walks to the door, tosses off an inside joke to the engineering officer, and leads you forward, back through the reactor compartment tunnel and into the crew's mess. As you emerge from the engineering spaces to the forward compartment, you realize your shirt is soaked with sweat. You follow the duty officer forward to the steep stairs to the upper level, emerging into the now-crowded control room. The captain looks up at the duty officer.

"Duty officer, station the maneuvering watch."

"Station the maneuvering watch, aye," he repeats, and picks up a microphone. His voice comes out of the shipwide PA system.

"Station … the maneuvering watch!"

"Follow me," he says. "We're going to the bridge. Now that maneuvering watches are stationed, I'm no longer the duty officer; I'm the OOD—the officer of the deck. That means I'm in tactical command of the ship."

"What's the bridge?" you ask.

"Top of the sail. Where we conn the vessel while on the surface. You don't drive a submarine, you 'conn' it. I'll have the conn on the way out of Norfolk."

He steps up to a ladder under a hatchway and climbs up. You follow him into a dimly lit tunnel, up 20 feet to another hatch. "OOD to the bridge!" he shouts, and a grating above the hatch is removed by someone above. He climbs up and you follow him.

Internal Communications

Here's all you need to know about IC, or internal communications: The shipwide PA system is called the 1MC. The similar circuit used in the engineering spaces is the 2MC. The 7MC circuit is for ship-control communications. The 4MC is a circuit that pipes in a sound-powered phone handset into the 1MC in the case of an emergency, sort of the submerged equivalent of dialing 911. For more about how to handle emergencies aboard a sub, see Chapters 5 and 6.

The sound-powered phone handsets are mounted in each compartment on each level. They don't need electricity to work—just the energy of a voice. They are the refined version of two soup cans with a string. The JA circuits are used up forward, and the 2JV are used back aft. A frequent 2MC announcement is "Engineering Watch Supervisor, 2JV," which means that the EWS needs to pick up the phone. The Dialex is a phone circuit that uses electricity, just like the phones at home, and that can dial station-to-station, including to the staterooms and goat locker.

The sound-powered phones use a crank-operated noisemaker. The crank is a small motor that, when cranked, generates a current that is sent via the selector switch to the station being called. If "maneuvering" is selected from the control room, the maneuvering JA circuit noisemaker suddenly goes "whoop!" That's yet another thing to startle the *nonqual rider*.

Subtalk

A **nonqual** is a landlubber or newcomer to the ship who is not qualified in submarines and, hence, somewhat dangerous (in addition, he steals the crew's air, water, showers, laundry, and ice cream). A **rider** is someone along for the ride. The rider may be qualified in submarines or a nonqual, but is not part of "ship's force" and therefore does not contribute to the ship's mission. Riders are sometimes sent to observe the ship (a report card function) or to perform their own mission. Admirals, squadron staff, antisubmarine warfare aviators, foreign navy officers, civilian VIPs, SEAL commandos, and wives are examples of riders. The worst riders are nonqual riders.

When a watchstander's phone whoops, he picks it up and announces the *station*, not his name. And he certainly does not say "hello." For example, he might say "Maneuvering" or "Control" or "Torpedo Room." By the way, on a phone circuit, the long, drawn-out pronunciation of *maneuvering* is said, "manurrn." Similarly, the officer of the deck is either called OOD, pronounced "OD," or is called "Off'sa'deck." The nonquals freak out when they hear on the phone circuit, "Off'sa'deck, manurrn."

The Officer of the Deck

The officer of the deck (OOD) does the captain's job, if your information comes from "Star Trek." He sits in the command chair, gives orders to the helmsman, the radiomen, the sonar chief, the engineering officer of the watch, and others.

The captain is above it all, supervising the actions of the OOD remotely from the aft part of the control room, from his stateroom, or from the end chair at the wardroom table while watching a movie with his officers (a good submarine captain loves movies and has memorized all the lines). Mischievous captains will sneak aft and attempt to surprise the nukes (the nuclear-qualified engineering watchstanders) by seeing if he can scram the reactor before they can stop him. (See Chapters 5 and 6 for more about submarine emergencies.)

The officer of the deck has the deck and the conn. Having the deck means being in charge of the ship's equipment. Having the conn means being in charge of the ship's course, speed, depth, and tactical weapon employment. You don't drive a submarine; you "conn" her.

Sometimes the OOD relinquishes the conn to the captain. If you are on watch as the OOD and the captain comes into control and sees that you are "standing into danger" (risking the ship's safety), he will give the helmsman a rudder or speed order. When he does, he has automatically taken the conn. You announce in a loud voice, "This is Lieutenant Smith; the captain has the conn, I retain the deck." The navigation technician will make an entry in the deck log: "0130: CO has conn." When you have the deck and the conn and are relieved by the oncoming OOD, he will announce, "This is Lieutenant Jones; I have the deck and the conn!" The watchstanders will all acknowledge: "Nav ET, aye!" "Radio, aye!" "Diving officer, aye!" "Helm, aye."

Mike's Corner

There's no bigger thrill than announcing that you have the deck and the conn on your first solo watch as a qualified OOD. I'll never forget the night, 410 feet beneath the Atlantic, at midnight, when I said those words for the first time. The first thing I did? I lit a cigar, of course, in violation of the captain's standing orders—but for those six hours, it was my control room and my ship.

View from the Bridge

The grating is lowered back over the hatch, and you stand on it, a bit nervous about being almost three stories above the deck below. Then you look around you. You are in a cubbyhole, surrounded on all sides by black metal walls up to your elbows. Far below you is the hull of the ship, the pier on the starboard side. Forward is the Plexiglas windscreen and the slowly rotating radar antenna. Aft is the top of the sail, where the two periscopes are raised, and behind them the radio mast is partially raised.

"Climb up to the top," orders the OOD.

You step up to the top of the sail, to a small area surrounded by stainless-steel handrails—the flying bridge. The captain is normally the only person allowed to stand there. The OOD remains down in the bridge cockpit, close to the bridgebox communication panel. You look around again, and from the crow's nest vantage point you can see for miles. A tugboat is lashed to the hull on the water side, the port side.

"Captain to the bridge," a voice calls from the access tunnel. The grating is lifted and the commanding officer climbs up to join you on the flying bridge.

After waiting for the lines on the hull to be singled up and the gangway to be removed, the captain nods at the officer of the deck. "OOD, your report?"

"Captain," the young OOD says, craning his neck to see the captain on the flying bridge, "the electric plant is in a normal full-power lineup, main coolant pumps running in slow speed, answering bells on both main engines, answering all stop and spinning the shaft as necessary to maintain the main engines warm. The fix holds us pier side, with visual fix in agreement with GPS navsat and SINS. All lines are singled up and the tug is tied up forward port. The subnote is received onboard, granting us permission to get underway. All pre-underway checks are complete and sat with minor discrepancies. All spaces rigged for dive with the exception of the deck and the bridge, rig performed by Ensign Rancourt and checked by me. The executive officer recommends getting underway." Taking a breath, the OOD concludes, "Captain, request permission to get underway."

Getting Underway

The captain's eyes squint in a serious war face as he looks down at the OOD. "Let's go," he orders.

The officer of the deck puts a megaphone to his lips and shouts down to the deck, "Take in all lines!" Down below, the deck crew frantically pulls in the heavy lines from the pier as the pier deck hands toss the lines over. As the last line is disconnected from the pier bollard (that's the post to which mooring lines are fastened), the OOD pulls on a lever, and a deep blasting horn blows from the sail. The OOD lets the horn blow for a full 15 seconds.

"Tells the harbor we're underway," the captain says as he lifts a pair of binoculars to his face and scans the channel.

"Shift colors!" the OOD barks, and the enlisted lookout hoists a large American flag from behind the flying bridge. The OOD talks into a radio: "Tug One, this is U.S. Navy submarine, stand by for tug orders."

The captain leans over to you. "He can't identify us as the *Hampton* for security reasons. On an open circuit, we'll always just be 'U.S. Navy submarine.'"

"Roger," the radio blasts.

"We use tugs to avoid breaking the fiberglass sonar dome," the captain explains as he watches the maneuver. "And also because submarines handle like pigs in shallow water next to a pier with no speed on."

"Tug One, back one third," the OOD commands. The tug's diesel engines roar as it throttles up and pulls the ship gingerly away from the pier.

"Tug One, ahead one third," the OOD orders. He picks up a microphone and says, "Helm, Bridge, all ahead one third, right full rudder."

The bridgebox crackles to life: "All ahead one third, right full rudder, Bridge, Helm aye. Maneuvering answers all ahead one third, my rudder is right full, no course given."

"Very well, Helm," the OOD says, "Steady course north."

"Steady course north, Bridge, Helm, aye."

Taking Her Out

Slowly the ship turns in the Elizabeth River channel. The piers of Norfolk Naval Station rotate around the vessel.

"Bridge, Helm, steady course north!" the bridgebox rattles.

"Helm, Bridge aye," the OOD replies. "Helm, all stop."

"All stop, Bridge, Helm aye. Maneuvering answers all stop."

"Very well, Helm." To the radio, the OOD orders, "Tug One, take in all lines."

The tug crew pulls in the lines. The OOD shouts down to the deck, "On deck, rig for dive!"

The bridgebox blares with a new voice. "Bridge, Navigator, hold us center of channel, recommend maintaining course north to the turn point."

"Navigator, Bridge aye," the OOD replies.

Mike's Corner

The smart destroyers, frigates, and cruisers of Norfolk Naval Station are an awesome sight. What a display of naval power. Farther north, the giant aircraft carrier *Nimitz* is tied up, towering over the other ships in the harbor.

The tug's lines are being coiled on her foredeck—the deck forward of the sail—as she backs away from the hull. Down on the deck, the watchstanders hurriedly coil the lines and stuff them into line lockers, closing the locker doors with huge wrenches. Even the deck cleats are rotated back into the hull so that the top surface of the submarine becomes completely clean and streamlined. It begins to look as if it has never been tied to a pier.

"Helm, Bridge, all ahead two thirds, steer course north."

The ship, now unencumbered by the tugboat, picks up speed in the channel until the aircraft carrier piers pass by down the starboard side.

"Bridge, Navigator, 200 yards to the turn point. New course, zero nine one."

"Navigator, Bridge aye."

The base fades astern as the ship approaches the opening of the bay. The channel buoys mark the channel leading to the first bridge-tunnel at Interstate 64, crossing from Norfolk to Hampton.

"Bridge, Navigator, mark the turn!"

"Helm, Bridge, right full rudder, steady course zero nine one!"

The helmsman answers and the ship turns into the new channel. The bridgebox squawks with another new voice. "Bridge, Control, topside rigged for dive, last man down."

"Control, Bridge aye. Helm, all ahead standard."

"Now that the topside deck hands have gone below, the OOD can speed up," the captain says. The wind of the ship's passage picks up, flapping the flag behind you. Down at the bullet nose of the bow, the water begins to flow smoothly over the curving hull and then breaks evenly down either side of the ship, roaring up into waves amidships astern, the wake turns a frothy white, marking the ship's past. The ship turns to another new course as the I-64 bridge fades behind you. The buoys line up on either side of the channel like lights marking a runway as the vessel points toward the right gap in the Chesapeake Bay Bridge Tunnel.

"This is Thimble Shoal Channel," the captain explains, shouting over the wind and the bow wave. "This takes us out to sea off Virginia Beach. We'll turn to the south to follow the traffic-separation scheme, then due east. Once we clear the channel we'll speed up to flank so that we can hurry to the dive point. We've got a six-hour surface transit ahead of us until we can get to the 600 fathom curve. Once we're at the continental shelf, we'll submerge the ship to test depth and then continue to the *op area* at flank."

Subtalk

Op is short for "operation." Never say "mission"—always say "op." The **op area** is the area shown on the classified chart where the ship will conduct the op. The unofficial term for op is **run,** as in, "After this run I'm going to buy a Harley," or "When the air conditioning unit went sneakers-up (broke), it turned into the run from hell," or "We went on a northern run and **snapped up** an **Akula**." (To "snap up" is to detect a submarine, and an "Akula" is a very capable Russian nuclear attack submarine.)

The next hour seems to melt away. All too soon Virginia Beach is shrinking in the wake. The captain orders the ship to speed up to flank speed.

Flankin' It

"Maneuvering, Bridge," the OOD orders, "shift reactor recirc pumps to fast speed."

"Shift main coolant pumps to fast speed, Bridge, Maneuvering aye!" A moment passes. "Bridge, Maneuvering, main coolant pumps are running in fast speed."

"Helm, all ahead flank," the OOD commands.

Almost immediately, the wind, already loud, roars into a hurricane shriek. The noise of the bow wave seemed as loud as a roaring truck before, but it soon sounds like your ears are being sprayed by the violent blast from fire hoses.

The bow wave climbs all the way to the forward edge of the sail and beyond, with the water curving down on either side of the cylinder of the hull and the salt spray in your face even up on the flying bridge.

Amidships, the bow wave breaks into a violent froth, covering the aft deck behind the sail. Further aft, behind the rudder, the ship's wake becomes over a hundred feet wide, an arrow pointing back to Port Norfolk.

Mike's Corner

It is fantastic to be aboard a submarine on a surface transit going flank. The sensation of pure speed, the feelings of the deck trembling with the power of 30,000-shaft horsepower, the blast of the waves and wind, the squeaking of the radar mast as it rotates once every second, and the mad flapping of the American flag behind you are addictive. You'll realize at that moment why the crew does this, why they go to sea for months on end and leave behind the sun and the wind and the weather.

Rig for Dive

The captain orders the flying bridge disassembled, and you spend the next hours in the bridge cockpit with the officer of the deck, watching the merchant ships lumber by on their way to the international terminal at Port Norfolk, waving at sailboats, and enjoying the day until the sun sets astern.

The surface transit comes to an end as the OOD slows to 10 knots and begins to break down the bridge. He transfers the OOD watch to the control room and passes down all the equipment brought to the sail, including the flag and flagpole, the windshield, the bridge communication box, the binoculars, the coffee cups, the grating over the hatch, the charts, and the compass alidade (*AL-ih-dade*).

You help him go through the bridge rig for dive checklist, and then watch as he closes the doors—the "clamshells"—that fair the bridge cockpit into the top of the sail. Before he shuts the last one, he tells you to stand up and take one last breath of real air, looking around at the dying daylight of the seascape.

Feeling silly, you do. Then you crouch down into the 4-foot-high cubbyhole as he shuts the last clamshell, plunging the cockpit into darkness. The bridge is gone now, and if the sail were viewed from above, it would appear completely streamlined.

Take Her Down

You step down the hatchway down the ladder and look up as the lieutenant shuts the upper hatch and spins the hatch wheel. Only the dim glow of single bulbs lights the way as you lower yourself into the lower hatchway and down the ladder to the control room.

The lieutenant shuts the lower hatch and then shuts the bridge access tunnel drain valve, checks it off on the checklist, and looks over at the watchstander outboard of the 747-style ship control seats.

"Chief of the Watch, bridge rigged for dive, last man down."

The chief of the watch repeats the news to the officer of the deck, who stands on the railed-in periscope stand at the starboard Type 18 periscope, his hands on the horizontal grips and his face pressed to the eyepiece. The two officers talk quietly for a moment, and then Lieutenant Phillips reassumes the OOD watch. He steps up and takes over the periscope. In the forward starboard corner of the room, a television screen shows the view out the periscope. It is a dimming seascape, only a sky and a horizon, with superimposed cross hairs.

"Two minutes to the dive point," a voice from the back of the control room calls.

Mike's Corner

You step up and grab the periscope grips. Only the right eyepiece has a view. Out of it you see the ocean in the twilight, the waves small from high above the ship. It looks like the view out of binoculars, but the cross hairs with their range marks remind you that it is a periscope view. The optical electronics console extends all the way to the floor, and is hot on your chest. The OOD makes a remark about periscope watch being called, "dancing with the fat lady."

"Very well, Quartermaster," the OOD replies. He beckons you to the periscope. "Take the periscope watch," he says. "Now that it's getting dark, we have to turn off the periscope video, so this way you can watch the ship submerge.

"The right grip controls the power. Click it up like this and the view is magnified." You try it, and the horizon jumps closer. "But keep it at low power. This button on the right grip helps you train the scope right. This one on the left helps you train the view left. Rotating the left grip will elevate the view up or down. Now, keep it in low power and do a slow circle search for surface ship contacts."

As you experiment with the periscope, the OOD shouts to the chief of the watch.

"Chief of the Watch, rig control for red!"

The overhead white lights click off, and the room turns red. The captain walks into the room.

"OOD, report," he says quietly.

"Mark the sounding," the OOD calls.

"Six five four fathoms!" the quartermaster replies.

"Captain," the OOD says. "Ship is on course one one zero at all ahead flank, making two zero knots. Ship is rigged for dive. We are one minute from the dive point, sir, with ship's inertial navigation tracking the GPS navsat, confirmed by the navigator with a stellar fix. We hold no surface contacts by visual or sonar. Sounding is six five four fathoms. Request permission to submerge the ship, sir."

"Very well, Off'sa'deck," the captain says. "Submerge the ship to one five zero feet."

"Submerge the ship to one five zero feet, OOD aye, sir."

"Thirty seconds to the dive point!"

"Very well, Quartermaster."

"Mark the dive point!"

"Diving Officer," the OOD calls, "submerge the ship to one five zero feet!"

I Have the Bubble

The diving officer sits in the center seat behind the helmsman and planesman at their ship control console. He acknowledges the order: "Submerge the ship to one five zero feet, Diving Officer aye, sir." He picks up the shipwide PA system microphone, and his voice rings out throughout the ship, "Dive! Dive!" He reaches into the overhead for the lever to the diving alarm.

You jump, startled at the sound of the diving alarm horn howling a deep OOOOOOOOOOH-GAAAAAAH just above your head.

"Dive! Dive!" the chief's voice announces a second time. "Helm, all ahead two thirds."

"All ahead two thirds, aye, maneuvering answers, ahead two thirds," the helmsman says.

"Very well," the diving officer says. "Opening forward main ballast tank vents."

"Train the periscope forward," the OOD whispers. When you do, you see four geysers of water screaming vertically up out of the bullet nose. "Now call, 'Venting forward.'"

"Venting forward," you say.

"Venting forward, aye," the chief says. "Opening aft main ballast tank vents."

You look aft and see the same phenomenon of an eruption of water from the aft hull, four fire hoses pointed upward.

"Venting aft."

"Venting aft, aye, sir. Rigging out the bow planes." A moment passes. "Bowplanes extended and locked. Helm, take control of your bowplanes."

"Bowplanes tested, tested sat," the helmsman said.

"Helm, ten degree dive on the bowplanes."

"Ten degree dive, aye, my bowplanes are down ten degree."

The bullet nose of the bow burrows deeper into the water, the geysers now submerged and some vapor still shooting up through the waves, until there is nothing forward except ocean. You train your view aft at the waves rising up the cylinder of the hull. The hull peeks out only between waves and then vanishes under the water.

"I have the sternplanes," the diving officer says. "Sternplanes tested in rise, tested in dive, sternplanes tested sat, I have the bubble, sir, and sternplanes to ten degree dive. Proceeding to ten degree down bubble. Flooding depth control one to the halfway mark, flooding commenced. Tank at five zero percent, hull valve shut, backup valve shut."

The deck angles downward slightly. You look downward at the forward deck and see the waves coming closer.

"Depth five five feet," the chief reports.

The waves are approaching your view, below by ten feet. You do a low-power search, and by the time your circle is complete, the waves are close.

"Six zero feet."

The down angle of the deck becomes steeper.

"Six five feet. Five degree down bubble."

The waves are much closer now, the speed of the ship making the water seem to zoom toward you. Soon the crest of a wave is above the level of your view.

To Test Depth

A burst of phosphorescent foam surrounds you for an instant, and the view comes out of the water again as the wave trough washes by. The view clears, and the stars and the sky come back before the next wave crest splashes the view. One final trough comes, and then the crest hits the view and it becomes surrounded by the fireflies of the foam and a storm of bubbles. The light particles clear and you see the underside of the waves. Three waves roll by overhead, and then the sea becomes dark. The OOD takes the scope and announces, "Scope's under, lowering number one scope."

You gaze over at the digital depth gauge on the ship control panel, feeling the down angle of the deck. The ship pulls out at 150 feet. The diving officer works with the chief of the watch for 20 minutes, trimming the ship to neutral buoyancy before turning the speed of the ship back to the OOD. Finally the OOD reports to the captain that he is ready to go deep.

"Take her to test depth, OOD," the captain orders. "Steep angle."

"Helm, all ahead standard. Dive, make your depth one three hundred feet," the OOD commands. "Twenty degree down bubble. Rig ship for deep submergence!"

"Thirteen hundred feet, twenty degree down angle on the ship, aye, sir, and rig for deep submergence, aye." The PA system barks: "Rig ship for deep submergence!"

The planesmen push their yokes to the panel, and the deck tilts dramatically downward. A clatter of dishes can be heard from the deck below. The captain glares at the OOD.

"We're not stowed for sea, OOD. Get the executive officer up here."

"Aye sir."

Suddenly a booming noise roars overhead, and you instinctively duck down, your hands on your ears. The crew sees you and shares amused looks.

"That's just the hull adjusting to the pressure," the OOD says.

"Sir, ship is rigged for deep submergence," the chief calls.

Finally the ship levels off at her test depth, and you realize that you are holding your breath, a quarter mile beneath the waves far above.

"Captain," the OOD says, "all spaces report—no flooding, no leaks. Recommend proceeding to depth 546 feet and follow point of intended motion to the op area."

The captain nods wisely. "Very well, Off'sa'deck, proceed to 546 feet and chase PIM to the op area."

The deck rises up as the ship climbs from test depth to her cruising depth. From this point on, the run should be routine. As routine as anything can be on a submarine, you think.

> **Mike's Corner**
>
> The deck is now tilted downward so far that it is like standing on a stairway. The handrails and tables look crazy pointed so far downward. You hang on by a conn platform handrail, shaking as another roaring boom is followed by a pop sound overhead. The noise turning into a sustained long, moaning sound and then rattles to a stop.

Buy Your Own Submarine

If your tour of a submarine made you want one of your own, and if you have a couple of hundred grand to blow, you could buy your own submarine. Lake Diver Submersibles in New York state sells personal submarines that use either a one- or two-person crew. The cheapest one-person sub can be purchased for $100,000, not counting the cost of shipping and handling, which could be considerable. The two-person sub with all of the options goes for $220,000.

The one-person sub is 12 feet long. The two-person sub is 2 feet longer. The diameter of the pressure hull is 3 feet. The vessels are capable of going 3 knots. They weigh approximately 1½ tons and have a reserve buoyancy of 600 pounds.

The engine is a 3-horsepower stern motor with two half-horsepower thrusters. The power comes from eight 85-amp marine batteries (for the smaller sub) and 10 batteries for the large one. Those batteries are mounted into two external pressure-proof pods.

Without options, the vessels can stay submerged for about an hour and 45 minutes. With air-revitalization equipment installed, the subs may stay submerged for longer. The variable ballast tank is mounted under the center of the submarine.

There are two external fiberglass free-flooding main ballast tanks. The conning tower has five acrylic viewports, four in trunk and one in hatch. The bottom view port is a 16-inch-diameter, 2½-inch-thick acrylic lens. Optional on the two-person model are two side-viewing acrylic lens for the passenger.

Optional equipment available includes a directional depth sounder and search sonar, the previously mentioned air-revitalization equipment, underwater lighting, and a mechanical claw.

The Least You Need to Know

- The bridge is at the very top of a submarine's sail.
- Submarines always start their mission on the surface and dive only when they are out to sea in deep waters.
- Submarines rise and sink by bringing aboard weight in the form of ballast water. This is done by venting air out and allowing water to flood into the ballast tanks.
- If you have the money and the inclination, you could buy your own submarine.
- It's a long way down to test depth.

Keep Water Out of the People Tank

In This Chapter

- The toughness of steel
- The importance of hydrodynamics
- The concept of ballast
- How to keep trim

The idea of a submarine is to allow trips to the waters under the surface in a controlled fashion. To do this, it is essential that the ship be watertight. Many people think this is done using high-strength steel, which is a misconception. It's not the strength that is vital; it's the toughness.

High Yield Strength and Toughness

The sub's hull is a pipe of HY-80 or HY-100 steel, meaning either 80,000 pound per square inch (psi) yield pressure or 100,000 psi yield. That means, if you took a bar of hull material that has a cross-sectional area of 1 square inch and made it support hanging weights, it would take either 80,000 pounds or 100,000 pounds before the bar of material began to stretch before elongating and rupturing.

This high yield strength means that the metal is extremely tough—and absorbs energy—while being moderately strong. A material is strong if it takes a large amount of load before breaking. Toughness is how much that material will stretch before breaking. Glass is strong but not tough, which is a condition called brittle. Salt water taffy candy is tough but not strong, a combination known as ductile. The idea with a submarine hull is to achieve acceptable strength with high toughness so that the hull can take the pressure of the deep without failing.

The hull is fabricated of this steel in 2-inch thick plates welded together. And although it seems that it would be easy to manufacture this 32-inch diameter pipe and be done with it, the hull has dozens of holes in it, including places where the hole leads to an internal pipe carrying seawater. Some of the piping carrying seawater into the ship is huge—up to 18 inches in diameter. The seawater is used to cool components of the engineering spaces or coolers in the forward spaces, and it is unavoidable. The water also goes to tanks that are used to *trim* the ship.

> **Subtalk**
>
> To **trim** the ship is to keep it level and at neutral buoyancy. This is done by pumping water back and forth between **variable-ballast tanks** or by flooding to or pumping from a variable-ballast tank. When this is done properly, the ship has a "one-third trim," meaning that it will maintain depth control with zero degrees on the bow-planes and sternplanes while at all ahead one third. A hovering trim is more precise so that the ship can come to a complete stop and remain motionless in the sea.

Why They Are All Shaped Like Cigars

Hydrodynamics is extremely important in submarine design. This is the science of minimizing the amount of power required to move the body of the submarine through the sea. It is the undersea equivalent of aerodynamics. In both sciences, the key to efficiency is to reduce drag (resistance force to motion).

In the days of the World War II diesel subs, the boat hull was designed for speed on the surface with its surface ship prow. Today's nuclear submarines are built for speed underwater. They are, in fact, speed limited on the surface. It takes more power to fight the drag of the water on the surface because of the wave action. Once fully submerged, the ship is streamlined so that water flows smoothly and evenly around the hull, which for the fixed power of the ship (30,000 horsepower for the Los Angeles class) gives the maximum speed (upward of 35 knots or nautical miles per hour).

A silhouette of the USS LaJolla, 1992.

Sub hull designs are tested using computer simulation and tow tanks. A tow tank is an elongated swimming pool with an overhead motor on a rail system. The motor is capable of hauling a model hull through the water, and strain gauges measure the drag forces on the model. Complex calculations are done to scale up the drag forces to the size of an actual hull. These forces correlate to the amount of power needed to propel the ship.

The requirements for sub hulls are that no objects can protrude above the cylindrical surface. Cleats (metal horns that hold the lines—ropes—that keep the ship tied to the pier) are mounted on hinges and rotate into cubbyholes in the hull.

Line lockers are larger cubbyholes that allow the lines to be kept (stowed) inside for use the next time the ship comes into port. The number of holes in the surface is at an absolute minimum because a hole can cause a "FIR," or flow-induced resonance (think of a hillbilly jugband musician blowing over the top of a bottle

Secrets of the Deep

The great inventor and artist Leonardo da Vinci designed an underwater warship but kept it secret out of fear that it would escalate the deadliness of future wars. He would have made a great submariner.

Secrets of the Deep

One thing about fluid drag forces: They rise with the square of speed. That is, they rise at the rate of their speed squared. If speed doubles, the drag on the hull quadruples. This means that even if a sub engine doubles in power, it may result in the ship getting only 10 percent more speed—or perhaps as little as 5 percent.

to make a whistling sound). This is important because a submarine's biggest asset is its stealth, or its underwater quietness.

Hydrodynamics for the possible speeds of a sub hull requires that the shape be curvingly blunt at the start of flow and sharply tapered as the flow leaves the body. Even the sail (formerly called the conning tower) is streamlined.

Mike's Corner

One rule of streamlined hydrodynamic design is that if a body looks streamlined, it is.

If you look at a sub's sail from above, it is wing-shaped, with a roundness forward tapering to a sharp point aft. The hull itself is elliptical at the bow, cylindrical in the middle, and tapered to a point at the screw, allowing the hull to gently push aside the water flow and then even more gently put the flow back in its undisturbed position.

Withstanding the Pressure of the Ocean's Depths

The submarine hull is a series of HY-80 or HY-100 plates, about 2 inches thick, rolled into curves at the correct hull diameter (usually 32 inches), and then placed over hoops of framing. The frames are thick I-beams of steel that are also rolled into a circular shape 32 inches in diameter.

Precise tolerances are required for how close to a circle the steel is. The hoops of steel are carefully rigged inside the cylinder formed by the plate, and the two pieces are welded together. Where plate and hoop simply touch, the weld is a fillet weld. Where a seam is formed between plates, a full-penetration weld is done. In a full-penetration weld, the two plates are placed next to each other and cut so that the seam is a V-shape.

Secrets of the Deep

As you might expect, it takes weeks to make a weld going all the way around the hull. But when it is complete and the x-rays are satisfactory, the crew can be satisfied that the hull will stand up to the stresses of the pressure of the deep.

The welding rig uses high-voltage electricity in an inert gas atmosphere to liquefy and vaporize a metal rod, and the liquid metal forms at the valley of the V-shape seam. As the metal cools, it freezes into solid metal.

The welding is done in layers, much like applying butter to toast (if you were going to make a 2-inch thick layer of butter on toast) and, in fact, is sometimes called "buttering." To make sure there are no inclusions or voids in the weld, the weld is x-rayed or radiographed, and the film is read.

If the weld passes, the area is "annealed" with a "post-weld heat treatment," which raises the area of the weld and the surrounding area to two thirds of the melting temperature of the plate. This allows internal stresses caused by welding to ease, and the "heat-affected zone"—a high-strength, low-ductility area—becomes a high-strength, high-ductility area.

All That Water Is Heavy

Where does this pressure come from? It comes from the weight of the water overhead. Seawater weighs about 64 pounds per cubic foot. Pretend for a moment that you are weightless. If you put your weightless self into a glass cube and the cube was 12 inches by 12 inches by 12 inches, and you lowered your cube into the water, when there is 1 foot of water over the top surface of the cube, there is a force of 64 pounds on the top of the cube from the gravity pulling down the water.

If the cube is filled with air and there is no water inside, there would be pressure pushing on the *underside* of the cube. That pressure would come from the weight of 2 feet of water depth, or 128 pounds of water overhead. (Wait a minute, you say—the underside surface has only 64 pounds of water on top because that's the top weight. This is incorrect; the bottom surface of the cube experiences the same water pressure as the *surrounding water* at a depth of 2 feet, which is 128 pounds over every square foot.) Since water is incompressible, at a single depth, each molecule of the water feels the same pressure, which is why the cube's underside feels the pressure of the adjacent water.

The mismatch between the pressure on the top surface pushing down (64 pounds per square foot) and the bottom surface pushing upward (128 pounds per square foot) would yield a net upward force of 64 pounds (this is called *buoyancy*). Your cube would fly out of the water like a beach ball because of the buoyant force unless you got some weight inside. If you were to put some lead weight into the cube equal to 64 pounds, you would keep from flying upward. Now at a depth of 1 foot, the cube has neutral buoyancy, and it floats along with the top surface 1 foot below the surface of the water.

How buoyancy is created by the weight of water.

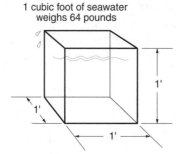

1 cubic foot of seawater weighs 64 pounds

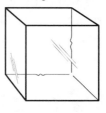

1 cubic foot of glass— assume weight is zero

Put glass cubic foot 1' below surface of the ocean:

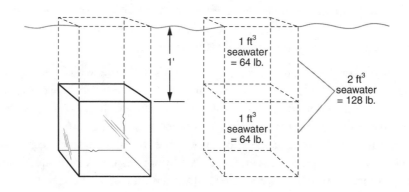

1 ft³ seawater = 64 lb.

1 ft³ seawater = 64 lb.

2 ft³ seawater = 128 lb.

Forces on glass cube

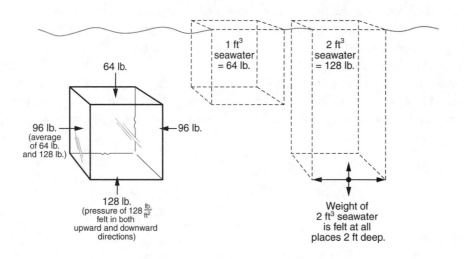

64 lb.

96 lb. (average of 64 lb. and 128 lb.)

96 lb.

128 lb. (pressure of 128 $\frac{lb.}{ft^2}$ felt in both upward and downward directions)

1 ft³ seawater = 64 lb.

2 ft³ seawater = 128 lb.

Weight of 2 ft³ seawater is felt at all places 2 ft deep.

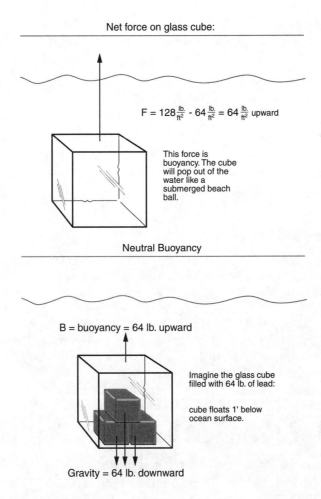

Net force on glass cube:

$$F = 128\tfrac{lb.}{ft^2} - 64\tfrac{lb.}{ft^2} = 64\tfrac{lb.}{ft^2} \text{ upward}$$

This force is buoyancy. The cube will pop out of the water like a submerged beach ball.

Neutral Buoyancy

B = buoyancy = 64 lb. upward

Imagine the glass cube filled with 64 lb. of lead:

cube floats 1' below ocean surface.

Gravity = 64 lb. downward

The Deeper You Go...

Now let's take that cube much deeper, to 1,000 feet below the surface. You still have 64 more pounds per square foot pushing up on the bottom surface than what is pushing down on the top surface. But now the top surface sees 64,000 pounds pushing on it downward, and the bottom surface feels 64,064 pounds pushing on it in the upward direction. The sides of the cube feel 64,032 pounds pushing inward. Let's hope your cube is strong enough to withstand those forces of pressure, or it will *implode* and squish you.

The curving cylinder of the hull is the best shape to withstand the forces of pressure. If you gently squeeze a raw egg in your hands, it will take quite a bit of squeezing before it breaks. This is the same principle as the arch in buildings, where a curved surface can bear up to a distributed load. However, a puncture force, such as a pin, will easily cause the eggshell to break. This is also true of a submarine hull—it easily takes the pressure of the deep, but it cannot take the puncture force of a collision with a surface ship.

When the submarine is taken to "test depth" (about two thirds of the design depth of the hull, but the hull could probably go deeper than the depth at which the calculations say she'll rupture and implode), the hull groans and shrieks and pops. For a first-time visitor, the sounds are terrifying and loud.

> **Secrets of the Deep**
>
> Submariners like to try this trick. Duct-tape a string to the hull at the widest part of the interior hull diameter (usually done in the torpedo room where you can gain access to the frames). Tape the string when the ship is at the surface; make it taut as a guitar string. Dive to test depth. The string will sag about 2 to 3 inches. When the ship gets back to the surface, the string will be taut. The sagging of the string at depth shows how much the pressure of the water forces the hull to contract and shrink. Bearing in mind that the hull is 2 inches of steel thickness all around, the forces required to shrink it are immense.

The Legend of a Sub, Test Depth, and Duct Tape

An old legend is told about a submarine, test depth, and duct tape. According to the story, in the old days a sub was being painted in the dry dock. This was in the days before the SUBSAFE program, and there was a 2-inch-diameter hole cut in the hull that had no quality-assurance paperwork. This hole was cut for a reason—probably a new pipe was going to a hot-running cooler.

For some reason, the installation of the new system was delayed, and the interior of the hull needed to be painted. The hole was covered with duct tape, sandblasted, primed, intermediate coated, and finish painted. The duct tape forgotten, the insulation material was placed into the frame bay, covering the hole.

The same thing was done on the outside as the shipyard prepared to paint the exterior. Somehow the new system—and its cut hull—was forgotten, and the ship was cleared for sea with no "closeout" paperwork.

The sub took an initial dive to test depth after the dry dock availability. Legend has it that the ship was watertight all the way down to 400 feet, when both pieces of duct tape suddenly let go and flooded the ship. The captain took her to the surface, where the bad hull cut was found. This was probably the incident that caused shipyard executives to be forced to ride a submarine down to test depth after an overhaul or new construction!

The Pressure Hull

American submarine hulls are considered to be "single hulls." This means the "people tank" has only one layer of metal between the interior and the seawater. The hoop frames are welded to the inside of the ship.

Russian submarines are typically double-hulled. The people tank pressure vessel is completely enclosed inside a larger shell, with the hoops welded to the outside of the inner hull plates. The outer hull is not pressure tight, but it is a "free-flood" envelope of inexpensive steel, which adds streamlining to the inner hull.

Double-hulled subs carry equipment in the space between inner and outer hulls, allowing the inner hull to have more useful space. There are trade-offs, as in any major design decision. A single-hulled ship is lighter and faster. A double-hulled ship must have its engines push the added weight of the water and the outer hull. But a double-hulled vessel can take more punishment from a torpedo, perhaps even surviving a direct torpedo hit, whereas a single-hulled vessel would puncture and flood from a single torpedo.

Secrets of the Deep

One of the first women to submerge in a submarine is said to have been the founder of the American Red Cross, Clara Barton. She may have been a pioneering woman and benefactor of all humanity, but she was still a non-qual airbreather.

Chicken Switches

Keeping the hull watertight is a major effort, especially since there are so many water pipes coming into the hull. American subs have "chicken switches" for safety. Chicken switches are hydraulic control levers that, when operated, direct hydraulic oil to the hydraulically operated ball valves at the hull penetrations for a seawater-piping system.

When operated by the engineering officer of the watch, the chicken switch shuts the valve and stops the flooding, but cutting off the seawater cooling flow will kill a major or minor portion of the propulsion plant—and loss of propulsion during flooding is lethal. For that reason, a great deal of skill is involved in being a good engineering officer of the watch: Knowing which chicken switch to throw takes wisdom. Failure at the chicken switch panel could doom the ship in a flooding casualty.

The Ballast Tanks

Submarines have main ballast tanks and variable-ballast tanks. *Ballast* is a mariner's word for weight that is carried solely to stabilize or control the rocking of a ship, and it is usually water or lead. (Subs have lead blocks placed at the bottom of the cylinder of the hull shape; this lead ballast keeps the hull more seaworthy so that when it rolls, it will roll back to the normal position instead of rolling all the way over like a log in river water.) The idea of a ballast tank is to help the ship submerge.

The main ballast tanks (MBTs) work to help the ship submerge or, when submerged, return to the surface. Think of the ship as the volume of the entire vessel including the ballast tank. When the ballast tanks flood, water comes in and the added weight of the water allows the ship to become heavier. This added weight counteracts the upward force of buoyancy, so the ship goes down into the water.

Alternately, think of the ship on the surface as including the ballast tank volume, but when the tanks are flooded, the volume of the ship decreases (the weight in this alternate example remains the same). Although the weight is the same, the volume shrank, and density is weight divided by volume. The ship, therefore, has become more dense—denser than the ocean water—and it sinks.

The main ballast tanks are open to the sea at the bottom through louvers. At the top of the tanks are MBT vents, which are very similar to the drain in your bathtub. They are poppet-type valves with a flat top that fit into a hole in the hull.

> **Beneath the Surface**
>
> Back in World War II, any piece of equipment that served to provide undersea communications was referred to as Gertrude. The underwater telephone is now called the UQC.

When the vents are opened, a mechanism pulls the poppet into the ballast tank, opening the hole. Water then flows in the bottom because air escapes out the top. When the valve is shut, the tank remains dry because of the air pressure inside the tank; the tanks can flood only if the valves are open to allow the trapped air to escape.

Variable-ballast tanks are interior to the submarine (as opposed to the exterior main ballast tanks, which are free-flood spaces). They are used to make small adjustments in the weight of the ship (or volume, in the alternate means of thinking) to control depth. At high speeds (over 5 knots), the ship "flies" through the water, with its depth control done by the sternplanes and bowplanes. But at low speeds, the airplane analogy of flying through the water no longer applies. The ship is more like a hot air balloon, relying on the exactness of its weight.

Stability and Why Submarines Make Everyone Seasick

A cylindrical submarine hull is not seaworthy and is barely stable. A surface ship has a hull design resembling a wine glass in cross section. If it heels over, the volume coming into the water progressively increases compared to the volume leaving, which forms a buoyancy "righting moment" that tries to torque—or twist—the ship back to level. This makes a surface ship stable and seaworthy. Subs don't have this benefit, since with a cylindrical hull the volume rolling into the water exactly equals the volume rolling out of the water.

If you step on a log in the river, the log rolls. But if you put an iron spike in the bottom of it (ballast), it will roll and then *very slowly* right itself, using only the horizontal distance from the centroid—the center of its volume—to the center of gravity (center of mass) as a "righting arm." For this reason, submariners are a seasick lot—a sub in high seas is a miserable place. It is no dishonor to cling to the periscope holding a vomit bag in one hand and saltine crackers in the other while on the surface. "Just get us the hell down, OOD," is frequently heard in control during a high-sea state surface transit.

Beneath the Surface
Life as a submariner has its compensations. A submarine submerged 546 feet beneath a hurricane won't feel a thing. The old girl will be as steady as the basement of an office building.

Trimming the Ship

At slow speeds (particularly at periscope depth), the ship's weight must be adjusted to exact requirements. This is called "trimming the ship." Other variable-ballast tanks are located far forward or aft, to keep the ship from being nose heavy or tail heavy. The ship's trim system is a series of pipes and pumps that transfer water between variable-ballast tanks and the sea.

The hovering system is also connected to the trim system. It consists of a series of valves and instruments that allow high-pressure air to "air load" one of the variable-ballast tanks called a depth-control tank (DCT).

Hard Tanks and Others

The DCT is a "hard tank" that can take full sea pressure even though it is inside the hull. When air pressure is admitted to the DCT and the outside hull valve is opened, seawater leaves the ship, the ship gets light, and the ship rises vertically. When the tank is vented of air pressure and the hull valve is opened, the tank floods and the ship gets heavy and sinks.

An "interlock" (a safety mechanism preventing a machine from doing something unsafe) shuts the seawater hull valve when the tank level rises to 95 percent, to keep the water from flooding from the vent valve. (On a ship to remain nameless, this interlock failed, flooding the lower level of the forward compartment and scaring the hell out of the officer of the deck.)

Uses of the Hovering System

The hovering system is used to vertically surface the ship to perform one of the following vital missions:

- Break through the polar ice cap

- Frighten sailboats

- Impress yacht girls

At 150 feet depth, with the ship trimmed and hovering, the officer of the deck gives the order: "Diving Officer, vertical surface the ship!"

The diving officer orders the chief of the watch to blow the hovering system to establish an upward 2 feet per second velocity, and the sub rises vertically upward and surfaces (even with the main ballast tanks flooded). Once on the surface, the ballast tanks are blown dry with the low-pressure blower. This is definitely not a normal evolution.

To surface the ship normally, the officer of the deck orders the ship to surface using speed and the action of the bowplanes and sternplanes. The ship "planes" to the surface, and the snorkel system (a series of pipes that brings air into the ship to the diesel or to the low-pressure blower) is lined up. The low-pressure blower is started, directing the air to the main ballast tanks. With the vents shut, the water leaves the tanks through the louvers at the bottom, and the ship is rigged for surface.

Emergency Blow: In Case of Flooding

In an emergency such as flooding, the officer of the deck orders an emergency main ballast tank blow, also called an EMBT blow or just an emergency blow. During an emergency blow, high-pressure air bottles (stainless-steel pressure vessels mounted inside the ballast tanks) exhaust their contents through large ball valves directly to the interior of the ballast tanks.

This puts air that is stored at over 3,000 pounds per square inch blasting into the ballast tanks. Even at test depth or deeper, the tanks "dewater" at tremendous rates.

After approximately 30 seconds of an EMBT blow, the ballast tanks are dry. With this gigantic amount of positive buoyancy, the ship tilts up to a 45 degree up-angle and rockets toward the surface.

If the ship has a high-speed bell on, the ship can almost jump out of the water during an EMBT blow. Perhaps the most dramatic thing a sub can do is an EMBT blow from test depth. It was the USS *Greeneville*'s EMBT blow from 400 feet that sank the Japanese vessel *Ehime Maru*.

> **Beneath the Surface**
>
> The Russians have used explosives to dewater ballast tanks, with the hot gas generated by a few grenades sufficient to blow the water out of the ballast tank. But in some cases the explosives have punctured the hull, losing the gases and rendering the ballast tank somewhat ineffective in saving the ship!

This evolution is conducted every six months for preventive maintenance (as proof that the system works). During one such emergency blow, a submarine to remain nameless checked the surface, verified the absence of traffic, went back to 400 feet, and emergency blew to the surface. Once the ship stabilized, the officer of the deck raised the periscope (it was 4:00 A.M.) and saw a sailboat close aboard. *Extremely* close aboard.

The sailboat hadn't been detected during the periscope depth sweep because its lights may have been off, and sonar had never detected the boat (sailboats tend to be somewhat quiet). For several tense seconds, the officer of the deck waited to see what the captain of the sailboat would do.

The sailboat's captain would either report the submarine and there would be courts-martial all around, or he would be thrilled. The sailboat captain leaped to his feet and raised both fists, dancing with excitement at the sudden appearance of the sub. The officer of the deck breathed a sigh of relief and decided not to bother the captain with the story.

After all, John Paul Jones once said that "discretion is the better part of valor."

The Least You Need to Know

- The most important qualities of a submarine are that it be watertight and keep the water out of the people tank.

- Subs are built with hydrodynamics in mind so that they slip easily through the water.

- Ballast is a mariner's word for "weight." Add ballast and a sub will sink. Lose ballast and it will rise to the surface.

- Trimming the sub means adjusting the weight to keep the craft level and at a particular depth beneath the waves.

Chapter 4

The Sail, a.k.a. the Conning Tower

In This Chapter

- ◆ Home for the periscopes
- ◆ Use of the radar set
- ◆ Snorkeling procedures
- ◆ Keeping the boat under control
- ◆ Exploring the bridge

The sail, formerly known as the conning tower, has the main function of enclosing the periscopes, antennae, and mast-mounted sensors so that the force of the water flow does not break them off. Submarine designs have been evaluated without sails, which requires antennae designs to "telescope" to extend out of the hull; this is a much more complex design problem. Since depth control at periscope depth close to the surface is extremely difficult, a sail allows greater stealth and greater antennae extension from the hull.

The sail also acts as a crow's nest vantage point to "conn" (drive) the submarine while on the surface. In addition, it acts as a point of diesel engine exhaust and a structure on which to mount the under-ice sonar transducers and cameras, as well as to mount running lights. It is used to mount layer depth–detection sonar and as a structure to punch through arctic ice.

The sail adds drag to the ship, but a sail-less submarine tends to want to spiral in the water from the torque of the screw, requiring fins or control surface corrections for countertorque. Alternately, a second screw with a concentric shaft can be used to cancel out screw torque so that the ship has two concentric counter-rotating screws, but this is a more complex, less robust design. Submarine sails will probably be around for some time.

The sail can be a pain because it takes a long time to "rig for dive," and there is always the danger of dropping something into it (coffee cups, binoculars, compass alidade, wrench or hammer, etc.) that will rattle in the free-flood space surrounding the masts. A sail rattle can require the shipyard or tender vessel to remove the sail, which is expensive and time consuming. But a captain can't live with the rattle, either, because it makes him less stealthy to a hostile sub, like a cowbell on a lion.

The Periscopes

Submarines are generally fitted with two periscopes. On some ships, one is an advanced electronic periscope (Type 23), while the other is a simpler World War II version (the attack periscope, but it is never used in an attack—only for surface navigation). On other ships, there are two Type 23 fully electronic periscopes. Newer ships are being fitted with *optronic* periscopes that do not use the conventional pipe with prisms and lenses; instead, they use electronics and fiber optics to pass the light signals so that the hull won't be penetrated by a conventional periscope.

The view out of the periscope is much like you'd expect from the movies, including the reticle with its cross hairs and division marks. There is only one eyepiece to the periscope, which takes getting used to. The view with the cross hairs may resemble the scope of a high-powered rifle, but the hairs have nothing to do with targeting; they're used to help the observer detect the range (distance) of another ship (a "contact"). The officer of the deck might call "three divisions in low power," which with a masthead height (waterline to the top of the contact's mast) of 100 feet would correlate to a range of 4,000 yards.

The periscope optics module extends from the overhead all the way to your toes. The electronics module below the eyepiece has knobs and switches controlling the still and video cameras.

On either side of the eyepiece are the periscope grips. The right grip controls the optical power. The left grip controls the angle of view. By rotating the left grip upward, your view inclines upward all the way to 70 degrees from horizontal, almost straight up. This allows the officer of the deck to look upward for ship hulls on the approach to periscope depth to avoid a collision, but also to do an air search for antisubmarine patrol aircraft. No one wants to hear the words: "Aircraft, *mark on top!*"

The right grip's selection of optical power begins at 1X, also called low power, or about the same thing you would see if you were standing on the bridge. Then the higher powers come in—2X, 6X, and 12X. That last one, 12X, is considered high power.

At periscope depth, the officer of the deck spends much of his time doing a low-power surface search for surface ship contacts, taking about three minutes to complete a 360 degree search. Then he explores 30 degree sectors of the horizon in high power, taking about three minutes, then another low-power search, then a low-power air search, and then another high-power search of another sector.

> **Subtalk**
>
> "Aircraft, **mark on top!**" means that an ASW (antisubmarine warfare) maritime patrol plane (MPA) has just done a fly-over and that, in all likelihood, the submarine has been detected. The words "mark on top" are almost inevitably followed by expletives!

> **Beneath the Surface**
>
> A doubler trigger on the right grip's index finger area is used to quickly double the optical power of the periscope's view. On 12X, the doubler that takes optical view to 24X is incredible. At 24X, what appeared to be a distant ship on the horizon gets so close that you can see into the bridge. But beware: High power causes the view to jump around.

As usual, during a search, if a close-aboard surface contact is sighted, which means impending collision is likely, the officer of the deck calls, "Emergency deep!" and the immediate evasive actions are taken.

The left and right grips have triggers to activate the training motor (*training* means rotating the scope). In port, rotating the periscope is easy; when at periscope depth, in a tossing sea state with the ship rolling and pitching, it may not be so easy. The motor allows rotation assistance during those times.

The cross hairs and divisions on the reticle (the circular field of view out the periscope with its superimposed cross hairs) are used for eyeball estimation of the

Secrets of the Deep

Submariner's rule of thumb: All ships have a masthead height of 100 feet except for those that don't.

Second submariner's rule of thumb: All merchant ships travel at 12 knots except for those that don't.

distance to surface ships. The observer measures with his eye the number of divisions from the waterline to the top of the ship's masthead.

The number of divisions allows calculation of the surface ship's distance (called range). For example, 1.5 divisions in low power could correspond to a range of 4,500 yards. Two divisions in high power might correspond to a range of 8,000 yards. These are surprisingly accurate ways to measure range, close enough to put weapons on the target.

Radar and Radio Masts

Forward of the bridge cockpit in the sail is the radar mast. This unit is used only on the surface—and then only in peacetime. The radar gives excellent shore resolution for navigation on the way in and out of port, and it also does a wonderful job of showing the course and speed of surface shipping. However, the Navy failed to purchase these units off the shelf from commercial selections.

This means that the radar sets are not only specially designed for the U.S. Navy, but they also are used only on submarines. Any rudimentary naval force would be able to analyze the radar's signal and identify it as that of a U.S. late-model submarine.

A good spy ship could even tell you what exact ship the signal is coming from. During the Cold War, Russian "trawlers" (they were actually spy ships disguised as fishing vessels) performed physical and electronic surveillance of warships leaving U.S. Navy ports and catalogued their radar signals. Each one has an individual voice, a fingerprint.

The Submarine Force combated this spying by using commercially available radars and clamping them to the flag mast. The same Raytheon radar that sailboats and motor yachts use close to land—there are thousands of them in a busy port—are used by subs to egress the base. They provide excellent navigation ability, although they are much worse at seeing oncoming shipping. On a clear day, during a period of high hostilities, the radar mast is retracted into the sail.

Secrets of the Deep

The sailor's badge or pin designating him as fit for sub duty depicts a dolphin. The British Royal Navy's sub school is known as HMS Dolphin.

Once submerged, radar is obviously useless and the anticollision sensor of choice is sonar.

Origin of the Snorkel

The snorkel was invented by the Germans for their U-boats, and they called it a *schnorkel*. The idea with a snorkel is to bring outside air (containing oxygen) into the ship to allow the diesel emergency generator to run. There are other uses, though. The snorkel can bring fresh air into the ship in the event of a fire that fills the boat.

The diesel takes air from the auxiliary machinery space, which for a 688 (Los Angeles class) submarine is aft of the torpedo room. Air flow from the ship is sucked into the diesel. The engine can pop your eardrums severely when it starts.

As pressure in the ship falls from the air going to the diesel, the snorkel mast brings air into the induction piping, past the outboard induction valve and inboard induction valves (there are always two valves when it is possible for water to enter the people tank) to the interior of the ship.

> **Beneath the Surface**
>
> The crew members of a just-commissioned vessel are called the plank owners.

The snorkel "head" has a "head valve." This is a poppet-type valve sort of like the drain on a bathtub. The valve is controlled by two things. The first is a permissive circuit from the control room telling the valve to open *if* the head is dry. The second is a "wet sensor," which is an electrical circuit that is allowed to be shorted out by seawater in the head. If the head goes underwater, the circuit shorts out and the head valve shuts, keeping water from an approaching wave that submerges the head valve from flooding into the ship.

While this is a wonderful system for ship safety, it is miserable for the crew. When a wave washes over the snorkel, the diesel keeps on chugging, sucking all air from the ship. In theory, when the air pressure falls to a very low pressure, the diesel engine will shut itself down from a pressure sensor. In reality, by the time that happened, your eyes would be sucked out of your head.

The diesel suction can be lined up to suck air from a particular compartment. For example, at the call on the 1MC to "Emergency ventilate the aft compartment with the diesel!" the ventilation will be lined up to take return air from the aft compartment straight to the diesel.

Air then comes into the boat to replace the air that is being sucked out of the smoke-filled compartment. This can also be done with the low-pressure blower.

To snorkel, the ship must be at periscope depth. The officer of the deck will order the chief of the watch to "Prepare to snorkel." The reason for this is that the reactor has been shut down (usually for a drill) and the power of the diesel generator is needed on the load centers.

While the reactor is shut down, the batteries supply all of the ship's loads, most of which are taken up by the reactor's main coolant pumps and the emergency electrical propulsion motor (EPM), used to maintain bare steerageway and depth control during snorkeling operations.

When the systems are lined up and all compartments report "Ready to snorkel," the chief of the watch at the ballast control panel in control raises the snorkel by reaching up to the console and clicking up the toggle switch marked SNORKEL to the UP position.

With the power of hydraulics, the snorkel rises out of the sail. It extends only about 8 feet above the sail, so the ship must be shallower than normal to snorkel. And since the ship is closer to the waves, the waves can exert suction force on the hull and make depth control difficult. This is why the head valve is so important—when operating on the sluggish EPM very shallowly submerged in a high-sea state, the waves come over the snorkel mast several times a minute.

Once the snorkel is up, the head valve comes open on the permissive from control. The chief of the watch requests that the officer of the deck test the head valve. The chief turns the permissive switch off, and the head valve should go shut.

The officer of the deck trains the periscope aft and down to look at the snorkel head and the position indicator of the head valve. This is a small rod protruding out of the flat head of the snorkel mast from the head valve. When the valve is shut, the rod is retracted into the head; when the head valve is open, the rod sticks up several inches out of the head.

The chief of the watch shuts the permissive switch, which shuts the head valve. The officer of the deck reports the head valve shut. The switch is then opened, the head valve opens, and the officer of the deck calls the head valve closing.

While that is going on, the auxiliaryman of the watch opens a drain valve that drains the water-filled piping from the snorkel mast to the bilges. (Bilges are unused spaces below the bottom deckplates that are used to store water that drips out of piping systems and that can be dewatered with the drain pump.)

When the mast is dry, the drain valve is shut and the outboard induction valve is opened. Then the inboard induction valve is opened. The auxiliaryman of the watch reports, "Control room ready to snorkel."

When all compartments report ready, the officer of the deck gives the order: "Chief of the Watch, commence snorkeling." The chief of the watch announces on the 1MC system, "Commence snorkeling!" That is the signal to start the diesel.

Commence Snorkeling

In the auxiliary machinery space, the auxiliaryman manually opens the outboard exhaust valve and then "rolls" the diesel on compressed air by opening a lever that admits 700 psi air to the cylinders, causing them to expand and begin to turn the diesel's crankshaft.

Immediately the watchstander opens the diesel exhaust inboard valve, and the air exhaust blows the exhaust piping dry, forcing out the seawater. At running RPM the fuel is injected, and if the gods are with you, the engine starts. Sometimes this takes a few tries, but eventually the diesel roars to life and does its sucking-the-air-from-the-boat thing. All eardrums pop, and almost immediately the boat begins to smell of diesel exhaust.

Remaining Undetected

The exhaust from the diesel goes through a pipe up through the hull to the aft part of the sail and out a "plenum" or discharge diffuser, which is designed to break up the exhaust gases into small bubbles below the surface. This helps the submarine remain undetected.

The trouble is that a following wind will blow the diesel exhaust into the snorkel intake. And since the snorkel is not a direct pipe to the diesel suction (the diesel sucks on the inside of the boat—the snorkel simply dumps air into the fan room), the boat can fill with smoke.

Secrets of the Deep

Motto of the U.S. Submarine Force: Remain undetected. This is because stealth is everything. Official Navy op orders usually start with, "Paragraph 1, remain undetected."

Warming Up the Diesel

The diesel takes 10–20 minutes to warm up to the point that its generator can be electrically loaded. In an emergency, it is loaded immediately, but that wears on the machinery. When the generator is brought onto the electrical buses, the battery can be unloaded and the diesel supplies all the ship's loads.

When the reactor is back online and the electric plant is in a "normal full-power lineup," the diesel generator is unloaded, its breaker is opened, and the diesel is cooled (run at no load for 20 minutes). In a "tactical situation," the diesel may be shut down immediately and the ship goes deep.

"Secure Snorkeling! Recirculate!"

To stop snorkeling, the officer of the deck gives the order and the chief of the watch gives the 1MC command, "Secure snorkeling! Recirculate!"

On this order, the ventilation system is brought back to normal steaming operation, with air recirculated throughout the ship from the fan room to the compartments and back to the fan room. The atmospheric control equipment operates to remove carbon monoxide and carbon dioxide and to add oxygen.

The diesel is shut down (by shutting off the fuel supply valve). When it stops turning, the inboard and outboard diesel exhaust valves are shut, as are the snorkel inboard and outboard induction valves. The snorkel mast is lowered, and the ship is ready to go deep.

Sternplanes and Bowplanes

In the forward port corner of the control room is the ship control station. The ship control console resembles a 747 cockpit. There are two seats with seatbelts set behind a large control panel that has an inclined section far overhead. A flat panel in front of each watchstander is stuffed with gauges and meters, and in front of each seat is a control yoke exactly as you'd see on a heavy jet.

Between the "pilot" seats is a horizontal console with several switches and controls. The central console contains the hydraulic controls so that the ship-control party can use normal or emergency hydraulics.

The panel above has all the instruments that report angle, depth, and control surface angle. Below the right yoke is the engine-order telegraph, where the dial selects the correct speed for the maneuvering (nuclear-control watchstanders) to make.

The station on the left side of the console is the sternplane operator, who has more influence on ship's depth, which is why he has only that task. The seat aft of the console is for the diving officer, who supervises the ship-control party and reports to the officer of the deck.

Farther off to port is the ballast control panel, where the ballast tank vents are controlled along with the emergency blow system, hovering system, and drain system. The chief of the watch (COW) takes his station here, trimming the boat's overall weight at the orders of the diving officer.

The Helmsman

The man in the right seat, on the starboard side, is the helmsman/bowplanesman. On the surface and when submerged, this watchstander controls the rudder and the ship's course, as ordered by the officer of the deck, by steering the ship exactly as you would steer a car. Instead of looking out the window at a highway, though, he looks at the gyrocompass.

The officer of the deck may give him rudder orders, such as "Right full rudder, steady course two seven zero." This means to turn the rudder to the right (full rudder is about 25 degrees, depending on the ship class) and watch the compass move toward course 270, which is due west.

As the compass rose rotates, the helmsman calls out each 10 degrees. "Passing one eight zero to the right, sir." The officer of the deck will acknowledge, "Very well, Helm." Eventually, when the helmsman is 10 degrees away from the final course, he will announce, "Passing course two six zero to the right, ten degrees from ordered course, sir." And then: "Steady on course two seven zero, sir."

The helmsman also controls the engine-order telegraph. As seen in the movies, there is a circular instrument face with two needles on it and a knob in the center. When the officer of the deck orders a speed change, the helmsman rotates the needle to the new speed order.

> ### Beneath the Surface
>
> The gyro is the size of a dinner plate, with a needle at the twelve o'clock position pointing to a mark on the plate. The marks start at 000 and are marked every 10 degrees (010, 020, 030), with each reading corresponding to the bearing relative to true north. The gyro is carefully set so that it reads the precise heading (or course or direction) of the ship.

This is the signal to maneuvering, the nuclear control room, to open the throttles and achieve the screw shaft RPM for the new speed. For example, the USS *Hampton* is at all ahead one third, making 6 knots at depth 546 feet. The officer of the deck orders a speed change to full speed by saying, "Helm, all ahead full." The helmsman answers, "All ahead full, aye sir."

Then he grabs the engine-order telegraph knob and turns it clockwise so that the dial moves from the ⅓ sector at about two o'clock on the instrument face to Full at the six o'clock position. Back aft in maneuvering, the throttleman sees his engine-order telegraph needle jump from ⅓ to Full at the same time a bell rings on the telegraph to get his attention.

Secrets of the Deep _____

U.S. submarines cruise at specific keel-depth levels, such as 410 feet and 546 feet. This was learned the hard way because our Russian friends cruise at even keel depths of 50 meters, 75 meters, 100 meters, 150 meters, etc. After one too many collisions, and based on Russian hull sizes, it was found that if U.S. subs restricted their cruising depths to these "air traffic control" depths, the risk of colliding with a Russian would be minimal.

He announces the speed change to the maneuvering crew and then answers the order by turning his knob and his needle to the Full position. Then he slowly cranks open his throttle to bring the ship's main engines up to speed until they crank the shaft at 150 RPM. This is done slowly to avoid *cavitation*.

Subtalk _____

Cavitation happens when the low-pressure side of the screw blade experiences such a low pressure that the water does not have sufficient pressure to remain a liquid; it becomes a vapor—steam. These steam bubbles move out into the wake and re-experience high seawater pressure and collapse, making a screeching noise audible for miles around. This must be avoided to remain undetected. When accelerating, it is mandatory that the throttles be opened slowly to avoid cavitation.

Sometimes maneuvering is ordered to cavitate, such as when there is a "torpedo in the water" fired by a bad guy. Then the OOD calls out on the 1MC, "Torpedo in the water, Maneuvering cavitate!" The throttles are then opened as fast as they can be without scramming the reactor.

He who cavitates becomes disqualified and yelled at by the captain. At 50 percent reactor power, the maximum power at slow-speed reactor coolant pumps, the ship is answering full (even if instead of 150 RPM this gives the ship 152 or 149 RPM).

The throttleman announces to the engineering officer of the watch, "Answering all ahead full." This is why the expression exists: "Answering bells on both main engines" means that when an engine order is received (it's a "bell" because the engine-order telegraph dings).

Meanwhile, back in the control room, at the helmsman's station, the engine-order telegraph needle from maneuvering dings and rotates to the Full position.

The helmsman calls to the officer of the deck, "Maneuvering answers all ahead full, sir."

One of the gauges on the helmsman's panel is the EM log, or electromagnetic log, which is like the car's speedometer. The needle climbs from 6 knots (nautical miles per hour—a nautical mile is about 2,000 yards or $\frac{1}{60}$ of a degree of latitude) to 22 knots.

The helmsman is also the bowplanesman. (For older ships with the planes on the sail, he is the fairwaterplanesman.) Bowplanes are the horizontal control surfaces that protrude from the submarine's hull at the bow. By pushing his yoke to the panel or pulling it back toward his waist, he controls the ship's depth. When he pushes down, the bowplanes rotate so the leading edge goes down and the trailing edge goes up. A gauge on his panel shows the bowplane angle.

The Sternplanesman

The left seat, or the port seat, is where the sternplanesman sits. The sternplanesman controls the sternplanes, which are the horizontal control surfaces at the tail.

By pushing the control yoke down, the ship takes a down angle, just as in an airplane. By pulling the yoke up, the ship's angle rises. The sternplanesman controls the ship's angle, or "bubble."

Subtalk

To **lose the bubble** is to cave in under pressure. When you say, "I've got the bubble," you mean that everything is under control. The term comes from the old-fashioned liquid-filled inclinometers that used a bubble in a water-filled tube, much like a level in the garage. There's still a bubble gauge mounted above the ship control panel in the event of an instrument failure, but the center of the panel shows the ship's angle in degrees, with each degree shown in fractions of a degree. (The human body can sense a quarter to a half of a degree of incline.) There is also a bubble gauge for left-to-right angle, or list.

The sternplanesman's job sounds easy, but he's the button man in case of severe emergency. When the ship is submerged and steaming at full or flank, a failure of hydraulics can force the sternplanes to a jam condition.

If the sternplanes jam in the down position, the sternplanesman shouts, "Jam dive!"

Without further orders, the other watchstanders take immediate actions to save the ship. The bowplanesman orders up "Back full" on the engine-order telegraph and pulls his planes back to full rise.

The chief of the watch prepares to emergency blow the forward group. If the watch-standers are lucky, they save the ship. If they aren't, the down angle plunges until the deck is vertically down, and the hull passes through crush depth.

Recently on a Ship of This Force …

Here's a story from my past—and an introductory note. The fleet administers a magnificent "lessons learned" program that publicizes mistakes made while making the stupid actions of other ships seem humorous. Those incident reports invariably begin: "Recently on a ship of this force, [the following stupid incident happened]." Without mentioning the ship the author happened to be on, here it is:

Recently on a ship of this force, the ship-control party was standing watch while the ship was in the trail of a Soviet Victor-class attack sub, sneaking behind him at 12 knots, dead quiet, rigged for ultraquiet, with watchstanders tip-toeing and main coolant pumps at slow speed. (These are giant car-size pumps that push water through the reactor core—they are quiet in slow speed but loud as freight trains in fast speed.)

The helmsman chose this time to cross his legs, and he hit the engine-order telegraph with his boot. The needle went from "ahead one third" to "ahead flank." Now "flank" is 100 percent reactor power, all out, 30 knots and then some, with the automatic order to the maneuvering guys to start the pumps in fast speed. I was on watch aft that night, and we were in trail of the Russian, a little tense; all of a sudden we get a flank bell.

Holy cow! Ivan's coming at us, or there's a torpedo in the water, or he's heard us and is coming around to ram us. It was an emergency. I leaped out of my seat and stood over the reactor operator as he immediately reached for the handle to main coolant pump 2 and pulled to start it in fast speed. The pump doubled its speed, which caused a check valve in a 12-inch pipe to slam shut to keep from reverse flowing the other pump.

Boom! The check valve slammed, the noise resounding in the sea. A tenth of a second later, the reactor operator started pump 3 in fast speed.

Another boom. Pump 4, then 5, two more booms. The throttleman started cranking open the throttle, feeding steam to the ahead turbines—the main engines—carefully, avoiding cavitation when sheets of steam boil up from the screw on the low pressure side and bubbles collapse in the sea and screech noisily.

We climbed from 35 percent power past 50 percent, as the pumps came to fast speed to 60 percent, 70 percent, 90 percent, and then leveled off carefully but quickly at 100 percent power. The speed indicator forward moved from 12 knots to 15, 20, and then 25 knots.

The officer of the deck, the navigator, heard the four check valve slams when rigged for quiet and felt the deck start to tremble. Then he saw the speed indicator climbing. The helmsman still didn't know what happened.

The OOD grabbed the phone to shout at me, in time to hear me crisply report, "Conn, Maneuvering, all main coolant pumps running in fast speed, answering ahead flank!"

"All stop!" The OOD shouts. "Switch your pumps to slow speed!"

Up forward, all hell broke loose. The captain came running from his stateroom, the XO showed up, and we almost rammed Ivan ahead right on his rudder.

"Right 5 degrees rudder!" the OOD shouted, trying to keep us off the Victor submarine's screw. We had pulled abreast of the Victor after slamming four check valves and blasting fast-speed pump noises out into the water. For the next 10 minutes we waited, panicking, wondering whether Victor heard us.

Russians have a nasty tendency to try to turn and ram trailing subs, for the purpose of deterrence. But Ivan steamed on, oblivious. "Thank God Dmitri was on watch," the OOD said later—the OODs have named each Russian watchstander, knowing their habits and routines. "If Sergei were deck officer, we'd be going home with a Soviet torpedo up our ass."

On the Bridge

The best way to understand the bridge is to imagine climbing the bridge access tunnel up through the sail just after the ship has surfaced. When you reach the top of the tunnel, you see in the light of the tunnel lamps a hatch with a wheel operator.

You turn the wheel counterclockwise ("righty-tighty, lefty-loosey") to open the hatch. Once the banana-shape metal "dogs" come off the hatch ring, you pull on the steel latch lever and push the hatch open. The spring assist on the hatch makes it easy to push the heavy steel hatch upward until it latches in the vertical open position.

You shine your flashlight upward into a dark cubbyhole. You climb up into the hole and reach for the middle latch on the central *clamshell*.

You lower the clamshell central section forward half and then the aft half. You reach to the port side and lower the clamshell port section and then the starboard side clamshell. The cubbyhole has been transformed into a crow's nest perch, about 4 feet fore and aft by 6 feet athwartships (athwartships means the width from beam to beam).

Subtalk

The **clamshell** is a fairing cover that makes the hole in the top of the sail hydrodynamic.

You reach down so the lookout can hand you the grating that is placed over the hatch opening, allowing you to stand on something over the maw of the hatch. Equipment is then passed up to you: first the bridgebox, the communication module that allows you to talk on an intercom to the control room's chief of the watch, helmsman, contact coordinator and navigator, the captain's stateroom, and maneuvering.

Next comes the compass alidade, a device that allows you to sight in on contacts and see their bearing from you, and to know the compass heading.

Then come the Plexiglas windshield and the Allen wrench to install it, the binoculars, chart, red-lens flashlight, and other needed items (coffee pot, coffee cup, grease pencils, and so on).

You climb down and rig out the red running light on the port side and the green running light on the starboard side. Then you valve in the service air to the ship's horn. You rig up the flagpole and the American flag, and you're done.

Now you can see for miles. You can see so far that the curvature of the earth prevents you from seeing the hull of the ship on the horizon; you can see only the superstructure and the masts ("hull down") at range 30,000 yards.

Mike's Corner

On a nice day, they have to pull you down from the bridge forcibly. On a miserable day, you'd rather be anywhere else.

The Least You Need to Know

- The sail encloses the periscopes, antennae, and mast-mounted sensors so that the force of the water flow does not break them off.

- A submarine usually has two periscopes.

- A sub's snorkel brings outside air (containing oxygen) into the ship, allowing the diesel emergency generator to run—in case of emergency, it also brings fresh air into the ship.

- The helmsman controls the rudder and the ship's course.

- The sternplanesman controls the sternplanes, which are the horizontal control surfaces at the tail.

Chapter 5

Emergencies: Part One

In This Chapter

- The worst that could happen
- Keeping priorities straight
- When everything is wet
- Living through an emergency blow

As many learned after the *Kursk* disaster, a submarine is a hazardous place to work. When you are standing on the deck of a nuclear submarine, submerged and underway, there is a chilling feeling that comes from the realization that the ocean floor is 2 miles beneath your sneakers—and there is nothing between you and the bottom but water.

What Could Possibly Happen?

If you really want to know, the list in general boils down to this:

- Flooding
- Fire
- Nuclear reactor accident
- Steam leak

+ Weapon warhead or fuel accident

+ Control emergency

+ Collision at sea

In general, for any emergency, the ship-control party (team) shall perform *immediate actions*.

Subtalk

Just as a pilot might execute emergency procedures without deliberate thought or reference to a checklist, a submarine crew will react immediately—that is, perform **immediate actions**—without a string of orders to save the ship during an emergency.

The submarine adage "Save the mission, save the ship, save the plant, save the men, in that order" applies to all emergencies. If the ship is in a "tactical situation," the emergency actions may be modified.

Save the Mission

For example, when in trail of a Russian Severodvinsk new-construction submarine in the Barents Sea, or on a surveillance mission taking place inside the 12-nautical-mile limit of a sovereign nation (in violation of international law), it may be inappropriate to emergency blow to the surface because the Russian Northern Fleet or the foreign government might take offense.

Other tactical situations may not be related to national security, such as a submerged transit through the Strait of Gibraltar, but the result may be the same—an emergency blow to the surface might risk collision with the hundreds of heavy merchant ships traversing the strait, none of them expecting 7,000 tons of nuclear submarine to come exploding from the deep directly in their path. In the absence of a tactical situation, the first part of the submarine code, "save the mission," is satisfied, and it is required to save the ship.

Save the Ship

The first step in saving the ship in any emergency (called a "casualty" in submarine language) is to alert the crew. This is normally done with a series of alarms with their actuators set above the ballast control panel at the station of the chief of the watch in the forward port side of the control room.

The general alarm may be sounded, which puts out a "bong, bong, bong" sound. Or the collision alarm, which sounds a swooping shriek. The third alarm is the diving alarm (OOOOHHHHH-GAH), which would be sounded three times during an emergency surface. If the casualty is flooding, the chief of the watch sounds the alarm, announces the casualty on the 1MC general announcing circuit, and then sounds the alarm again.

The next step is to order the *casualty assistance team (CAT)* to go to the scene of the emergency.

Subtalk

The **casualty assistance team (CAT)** is composed of members of the off-going watchsection (the watchsection that just got off watch). They are considered to be in the loop on the ship's tactical situation, but they may be eating their post-watch meal or working on their divisional duties.

Finding Out What's Wrong

The off-going officer of the deck and the ship's second-in-command, the executive officer (XO), rush to the scene. As the senior member of the CAT, the XO usually assumes command at the scene after receiving a hurried "turnover" or brief on what is being done to fight the casualty by the watchstanders already at the scene.

The second-ranking CAT member, the off-going OOD, dons a sound-powered phone headset to relay instructions from the control room to the CAT leader and information from the scene to control. The other members of the CAT take orders from the scene leader.

Secrets of the Deep

It is never a good idea to say, "Good news, Captain—the flooding put out the fire." Submarine commanders don't have a sense of humor about emergencies.

You Find a Leak; Flooding Finds *You*

The first thing that can go wrong submerged is to lose the watertight integrity of the ship. Water can come rushing into the ship much faster than the scenes in the movies, particularly at deep depth.

In *Ice Station Zebra*, flooding comes in through an open 21-inch torpedo tube breach door. If this happened in reality, anywhere near test depth, it would scatter the weapons in the room and perhaps even rupture compartment bulkheads.

This also points out the need to define flooding: "You find a leak. Flooding finds you." A leak is a dripping or even a streaming from an affected system. Flooding risks ship survival.

You Found It, You Report It

The person who finds flooding is responsible for reporting it to the control room. In lieu of a 911 system, submarines have the circuit 4MC, which is a sound-powered emergency way of getting the word out to the other watchstanders. From any 1JV or JA phone handset, located conveniently in each space of each compartment aboard, the 4MC panel is located.

Pull the switch to the right and shout into the phone the appropriate announcement: "Flooding in engineroom lower level! Flooding in engineroom lower level!"

Mike's Corner

In an emergency, try speaking slowly and distinctly, even though your heart is in your throat and you're certain that you're confronting the Grim Reaper at test depth.

Upon receiving your announcement, the chief of the watch repeats the word on the much louder 1MC general announcing circuit: "Flooding in engineroom lower level! Casualty assistance team lay to engineroom lower level!"

He then punches the general alarm, waking up all sleeping off-watch personnel and alerting the casualty assistance team.

Causes and Remedies

If the cause of flooding is collision, the only emergency action that will save the ship is a desperate emergency blow to the surface.

If the cause is seawater flooding through a seawater system, the engineering officer of the watch isolates the offending seawater system. In this case, it is vital that the engineering officer of the watch get an accurate report of which system is flooding. The correct report is "Flooding from port auxiliary seawater" rather than "Flooding port side"—if main seawater is isolated, the ship will have less power to sprint to the surface.

The engineering officer of the watch reaches into the overhead above his watchstation and throws a small lever that shuts the hydraulically controlled hull and backup isolation valves for that system.

He listens for the report of "Flooding stopped" or "Flooding continues." In the former case, he must recover the reactor plant with the impaired cooling system. In the latter case, he must throw another lever and further isolate the ship's seawater systems.

If flooding still continues, the flooding might be so severe that he has to button up all seawater systems—which is a severe casualty in itself because all propulsion is lost. The *Thresher* disaster pointed out the need to keep power during flooding.

If the flooding is not from a seawater system or collision, it may be from a torpedo tube. Shutting the muzzle door may be called for from the control room's weapons control panel if the ship is running with open muzzle doors in a tactical situation. Sometimes *cycling* the door will help.

Subtalk

Cycling is opening a valve, hatch, or door and immediately shutting it again.

Snorkel Induction System

The other cause of flooding is from the snorkel induction system from a poor rig for dive. An open induction valve will flood the fan room, shutting down the fans, and seawater will pour out of the air-conditioning ducts.

The manual inboard induction valve should be shut again if this is the case. Another cause of flooding is a ripped-off periscope, which can be caused by collision with a ship hull or the polar ice cap.

In this case, all that can be done is an emergency blow. The final cause of flooding is a shearing off of the shaft, creating an 18-inch hole far aft in the ship when the screw falls to the bottom. This could happen in a collision or from an unlikely but possible fatigue failure of the shaft metal. Odds in this case favor loss of the ship, since flooding far aft of the center of gravity will tilt the ship violently into an up angle and spill the air out of the ballast tanks.

How to Conduct an Emergency Main Ballast Tank Blow (EMBT Blow)

The officer of the deck orders the chief of the watch to emergency blow all groups (there are only two groups: forward and aft). The chief of the watch reaches into the overhead to the two stainless-steel levers that point vertically down. He pulls the *interlock plunger* down off both levers.

With the interlock plungers pulled down, the chief of the watch rotates the levers from straight down to straight up. Immediately afterward, the chief of the watch sounds the diving alarm three times to indicate an emergency surfacing (three OOOH-GAH alarms) and says on the 1MC, "Surface, surface, surface!"

Subtalk

The **interlock plunger** is a cap on the end of the lever handle that prevents it from being operated inadvertently. The blow must be deliberate.

As soon as the EMBT blow valve plungers are opened, air from the 3,000 psi high-pressure air bank is admitted to control pistons and cylinders of the EMBT valves, which cause the large 8-inch full-port ball valves to open.

When they do, a shut-off piping system becomes a straight shot for the high-pressure air to roar from the bank of bottles in the ballast tanks themselves directly into the tanks. The vents are shut, so the air collects at the top of the tank and fills the tank, blowing the water out the always-open louvers at the bottom of the ship (the keel).

When the tanks go dry, the blow is stopped ("secured"). Usually the forward group is blown first so that the bow of the ship points upward with the ahead motion of the ship. Then the aft group is blown. Exceptions to this rule are when flooding is catastrophic, when both groups are blown simultaneously; or when the ship is going backward with a down angle in a recovery from a jam dive, and the aft group is blown by itself to stop the backward plunge.

> **Secrets of the Deep**
>
> As the forward group deballasts, the ship takes on an up angle. The control room may fill with fog from condensation caused by pinhole leaks in the inboard part of the system.

The EMBT blow system is extremely loud as the air roars into the ballast tanks, but it is a comforting sound, like the vicious bark of your watchdog fighting a burglar. You grab a handhold in the control room as the deck rises below your boots to 10 degrees up, then 15 degrees, 20 degrees, 25 degrees, 30 degrees—steep as a staircase.

The world begins to look odd, with consoles and platforms and watchstanders suspended far over your head when they used to be simply across the room. The digital depth gauge rolls out the depth indication, starting slow at first and then gathering momentum.

The bowplanesman and sternplanesmen try to keep the up angle gentle, since above 40 degrees the ballast tanks will lose air, but sometimes it is impossible, particularly if the flooding happens in the aft compartment. The diving officer calls the depth: "One thousand feet, sir. Eight hundred. Five hundred. Three hundred, broach!"

The ship explodes through the surface. In a two-group EMBT blow from test depth at flank speed, with the flank bell maintained, the ship will fly so far out of the water that only the screw remains submerged; then the ship will fall back into the water, creating a huge violent foamy wake.

The vessel takes a depth excursion back down to 200 feet and disappears from view on the surface; then it pops back up. It is an amazing experience from the control room, but it's even more dramatic from the surface.

Tragedy of the *Greeneville*

In a recent tragedy, the USS *Greeneville* collided with the *Ehime Maru* during a practice EMBT blow from 400 feet, sinking the Japanese vessel with barely a scratch to the submarine. This shows the buoyant power of the EMBT system.

When an emergency blow is conducted for training or for preventive maintenance every six months (to make sure it's still working), it is vital to check the surface traffic to ensure that no ship is in the area.

After an EMBT blow, it is necessary to recharge the high-pressure air banks as soon as possible, in case another emergency blow is required.

Fire Aboard Ship

Fire aboard the closed environment of a nuclear submarine is extremely dangerous. As the *Kursk* disaster showed, a fire in the torpedo room can ruin your day. A fire in the torpedo room is doubly dangerous because of the weapon fuel (peroxide or Otto fuel has its own oxygen and will burn underwater) and weapon warheads.

In addition, cruise missile solid rocket fuel will melt a 4-foot-diameter hole in the hull, a catastrophic event that no amount of firefighting will fix. If a Tomahawk missile first stage lights off, you are standing on an express elevator headed to the ocean floor, with barely enough time to say a prayer before the unflooded sections of the hull implode.

Cook the Food, Not the Crew

The main source of fire aboard is the galley. The grease of cooking meat, such as *sliders*, will start cooking fires sometime during a sea tour. A second source is an electrical fire, which is rare under normal operations in the U.S. Navy but not in foreign fleets. Russian submarines frequently have succumbed to fires at sea.

In 1970, the Soviet navy lost *K-8*, a November-class sub in the Bay of Biscay when fires broke out in the third and eighth compartments. The sub surfaced, but the crew could not extinguish the fire. The reactor was shut down and the emergency diesels would not start, leaving the ship on the batteries. Part of the crew was evacuated, but the ship lost buoyancy and sank in 4,700 meters of water, killing 52 people, including the captain.

Subtalk

Sliders are hamburgers that slide down the throat from the grease used to cook them.

In 1986, the ballistic missile submarine *K-219*, Yankee class, sank north of Bermuda in the Atlantic during strategic patrol after an explosion in a missile tube from the mixing of leaking fuel and seawater.

The fourth compartment fire was set by the explosion and further leaking of missile fuel. One reactor had been shut down for silencing. The sub surfaced and the other reactor was started. The fourth compartment experienced a fire, probably from a short in the equipment from water used in firefighting or a flooding in the third compartment. Air leakage from the main ballast tanks caused the ship to sink, killing four.

> **Secrets of the Deep**
>
> Fires can be caused by electrical shorts. Such shorts or grounds are hunted down with determination in the U.S. Submarine Force and consequently have not been a large problem.

In 1989, in the Norwegian Sea off Bear Island, the attack submarine *K-278 Komsomolets* experienced a fire in the seventh compartment, later thought to be due to a high concentration of oxygen and an electrical short. The ship surfaced. The fire shorted out reactor control circuitry, and power was lost. The fire breached a high-pressure air pipe, which blew high-pressure air into the flames and spread the already roaring fire. On the surface, the ship lost stability and sank in 1,700 meters of water. There were 41 deaths, including that of her captain.

In the mid-1980s, the U.S. submarine *Guitarro* experienced a severe battery fire probably caused by an electrical fault in the presence of hydrogen. Hydrogen is generated by battery-charging operations. The crew battled the fire for days before the ship was considered saved. A similar incident on a Russian Golf submarine in the Pacific led to its sinking. This was the submarine partially raised by the *Glomar Explorer* during the Nixon administration.

The Bomb

One source of fire is "the bomb," or the oxygen generator. Its nickname comes from the fact that its hydrolysis process breaks down distilled water, using high direct-current voltage, into hydrogen gas and oxygen gas. The gases are in a *stoichiometric proportion.*

The hydrogen is dissolved in seawater and taken overboard using the auxiliary seawater system. The oxygen is pressurized and stored in large stainless-steel oxygen bottles. The ship's oxygen content is regulated using the oxygen bleed, an unsophisticated method that simply involves opening up a manual bleed valve a few turns on the oxygen manifold. Oxygen comes into the ship in the auxiliary machinery room and is distributed to the ship by the ventilation system. Poorly distributed oxygen, in the presence of a spark from a motor starter or circuit breaker, could cause a severe fire. In the event of a fire, the casualty assistance team (and the rest of the ship) don *EABs*.

Fire hoses are strung throughout the space, pressurized by the auxiliary seawater system. If the fire is electrical, the applicable circuit or load center must be de-energized. If the fire is in the torpedo room, chemical extinguishers may also be used. When firewater is used, it is necessary to dewater the compartment using the drain system, or else seawater will rise in the bilges of the compartment and do as much damage as the fire itself.

Subtalk

A **stoichiometric proportion** is an optimum mixture to cause a violent explosion. For every atom of oxygen, there are two atoms of hydrogen so that neither reactant is wasted in the chemical reaction, which would take heat energy away from the explosion.

Subtalk

EABs are emergency air-breathing masks, full-face respiration devices with regulators mounted on the wearer's belt and plugged into an overhead manifold. A newcomer who is a nonqual (not yet qualified in submarines) is forced to find these manifolds while blindfolded, in each compartment and space aboard, so that he will be able to survive a fire.

Submariners will say they are **sucking air** when wearing EABs, or just **sucking**. One reason for this is that the air doesn't come until you inhale hard; after an hour in an EAB, the effort of pulling in air is exhausting. The other reason for this is that, frankly, being in an EAB sucks.

Dealing with Smoke

The danger of fire is exacerbated by smoke filling the ship. The ventilation systems are secured (shut off) as the ship is rigged for fire, with the compartment hatches shut and dogged. The officer of the deck rises to 150 feet in preparation for coming to periscope depth. The officer of the deck clears baffles and comes to periscope depth. This is difficult with a space filled with seawater from firefighting, with smoke filling control, and with an EAB mask blocking the periscope eyepiece. At periscope depth, the crew prepares to snorkel. As soon as the fire is declared out and the *reflash* watch sets, the crew emergency ventilates the compartment using the diesel.

Subtalk _____

A fire can easily **reflash** after it has been put out. The water is heated to steam and is carried away, and the components of the fire—a combustible, oxygen, and high temperature, or heat—remain present. Just when you thought it was safe to go back to your **rack** (bed), the general alarm sounds (bong, bong, bong), because the fire started again.

This is the reason a reflash watch is set: A person stands there and stares at the ashes. If the fire restarts, he passes the word.

The compartment experiencing the fire is the suction point for the diesel, which pushes out (exhausts) the air from the compartment out the diesel exhaust in the sail. When the atmosphere is acceptable in the compartment, the ship is rigged for surface ventilation, pulling air out of all compartments and pulling in fresh air. When all atmospheric readings are acceptable ("in spec"), the atmospheric control equipment is turned back on, the ship is rigged for recirculation, snorkeling is secured, and the ship is rigged for dive and goes back deep to continue the mission. (Source for Russian incidents: www.bellona.no, Report 2, 1996, "Nuclear Submarine Accidents.")

The Least You Need to Know

- A nuclear submarine can be a very hazardous place to work.

- The submarine adage "Save the mission, save the ship, save the plant, save the men, in that order" applies to all emergencies.

- The first thing that can go wrong submerged is to lose the watertight integrity of the ship. This results in flooding.

- As a last resort against flooding, an emergency blow might bring the sub to the surface.

- Fire in a submarine is always potentially deadly, but especially if it breaks out in the torpedo room.

Chapter 6

Emergencies: Part Two

In This Chapter

- ◆ The hazards of radioactivity
- ◆ Keeping neutrons from leaking
- ◆ Scramming the reactor
- ◆ Undergoing and emerging from a jam dive and emergency deep

Radioactivity is a serious problem aboard a nuclear submarine. The result is that ionizing radiation passes through the human body, causing cellular damage. Such radiation is in the form of gamma rays (electromagnetic waves much like x-rays) and neutrons (neutrally charged, massively heavy subatomic particles that can decimate tissue). At times alpha radiation is a hazard (alpha is a helium atom without its electrons). If you get alpha particles in your lungs, you're in deep trouble.

Nuclear Reactor Accident

The reactor is heavily shielded by lead and water (lead attenuates gamma rays, while water's hydrogen molecules slow down and attenuate neutrons) in the shield tank. The forward and aft bulkheads and tunnel walls of the reactor compartment are shielded by lead and polyethylene.

In normal operations, these shields contain the dragon, and all is well. Low levels of radiation from neutrons and gamma rays get by the shielding, but these levels are monitored by taking radiation measurements in the compartments and by keeping track of individual exposure using the (repeat after me, slowly) thermoluminescent dosimeters (very good!) distributed to each person.

> **Beneath the Surface**
>
> Some might say, "Why not just shut down the reactor?" That would not be enough. A core at 100 percent power that is shut down still remains at about 8 percent power due to "decay heat," the heat produced by the continuing decay of the products of fission and spontaneous uranium fissions. Unless this heat is removed, the fuel can melt.

> **Subtalk**
>
> The term **critical** in the phrase "the reactor is critical" means that the level of neutrons in the core is able to sustain a nuclear reaction without the number of fissions declining. Criticality is achieved in the intermediate range just before entering the power range. In the power range, the reactor core has the ability to change the temperature of the primary coolant. If the core goes subcritical, the level of neutrons is declining with each fission "generation" so that power level goes down.

Several families of emergencies can take life or even doom the ship. One general category is loss of coolant accidents, such as Three Mile Island. Another is loss of reactor control.

Loss of Coolant

In a loss of coolant accident, or LOCA, the primary water loop circulating through the reactor to cool the fuel modules is ruptured and water is lost from the primary. In many cases, this can cause loss of pressure in the system.

As the pressure and the water inventory is lost, the water in the reactor vessel boils to steam, "uncovering" the fuel modules. Uncovered fuel rises in temperature until it melts. Hydrogen is formed in the steam bubble from a heat reaction with the zirconium fuel cladding, and it can be ignited and breach the reactor system. Melted fuel in a breached system releases severe levels of radiation into the atmosphere.

Things *can* get worse. The fuel in a naval reactor is "bomb grade," unlike a civilian reactor; it uses U-235, the high-octane variety, instead of natural uranium (95 percent U-238 that sits around and 5 percent U-235 that fissions and produces heat). If a U-235 bomb-grade uranium core melts in a loss of coolant accident, there is a possibility that it could form a *critical* mass at the bottom of the core. It is further possible that an uncontrolled nuclear reaction would then take place. In the least likely case, it would explode like a fission bomb and vaporize the ship. In the more likely case, it would cause a "prompt critical rapid disassembly," which is an uncontrolled run-away reaction that causes the nuclear fuel to thud in less than a full explosion but that is strong enough to blow open the reactor vessel and the hull.

In a loss of coolant accident, the crew attempts to pump more water into the primary system and into the core. It is vital to use pure water because seawater would tear the stainless-steel components apart in a matter of hours from chloride stress corrosion. If water cannot get to the core due to the pressure of the steam or hydrogen bubble in the vessel, the accident cannot be stopped.

> **Secrets of the Deep**
>
> Even when the nuclear fuel does not experience a nuclear reaction, it could be hot enough to melt through the reactor vessel and the hull. In this case, the reactor compartment would flood uncontrollably. The hole's size would matter because a large enough hole could cause the ship to crack in half.

Loss of Reactor Control

The other accident variety is a loss of reactor control. This can happen in various ways that increase the reactivity in the core. Reactor power is controlled by control rods. If the rods are inadvertently withdrawn, reactor power increases to the point of a steam explosion. A steam explosion happens when the reactor fuel adds more energy to the water than it can accept, so the water immediately turns to high-pressure, high-temperature steam. In some scenarios, the steam explosion blows apart the reactor as it did at the SL-1 test site at Idaho Falls, killing three operators (see the following section "The Idaho Falls Tragedy: SL-1").

In one Sturgeon-class submarine, a reactor *scram* drill was being conducted and tripped the reactor offline.

Immediate actions are taken during a scram to restore power and to avoid damage to the reactor. The crew began restoring the reactor to the power range from its shutdown state in an emergency recovery procedure called a fast-recovery startup or fast-scram recovery. In a fast-recovery startup, the reactor reapproaches power so fast that it is about 50 times the

> **Subtalk**
>
> The term **scram** comes from the old days of the carbon-moderated piles, in which the single control rod was controlled by a rope. A man was stationed above the pile to shut it down in an emergency. This required dropping the control rod into the pile by cutting the control rod's rope with an ax. Legend has it that the man was called the Safety Control Rod Ax Man, or SCRAM, for short. Since then a reactor isn't "tripped" offline; it is scrammed.

startup rate as a civilian core. The procedure is so dangerous that it is done only at greater than 50 miles from shore. The rod control lever suddenly broke off during the recovery.

The maneuvering room crew was so shocked by this odd event that they focused completely on the broken lever rather than the fact that the switch had frozen in the "rods out" position. The reactor's power level was still rising, with the rods being withdrawn from the core. Instead of the controlled 5 decades (or multiples of 10) per minute startup rate, the core came screaming out of the intermediate range at 10 decades per minute. Later calculations showed that the reactor was six seconds away from a prompt critical rapid disassembly—and the consequent steam explosion and hull breach.

At 10 decades per minute, the reactor protection circuitry tripped and rescrammed the reactor. After the incident report was written and the calculations were performed, the leader of the engineering crew at the time, the engineering officer of the watch, invented a new ceremony in which he kneeled before the RCP reactor control panel containing those channels of nuclear instrumentation that saved the ship and then kissed the circuit boards.

Ranges of Power

The startup rate of a nuclear reactor refers to the fact that when a reactor shuts down, its nuclear reaction level goes down by decades. The level drops out of the power range (in which the nuclear reactions have the capability to raise coolant temperature) to the intermediate range (in which the reactor has quite a bit of reactivity but is not able to raise coolant temperature) and finally to the startup range (in which the power is extremely low). The intermediate range is about 11 decades wide (the top might be 10^{-5} and the bottom would be 10^{-14}). The startup range is about 15 decades wide, from 10^{-3} to 10^{-18} (different units). At the bottom of the startup range is the fiduciary level, in which reactivity is so low that it cannot be measured—but it still exists.

When you fast-recover a reactor from a scram, you bring power that is in the startup range into the intermediate range by pulling out control rods and watching the startup-range startup-rate meter. You maintain 5 decades per minute, and up she goes. At the top of the startup range, you cut out the meter and switch to the intermediate range readout, maintaining 5 decades per minute startup rate. As core power approaches the top of the intermediate range, you can see the power meter budge from 0 to 1 percent—you are in the power range and can bring steam into the engineroom.

Cold Water Accidents

Another kind of loss of control is a cold water accident. Most reactor dynamics are conducted at operating temperatures of 500°F. It must first be recognized that the main thing that is different between a nuclear reactor and a nuclear weapon is leakage of neutrons.

A nuclear fission happens when an unstable uranium −235 nucleus is hit by a slow neutron (a fast neutron will whiz right by). In the fission, the nucleus splits in two and produces either two or three fast neutrons. The neutrons must be slowed or "moderated" for the next fission to happen. If all but one of the fast neutrons leaks out, and if that single nonleaker becomes slowed, it can cause another fission and reactor power remains the same. If that neutron leaks, the next generation of fissions does not happen and reactor power declines. If the leakage qualities of the core are changed, and if fewer neutrons leak and more are slowed by the moderator, reactor power rises.

The moderator is what minimizes leakage and slows fast neutrons to be slow or thermal neutrons. In a pressurized water naval reactor, the moderator is the water that flows through the core on the way to the boilers to boil steam—the water is a dual-purpose coolant.

In a gas-cooled reactor, the coolant that transfers heat to the boiler does not act as a moderator, and moderation material must be added to the core in the form of graphite. The part of water that moderates is the hydrogen end. The oxygen atom in water hogs the electrons of the two hydrogen atoms, so the hydrogen atoms sticking out the sides of a water molecule are really bare protons, with the same molecular weight as a neutron. And just like a billiard ball, a neutron is slowed when it hits something of the same size. A billiard ball hits the side of the table and bounces right back, transferring minimal momentum to the massive table. If it hits a cluster of like-massed objects, however, its momentum is transferred to the other balls that the first ball slows. So the hydrogen of a water molecule slows the neutrons and makes them slow enough to hit another uranium nucleus and cause another fission.

Now, water density has a lot to do with the effectiveness of water as a moderator. At 300°F, water is much more dense than it is at 500°F. So, if a reactor is at a steady power level ("critical") at 500°F and suddenly 300°F water is injected into the core, the colder water moderates neutrons much better, fewer leak out, and more are slowed, causing more fissions; reactor power then rises. If one loop of the dual-loop primary becomes idle and cools to 250°F and suddenly the idle loop's pumps are started, and if that 250°F water is injected into the core, the reactor power level would climb to about 10,000 percent. A steam explosion would result and hull breach would be virtually guaranteed. This is called a "cold water accident," and this is the reason why a reactor running on one loop is a dangerous thing.

To recover an idle loop, the reactor is intentionally scrammed. The idle loop pumps are started, and only then is the reactor restarted with a fast recovery startup. This is called a down-and-up, and it can be conducted submerged without snorkeling.

Other Types of Nuclear Accidents

Other nuclear accidents can happen, but by comparison they are garden variety:

- A loss of shielding accident occurs when water in the reactor shield tank leaks and the levels of radioactivity increase.

- A loss of coolant purification occurs when the ion-exchange resin that cleans and filters the coolant of highly radioactive microscopic metal fragments fails. The radioactivity of the coolant rises, radiating the crew.

- A rod jump can be caused by a malfunctioning control rod drive mechanism, locally melting fuel and increasing radiation levels.

- A rod ejection could be worse, a combined loss of pressure accident and rod withdrawal accident.

- A fuel module could corrode, putting radioactivity into the primary coolant. This is called a fuel element failure.

- Finally, a primary-to-secondary leak could develop in the tubes of a boiler, which would make the steam loop radioactive. Since part of this loop is vented to the atmosphere by devices in the engineroom that take gases out of the steam loop, the hull would become radioactive from this sort of leak.

These minor kinds of radiation accidents can be lived with until the ship can get to shore. Otherwise, the reactor can be shut down and the ship can snorkel on the diesel and use the emergency propulsion motor for steerageway until a tow can arrive.

Russian Accidents

The U.S. Navy has never suffered a serious reactor accident involving equipment damage or personnel injury. This is not true of the Russian fleet. Over 500 men have been killed in Russian accidents, many of them nuclear accidents. Some happened in construction or refueling; others happened at sea.

- In 1960, the November class submarine *K-8* suffered a primary-to-secondary leak that contaminated the entire vessel and exposed the crew to 200 *rem* or more.

◆ The accident of the Hotel I class strategic missile sub *K-19* occurred in 1961, when a loss of pressure and loss of coolant accident happened at sea. The crew had to make a reactor compartment entry to attempt a jury-rigged repair to feed water to the leaking core and take away "decay heat." The attempt did save the ship, but the crew members were exposed to severe radiation; eight men died of radiation sickness after receiving more than 5,000 rem.

◆ In 1968, the *K-27* suffered a loss of reactor shield tank water. When the indications at the reactor control panel showed dropping power, it was due to the loss of water in the shield tank. The nuclear instruments were no longer reading true reactor power. Instead of reading increasing power the way they would if the shield tank were full, they read lower levels of radiation and hence lower power. The water of the shield tank "thermalizes" neutrons (slows them down and prevents them from leaking), allowing the nuclear instrument to read the power level. Without the shield water, the nuclear instrument loses sight of the neutrons because they leak and are not slowed down. The loss of tank water caused the instrument to read a lowered power level, but the true power level in the core was rising. To bring back apparent reactor power where the operators thought it should be, they withdrew control rods (but true reactor power was actually high). The rod withdrawal overpowered the core, melting 20 percent of the fuel assemblies. Soon they learned that they had experienced a loss of instrumentation, but by then the damage was so severe that the ship had to be scuttled in the Kara Sea some years later.

◆ In 1982, the Alfa class submarine *K-123* had a primary-to-secondary leak, but the Alfa's reactor was cooled by liquid metal (a lead-bismuth mix). The leak caused 2 tons of coolant to fill the reactor compartment, and the reactor experienced a loss of coolant accident and melted fuel. The reactor was so severely damaged that it took nine years to restore the ship to operational status.

◆ In 1985, the Victor-I class submarine *K-314* was being refueled at Chashma Bay outside Vladivostok. During the refueling operation, the reactor vessel head was lifted improperly, which raised control rods. The reactor experienced a prompt

Subtalk

A **rem** is a roentgen equivalent man, an attempt to somehow standardize radiation dose measurement for gamma and neutron radiation. A lethal dose for half of the people exposed is 1,000 rem. Survival with more than 1,500 rem is doubtful. Experiencing 10 rem to the head can be extremely damaging. The normal dose is less than 0.1 rem per quarter—and less, if it can be managed.

critical rapid disassembly that contaminated 6 kilometers of the Shotovo Peninsula and killed 10 people.

◆ In 1989, the Echo II class submarine *K-192* suffered a severe loss of coolant accident that polluted the waters of the Norwegian Sea and the Barents.

Fourteen other nuclear accidents took place aboard Russian attack submarines, but these were less severe than the ones described.

Protecting a Nuclear Reactor

A naval nuclear reactor must be protected by four things:

◆ Excellent design that takes into consideration safe operation and maintenance

◆ Excellent training of operators and maintenance personnel

◆ Continuous examination of operating and maintenance procedures by a nuclear safety organization

◆ Education and feedback to the operations and maintenance personnel of lessons learned during near-miss incidents that happen to the fleet

These four things were all instituted by Adm. Hyman Rickover, the father of the U.S. nuclear navy, and all four were lacking in the Soviet fleet. (Source for Russian incidents: www.bellona.no, Report 2, 1996, "Nuclear Submarine Accidents.")

The Idaho Falls Tragedy: SL-1

The SL-1 reactor was a prototype of a naval-type reactor able to be moved by railcar. At the Idaho Falls government reactor compound, the initial unit of the class was undergoing maintenance when radiation alarms were received at a distant firehouse. Rescue crews found radiation levels too high to pursue. Eventually they recovered the three bodies of the operators. Later investigation revealed that faulty design contributed to the incident because the reactor could go prompt critical on one control rod.

Second, the chemistry control of the reactor was poorly designed: The control rods could be bound up by corrosion. Finally, operator error contributed because when one of the operators pulled a sticking control rod out of the core to mate it to the control rod drive mechanism, it came out to far and too fast. Reactor physics calculations show that the speed of control rod withdrawal is more important in adding reactivity to the core than the amount of withdrawal itself, so a rapidly pulled rod for a millimeter could be worse than a slowly pulled rod withdrawn 10 times as far.

In any case, the reactor experienced a prompt critical rapid disassembly in which it went from about 1,000 percent to 10,000 percent power in a few milliseconds. This caused a massive steam explosion and blew the reactor out of the ground about 9 feet. The two operators on the reactor vessel head were killed; one was impaled by a rod blown out of the vessel. A third operator in the remote control room was killed by the intense radiation before he could pick up the telephone to call for help. It took years to clean up the incident, and it was kept classified for decades after it happened, to spare the government embarrassment and to avoid jeopardizing civilian nuclear power efforts.

Steam Leak

A special category of engineering casualty is a steam leak. Steam piping is carefully designed and is over an inch thick in places, to take the internal pressure of the steam and to stand up to erosion over time. This is because the steam from the boilers is not completely vapor, but it has moisture in it. The entrained moisture causes erosion that can rupture even the heavy wall piping. Steam piping must grow as the temperature of the piping rises from ambient 60°F to its operating temperature of more than 460°F. This great temperature difference makes the steel of the piping expand, and the pipe can become longer by several inches. To allow for piping growth, large "racetracks" are built into the piping system above the turbines. But despite these cautions, sometimes power piping ruptures.

A steam leak from a piping rupture is a double casualty. First, the steam from a main steam line will fill the engineroom with steam, roasting the engineering crew like lobsters. Steam in this case is not the wafting fog coming from the tea kettle; it has enough energy to cut a man in half or burn him to well done in seconds. A complete shear of a steam pipe is calculated to kill every watchstander aft within 30 seconds.

The reason it is a double casualty is that it overpowers the reactor by taking so much energy from the primary coolant that the primary water returning to the reactor is excessively cold; this moderates neutrons and allows more fissions. Reactor power therefore automatically responds to steam demand. As the throttleman calls for power by opening his main engine steam throttles, the reactor sees cold water returning from the boilers, and reactor power escalates. In the case of a steam leak, the steam takes a shortcut from driving the turbines and simply empties into the engineroom. Reactor power screams upward, providing even more steam, and the entire system runs away.

A dead engineering crew means that the reactor protection circuits must shut down the reactor during the overpowering, but a sudden steam leak will probably melt fuel before the circuits scram the core. Then the problem arises that decay heat from fission products must be taken away by the emergency cooling system, or else fuel melting will get worse. A dead engineering crew and a reactor without emergency cooling make for a ship-threatening disaster.

The immediate action for a steam leak, assuming that the crew survive the initial blast of steam, is for the reactor operator at the RPCP (reactor plant control panel in maneuvering) to flip shut the switches for main steam bulkhead isolation valves MS-1 and MS-2.

Unfortunately, it takes about 20 to 30 seconds for these valves to shut off the steam, and shutting them means losing propulsion in the case of a double emergency such as flooding. The second action is to open the throttles to attempt to "bleed down" the steam headers to the main condenser.

The next action is to find the leak and then isolate that part of the system and recover the unaffected part of the plant. If the leak is in the port turbine inlet, main steam valve MS-4 must be shut to isolate the port turbine, and then the steam headers must be repressurized by bypassing MS-1 and MS–2 to check that the isolation is working. Then MS-1 and MS–2 must be reopened and started up on the starboard side of the engineroom; propulsion capability then can be returned to the control room.

Weapon Warhead/Weapon Fuel Accident

In 1968, the Skipjack class attack submarine *Scorpion* was returning from patrol in the Mediterranean after a long deployment. She never showed up at the pier. It took the analysts and mathematicians some time to theorize her location, and when they did, they took a deep-diving submersible down to the ocean floor. The decapitated sail of the *Scorpion* lay on its side, with one fairwater plane buried in the sand The bow compartment had a hole in the side and had apparently flooded, since it did not get crushed by pressure.

The aft compartments were in much worse shape. The pressure had been so great that the tip of the ship at the screw had been rammed all the way into the wider cylindrical portion of the hull, as if a witch's hat had been crushed into itself. The submersible concentrated on the bow where the blown-out hole had been. The first reports came back that the *Scorpion* had been torpedoed, which meant that a Soviet attack submarine had put her down.

A more detailed investigation revealed that the explosion had come from *inside* the ship, from one of her own weapons detonating. The reconstruction of the event holds that a torpedoman was conducting preventive maintenance on a Mark 37 torpedo and was verifying that its circuitry was working correctly. This involved removing a cover and inserting the probes of a test meter into the weapon. The test meter would simulate to the weapon that it was in the water and was homing to the target. The procedure may have been flawed, or the weapon may have actually been malfunctioning, or the procedure may have been done incorrectly, or all three. In any case, the weapon decided that it was in the water homing toward a target. The weapon's engine started inside the torpedo room.

This is called a "hot run," and the emergency procedure calls for the officer of the deck to turn the ship in a tight circle as fast as possible. If he could turn the ship more than 180 degrees, the ACR feature of the torpedo would shut it down. ACR is an anti-circular run, an interlock keyed off the torpedo gyro in which a torpedo that turns back around toward the mother ship is shut down to avoid homing on the launching sub.

But either the maneuver was incomplete when the torpedo fully armed itself or the ACR circuit was jumpered out or was malfunctioning. When the weapon armed itself, the only thing missing before warhead detonation is the detection of a magnetic hull. With the weapon in the torpedo room surrounded by a magnetic hull, the proximity sensors lit off, telling the weapon computer that it was near a magnetic hull, and the torpedo exploded. Neighboring weapons and torpedo fuel likely also exploded, adding to the damage in the torpedo compartment and probably breaching its aft compartment bulkhead to the ops compartment, which was flooded and thus unimploded at the bottom. The flooded forward compartments dragged the ship below crush depth, which imploded the reactor compartment, the machinery two compartment, and the engineroom compartment.

Tragedy of the *Kursk*

On August 12, 2000, the Russian Northern Fleet SSGN *Kursk*, an Oscar II class cruise missile submarine, approached periscope depth during fleet exercises intent on launching a 1957-design torpedo.

The *Kursk* crew experienced a problem when the hydrogen peroxide fuel of the torpedo leaked and came into contact with metal parts of either the weapon or the tube. In such an instance, the oxygen generated is easily ignited, lighting off the leaking peroxide and causing a fire that is nearly impossible to fight.

Within two minutes, the other weapon warheads and fuel systems detonated, destroying the first compartment and breaching and flooding the second and perhaps third. The fires generated carbon monoxide and smoke, which killed most of the crew.

Twenty-three members of the crew survived for about eight hours and evacuated to the ninth compartment. They died and the compartment flooded long before submersibles and diving crews could get the escape hatch opened.

The incident attests to the severe danger of a ship's own armament sinking her. As a result, weapons designs have focused on ship safety, and crew training has been intensified. The Russian use of hydrogen peroxide liquid fuel was ill advised, as was the use of a fueling system internal to the ship. American weapons are self-contained, maintenance-free fuel systems with canned fuel tanks. This has led to fewer incidents. The newer Mark 48 torpedoes have been vastly improved in safety over the Mark 37s, which has also boosted the U.S. Navy's safety record.

Control Emergency ("Jam Dive")

A control emergency happens when the bowplanes or sternplanes have a hydraulic oil system casualty. A hydraulic failure that causes the planes to put the ship in a dive are the most serious of these emergencies and are called "jam dives." A sternplane jam dive is the worst accident: The sternplanes have the most power to tilt the ship downward because they are so far away from the ship's center of gravity, which gives them great power to force the ship into a dive.

A word needs to be said at this point about the Submarine Operating Envelope. This is a graph of speed vs. depth. It shows that the deeper the sub goes, the more restricted the ship is in speed. For example, at 546 feet keel depth, the ship can cruise at any speed between all stop (hovering at 0 knots) and all ahead flank (four main coolant pumps in fast speed, reactor power at 100 percent, submarine going flat-out). But below 600 feet, the ship is rigged for deep submergence and must move forward at a minimum speed. Deeper still, the ship's minimum speed rises until at test depth the ship must be going at least 10 knots—no slower because, in the event of flooding, there may not be enough forward momentum to plane up to the surface, even with an emergency blow.

At 600 feet, the maximum speed becomes limited, and deeper still the ship is further restricted in speed, until at test depth the ship is allowed to go no faster than about 20 knots. This speed limit is based on a sternplane jam dive. If the ship was going all ahead flank at test depth and the main hydraulic system failed and put the sternplanes in a jam dive, the ship would go below crush depth before the crew could recover.

That said, all fast-attack boat submariners have been at test depth at ahead flank because, in a "tactical situation," the Submarine Operating Envelope is thrown into the TDU (trash disposal unit). This is why almost all submariners will begin a sea story not with "Once upon a time," but rather with the words, "There I was, test depth, all ahead flank, when suddenly ...."

Safety Checklist

Here are the immediate actions for a sternplane jam dive:

- ◆ The sternplanesman calls "Jam dive, sternplanes!"

- ◆ The diving officer orders "All back full!"

- ◆ The chief of the watch sounds the general alarm (*bong, bong, bong*) and announces, "Sternplane jam dive!" on the 1MC. (By this time, the down angle could be as much as 40 degrees down, with the ship headed straight for the ocean bottom.)

- ◆ The bowplanesman pulls up his control yoke to full rise, in an attempt to counteract the sternplanes.

- ◆ The chief of the watch stands by the emergency main ballast tank blow levers.

- ◆ The officer of the deck makes a snap decision whether to emergency blow. Odds are, he will order an EMBT blow of the forward group to get buoyancy in the forward ballast tanks to counteract the downward plunge of the ship.

- ◆ The sternplanesman attempts to switch to auxiliary hydraulics and pull up on the sternplanes. If that fails, he switches to emergency hydraulics and pulls up. If that fails, the engineering watchstanders aft begin to prepare to take local control of the sternplanes and troubleshoot the problem with the hydraulic system.

Recovering from a jam dive can be hairy even if these immediate actions work because the back full bell and bubbling of the forward ballast tanks can give the ship an up angle while going backward.

In the diving trainers at the Submarine School at Groton, Connecticut, ship-control parties practice this casualty over and over, and more than a third of the time the ship goes below crush depth going backward.

The diving trainers are mounted on large hydraulic struts that give the mock control room the ability to take up angles and down angles. A severe jam dive training run can be a chilling experience. If you go through the berthing spaces and shout in the ear of a sleeping watchstander, "Sternplanes jam dive," he will shout back "All back full!" before he is fully awake.

Mike's Corner

When I first watched the movie *Das Boot*, when the U-boat had a jam dive, I found myself saying aloud, "Back full!" A second later, the U-boat commander ordered—you guessed it—"Back full!"

Other control casualties, such as a jam rise on the planes, can be troublesome during a tactical situation, since a jam rise can cause the ship to broach the surface. This is bad style if the ship is shadowing a foreign fleet or trying to sneak up on another submarine. Generally, control emergencies that do not involve the sternplanes can be dealt with easily.

Collision at Sea (Emergency Deep)

As the lore suggests, a collision at sea can ruin your whole day. Collision prevention is done with extensive training. But sometimes, as soon as the periscope breaks the surface, the officer of the deck will see a close-aboard contact and will order an emergency deep.

Collision remains a terrible accident because it can cause other accidents, such as flooding and fire. If the ship experiences a collision and is flooding, the ship-control party may emergency blow or plane to the surface. If flooding is catastrophic, the affected compartment may be abandoned and isolated, but with only three compartments on the Los Angeles class submarines, this is no longer a viable option. The crew will attempt to stop flooding and may succeed if the flooding is from a piping system, but flooding from a ruptured hull may be catastrophic.

In conclusion, a nuclear submarine is a front-line weapons system, but it remains one of the most dangerous duty assignments in the military, topped only by naval aviation.

The Least You Need to Know

- Radioactivity is a serious problem aboard a nuclear submarine.

- A nuclear accident can have several different causes.

- Immediate actions are taken during a scram to restore power and to avoid damage to the reactor.

- A steam leak on a sub could be as deadly as a fire.

- Although collision prevention is a key part of a submariner's training, it remains a terrible potential.

- A jam dive occurs when a sub's control system puts it into an unwanted dive.

Flooding: Loss of the *Thresher*

In This Chapter

- ◆ The worst submarine disaster
- ◆ The dangers of safety shortcuts
- ◆ Changes made

The worst U.S. Navy submarine disaster during the nuclear era occurred on April 10, 1963, in the Atlantic Ocean when the USS *Thresher* was lost with 129 men aboard. The sub, which at the time was the most advanced in the world, had just undergone a complete overhaul at the Portsmouth, New Hampshire, naval yard.

The *Thresher* was on its way to a rendezvous with the USS *Skylark* at a spot about 200 miles off the Cape Cod coast where the continental shelf dropped to the ocean floor. In case of emergency, if the *Thresher* had to surface quickly (blow ballast), it would have been the *Skylark*'s job to make sure the surface was clear of passing ships. And, if there were problems with the *Thresher*, the *Skylark*, in theory, would be in a position to attempt a rescue.

Attempting to Blow

Here, according to "*Thresher* Down," in the February 1987 edition of *Mechanical Engineering,* is what occurred that morning:

> 6:35 A.M. *Thresher* rises to periscope depth, spots *Skylark,* and reports to the surface vessel by acoustic telephone. Captain John Harvey is ready to take *Thresher* down for testing at her maximum serviceable depth—about 1,000 feet. The descent is made in stages of several hundred feet at a time. At 400 feet *Thresher*'s crew checks for leaks in the hull, fittings, and piping system. Any rupture could be disastrous, blasting water into the interior at 600 psi.

> 7:54 A.M. Harvey notifies *Skylark* that future references to his depth will be encoded—"half test depth, three quarters test depth," and so on—because of the numerous Russian trawlers that cruise along the U.S. coastline.

> 8:09 A.M. *Thresher* is at one-half her test depth.

> 9:02 A.M. The submarine requests *Skylark*'s navigator to repeat a course reading.

> 9:03 A.M. The following message is received from *Thresher:* "Experiencing minor problem. Have positive angle." And then: "Attempting to blow (ballast)." *Skylark*'s telephone picks up the sound of air under high pressure as *Thresher* attempts to push seawater from her ballast tanks. Then there is silence. For the next 10 minutes *Skylark* attempts to make contact with *Thresher,* but there is no reply.

> 9:17 A.M. *Skylark* receives a garbled message. It is mostly unintelligible, but it ends with the distinct and ominous words: "… test depth." *Thresher*'s acoustic phone has remained open, and *Skylark*'s navigator, a veteran of naval combat in World War II, is astounded by what follows. He hears the distinctive groans and clanks of a doomed ship. *Thresher* is breaking up.

Secrets of the Deep

James L. McVoy, a former submariner and once editor of the *Naval Engineering Journal,* says, "When the Navy tried to determine the cause of *Thresher*'s loss, we found so many things wrong it was almost a good thing we didn't know what happened."

Vice Admiral Elton Grenfell, one-time commander of the Atlantic fleet's submarine force, wrote about the *Thresher* disaster in the March 1964 issue of the *U.S. Naval Institute's Proceedings:* "The casualty must have occurred when the ship was at or near test depth, which subjected the interior to a violent spray of water and progressive flooding. In all probability, water and spray shorted out vital electrical circuits, causing a loss of propulsion power. The *Thresher* presumably blew main ballast, started to rise, and began to sink. Shortly thereafter, she undoubtedly exceeded her collapse depth and plunged to the bottom."

Garbled Voices

The *Skylark* traveled in a crisscross pattern in the area where the *Thresher* was supposed to be, calling for a response but receiving none. Dozens of rescue planes and ships were sent by the Navy to the area immediately.

The *Skylark* eventually found an oil slick near the spot where the Thresher had been last reported. Soon thereafter, floating debris was discovered by other ships arriving on the scene. The debris included yellow gloves such as those used on nuclear submarines, and the same sort of cork used to insulate submarine hulls.

A report from a search-and-rescue submarine indicated that garbled voices were being picked up through the *Thresher*'s UQC, or underwater telephone. It was later suggested that the voices were coming from trapped men who had been on a forward section of the sub, blown clear of the rest of the sub.

Some said the *Thresher* had gone deeper than her test level and had imploded, which is exactly the opposite of exploded. In explosions, the pressure inside an object is excessively larger than the pressure on the outside, so the object blows apart outwardly. When something implodes, there is more pressure on the outside of the sub than on the inside and the entire structure caves in.

A theory also held that the implosion was followed by an explosion, which might have been caused when the wall of air and water caused by the implosion struck the sub's diesel fuel supply.

Secrets of the Deep

The Navy and those in the free world who were aware of the situation grieved over the loss of the *Thresher*—and not just because of the sailors and civilians who were lost. The *Thresher* had been a key element in the Cold War, which was close to its peak in intensity in 1963, and was expected to neutralize the growing threat from the submarines of the Soviet Union.

Beneath the Surface

The *Thresher* had more fire power than all of the U.S. submarines during World War II put together.

The Navy's investigation concluded that while the *Thresher* was operating at test depth, it developed a leak at a silver-brazed joint in an engine room seawater system. Water from the leak, they say, short-circuited electrical equipment, causing a reactor shutdown.

This left the submarine without propulsion. Unable to blow its main ballast tanks, the submarine didn't have enough power available from the emergency propulsion motor to raise it to the surface.

Columbus O. D. Iselin, of the Woods Hole Oceanographic Institution, has another theory. He suggests that the *Thresher* was lost because of a large underwater swirl. A major storm had crossed the Gulf of Maine on April 8, and perhaps may have created a subsurface eddy.

Such an eddy could have caused 300-foot underwater waves. If the sub dove at just the wrong spot, Iselin said …

> [S]he might have been first caught in the eddy and then been pummeled by the waves. This would have considerably hastened the vessel's descent, sweeping her down to close to crush depth before the crew had time to respond …. [I]f *Thresher* then experienced a failure in her ballast-blow system, she would not have had time to recover before imploding.

It was several weeks before the wreckage of the *Thresher* was floated by a small search submersible. The *Thresher* was first rattle out of the jar of a new class of nuclear submarine. The loss of the sub was a major blow to the program because the new subs were designed to dive significantly deeper than their predecessors.

Now one had gone down and hadn't come up. The whole nuclear submarine program might have been in jeopardy if it weren't for the Cold War.

Beneath the Surface

Here are the designations for the different types of submarines:

- SSN: fast-attack submarine
- SSBN: ballistic-missile submarine (boomer)
- NR-1: deep-submergence research craft
- DSRV: deep-submergence rescue vehicle
- T-AGSS: research submarine

Procedure Flaws That Doomed the *Thresher*

The Navy investigation revealed that the designers of the *Thresher* had not met standards to ensure safe operation.

Design and Construction

The engineers put too much of their safety focus on the nuclear reactor in the submarine and not enough to the structure of the sub itself. While great safety consideration was given to all elements of the sub's nuclear power plant, comparatively little was given to its steam and saltwater systems.

Silver Brazing

This is a method of sealing fitted joints in pipes. Metal parts are joined by heating them to the temperature at which a filler material, usually silver, will melt and flow into the tiny spaces between the closely fitted parts. This is a safe method of sealing joints, but it was not used everywhere in the *Thresher*.

The best brazing is done thorough a process called heat induction. But this system was not used on all of the metal joints in the sub. For the hard-to-reach joints, builders just gave the joints a blast with a hand-held torch and called it sealed.

Subtalk

In **ultrasonic** testing, special sound waves are used to look for cracks in the joints.

Quality Assurance

A number of indications already showed that the testing of the brazing on a sub was insufficient. The Navy referred to these as "near misses." But the testing standards for the brazing done on the *Thresher* was not stepped up. The old method, called *hydrostatic* testing, was used instead of a newer and more reliable method called *ultrasonic* testing.

The troublesome thing about this safety failure is that the tests started being done with the ultrasonic system—145 joints were tested by the system, with a frightening 20 of them failing—when it was decided that the ultrasonic system was too time consuming and cumbersome. The remainder of the joints were tested using the *hydrostatic* system. The remaining joints passed the test.

Subtalk

A **hydrostatic test** is when a piping system is filled with water and pressurized (using a pump) to see if any joints fail or leak. This is a safer way to test a system than a pneumatic test, which fills a system with pressurized air—in the latter test, a system leak could cause injury or death because the energy of the pressurized air remains after the leak, while a "hydro" system failure results in an immediate lowering of pressure on a leak or failure.

Procurement

Strict rules govern the military and procurement. Although the Pentagon has been known to spend $20 for a paper clip, you can be pretty sure that it is a safety-approved paper clip. When it came to constructing and overhauling the *Thresher*, however, the rules of procurement were not followed.

After the *Thresher* went down and the wreckage was recovered, the Navy found that the reducing valve components installed in the pressurized air systems (these were used to blow the main ballast tanks) failed to meet design specifications.

The Navy also found that a design flaw in those reducing valves had caused moisture to accumulate inside; this moisture froze and blocked the air flow through the valve. It was determined that this could have been a contributing factor to the *Thresher*'s inability to get back to the surface.

Safety Changes Made

New safety standards have been implemented since the *Thresher* disaster 40 years ago. Today, although the engineers, designers, and construction workers who build nuclear submarines are still infinitely respectful of the possible dangers of a nuclear accident, they also give top priority to non-nuclear safety features.

> ### Beneath the Surface
>
> The USS *Thresher* that went down in 1963 had a namesake in World War II. This WWII version (SS-200) displaced 1,475 tons when surfaced and 2,198 tons when submerged. It was 308 feet long, with a beam of 27 feet and a draft of 13 feet, 9 inches. It could travel at 21 knots on the surface and at 9 knots when submerged. It was armed with 6 bow and 4 stern torpedo tubes and 24 torpedoes, each 21 inches long. The sub also had both diesel engines and electric motors. It was built at the Electric Boat Company and was commissioned on August 21, 1940.

No longer are safety precautions downgraded routinely because a project is behind schedule or budget. Today, when a "near-miss" occurs and causes a rethinking of safety precautions in that particular area, improved communications ensure that everyone who needs to know about the possible upgrade in safety precautions knows as soon as possible.

And today, better systems are in place to make sure that the parts that are called for in the design are actually the parts that are being used, not something "just as good."

U.S. Submarine Force Inside Story of the *Thresher*

Note: This account is the U.S. Submarine Force mouth-to-ear inside "tribal knowledge" of the *Thresher* disaster. It is considered reliable but not guaranteed.

The *Thresher*'s initial dive to test depth after a shipyard availability proved disastrous. On the way down, an auxiliary seawater system in Machinery Two upper level (the compartment aft of the reactor compartment and forward of the engineroom) ruptured and flooded the space. Apparently, at the time of flooding the ship was deeper than the depth of rig-for-deep-submergence, which was 600 feet by procedure.

It is possible that the flooding occurred when the ship was near test depth, the deepest operating depth a submarine is allowed to dive. Test depth is assumed to be about two thirds of the depth that the sub should theoretically crush (this is not a known depth because it is based solely on calculations). At this extreme depth, the pressure of the seawater was immense, and when the auxiliary seawater piping let go, a hole approximately 2 to 3 inches in diameter opened up.

The Power of a Leak

It is difficult to imagine the water stream that would come from a leak of this size at or near test depth. The stream from a firewater hose would seem tame by comparison: If a leak like this hit someone in the chest, it would be capable of cutting the person in half. It would rip open electrical panels and short out electrical equipment. The rocket thrust on the damaged piping system would be capable of ripping the section of piping completely loose. This would make a 3-inch diameter break into a "double-ended shear," which means that the pipe would be completely open to sea. The auxiliary seawater piping is 6-inch or 8-inch pipe, and a double-ended rupture would doom the ship if the hole was not isolated.

> **Secrets of the Deep** _____
>
> The original idea of the procedure was well thought out. After all, if steam were taken from a shutdown reactor, the reactor coolant loop's water returning from the boiler (steam generator) would continue to get colder as the boiler withdrew energy from the primary loop water to make steam to drive the turbines.
>
> Normally, returning cold water back to the reactor is fine because the cold water would be heated by the critical reactor fuel modules and would return to the steam generators hot. But since the core is scrammed, the water is not heated appreciably by the core, and the reactor coolant steadily cools drastically from the energy withdrawal of the boilers.

The flooding at that point damaged and flooded out the reactor control circuitry. Shorted reactor-protection circuits would "scram" the reactor (shut it down by slamming the control rods into the core). On a scram, the controlling rod group's rod-drive mechanisms would lose power, opening alligator mechanisms that allow compressed springs to drive the rods into the bomb-grade uranium fuel modules. At the instant of a scram, the nuclear reactions stop, and only the heat of the vessel and residual fission reactions heat the primary coolant water. A scram from 100 percent power would make thermal power go down to about 8 percent and stay there. Because of complicated reactor-protection procedures, the nuclear Navy insisted that the moment a scram happened, the steam isolation valves MS-1 and MS-2 be shut so that no energy is taken from the reactor coolant.

The Danger of Power Spikes

Finally, the reactor coolant is so low in temperature (perhaps 275°F–300°F, down from 500°F) that its density gets much better at moderating fission-causing neutrons that at higher coolant temperatures would leak from the core. Denser water means less neutron leakage and more fissions. More fissions mean more power. Once the ultra-dense coolant moderates the neutrons, the core can climb back into the power range by itself. This is called a "restart accident," and it is extremely dangerous because the reactor is now out of control and is capable of experiencing a power spike in the thousands of percent of rated power.

On a good day, the accident melts fuel and contaminates the reactor compartment, and the ship is without propulsion; it takes years to repair the damage. On a bad day, the power spike adds more energy to the primary coolant system than it is capable of accepting, and the resulting steam explosion blows apart the reactor vessel, breaches the hull—perhaps even making a hole large enough to drive a car through—and sinks the ship. In any case, enough radiation is scattered into the environment to kill a moderate-size ecosystem. To avoid this, Admiral Rickover's procedures ordered that on a reactor scram, the main steam bulkhead cutout valves (MS-1 and MS-2) be shut by the emergency switches on the reactor plant control panel (RPCP). These operator switches drive the valves shut by hydraulics, taking only a few seconds. Once they are shut, it takes 10 minutes to reopen them, so shutting them in a casualty is irreversible.

Unfortunately, the Rickover scram procedure was incompatible with a flooding accident. Even at risk of a restart accident, when the ship is flooding, the operators can use the residual heat of the core to propel the ship to the surface. The submarine mantra is: "Save the mission, save the ship, save the plant (the reactor), save the men, in that order." Shutting the MS-1 and MS-2 steam valves would save the plant but not the ship. Later procedures revised the shutting of MS-1 and MS-2 so that during a scram, the steam side remains ready to propel the ship for up to three minutes at 50 percent power, which was judged to be as much as the reactor can provide without a restart accident. These later procedures were inspired by the *Thresher*, but that did not help the crew of that ship that day.

No Chicken Switch

Back to the *Thresher* accident. The water flooding Machinery Two had shorted out the reactor electronics and scrammed the reactor. By procedure, the maneuvering crew shut MS-1 and MS-2, the main steam bulkhead cutout valves, so that there was no hope of using steam and propulsion to approach the surface.

An attempt may have been made to shut the valves of the auxiliary seawater system and isolate the flooding. Later submarines had a SUBSAFE "chicken switch" panel (emergency valve-closure panel) mounted in the overhead of maneuvering so that the engineering officer of the watch could immediately reach up and shut the hull and backup valves of the individual seawater systems using hydraulics.

Without such a panel, and with any time lag in isolating the auxiliary seawater system, so much water would have flooded Machinery Two that the ship would have had trouble surfacing without power unless the emergency blow system were used.

Three Legs to Disaster

They say all accidents are like stools: One leg or even two are not enough—to stand up, a stool needs three or more legs. Similarly, an accident needs three simultaneous malfunctions to become a disaster. Here, the first malfunction was the seawater flooding. The second was the act of abandoning the steam system to protect the reactor, missing out on the power that could have driven the crippled and flooding sub to the surface. The third may have been late isolation of the auxiliary seawater system or the continual flooding of the system. The fourth malfunction proved worst of all—if not for it, the *Thresher* would have steamed back to Groton while writing a sobering incident report.

That last malfunction was a failure of a desiccant tower downstream of the high-pressure air compressors, or "hi-packs," a pronunciation of HPAC. When the high-pressure air banks are filled, air from the ship is compressed by piston-type compressors up to 3,000 psi. This is done when the ship is on the surface or when snorkeling to avoid depleting the atmosphere of the ship. But the problem is that the moisture in the air can be deadly in a high-pressure air bank. The air goes through a desiccant tower, a bottle filled with powder that absorbs moisture from the air. When the powder is saturated with moisture and can accept no more, the system is supposed to switch to a fresh bottle and regenerate (dry out) the exhausted bottle. Somehow this system failed, and moist air left the HPACs and desiccant towers and filled the high-pressure air bank bottles.

When the officer of the deck in control ordered a main ballast tank emergency blow, the moist air in the high pressure air bank went through large valves and some 90 degree elbows to get to the ballast tanks. This caused trouble because of the Joule-Thompson coefficient, or J-T effect. When high-pressure gas is taken suddenly to a low pressure (in a process called throttling in thermodynamics), the equation describing conservation of energy requires that, as the pressure decreases and the density decreases, the property called internal energy of the gas falls. Internal energy is proportional to the absolute temperature of the gas. Therefore, as the gas goes from high pressure to low pressure, the gas's temperature goes from ambient (say, 45°F in the ballast tank-mounted air bottles) to subzero (to perhaps −100°F). You can immediately see why this would be a bad idea with moist air. Onboard the *Thresher*, moisture in the bottles instantly froze to a gigantic ice ball inside the piping, at the valve and the elbows of pipe, stopping all flow of high-pressure air to the ballast tanks.

Without the ability to deballast the main ballast tanks, with no propulsion due to shut steam bulkhead valves, and with the extra weight in the Machinery Two compartment, the ship was doomed. Reportedly, the junior officer of the deck was calling off telemetry on the UQC underwater telephone, a sonar device that sends voice signals instead of pulses. One of his transmissions was rumored to be that *Thresher* was passing backward through test depth with a severe up angle, which would have been the case with Machinery Two flooding, since Machinery Two is abaft the center of gravity. The fact that this officer kept calling off data when he knew he was going to die constitutes extraordinary devotion to duty.

The *Thresher*'s hull broke apart at crush depth and created a huge debris field on the ocean floor. Robert Ballard, the oceanographer who discovered the *Titanic*, took his submersible *Jason* and remote camera robot *Alvin* down to the *Thresher* sinking site. The secret-classified video of the debris field is chilling. Other than pieces of equipment—tanks, valves, piping, and cables—little can be recognized.

Lessons Learned

The *Thresher* lessons learned included these:

- Never shut the steam bulkhead valves MS-1 and MS-2 on a scram. In a ship-threatening emergency, be prepared to open the ahead throttles and use the steam to get the ship to the surface.

- Install and be prepared to use a SUBSAFE chicken switch panel in maneuvering to hydraulically slam shut all hull openings in the event of flooding.

- Make sure that all compressed air is being dried in the desiccant towers.

♦ Make all emergency main ballast tank blow valves full-bore ball valves with no internal passages or corners to turn. ("Full-bore" valves do not constrict the diameter of the pipe; there is no change in pressure or temperature—so there is less chance of freezing moisture into an ice ball.) Also make the piping from the high-pressure air bottles to the destination ballast tank as short as possible, with minimal or no elbows—a straight shot—so that even with moist air there is a fighting chance to get air into the ballast tank.

♦ Train every member of the dolphin-wearing community about these lessons learned so that this disaster will never happen again. In teaching these lessons, we ensure that the men of the *Thresher* did not die in vain.

The Least You Need to Know

♦ The biggest disaster in the U.S. nuclear submarine fleet was the loss of the *Thresher* in 1963.

♦ Many theories try to explain why the *Thresher* went down and broke apart 200 miles off the coast of Cape Cod.

♦ The U.S. Submarine Force mouth-to-ear inside "tribal knowledge" of the *Thresher* disaster doesn't completely jibe with the official version.

♦ Many lessons were learned, and submarines became safer because of the *Thresher* disaster.

Part 2

The Atomic Age

If the definition of a submarine is a "a submerged vessel independent of the surface," the first true submarine is the nuclear powered *Nautilus*. This was one of the most significant scientific achievements of the twentieth century. It proved incredibly difficult to get from point A (Enrico Fermi creating the first nuclear chain reaction) to point B (the launching of the *Nautilus*, the first nuclear submarine).

In this section, we'll be charting the course from point A to point B. The story has great historical value, of course, but it is of personal interest to me as well, because I met the hero responsible for it all: Admiral Hyman G. Rickover. Rickover not only had the idea of using nuclear power to operate submarines, he hung around for the next 30 years as head of the Naval Reactors Branch to watch the nuclear fleet grow from the *Nautilus* into a large force. As guardian of the nuclear fleet, he screened every officer to enter the nuclear program. In these pages, you'll see how he performed this miracle.

Chapter 8

Entering the Nuclear Age

In This Chapter

- Atom splitting time
- Building power plants
- Placing a power plant in a sub
- The perfect test bed

Radioactive, or molecularly unstable, materials were first discovered in 1895, when William Conrad Röntgen discovered x-rays. The following year, Antoine Henri Becquerel found that uranium salts caused fogging and images on photographic plates. But mankind did not learn to use radioactive materials to create power until more than 50 years later.

Today, most submarines run on nuclear power. A nuclear reactor's air-independent method of creating electricity allows today's modern submarine to stay under the water for so long without surfacing. Submarines are less than ever like dolphins and more than ever like fish.

We will return to the point later in the chapter, but briefly, here is how nuclear power is made: Nuclear power results when radioactive material undergoing a nuclear fission reaction releases energy and hence transfers heat; this heat is used to turn water into steam. The steam pushes a turbine connected to a generator that converts the energy into electricity.

Fermi Was First

The ability to harness power in this way was discovered on December 2, 1942, when Enrico Fermi first achieved a controlled nuclear chain reaction. The first usage of the new technology was to make a bomb, two of which were used to blow up Nagasaki and Hiroshima and thus hasten the end of World War II.

More than two years after the end of the war, the U.S. Atomic Energy Commission first considered using nuclear energy for something other than making war, such as creating electricity to light cities or operate huge machinery.

> **Beneath the Surface**
>
> Enrico Fermi's first nuclear reactor was called the Chicago Pile 1.

The first nuclear reactor to produce electricity functioned on December 20, 1951. It was built on a very small scale, however. In fact, it produced only enough electricity to light four light bulbs—think of this as something akin to the first nuclear battery.

Making Power

The Atomic Energy Commission was formed and began a program to fund nuclear power plants, the usage of which would be split between the government and the private sector. The building and maintenance of those atomic energy plants remains controversial because the consequences of a possible nuclear disaster outweigh the benefits of the cheaply produced power, according to some.

The first nuclear power plant was built in 1956, on the Cumberland coast. Called the Calder Hall Power Station, it used uranium as its fuel. The first full-scale plant opened the following year in Shippingport, Pennsylvania.

Secrets of the Deep

Here's how nuclear power is made:

- Fissionable materials (plutonium or uranium) experience fission (their nuclei break apart) and release energy.
- Energy is released in the form of heat, or thermal energy.
- Water flowing around uranium fuel modules absorbs the heat of fission.
- The water turns to steam if this is a boiling water reactor, or transfers heat to a secondary water loop that generates steam. At this point, the nuclear reactor becomes a big steam engine.
- The steam turns a turbine, which creates electricity by converting the thermal energy of steam into the mechanical energy of the turbine shaft. This electricity is then converted to electrical energy in the electrical generator.

In the meantime, the study of radioactive materials led to effective cancer treatments and other medical benefits. Industry uses radiation to study the structural integrity of aging buildings and the integrity of pipe welds (see Chapter 7 about the *Thresher* disaster). The use of radioactive materials has even influenced the art world, and it is now possible to date old materials, thus exposing hoaxes.

How do we get from making nuclear power in plants on the ground to having submarines running under the sea with nuclear reactors in them? Well, that seemingly gigantic leap was pretty much accomplished by one man, Adm. Hyman Rickover. (See Chapter 9.)

The first nuclear submarine in the British fleet was the HMS *Vanguard.*

Albacore

Before we get to Rickover and the first nuclear sub, we have to talk about a sub that bridged the gap between the archaic subs of the World War II era and the modern nuclear subs that we have today. That's the *Albacore*.

One of the most influential submarines of the early 1950s, the USS *Albacore* was an experimental submarine. Using it, submarine designers first tested a lot of ideas that have now become standard features on state-of-the-art submarines. The *Albacore* was different because it was a "body of revolution" rather than a waterproof surface ship. The "potential flow field" around this body of revolution minimized the vessel's drag, squeezing every bit of velocity from a given amount of ship's power.

In the modern history of submarines, the *Albacore* was the link between the submersible warships of World War II—which were basically surface vessels with the capability to submerge, doing so only when they needed to hide or attack—and the nuclear-powered submarines that followed. The WWII subs were designed to run along the top of the water and to move quickly. Their ability to move quickly diminished greatly when they submerged, however. Under the waves, the submarines of World War II became pokey and, like dolphins and whales, had to surface regularly for air.

To Move Swiftly Through the Deep

After the war, the Undersea Warfare Committee of the National Science Foundation (NSF) recognized that a submarine's speed while underwater was essential to its ability to escape from or attack the enemy, and to position itself for that attack across global distances.

The NSF report resulted in a feasibility study. Could a submarine be built that moved swiftly under the water—a submarine with a fully rounded hull, a single propeller located along the axis, and a pressure hull constructed of *HY-80*?

A debate began among the brightest and best minds in submarine design about which was better, a single propeller or a double propeller. It was decided that a test submarine would be built, and different systems would be used on the same sub at different times, thus definitively determining which of the systems was superior.

> **Subtalk**
>
> HY-80 was, at the time, the newest, toughest, and strongest form of steel known to man. The name stands for "high-yield 80,000 psi," for the yield point of the steel. Yield strength is the point at which the material stops its elastic behavior (snapping back to its original shape at the relaxation of the stress) and begins behaving plastically (at the removal of the stress, the material doesn't return to its original shape).

> **Beneath the Surface**
>
> Royalty beneath the waves: The king of England and the king and queen of Spain have made submerged cruises in submarines.

USS *Albacore*, a Test Bed

The USS *Albacore* was laid down on March 15, 1952, launched on August 1, 1953, and commissioned on December 5, 1953. She served for the next 20 years, mostly as a test bed for many of submarine development's new concepts.

Most notable of the new concepts that the *Albacore* tried first was the teardrop-shape hull. The shape of the hull proved to be so effective that nearly all modern submarine designs use it. Tests proved that subs with a teardrop-shape hull are faster and more maneuverable than those with hulls of another shape.

Beneath the Surface

Facts about the *Albacore:*

- ◆ Length: 203 feet, 10 inches
- ◆ Width: 27 feet, 4 inches
- ◆ Draft: 18 feet, 7 inches
- ◆ Displacement: 1,242 tons surface, 1,847 tons submerged
- ◆ Speed: 15 knots surface, 30+ knots submerged
- ◆ Armament: None carried
- ◆ Complement: 5 officers, 50 enlisted

Because it was used for continuous design experimentation, the *Albacore* functioned under a number of configurations during its lifetime. When it was first built, it had a single propeller. That configuration also featured a dorsal rudder on the aft edge of the sail with small bow planes. Control surfaces extended to the rear of the prop.

The first version of the *Albacore* was powered by two diesel engines. These were coupled to a 7,500-horsepower electric motor on the propeller shaft. When the submarine needed to propel itself underwater, batteries supplied the power.

The submarine was redesigned in 1956. Now the stern control surfaces were forward of the prop. The bow planes were no more, and the dorsal rudder was deactivated. The sub's third look was completed in 1961, when the stern control surfaces were made into an "X" formation. Speed brakes were installed on the hull. The dorsal fin continued its on-again/off-again existence and was reactivated.

New stern surfaces were installed in 1961, which greatly improved the sub's maneuverability. The increased maneuverability came at a price, however: Crews found the new control system complicated and hard to learn.

Later in the 1960s, the *Albacore* worked under yet a fourth configuration. She received a new battery and props that counter-rotated. A second electric motor was put in as well. The extra prop had a second propeller shaft inside the first. These changes made the *Albacore* faster.

The *Albacore* was used to test new ballast control systems following the loss of the USS

Beneath the Surface

As the result of a trip in an early U.S. submarine, President "Teddy" Roosevelt ordered extra compensation for personnel serving in the "Silent Service."

Beneath the Surface

President Harry Truman made a 440-foot dive in a captured German submarine.

Thresher in 1963. The sub remained on active duty until September 1, 1972. At that time, she was decommissioned and sent to Philadelphia, where she was placed in reserve.

> **Beneath the Surface**
>
> The first president to cruise aboard a nuclear submarine was President Eisenhower, who rode the USS *Seawolf* out of Newport, Rhode Island, on September 26, 1957.

She remained in Philadelphia until 1984. She was then towed back to Portsmouth, New Hampshire, and was converted into a museum. She now lives a quarter of a mile inland. Getting her that far from water was no easy trick that involved getting through a railroad bridge. She currently rests 27 feet above the water level in a dry basin, on a cradle. The museum was opened to the public in 1985.

The Original *Albacore*

The *Albacore* was named after the submarine USS *Albacore*, which was lost in the Pacific during World War II with 86 men aboard. With Lt. Cmdr. H. R. Rimmer in command, the original submarine *Albacore* left Pearl Harbor on October 24, 1944; topped off with fuel at Midway on October 28; and departed there for her eleventh patrol the same day. She was never heard from again.

The sub's operation area was northeast of Honshu and south of Hokkaido. Because of the danger of mines, she was ordered to stay outside of waters less than 100 fathoms deep. She was to depart her area at sunset on December 5, 1944, and was expected at Midway about December 12. Information now available from the Japanese indicates that the sub sank after hitting a mine. The explosion occurred on November 7, 1944, while she was submerged, and it was witnessed by an enemy patrol craft. A Japanese craft reported seeing much heavy oil and bubbles, cork, bedding, and various provisions after the explosion.

The Least You Need to Know

- Enrico Fermi is the scientist who first created a nuclear chain reaction.
- The first full-scale nuclear power plant was built in Shippingport, Pennsylvania.
- Because of nuclear power, today's submarines can stay underwater for long stretches of time, less like dolphins and more like fish.
- The USS *Albacore* was the test-bed submarine upon which many of today's state-of-the-art systems were first tried out.
- The *Albacore* formed a bridge between the outdated subs of WWII and today's nuclear-age submarines.

Nautilus: Admiral Rickover's Baby

In This Chapter

- ◆ The first nuclear reactor
- ◆ The first nuclear sub
- ◆ Interviewing with Admiral Rickover
- ◆ The *Nautilus* grows old

Although it may have been a group effort to discover radioactivity and then build a nuclear bomb, no committee was responsible for the idea of putting a nuclear reactor in a submarine.

That light bulb went on over the head of one man and one man only: Adm. Hyman G. Rickover.

Rickover: Father of the Nuclear Navy

Hyman G. Rickover was born on January 27, 1900, in Makow, Russia. When he was six, his family moved to Chicago, Illinois. Rickover entered the U.S. Naval Academy in 1918, and was commissioned as an ensign in June 1922.

Following sea duty aboard the USS *La Vallette* (DD-315) and the USS *Nevada* (BB-36), Rickover attended Columbia University, where he earned a Master of Science degree in electrical engineering. His career with submarines began in 1929, when he qualified for submarine duty and command.

Years Submerged

Rickover spent the next four years aboard the submarines S-9 and S-48. He assumed command of the USS *Finch* in June 1937. A few months later, he was selected as an engineering duty officer, which remained his specialty for the remainder of his career.

After the Japanese attack at Pearl Harbor brought the United States into World War II, Rickover became head of the Electrical Section of the Bureau of Ships. After the war he was the commanding officer of the Naval Repair Base in Okinawa.

Hyman Finds the Atom

In 1946, Rickover was assigned to the Atomic Energy Commission laboratory at Oak Ridge, Tennessee; in early 1949, he was assigned to the Division of Reactor Development, U.S. Atomic Energy Commission. It was as director of the Naval Reactors Branch that Rickover developed the world's first nuclear-powered submarine, the USS *Nautilus* (SSN-571), which went to sea in 1955. For many years, Rickover directed all aspects of building and operating the nuclear fleet.

Launching of the USS Nautilus, January 21, 1954.

Rickover's numerous medals and decorations include three Distinguished Service Medals, the Legion of Merit, the Navy Commendation Medal, and the World War II Victory Medal. He also received 61 civilian awards (including the prestigious Enrico Fermi Award) and 15 honorary degrees.

They Named a Submarine After Him

Rickover was twice awarded the Congressional Gold Medal for exceptional public service. In 1980, President Jimmy Carter presented him with the Presidential Medal of Freedom, the nation's highest nonmilitary honor, for his contributions to world peace. Rickover retired in 1982 after 63 years of service. A building at the Naval Academy is named after him, and the attack submarine USS *Hyman G. Rickover* (SSN-709) is named in memorial to him.

When it comes to people whose ideas and drive shaped the twentieth century, Rickover's name is frequently overlooked. However, it was Rickover who envisioned and implemented the atom as a source of energy rather than destruction.

> **Secrets of the Deep**
>
> Before nuclear power was used, submarines were invented that were propelled by cars, sails, treadles, hand-operated screws, clockwork, springs, steam stored in tubes, chemical engines, compressed air, stored gases, and electric motors.

> **Beneath the Surface**
>
> According to historian Terri Hardin, writing in the *Military Technical Journal*, "[Rickover's] ability to chart his course of action through the sea of red tape created by the Navy and Washington are equally legendary."

Former U.S. President Jimmy Carter described Rickover as an "iconoclastic Navy figure who had overcome all obstacles." Without Rickover, it is unlikely that nuclear energy would have been launched as expeditiously or as safely as it was. Rickover was a maverick and a charismatic figure. He was able to charm and entreat an unwilling military and Congress into building the prototype nuclear-powered submarine, which turned out to be the USS *Nautilus*.

Rickover's efforts were duly rewarded. Every pain that the *Nautilus* project bought him early on was replaced by glory in long and distinguished service.

Prototype Reactor Built

Rickover started his military career in the 1920s. After World War II, he was convinced that nuclear power was essential to the naval fleet, and he lobbied for the chance to prove it.

In 1947, the Naval Reactors Branch of the Navy was created, with authority shared by the newly formed Atomic Energy Commission. Then a captain, Rickover was in command of the branch and was entrusted with the task of developing the first nuclear reactor. Construction of the *Nautilus* reactor took place in Idaho, with an initial budget of $30 million. The prototype was a uranium-based reactor that cycled water through a steam and cooling process. Steam actually powered the sub, but power was made almost limitless by the addition of nuclear energy.

The Admiral and I

Admiral Hyman G. Rickover, the father of the nuclear Navy, had pledged to Congress that not a single naval officer would be admitted to his program unless he personally approved of him. Every single candidate would be interviewed personally. The trouble was that Rickover was so eccentric that he tended to throw candidates out of the program for reasons only he knew. And once Rickover flunked someone, there was no appeal. The door was shut forever.

Anyone else would have done a cursory examination of the huge number of interviewees, but Rickover took his promise quite seriously. The result of his interviews is legendary. A pre-interview was done by Rickover's staff members. These engineers from various disciplines probed for strengths and weaknesses in a candidate's knowledge, but more important, they trolled for character flaws and then reported them to Rickover.

Rickover's office swarmed with people rushing around in a panic. His office was huge, a cheap government-issue desk in the center, with the top cluttered with papers. In front of the admiral's desk was a wooden chair. The front legs of the chair were shorter by 2 inches than the back legs, intentionally keeping a candidate off balance. Rickover might begin roaring at a candidate immediately; if snappy answers weren't received, he threw the interviewee into "the cooler," a small closet with a few filing cabinets and a hard chair. The candidate was supposed to be rethinking his answers during his time in this penalty box. Many people logged hours in the cooler.

Stories Galore

Every submariner had a story about his Rickover interviews. One weapons officer recounted the tale of when he was brought in to see the "kindly old gentleman." He did a poor job answering a question, and the admiral became enraged.

He picked up a pile of papers and threw them to the overhead. Papers rained down all over the office. Aides scurried to pick them up, but Rickover screamed at them to let them be. Several sheets of classified information flew out the open window. One sheet landed right on top of the admiral's head. *He kept it balanced there for the rest of the interview.*

Rickover hated jocks and "stripers," who are midshipmen charged with the authority to govern the academy's Brigade of Midshipmen. But most of all, he hated to see a declining trend in class rank. If he found someone with that down-sloping rank, he insisted that they commit to a study program and report to him by letter every week. Seniors were contracting to study 40, 50, even 60 hours per week in addition to classes, sports, and drill. Woe to the man who didn't keep up with his promised hours, or who failed to write the required "Rickover letter," or one whose class rank did not improve.

Rickover Tales

One midshipman had a hobby as a poet. Rickover asked him if he thought he was creative. Feeling boxed in, the midshipman answered that he did. Rickover ordered him to stand on a chair and think up a creative poem about the interview. After the youth stuttered his way through something lame, Rickover called in one of his female assistants, who was pregnant. Rickover pointed at her belly and roared, "That, *that right there*, is creativity!"

A timid youth was sent in to see the admiral. The report from the staff was that he was shy and fearful. Rickover looked up from his desk and calmly said, "You have exactly 30 seconds to piss me off." The midshipman panicked as he looked around the room, wondering how he would anger the admiral. He thought he could find a family picture and say something rude about the people in it, but with Rickover it might backfire. The crusty admiral might laugh or agree with him.

Desperate and out of options, the kid saw Rickover's 3-foot-long shiny model of the USS *Nautilus*, the first nuclear-powered submarine. He ran over, grabbed it, hoisted it over his head, and with a shriek from hell smashed it on the admiral's desk. Pieces of the submarine flew all over the room. One shard cut the admiral's wrist, and the old gentleman bled onto his shirt. The admiral's face went pale in fury. The midshipman's eyes grew wide in terror—what had he done?

The admiral stood up and screamed, "Get out! Get the [bleep] out of my office! *Now!*"

The youth sprinted for the door, his hand trembling on the knob. Finally he got the door open. Just as he had almost reached the safety of the other side, the admiral shouted, "Freeze! Hold it right there!"

When the midshipman did, the admiral said gently, "Good job, son. You've got real spunk after all. You're hired."

The midshipman blinked, not quite believing his luck. Just as it seemed that he had turned the tide of the day, Rickover shouted, "Are you deaf? I told you to get the [bleep] out of my office! Now *go!*"

In another round of interviews, two midshipmen arrived with the same major and similar academic careers, both suitable for the nuclear Navy. Both candidates had serious girlfriends, and both were engaged to be married at the academy chapel after graduation.

When the first came in, Rickover informed him that his grades showed that he was not capable of passing the demanding program while devoting time and energy to a new wife. Rickover ordered him to phone his fiancée on the speakerphone and tell her that he would be delaying their wedding by a year.

Obediently, the midshipman complied, explaining to his upset girlfriend that the admiral insisted that the wedding be postponed for a year and a half. Afterward, Rickover sent the candidate back to the waiting room and called for the second midshipman.

Again, Rickover gave the speech about how demanding the nuclear-training pipeline would be and said that the candidate would have to delay his wedding until after he completed the program. Rickover turned on the speakerphone. When the midshipman's girlfriend answered, the mid told her, "Honey, I've changed my mind about going into the nuke Navy. I'm going Navy Air. We'll be in Pensacola for flight training after the wedding. Talk to you later."

The midshipman clicked off the connection and left the room, turning his back on the admiral.

The admiral hired the second midshipman and rejected the first. To Rickover, strength of character was everything.

My Own Personal Rickover Story

While a first-class midshipman at the Naval Academy, I applied for nuclear power training, the prerequisite to becoming a submarine officer. The first stop was Naval Reactors, in Crystal City. It was like having an audience with the Pope. Strike that—it was like being ushered in to see God the Father.

I entered Rickover's office so nervous I could barely speak. The admiral mumbled something. "Excuse me, sir?" I asked, swallowing.

"Why?" Rickover roared. "Did you fart?" Rickover glanced down at a card in front of him showing my class rank. "Now, are you going to maintain this academic standing all the way to graduation?"

"Yes, sir," I shot back, on solid ground. I had been first in the class—academically, anyway—since plebe year, although my military conduct grades were abysmal and I'd just been "fried" and restricted to Bancroft Hall for parking my hot rod in the commandant of midshipmen's space. I hoped the admiral wouldn't mention that.

"DiMercurio ... DiMercurio," Rickover mused. "Sounds like Mercutio from Shakespeare. You read much Shakespeare?"

"Um, no, sir," I said, back in trouble. "A few plays in high school."

"What? You call yourself an engineer and you've barely read Shakespeare? You call yourself a well-rounded person? You call yourself an *adult*, dammit?"

"I, well, sir, I could improve in this area." What else could I say?

"I can't believe what the academy calls an education these days. You're ignorant! Do you hear me? *Ignorant!*"

"Yes, sir," I agreed, feeling absurd.

Suddenly the admiral mellowed. "Fine," he said gently. "Write me a book report on Shakespeare every month. Now get out."

I wasn't prepared for the interview to be over so soon. "Excuse me, sir?"

"*Get out! Get the hell out!*" he screamed.

I ran from the room, managing to make it out the door before he shouted something else for me at the doorknob.

The Hard Part: Building It to Last

Vice Admiral (then Captain) Eugene P. "Dennis" Wilkinson—who worked with Rickover on the development of the *Nautilus* reactor and later became its first captain—explained, "Actually, the reactor physics was relatively simple. The hard part was the engineering to design and build equipment that would work under the stress of pressure, temperature, corrosion of high-temperature water, and radiation for year after year without failure.

"To accomplish this," Wilkinson continued, "Admiral Rickover reshaped engineering standards in America, in such areas as pipe and material marking and identification. He was responsible for the commercial development and application of *zirconium* ...."

Subtalk

Zirconium is a material that has a low neutron absorption cross-section. This means that it doesn't lower the level of neutrons, which are the lifeblood of a nuclear reactor, and it doesn't corrode even when exposed to extremely hot water for long periods of time.

Connecticut-Born

Meanwhile, the actual submarine was being laid out in Groton, Connecticut, where the first naval submarine had also been built by the Electric Boat Company (later the Electric Boat Division of General Dynamics). New England's deep-water harbors, particularly those in Connecticut, made the area ideal for submarine building.

> ### Beneath the Surface
>
> The *Nautilus* was based on a design by Farrington Daniels, a professor at the University of Wisconsin.

The *Nautilus* was not extremely different from the diesel submarines that preceded it when it came to length and beam. Wilkinson explains: "But she was an anomaly, being the same size on the outside but twice as large inside. Her 27 feet in beam was all ship, whereas the diesel subs had a 16-foot diameter hull, surrounded by fuel tanks."

> ### Subtalk
>
> A **fast cruise** is anything but fast. The ship is tied up to the pier with the hatches shut, with the reactor critical and steam brought into the engineroom. The underway watchsection is set, and the nukes back aft steam the engineroom at low power. Forward, the crew stares at blank screens, so bored they could scream.

First Test: Threat of Meltdown

Rickover's involvement in the *Nautilus* was hands-on and often very flamboyant. The reactor was first tested in 1953 in an underwater simulation called a *fast cruise* that lasted for several days. During the tests there were warnings of a meltdown.

In spite of the dire situation, Rickover insisted that the testing continue, reasoning that the results of the simulation were important enough to narrow the margin of safety granted the Idaho site. The reactor passed without disaster.

Psychodrama

Rickover also practiced psychodrama during the *Nautilus*'s sea trials, which he felt was necessary to test the crew's ability to adapt and function in a crisis.

In 1986, crew member Bob Bell told *Yankee Magazine* that "during sea trials, Rickover might suddenly say to the engineering officer, 'Don't move. You just died.' And then turn to the nearest sailor, tap him on the shoulder and say, 'Take over.' If you couldn't do it, you would find yourself off the boat."

Christened by Mamie

The SSN-571 *Nautilus* was launched in 1954 and, when completed in 1955, was christened by then First Lady Mamie Eisenhower. According to Wilkinson, Mrs. Eisenhower had been a strong supporter of the submarine's name.

The completed *Nautilus* was 324 feet long and 27 feet wide at its widest (this measurement is called the *beam*). It could carry a crew of more than 100. Its technological achievements were its S2W reactor, and the inertial navigation system had been designed by scientist (and Rickover confidant) Edward "Ted" Rockwell, who was also a shielding expert.

The *Nautilus*'s nuclear reactor ensured it nearly unlimited amount of energy, and speculation was that it could go around the world without surfacing.

According to Wilkinson, "We could make our own air and water, and our only limiting characteristic was food for the crew we carried."

> **Beneath the Surface**
>
> The firing of the *Nautilus*'s six 21-inch torpedo tubes was controlled by one of the first computers.

Wilkinson recounted other abilities as well: "*Nautilus* had a twin-screwed 15,000-shaft horsepower steam propulsion plant …. Submarine operating depths over 400 feet and submerged speeds over 20 knots are classified, so her operating depth and speed are classified. She had the best sonar and weapons available at the time. In retrospect, it is amazing that the very first nuclear-powered ship operated astoundingly well."

Early Problems

In other respects, however, the *Nautilus* was still far from perfect. In its first trials, the system by which fresh oxygen flowed was faulty and had to be adjusted. The *Nautilus* was also employing the same armament—Mark 14 unguided torpedoes—that had been used on diesel subs since World War II, and it had an old-fashioned interior communication system made out of brass funnels.

In one sense, the *Nautilus* was a true child of the 1950s. It had all of the labor-saving devices of a tract house and more: clothes washers and dryers, vending machines, and complete air conditioning. To keep morale high, it had a multitude of extracurricular activities, such as movies twice a day, a photography dark room, a daily newspaper, a library, and a nickel juke box.

Considered an Ugly Duckling

Admiral Wilkinson has no problem remembering his most thrilling moment as the captain of the *Nautilus*. It was the ship's first voyage.

He recalls, "*Nautilus*, with our country's eyes on her, first went to sea on 17 January 1955 and sent the flashing light message, 'Underway on nuclear power.'"

Even though the *Nautilus* had been successfully completed, it was considered an expensive ugly duckling, and the future of a nuclear Navy was still far from ensured.

Secrets of the Deep

The first diesel engines built by Electric Boat for submarines were installed in 1913 in the USS *Nautilus* and the USS *Seawolf*, namesakes of the first nuclear-powered submarines (also built by Electric Boat).

"We operated directly under the Commander Submarine Forces Atlantic Fleet, who gave us great support," Wilkinson said. "The other submarines nicknamed us Lola, as in 'Whatever Lola wants, Lola gets.' We didn't think that was quite fair, as we worked very hard."

There was much speculation and envy, since the then-current antisubmarine forces did not like to think of themselves as obsolete. And yet they were.

Nautilus Specifications

Milestone	World's first nuclear-powered vessel
Launched	January 21, 1954
Commissioned	September 30, 1954
Decommissioned	March 3, 1980
Overall length	319.42 feet
Maximum beam	27.67 feet
Maximum draught	25.42 feet
Displacement	Surface: 3,764 tons; submerged: 4,040 tons
Number of reactors	1
Number of screws	2
Maximum speed	Surface: 20+ knots; submerged 23+ knots
Armament	Six 21-inch bow torpedo tubes
Crew	12 officers, 124 enlisted men

Commenting on the *Nautilus*'s superiority over the submarines that had preceded her in the U.S. fleet, Vice Admiral Wilkinson described one practice: "Some 5,500 antisub rounds were fired at her, and none ever touched the hull. On the flip side, in fleet exercises, we put exercise torpedoes under nine ships in 51 minutes."

Public Relations

Rickover was also very good at public relations, and he worked ceaselessly to win public support. When in port, the *Nautilus* was constantly toured by the most important and influential people in the nation. At another level, Wilkinson and his crew labored to win and keep the hearts of the rest of the civilians.

"On the average," Wilkinson explains, "we got 43 letters a day, 14 of which required an answer. If we'd been out for 30 days, that meant 1,290 letters saved up, and 420 of them needed an answer. We were a little ship, but we read our mail. We had 24 Girl Scout troops that named themselves after the *Nautilus* and who sent pictures and cookies. You always answered those."

Launch of the USS *Skipjack*, 1956

The USS *Skipjack* (SSN-585) was the first submarine designed from the keel up for top underwater performance using nuclear power. It was the first Navy SSN sub to have a teardrop or *Albacore* hull.

An earlier *Skipjack* was the first submarine to cross the Atlantic Ocean under her own power. That trip occurred in 1917, starting in Newport, Rhode Island, and finishing at Ponta Delgada, in the Azores, off the coast of Africa.

Secrets of the Deep

The USS *Skate* (SSN-578) was the first vessel ever to surface at the North Pole. On March 17, 1959, she surfaced there to conduct memorial services for the renowned Arctic explorer Sir Hubert Wilkins. The sub was also one of the first to rendezvous at the North Pole. The USS *Skate* and the USS *Seadragon*, after executing a historic rendezvous under the ice, surfaced together at the North Pole through an opening in the ice in August 1962.

Cruise Beneath the North Pole

In 1956, U.S. Senator Henry Jackson proposed that the *Nautilus* explore the North Pole. The novel idea caught fire with Rickover and others. Wilkinson left the ship to attend Naval War College. Soon thereafter he assumed command of the USS *Long Beach*. So, the *Nautilus* got a new skipper, her second, in Commander William R. Anderson. Anderson's first assignment was to head north.

On July 29, 1958, the *Nautilus* entered the Bering Strait and then the Chukchi Sea, on its route to the polar ice cap. On August 3, under ice that was sometimes more than 65 feet thick, the *Nautilus* reached its objective. Since then, more than 40 subs have reached the North Pole, which has been considered the proving ground for submarine exploration.

> **Beneath the Surface**
>
> The USS *Nautilus* made history by cruising submerged from the Pacific Ocean to the Atlantic Ocean, passing under the North Pole at 11:15 P.M. EDT on August 3, 1958.

Future of Nuke Vessels Assured

This bold expedition assured the future of nuclear-powered vessels. Rickover remained the head of the Naval Reactors Branch for the next 30 years, where he oversaw the nuclear fleet grow from the *Nautilus* to a large force, including the Los Angeles, Polaris, Poseidon, Permit, Sturgeon, and Trident submarine series.

Ever resourceful, Rickover was able to quell Washington's concerns over *Nautilus* expenditures by double-selling the reactor as a civilian project. The sub's S2W reactor became the lightwater reactor (LWR), designated for commercial use, the first of which was used in Shippingport, Pennsylvania.

> **Secrets of the Deep**
>
> Were U.S. subs effective during World War II? You bet they were. U.S. subs destroyed a total of 1,314 Japanese ships during WWII, including 1 battleship, 8 aircraft carriers, 15 cruisers, 42 destroyers, and 23 submarines. On the other side, 52 U.S. submarines were lost.

Vice Admiral Wilkinson, who retired in 1974, became the first chief executive officer of the Institute of Nuclear Power Operations, which now sets standards for the nation's nuclear electric generating plants.

Also, due to Rickover's influence, all major warships built since 1974 (except destroyers and frigates) are nuclear powered. This now amounts to more than 120 vessels, including submarines, cruisers, and aircraft carriers. This has been done in spite of the fact that it is easier for nuclear subs to discover and destroy nuclear-powered surface craft.

Nautilus Becomes Antiquated

Rickover outlived his creation. In 1980, at the time of the *Nautilus*'s retirement, Rickover was still in the Navy. Rickover died in 1986, a legend among his many high-powered associates. (As nuclear submariners tell it, three days after his death, he was back ....)

Strangely, after doing its part to usher in the Nuclear Age, the ship has most recently been affected by toxic chemicals that are leaking from the nearby Goss Cove Landfill.

Beneath the Surface
The *Nautilus* is now a national historic monument. It is a public museum, moored at Groton, Connecticut, the place of its birth. But these honors do not ensure its fate.

The Least You Need to Know

- ◆ Admiral Hyman G. Rickover envisioned and implemented the atom as a source of energy rather than destruction.

- ◆ The first nuclear sub, the SSN-571 *Nautilus*, was launched in 1954 and, when completed in 1955, was christened by then First Lady Mamie Eisenhower.

- ◆ The USS *Skipjack* (SSN-585) was the first submarine designed from the keel up for top underwater performance using nuclear power.

- ◆ Rickover remained the head of the Naval Reactors Branch for 30 years as the nuclear fleet grew from the *Nautilus* into a large force.

Part 3

How Nuclear Subs Work

Odd as it may seem, a nuclear submarine is no more complex than your house or your car—or the space shuttle. It's just that you need to memorize 100,000 systems before you can become qualified in submarines. The information presented in this part is a small fraction of what a nonqual must learn in the first few months aboard a submarine.

When this information is down cold, the nonqual will progress to the point that he no longer is breathing the engineering department's air, eating the supply department's food, drinking and showering in the engineering department's water, or sleeping in the supply department's bunks. Instead, he will be pulling his own weight as a watchstander.

When that day arrives, the individual becomes a true submariner (this is correctly pronounced "sub-muhr-REEN-er"—a "sub-MARE-en-er" is a watch made by Rolex, which is popular among submarine commanders).

So, let's get qualified.

Chapter 10

Sensor Systems

In This Chapter

- ◆ Serious listening
- ◆ Finding needles in haystacks
- ◆ Screening out the noise
- ◆ Serious vision, too

It is dark about 70 to 100 feet below the surface, and little can be detected underwater using the visible light spectrum. Rather than drive blind, much of submarine history has been devoted to coming up with the sub's ability to sense its environment. The result is called its sensor systems, which function as the eyes and ears of a submarine.

Forget Everything You've Seen in the Movies

First, forget everything you've seen in the movies. There is no "radar" scope that shows direction and distance of a target. The closest that a submarine can come to that kind of realization of the outside world is through the use of active sonar, in which the sonar sphere in the bow transmits a sonar sound pulse into the water and then switches off to wait for a ping return from the target. Although this system is installed and submarine crews do train on it, it is not tactically useful. Transmitting active sonar gives the ship away, and stealth is everything. It's like a burglar calling out, "Hey, is anyone there?" Not a great idea.

Some tactical situations can take advantage of active sonar, such as when the bad guy already knows you're there and instead of dancing around him, you decide to ping a few blasts at him to confirm his range just before nailing him with an ADCAP Mark 48 torpedo. The active sonar pulse then is transmitted, and the ping travels at the speed of sound in water, bounces off the target, and returns to the sonar sphere's "ears," called hydrophones. The time between ping and return is measured to the millisecond, and since the computer knows the speed of sound in water, the distance (range) to the target is equal to sound speed times the time interval.

This works well in theory, but not so well in practice. The target returns an echo of the ping, but so does the underside of the waves at the surface and the water impurities themselves.

Helping to filter out real objects from echoes are Doppler filters. These are electronic circuits that discard all return sounds except those that are upshifted or downshifted by target motion.

Secrets of the Deep

The potential for sonar error is even worse under ice, where large ice structures return the ping from all around your own ship. The ping return is a blurry mess on the scope.

The Doppler effect is also at work when a train blows its horn as it approaches. The sound waves compress, making the sound higher in pitch than when it passes. Its speed away from you causes the sound waves to spread apart, lowering the tone of the whistle. In the same way, a target moving toward your own ship upshifts the frequency of the sonar active pulse, while a retreating target downshifts the frequency.

When the computer throws away all frequencies close to that of the transmitted pulse, the target shows up. The display is a graph of probable range vs. probable azimuth angle. This is displayed not in circular coordinates like a radar screen, but on a rectangular plot.

Beneath the Surface

The Russians have nearly perfected active sonar. They use a high-frequency active system to confirm the target range just before they shoot a torpedo. Their main active sonar has been named by NATO "Blocks of Wood" because it makes a clinking noise like two blocks of wood knocked together. If you hear Blocks of Wood sonar, call the officer of the deck and tell him to execute a snapshot—a quickly fired torpedo or missile, without a heck of a lot of aiming—because you are about to eat a Russian torpedo.

Bearing 000 (north) is in the center, with increasing bearing angles to the right up to 180. Bearings from 181 to 359 are on the left of center. Active return intensity and range is plotted vertically using dots. The bearing with the most dots is the active return bearing, and the vertical position of the preponderance of dots is the target location. In real time, with the survival of the ship at stake, reading an active sonar plot is like trying to read tea leaves and can take more practice than the result is worth. It is generally better to execute target motion analysis (TMA) to use passive sonar.

The Submariner's Edge: Passive Broadband Sonar

Passive sonar is the submariner's edge. It consists of a set of microphones that listen to underwater sounds (those in the know call them *hydrophones*). The hull arrays, or conformal arrays, are plates of hydrophones laid on the metal of the cylindrical hull. These listen to the sounds of the ocean at all frequencies.

The spherical array is a sphere about 12 feet in diameter that is set inside the fiberglass nosecone of the submarine. The sonar dome is a free-flood area, so the sphere is always submerged with its hydrophones listening to the environment, again, on all frequencies. This listening at all frequencies at once is called *broadband*. It would be like listening to a special radio that played all stations at once, and you have to try to pick up the sound of a ship out of the static.

Subtalk

Hydrophones are the sub's ears. In the spherical array, they are tiles that cover the sphere. In the hull array, they resemble rubbery plates. In the towed array, they resemble thick cables.

If you are on the headphones listening to the sea at a selected bearing (the sphere allows this by selecting certain hydrophones pointing at that bearing), you will hear the sound of rain or a babbling brook or wind blowing in the trees or waves breaking on the shore—all of these are "white noise," or broadband noise. The broadband noise will be loud at the bearing of a ship, either close or distant.

The display of the broadband sonar system is on what is called a *waterfall display*. This is simply named because it looks like a waterfall. It is essentially a visual depiction of the sound around the ship. At each second, the sphere hears noises at each bearing. Some are loud and some are quiet. The loud noise is plotted as a brighter dot than a quiet one. The display shows bearings going across, with 000 (north) in the middle, bearing 180 on the far right, and bearing 181 on the far left. Time is depicted vertically, so the data "cascades" downward. If there is a ship at bearing 045 and another at bearing 120, these bearings light up with a bright line extending vertically downward.

The recent data is on the bottom; the old data is at the top. If the ship at 045 used to be at 040, the line will slope to the right (this is called a right-bearing drift).

The disadvantage of passive sonar is that it indicates only the bearing of the target, not its distance from your own ship. When I found this out, I couldn't believe it—what good is it just knowing the direction to the target? You need to know its distance to be able to put a weapon on the target. It turns out that to find the range to the target, you need to maneuver back and forth while taking data on the target and observing how the bearing behaves. You've got to be kidding me, right? I asked. You have time in combat to pace back and forth and take data?

The answer is twofold:

- First, yes, you do have time. You have the acoustic advantage over the target, so you hear him long before he hears you. You do all this covertly.

- Second, it takes only about three to four minutes, and that's about how long it takes to warm up a torpedo and line up the tube anyway.

This determination of range by maneuvering your own ship is called *target motion analysis*, or TMA. The target's bearing rate is the key variable coming from this maneuvering. The higher the bearing rate is—the more horizontal the contact line becomes on the waterfall display—the closer the contact is. An example of this in landlubber life is that a close car whizzes by you on the highway, while a distant skyscraper appears to stay almost at a constant bearing from you.

The waterfall screen is usually divided into three areas:

- The top one displaying the last hour of data

- The middle one displaying the last 10 minutes of data

- The bottom one displaying the last two minutes of data

This way, a contact zooming quickly across the bearings (a high bearing rate) will show up in the short time display, while a far distant ship can be shown to change in bearing using the long time display.

A maritime patrol aircraft (MPA) such as a P-3 Orion can be tracked on the short time display as it moves from one side of the ship to the other. Sonar can even call a "mark on top" when the ship is deeply submerged from hearing close-range propellers.

God Said, "Let There Be Narrowband"

Broadband was the technology of the 1960s. With a good, quiet Sturgeon class going up against a nice, loud Victor class, broadband would normally be enough to detect the Victor inside 6,000 to 8,000 yards (3 to 4 miles).

In today's technology, this is a ridiculously short range. In the late 1970s, God said "Let there be narrowband," and he saw that it was good. We had it. The Russians didn't. We therefore had them in our sights.

If passive broadband sonar is like listening to all stations on the radio at once, imagine the tremendous noise you'd hear—music and news and commercials and static. The sea is like this, full of noise, including waves, whales calling to each other, loud merchant ships, and even far-distant volcanic activity. Now imagine if you knew the exact frequency of the radio station that you wanted to listen to, you could dial in and focus on it, and get rid of the static and interference from other channels. This is exactly what narrowband sonar does. If you know what tonal frequencies are put out by the target you seek, you can slice through all the useless noise in the ocean and find the target many miles away. We have detected quiet-running submerged bad guys as far away as 80,000 yards, or 40 nautical miles. That's quite an improvement over the 6,000-yard detection range of the broadband systems.

Like the passive arrays, the narrowband processor listens to the ocean environment and uses hydrophones in arrays. There all similarity ends. A narrowband array is towed behind the ship on a mile-long cable. The array is linear, meaning that it is arranged in a line like a very thick cable. The array receives all frequencies of ocean noise, but the real improvement is in the computer itself, called a *narrowband processor.*

Subtalk

A **narrowband processor** screens out all noise but the frequency "bucket" that it wants to hear. The frequency bucket is just a small range of frequencies, say from 249 hertz (Hz), or cycles per second, to 251 Hz.

The processor works so well because of *tonals.* Any ship is full of rotating machinery, including the screw, seawater pumps, other pumps, turbines, and diesel engines. This machinery rotates at a fixed speed governed by the electrical AC frequency (which in Western applications is 60 Hz and in Russian ones is 50 Hz). This rotating equipment puts tonals into the water.

Subtalk

A **tonal** is simply a pure sound at a fixed frequency, like a bell tone from a musical instrument.

The only way to avoid making tonals is to put equipment on sophisticated sound mounts, but that only quiets the tonal—it still is transmitted out into the water for a narrowband processor to pick up.

The narrowband processor takes the sounds from the linear towed array and screens them for a small interval of frequencies, based on known tonals emitted from a particular target submarine. The computer then displays a graph with frequency on the horizontal plot and intensity on the vertical plot, and the graph is integrated over 15 minutes.

After 15 minutes of looking at a slice of ocean at a particular frequency, the absence of a target shows a flat graph. The presence of a target shows a spike or pattern of spikes. A frequency spike can be present only when a man-made object is in the area. You stare at the spike on a graph on the display screen, thinking that you've just hooked your first enemy submarine, and that thought makes you forget how unglamorous-looking the display is. It would never play in Hollywood, where directors want sexy radarlike displays so that people know where the target is.

The Narrowband Paradox

This points out the paradox of narrowband sonar: You have to know what frequency you're searching for to pick up a target. This is because of the processing limitations of the supercomputers onboard. They cannot listen to and analyze all frequencies at all bearings. That would choke the most powerful computers in the world. Instead, they listen to a particular direction at a particular frequency chosen by the sonar operators. Only then can they be effective.

How, you ask, do you know what frequencies to look for? This is done by having a U.S. boat trail a new-construction hostile submarine when it initially leaves port on sea trails. The U.S. sub does an SPL, or sound pressure level, measurement of the target sub by literally driving circles around the bad guy. The tapes are analyzed later by the sonar eggheads, and the new class of hostile sub's emitted frequency tonals are analyzed.

An Example

For example, imagine that on March 14, the National Security Agency gets word that the new Russian *Severodvinsk* submarine will be departing from the Sevmash shipyard in northern Russia on or about April 1. The word is relayed to the Defense Intelligence Agency, from there to the Office of Naval Intelligence, then to the Chief of Naval Operations, and from there to Commander Submarines Atlantic. The message goes out that afternoon to the U.S. submarine *Oklahoma City*, which is lingering on-station north of Russia's Kola Peninsula, a hotbed of submarine bases and shipyards. Within hours, the *Oklahoma City* is in position off the channels from the Sevmash harbor, her crew alert and the submarine rigged for ultraquiet.

On April 1, nothing happens; on April 2, the seaway is quiet. Perhaps there's a problem with a steam generator–level detector? On April 3, bingo! *Severodvinsk* unit 1 is detected by periscope observation leaving port. The *Oklahoma City* shadows her and, during the Russian's surface transit, does an underhull (a close-up periscope video of the sub's underwater features) and an SPL, in which the sonar system records the sounds as the *Oklahoma City* drives around the Russian. How is it that we get away with doing this?

Two words: acoustic advantage. American subs are quieter than Russian subs, so we hear them and they can't hear us. The *Oklahoma City* trails the Russian, watching her sea trials, and then eventually breaks trail and brings the data home for analysis. It turns out that the *Severodvinsk* puts out a 354 Hz "doublet," or dual-frequency spike, with one spike at 353.5 Hz and the other at 354.6 Hz.

This information is passed on to the fleet. The next time a U.S. sub is in the Barents and intelligence indicates that a Severodvinsk-class sub will be in the area, the U.S. sonar team inserts the Severodvinsk "search plan" that hunts for that unique 354 doublet. When the narrowband processors find it, they know that there is a Severodvinsk out there.

Unless this surveillance is done on a hostile submarine, there is no way to catch it with narrowband. To find a needle in a haystack, you have to know exactly what the needle looks like.

LOFAR

LOFAR stands for low-frequency analysis and ranging. It is a rough frequency analysis done to broadband input seeking a "turn count" or propeller speed. On surface ships, the propellers are so loud that the turn count can be done using the headphones and a stopwatch. When the turncount is not so obvious, the computer takes care of it. The result yields target screw RPM and number of blades per screw.

Secrets of the Deep

The *R* in LOFAR is a mystery because LOFAR doesn't do squat to find range. Apparently, "LOFAR" sounded better than "LOFA" when they were making up acronyms.

A screw blade count can be extremely useful because all merchant ships have three blades per screw, with the occasional upscale four-bladed screw. A five-bladed screw is always a warship. When LOFAR puts out a seven-bladed screw, man battle stations, spin up two torpedoes, and make tubes one and two ready in all respects: The contact is a submarine.

On the Rocks: Under-Ice Sonar

Navigating under ice is tricky in good times and treacherous otherwise. It is done using two frequencies of under-ice sonar. One uses a set of hydrophones mounted at the top of the sail that ping upward with a short, high-frequency, secure tone. One ping return is from the bottom of the icepack. The second is from the top. The display shows both, and the difference between them is ice thickness.

This is vital to know because thick ice is dangerous to the ship. Thin ice, called a polynya, is where the ship can vertically surface through the ice. The topsounders can find a polynya; its location then is logged so that in an emergency, the ship can return to it.

Such an emergency would include …

- A fire, in which the ship needs to ventilate the smoke and carbon monoxide out and needs to use the snorkel mast to bring in fresh air.

- A reactor casualty that requires the emergency diesel to run.

- A medical emergency requiring a medical evacuation.

The forward-looking sonar is used to drive the ship through the ice rafts and stalactites, which even at a speed of 4 knots could smash the sail or ruin the sonar sphere. The forward-looking sonar is an active transmitter that transmits and receives at the same time. This is done by transmitting a tone that steadily rises in frequency and then falls back down, somewhat like a police siren. This way the unit measures the time difference from when the lower-frequency pulse echo is received even while it is transmitting the higher-frequency pulse. The unit also looks left and right by 15 degrees, illuminating a swath of ocean in front of the sub 30 degrees wide.

The display is a radarlike scope that shows blips where ice rafts hang down in the ship's path. The officer of the deck steers the ship from the under-ice console, driving the ship slowly ahead and maneuvering around the ice rafts.

While this is an active system, it runs at high frequencies, which attenuate quickly in the ocean and are not detectable outside close range. In addition, the icepack itself is extremely loud; the groaning and creaking of the ice is so noisy that it can be heard through the hull with the naked ear (a very spooky feeling). The under-ice sonar is therefore stealthy even though it is an active system.

Electronic Countermeasures (ECM)

If the skimmer pukes (surface warfare sailors) and Airedales (naval aviators) only knew how much intelligence submariners obtain from surface ship and airborne radars, they would permanently shut them all down. Each radar broadcasts a pulse at a frequency that identifies the transmitter—you might say that each one has its own voice.

Even ships of the same class with identical radar sets can be distinguished because each transmitter is slightly different. Good *ESM* operators can tell the difference between different hulls of identical surface warships by a notch or characteristic of the radar pulse.

The ESM room is usually situated close to the radio room and the control room. The antenna that receives this information is mounted on the periscope, so there is no need to raise another mast that would attract unto-ward attention.

Subtalk

ESM stands for electronic signal measures. Most of the duties of the ESM technician involve classifying and identifying incoming radar pulses.

If more refined analysis of the signal is required, the ESM operator requests the officer of the deck to raise the ESM mast, which is a fat telephone pole mounted in the sail. Although it is large, it needs only a few seconds to sample the electronic environment. The mast comes up, sniffs the air, and comes back down, capturing a wealth of electronic intelligence.

The officer of the deck can tell if his periscope is being painted by a radar beam, with the ESM signal piped into a special speaker by the periscope. You can tell that the situation is tense when you come to periscope depth and the periscope ESM speaker is blooping and bleeping like crazy. When it emits an angry buzzing sound, it means that the periscope has been "painted" by a high-frequency polarized radar, one that is designed to find periscopes.

The officer of the deck usually "dips the scope" and minimizes periscope exposure. Fortunately, the periscope is packed with RAM, or radar-absorptive material. Still, when you're sneaking up on a hostile Chinese surface force exercise in the Bo Hai Bay, it's nice to know that the bad guys are looking for you, and you are careful how you peek around the corner at them.

Infrared (IR): Detecting Heat Radiation

Infrared is sometimes used as a separate mast wired to a console in the control room. The mast detects light below the visible spectrum in the form of heat radiation. It distinguishes between hot shapes and cold ones.

The console has a television display with a view that can be turned with a computer control. It is a freaky system because it looks through objects. If an MPA (maritime patrol aircraft) flies overhead, you can see into the skin of the plane at the consoles, the people, and the various parts of the engines. It is very much like x-ray vision.

Against a surface ship, it shows the hot hull against the cold background of the sea. It has not been used extensively because it is blurrier than the periscope unless the object is up close. So far, nothing beats the periscope.

Visual: Up Periscope

Everyone knows what a periscope is: an eyepiece, with handgrips left and right. Optic power on the right, the angle of view is on the left, and cross hairs are on the reticle. The modern periscope also is …

 ◆ A receive-only radio antenna.

 ◆ An ESM mast.

 ◆ A device that takes still photos and video.

A video repeater panel is mounted in the control room, the captain's stateroom, and the wardroom, showing the view out the periscope if the scope is up during the day-time (and if classification permits).

The still pictures can be dramatic. Submarine commanders love to send framed periscope photographs, signed by the crew, to the captains of skimmers (surface war-ships) caught in periscope cross hairs—particularly after exercises won against said skimmers.

Low Light

A little-known feature of the periscope is the ability to shift to low light. This is also seldom used, since it can get "over-ranged" or blown out by a sudden bright light, which will display as a blinding white light in the periscope eyepiece and will ruin the officer of the deck's night vision. But when used, low light is much like an Army starlight scope. It is extremely cool to use just after the periscope goes underwater—you can look down on the hull and see the ship submerged. It's a bit spooky.

Laser Ranging

Sounds like a good idea: When you observe a contact on the periscope, don't bother with the range marks on the reticle; just shoot a laser beam at the contact to determine his range. The range will read out to the inch. This has the same drawbacks as active sonar: It transmits a pulse of energy that had to come from somewhere; it therefore violates stealth. It can be detected by sophisticated equipment. Imagine sneaking up on a skimmer, thinking that you see him but he doesn't see you. You shoot the laser range-finder at him, and suddenly he turns toward you and launches the RBU (rocket-guided depth charge battery) at you. Suddenly the ship is surrounded by underwater explosions. The torpedo is next; then comes the underwater missile. It's all over.

You should have used your "seaman's eye" and estimated the range. A good officer can get an extremely accurate range by visual estimation to a surface contact. How accurate? Good enough to use to shoot at the skimmer and hit him. This is called a "firing solution."

Secure Fathometer

This is another active sonar system, but it is mounted in the keel, pointed downward, and pings at high frequency with a very short pulse sent at low power. It is minimally detectable, but it is not used during a tactical situation. The pulse bounces off the bottom and returns. The time difference between ping and return is used to calculate the distance to the bottom. As part of the secret handshake of the Navy, and in accordance with tradition, the depth is read not in feet or meters, but in *fathoms*.

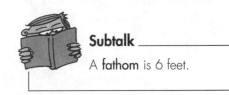

Subtalk

A fathom is 6 feet.

If the readout shows less than a hundred fathoms, you are either in deep trouble with the captain because you could go aground, or you are in a tactical situation in littoral (less than 100 fathoms deep, near a coastline) waters, lurking in someone's port.

Future Sensors

Optronics, also called photonics, are being engineered now for the Virginia class attack submarines. This technology will eliminate the hull penetration of the periscope and enable the control room to be relocated to somewhere other than the upper lever beneath the sail.

With optronics, images from the surface are transmitted into the hull using fiber-optic cables instead of a big tube with prisms. This means that only the cable penetrates the hull. The rest of the optronic mast will be installed in the sail.

Future sonar systems will build on the current technology, with more effort being directed at the computer side of the sonar equipment suite. Narrowband processors currently divide the ocean into segments called beams and search for specific frequencies. More powerful computers will be able to search for frequency tonals all across the spectrum, requiring processors to handle a hundred million to a hundred billion times as much data per second as they do today. Later computer generations will allow wideband frequency searches around the azimuth rather than in specific beams. A future towed array system could be articulated, with each "node" of the array knowing its spatial relationship to the other nodes. The wiggling of the array will do miniature time-motion analysis (TMA) to determine a rough range to the target without requiring the ship to maneuver.

> ### Secrets of the Deep
>
> The Seawolf class control room is on the middle level, but other ships put control in the upper level, largely because of the periscope. Seawolfs get away with this because their hull is much fatter than in the Los Angeles or Virginia classes.

Offboard sensors will start to make their appearance in the next decade, with remote sonar systems launched by the ship or dropped by surface ships, helicopters, or even permanent remote sonar arrays anchored to the ocean floor. This will essentially wire a particular area for sound, and the submarine will be able to monitor that area from far over the horizon.

Offboard weapons-delivery vehicles are being developed that will allow a submarine with offboard sensor capability to direct weapons to hundreds of miles away. In future years, a minisubmarine will depart from the mother ship to carry weapons to the remote battle area, using the submarine as a command-and-control platform. Alternatively, weapons could be forward deployed to a trouble spot, in a remote pod that keeps the units safe and ready for action, with a link to the remote submarine in case they need to be fired.

The two offboard scenarios begin to eliminate the need for a submarine at all—with remote sensors and remote weapons pods, the over-the-horizon platform could well be a destroyer or a cruiser. What will keep this warfare specialty under dolphin-wearer control is that the remote platform needs to have as much degree of stealth as the weapons and sensors in the operation area—and the only ship with true stealth is a submarine.

Radio and Communications Suite

Submarines are much different than other ships or units of the fleet when it comes to communications. The submarine commander is one of the world's last tyrants: He is in sole command of his unit, without the leash of constant orders from headquarters. This is because an attack submarine is out of communication most of the time.

Only one brand of radio wave will penetrate the dense ocean water, and that is ELF, or extremely low frequency. Attack subs have the capability to receive an ELF transmission off a loop antenna in the sail. The trouble with ELF is that the transmitters are gigantic, requiring multiple thousand-foot-tall towers at each installation, with transmitting facilities located on each ocean shore.

The "data rate" of an ELF transmission is so slow that it takes up to 20 minutes to transmit a single letter of the alphabet. ELF remains useful because it can call an attack sub to periscope depth, where the rest of the electromagnetic spectrum awaits.

At periscope depth (PD), the radio waves are received through the periscope for UHF and VHF. A better reception device is the AN/BRA-34, a fat telephone pole that is an excellent receiver of UHF, HF, and now EHF. These higher frequencies all have different transmission characteristics. HF, or high frequency, is not that useful. Think ham radio— the transmission can jump through the atmosphere, and you might reach Shanghai but not be able to hear Norfolk when you're off Charleston. UHF, ultrahigh frequency, has excellent transmission qualities but is limited to line-of-sight use. If you can see it, you can transmit to it and receive from it; it doesn't work for over-the-horizon use. But add a communications satellite in orbit, and line-of-sight transmission becomes an advantage. You can get your messages from the bird without the bad guys overhearing. Plus, the message comes down in a "burst comm," or burst transmission,

> ### Beneath the Surface
>
> One ELF transmitter is at Annapolis, Maryland; another is at Cutler, Maine; and a third is in Michigan for use in transmitting to the polar ice cap (the Arctic Ocean and the Barents Sea). Submarines cannot transmit on ELF; they can only receive on it. ELF takes enormous power to transmit, requiring dedicated power plants to be built nearby.

> ### Secrets of the Deep
>
> During the Cold War, the Russian commando groups (*Spetsnatz*) had secret war plans to break into American ELF facilities on the eve of war and disable the power plants or even knock down the ELF communication towers. These plans were countered by the American use of TACAMO (take charge and move out) aircraft that can transmit an ELF signal with less power and range.

which means that in a few seconds you can get reams of messages. This minimizes BRA-34 exposure time. In addition, uplink to the satellite is quick.

Submarines try to avoid transmitting, if at all possible. Maintaining radio silence is a big part of stealth, and the motto of the Submarine Force is "Remain undetected." Submarine captains love this because they do not get "rudder orders" (annoying and specific minute-by-minute instructions from headquarters). They are in command not only of the ship, but also of the tactical situation. A sub captain goes out and does stuff and tells the boss about it later. No other element of the military can brag that.

Perhaps it is unfortunate that the Pentagon is working hard on real-time continuous communication systems for submarines, using buoyant wire antennae and EHF buoys trailed from cables in the sail.

The current passive way of getting radio traffic is to come to periscope depth once every 8 to 10 hours, at random intervals. At periscope depth, there is housekeeping to do: Every week or two weeks, the engineer (Eng) wants to blow down the steam generators (boilers) to get rid of nasty chemicals; every day, the supply officer (Suppo) wants to discard trash through the trash disposal unit (TDU); the navigator (Nav) wants to get a fix (see Navigation); and the communications officer (Commo) wants to get the ship's messages. At periscope depth, or PD, the goal of the officer of the deck is to get the BRA-34 dry one minute before the communications satellite's broadcast, which occurs four times an hour at a classified interval. If he can do that, he knows that a minute later the broadcast burst communication will come down the antenna in about 60 seconds and go to the computer memory (buffer). Then the radiomen lower the BRA-34, and the officer of the deck can go back deep.

The ballistic missile submarine fleet is in constant receptive radio communication using the wire or the buoy so that any orders from the White House or Pentagon to fire submarine-launched ballistic missiles will be heard and acted on at any time. If the land-based transmitters are nuked, the TACAMO aircraft fly out and transmit the "go code" to the boomers to launch missiles.

Secrets of the Deep

A word about radio security: When in the channel leaving or entering port, the submarine uses the international frequencies on the VHF bridge-to-bridge radios. Under no circumstances will a submarine identify itself by hull or name (to do so would allow a spy ship to link a hull number with radar-emission characteristics). When a U.S. submarine identifies itself on a nonsecure VHF circuit, it calls itself "U.S. Navy submarine."

In a tactical situation, if a transmission becomes necessary, a submarine commander will often use a SLOT buoy, for submarine launched one-way transmitter. A SLOT buoy is the size of a baseball bat and can be loaded from a computer to transmit a coded message to the overhead communication satellite. The buoy is ejected from one of two signal buoys, each sort of a small torpedo tube that is flushed by auxiliary seawater to pop it out of the hull. The buoy rises to the surface, waits a preset interval (an hour is good), and then transmits its message. Then it floods and sinks.

On the periscope stand (the "conn") is a small red box with a red phone handset mounted on it. This is the remote NESTOR satellite secure voice system, which uses UHF to transmit through the encryption machines in radio, scrambling the user's voice. It takes a second or two for the transmission to make it through the encryption machine. The voice is distorted, but it allows a submarine captain to chat with a P-3 Orion antisubmarine warfare plane about the location of a submarine being trailed. One sub can "turn over" to another sub a hostile submarine being trailed using a P-3 and the NESTOR system. "I had it, you got it, I'm goin' home."

The Least You Need to Know

- In the 1960s, using broadband sonar was like trying to hear a needle in a very noisy haystack.

- Today's technology allows us to screen out the noise and hear only what we want to hear.

- Modern periscopes do more than allow the officer of the deck to see what's on the surface.

- Subs are able to receive ELF radio waves because they are the only ones that can make it through the ocean's dense water. The ELF signal is like a beeper to page a submarine to come to PD and get her messages from the satellite UHF.

Chapter 11

Weapons Systems

In This Chapter

- ◆ Going on the attack
- ◆ Torpedoes: inside and out
- ◆ Firing missiles
- ◆ Firecontrol and navigation

You first toured the control room in a submarine in Chapter 1. Now we are going to return there and take a more detailed look at a submarine's weapons systems.

You walk into the control room from the forward entrance near the entrance to the sonar room and the ladder to the bridge access tunnel. You are facing aft, toward the rear of the ship. The first thing you notice is the railed-in periscope platform with its side-by-side Type 18 periscopes. Tempted, you step up to the platform and put your eye to one of them. You can see all the way to Maryland, the view framed in cross hairs.

Control Room Layout

Mounted in the overhead are video screens, which are sonar repeater screens. They are "slaved" to the indications in the sonar room, but you can select which display you want to see, such as waterfall, narrowband frequency bucket, or active bearing vs. range.

Also in the overhead are several microphones hanging from cords (1MC shipwide announcing system, 7MC circuit to the bridgebox on the bridge if on the surface and to the maneuvering room) and a phone communication box for dialing up the captain. The red-painted box mounted next to it with a handset is the NESTOR secure voice UHF circuit, for chatting with P-3 Orion MPA (maritime patrol aircraft) pilots, or for calling the satellite on UHF secure voice. Finally, a circuit with a microphone is tied into the sonar gear—the UQT underwater telephone. This is a misnomer: It is simply a system that makes the BQQ-10 sonar system a big megaphone to transmit your voice into the ocean.

Mike's Corner

The UQT underwater telephone is pretty cool. When your voice bounces off the ocean floor, it sounds like the voice of God.

When you turn back to look forward, you see what appears to be the cockpit of a 747 in front of you on the forward bulkhead. This is the ship control panel. The "pilot" on the left is the sternplanesman. The one on the right is the helmsman/bowplanesman. Each watchstation has a control yoke much like an airplane. You scan the panel. The console between them has protruding sticks, the emergency hydraulic controls for the rudder, bowplanes, and sternplanes.

Also mounted on the console are the hydraulic control valves to shift from main to auxiliary hydraulics, and from auxiliary to emergency. The panel above is crowded with all the instruments that report angle, depth, and control surface angle. Centrally mounted is the digital depth gauge.

Below the right yoke is the engine-order telegraph, where the dial selects the correct speed for maneuvering (nuclear control watchstanders) to make. The seat aft of the console is for the diving officer, who supervises the ship-control party and reports to the officer of the deck.

Farther off to port is the ballast control panel, where the ballast tank vents are controlled in addition to the emergency blow system, hovering system, drain system, 1MC shipwide announcing system, and emergency alarms. This panel also has indications for the high-pressure air banks, and it shows hull openings. Called the "Christmas tree," this panel has a number of red circles (for an open indication) and green bars (to indicate shut). There is a light for each hatch and main ballast tank vent. When the panel shows all green bars, the ship is rigged for dive and can be submerged (naturally, this condition is called having a "green board"). The chief of the watch (COW) takes his station here, trimming the boat's overall weight at the orders of the diving officer.

Behind the chief of the watch on the port side of the control room are the navigation consoles for the ship's inertial navigation system and the fathometer. Immediately aft of the periscope stand are the twin plotting tables, one for navigation and the other for target plotting.

The Attack Center

The business end of the control room is on the starboard side. A mean-looking row of consoles with video display screens forms the attack center. The forward end of the row is Pos One, where an officer sits and "stacks dots" on the display to obtain a target solution. The next console is Pos Two, where the officer maintains the geographic plot. Then comes Pos Three, another dot-stacker. Finally is the *WCP*, which is used to line up and program torpedo tubes and weapons and, once a torpedo is launched, to monitor what the unit says and steer it, if required (see the following section "Torpedoes").

Subtalk

WCP stands for "weapons control panel."

Scattered through the room are status boards marked with grease pencils and tactical plots that fold away when battle stations aren't manned. The control room becomes Times Square on New Year's Eve during battle stations. And since the air-conditioning system is set up to cool off all the battle electronics plus two dozen men crammed into a space the size of your dining room, when it's just you and the normal underway watch section, the room is a refrigerator.

Torpedoes

The Mark 48 ADCAP variant torpedo, the one predominantly used by submarines of the U.S. Navy, has been refined through the years to the point of near perfection. If you are standing in the torpedo room patting its cool, gleaming green flank, you can tell it's a killer. Slender and streamlined, it's a cylinder 21 inches in diameter and 21 feet long. The bow tapers elliptically and then suddenly becomes flat, the shiny green skin yielding to a rubbery transducer.

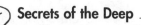

Secrets of the Deep

Stenciled on the weapon is the magnificent word *WARSHOT,* in white block letters.

You follow it aft, disappointed that the stern of it is covered by a gray fiberglass canister. If you pulled off the canister, you'd see the ducted pumpjet propulsor set inside a shroud, with a long coil of stereo speaker wire. The torpedo is linked to the ship by this thin filament of an umbilical, which transmits signal information back and forth.

If you could see inside the torpedo, you'd see that the first sixth of its length is taken up by the nose transducer and the weapon-guidance computer. Immediately aft is the warhead, which is three quarters of a ton of specially formulated, densely packed HBX explosive. Aft of the warhead is the fuel tank and finally the engine.

The Torpedo's External Combustion Engine

The engine of the weapon is perhaps the most interesting thing about it. It is an external combustion engine, where the combustion happens away from the work of the engine. Your car is an internal combustion engine, in which the combustion actually happens on top of the pistons that do the work of pushing the flywheel and the drivetrain.

A jet engine is an external combustion engine. The fuel and air combine and combust in a combustion chamber and the hot gases that result go to a turbine that spins the compressor. Then out they go to provide thrust (this will come up again in the Tomahawk discussion).

A torpedo engine is something like a jet. Instead of fuel mixing with air in a chamber and being lit by a spark plug, however, the fuel, called Otto fuel, is a peroxide derivative. Otto fuel contains its own oxygen and doesn't need the oxygen in the air. That's great for a torpedo, but God help you if it spills into the bilges and lights off—you'll never get it out (see Chapter 5 for more about onboard fires).

Building a Hydraulic Motor

The Otto fuel is atomized and lit off by a spark plug in the combustion chamber. The hot gases travel to the turbine part of the assembly. But this turbine isn't like any you'll see on a jet. It's a "B-end" hydraulic motor, stolen from servomotor technology. Two dozen little pistons are put into two dozen cylinders and arranged so that the cylinders are in a circle fixed to a steel circular plate the size of a dinner plate (the mounting plate). Now the pistons inside the cylinders are connected by connecting rods to a second plate. This plate is intentionally tilted with respect to the mounting plate so that when the assembly rotates, the pistons will be at the top of their cylinders at the three o'clock position of the mounting plate and at the

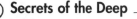

Secrets of the Deep

When a torpedo is fired quickly, without careful aim or consideration and usually in reaction to an emergency situation, it is called a snapshot.

bottom at the twelve o'clock position, then back at the top at the nine o'clock, and again at the bottom at six o'clock. You've made the beginnings of a B-end hydraulic motor.

Now drill a hole in the mounting plate to let hot exhaust gases into one of the cylinders at the three o'clock position. The hot exhaust, which is dying to expand and willing to do work by pushing a piston against resistance, goes into one of the cylinders where the piston is near the top of its stroke. The gas expands the piston downward in its cylinder. The way the tilted swash plate is made, the cylinder drags the 24-cylinder assembly with it in a circle where, at the twelve o'clock position, the cylinder is fully at the bottom of its stroke. The swash plate is connected to a shaft that spins the propulsor. (The "propulsor" is a fancy term for the screw.)

The assembly keeps turning on the swash plate and compresses the spent exhaust gas to a pressure just above the outside pressure of the seawater. It takes energy away from the swash plate to do this, but other cylinders are constantly coming into the inlet port area where the hot gases want to expand. When the cylinder arrives at the exhaust port, the exhaust leaves through another hole drilled in the mounting plate and is conveyed to a pipe that takes it to the aft skin of the torpedo. A special nozzle is made so that the gas is broken up into fine bubbles, making the torpedo less detectable.

Loading the Tube

To load the torpedo into the tube, the watchstander must coordinate with the control room, open the breach door from the torpedo control console, check it for any problems with a flashlight, and then line up the weapon to the hydraulic ram. At the torpedo control console, the watchstander selects the ram and nudges the controller slowly forward. Under hydraulic power, the torpedo will be rammed into the tube until only the gray canister is showing.

The watchstander will then take the power cable from the canister and plug it into the door. Then he does the same with the signal cable, making sure it's snug, and then he'll shut the door by hand.

At the torpedo control console, the interlock collar will rotate over the door, shutting and locking the tube. Now the system is ready for the tube to be flooded At the console, the watchstander flips up the toggle switch that vents the top of the tube to the torpedo room

Secrets of the Deep

Your own ship's weapon is called a unit. A "torpedo" is the weapon of a hostile ship. Never say "torpedo"— always say "unit" or "own ship's unit." If you say, "Torpedo bearing zero five five," the captain will assume that a bad guy has just launched at you and that he must "fight the ship" to combat the enemy sub.

and opens the flood valve. Now there's nothing between the crew and seawater pressure. If the valves and interlocks fail, the ship is flooding.

Flooding in the Torpedo Room!

In this case, the watchstander grabs a phone, hits the 4MC toggle, and yells loudly but clearly, "Flooding in the torpedo room! Flooding in the torpedo room!"

While it may be embarrassing, it may not be the watchstander's fault. And if he can't stop it and he's failed to notify the crew, he's just killed 130 people. Then and only then, the watchstander hits the toggle to shut the vent valves. (If the tube flooded, the interlocks have failed, so hitting the toggle won't help.)

If that doesn't work, the watchstander will run forward to the manual isolation valves and see if he can stop the flooding. If that doesn't work, he will rig the compartment for flooding and report to the casualty assistance officer.

If the vent valve interlocks are working, the tube will fill with water and then stop when the tube is full. The watchstander will check the water-round-torpedo (WRT) tank. This is a tank of seawater that surrounds the aft end of the torpedo tube. The tube has louvers that open it up to the WRT tank on command from the firecontrol system.

Now the watchstander will inform control that all is well with the torpedo. Control may power up the weapon in the tube; if the tactical situation is tense, it may pressurize the tube (reopening the tube flood valve with the vent valve shut) and open the *muzzle door* (other navies may call this a "bow cap").

Beneath the Surface

The muzzle door is an odd contraption, not like a lid, but more like a bookcase on a horror movie that rotates when the statue head is moved. The assembly rotates 180 degrees to open up a hole in the hull and expose the interior of the tube to the sea. When it rotates back, it is faired back into the streamlined shape of the hull. The ship may run with two torpedo tube muzzle doors open and two weapons powered up, with firecontrol solutions locked onto the bad guy. That way, if the bad guy pulls anything (such as impolitely preparing to launch intercontinental ballistic missiles to fall on Chevrolets and apple pie), you let him have a couple of Mark 48s up the tailpipe.

Up in the control room, the firecontrol party goes through a routine that is much the same on every launch. The routine ends as they hit the trigger to launch the weapon.

Launching the Torpedo

At the moment the control room firecontrol party launches the torpedo, the 3,000 psi high-pressure air system is suddenly piped into a big steel ram through a quick-acting solenoid valve. The air loads one side of the ram's piston, and the other side is wet and connected to the WRT tank. Immediately when the high-pressure air hits one side of the ram, the piston desperately wants to expand, and it has nowhere to go except to push against the water side of the piston.

The pressure in the WRT tank, previously at low pressure, soars to 3,000 psi. Because of the way water behaves, if one part of water in a level situation feels pressure, *all* of the water feels that pressure. The louvers to the aft part of the torpedo tube then come open, and the pressurized water in the WRT tank pushes against the aft part of the torpedo. Even all the way down to test depth, the pressure outside the ship is less than the pressure in the WRT tank; the only thing separating the high pressure from the low is the torpedo. The torpedo becomes a spit wad in the soda straw of the tube. The WRT tank is the boy's mouth, and the seawater is the air of the classroom. The torpedo pops out of the tube, accelerating madly until the 2-ton weapon is going 25 knots as it leaves the tube muzzle.

> **Beneath the Surface**
>
> If a crew waits too long to fire a weapon by trying to "over-refine the solution to the target" and thus loses a firing opportunity, it is said that they were polishing the cannonball. (Cannonballs work just fine whether they are dirty or not.) This is entirely different from polishing a turd, which is wasting time on a hopeless situation.

Now the fun starts. The engine pressurizes Otto fuel, the spark plugs light off, and the propulsor starts spinning. At engine start, the torpedo feels immediate thrust from the propulsor. Torpedo programming kicks in here. If the situation is tense and you don't want the enemy sub to hear your torpedo coming, you launch it in low transit speed with a passive search. If he's already detected you and you're in a melee situation (think barroom brawl, but between two submarines), just launch the torpedo in a high speed transit with an active search.

During transit or run-to-enable (RTE), the torpedo dives to its ordered transit depth and speeds up to the ordered transit speed (high, medium, or low). On the way, it just hums along, letting signal cable out the aft end to the mother ship. It doesn't do any talking; it just listens. If the launching sub wants to change the programming—speed it up or turn it or change it from passive to active—the word comes down the signal wire. The torpedo counts turns of its screw, and it knows how many revolutions add up to a mile. It checks its instructions and patiently drives on to the point at which the run-to-enable is over and the torpedo reaches the enable point.

At the enable point, everything switches on. If the instructions called for an active search, the torpedo starts pinging a high-frequency pulse in a "shark-tooth" pattern much like the under-ice sonar. It also executes a search pattern. One doozie of a pattern is the snake. In a snake pattern, the torpedo slowly climbs up a ramp about 100 or 150 feet and then dives back down. At the same time, it turns in a sine wave to the right and then to the left, its sonar illuminating a cone shape in the sea from this snake-pattern corkscrew. If the instructions call for a passive stealthy search, the torpedo only listens (so when it hits—surprise!). In a passive search, it still does a snake pattern. The torpedo continues its spiral search until it finds something.

Leading the Target

Although this sounds like a sure thing, shooting a torpedo is exactly like throwing a touchdown pass in football. You don't throw the ball at the runningback; you throw it farther downfield where he will be when the ball gets there. Sometimes you misjudge the speed of the running back—or worse, he turns suddenly. When a target changes direction or speed, the torpedo misses. The change of the target is called a "zig."

When the target zigs, it is necessary to turn the torpedo, or else the torpedo will miss. If the firecontrol party can determine a new target solution, a turn is "inserted" into the torpedo from the weapon control panel. Even if the firecontrol party comes up short, a million-dollar torpedo is out there—may as well guess as have it miss. The weapons officer, on the order of the coordinator, inserts a steer command into the weapon. The computer screen to do this is not sexy—just a functional display of torpedo course and desired steer angle. Once the weapons officer clicks the turn command confirmed, the weapon control computer sends the command to the torpedo tube, which relays it down the miles-long wire to the weapon, and it turns to the new course and continues the search.

After this, the unit either succeeds or fails If the turn is inserted skillfully, the unit either finds the target or runs out of fuel, shuts down and sinks. If it gets a sniff of the target, a "detect" (which is defined as four "left-to-right tag reversals"—think of this as hearing a distant sound and turning your head left and right to try to identify the noise source)—it starts "homing" during its "terminal run."

The "detect" signal is relayed through the signal wire to the submarine's control room. The weapons officer calls "Detect!" and the firecontrol party holds its breath. Most of the time, the unit will get another hard detect; if not, it goes into "reattack," a mode in which it turns a few circles trying to reacquire the target. A second detect is an excellent sign. After the third, the target is a ship of dead men. The weapons officer calls "Homing!" and the unit continues until the proximity detectors light up.

Speeding Up to Attack Velocity

At the homing point, the torpedo speeds up to attack velocity, which for the ADCAP is about 63 knots—up from 45. The 63-knot screamer was built to home in on the Alfa submarine, the fastest, deepest diving submarine in the world. It also can dive to an unprecedented depth so that the Alfa can't go to emergency depth and thumb its nose at the American attack. But by the time the ADCAP came out, it was clear that the Alfa was no longer a threat: Most of the seven hulls had already had nuclear accidents and were decommissioned. At 63 knots, nothing will outrun the torpedo. As long as the unit smells the target and has fuel, the target is going down.

At homing, the torpedo arms itself, lining up an interlock plate between the low explosive and high explosive. Low explosive is touchy and flashes without much energy input, but it is weak. High explosive is normally inert but, when ignited, blows things to hell. When the low explosive lights up the high explosive, good things happen.

Now fully armed, the torpedo awaits input from the proximity detector. A proximity detector is a device that senses changes in the Earth's magnetic field. When it is in open ocean, the magnetic lines of force are evenly spaced. Close to a submarine or a surface ship hull, though, with all its iron on the outside and empty air on the inside, the magnetic lines of force dramatically concentrate and the proximity detector knows that it is near a hull. The low explosive lights off, the high explosive detonates, and the detonation punches through the bad guys' hull.

Too bad there's no beer on board—this would be a great time for one.

Cruise Missiles

There are two ways to sink a ship: Either let the water in the bottom or let the air out the top. Cruise missiles are good for the latter method. They tend to be flashy, and low-profile submariners tend to find them flamboyant. If you've got a fleet of over-the-horizon skimmers, though, it might be best to get it over with and launch a half dozen Tomahawks at them. The surface-attack Tomahawk missile, the SACM (for ship-attack cruise missile) is a handy weapon when there are hostile skimmers lurking about and all your torpedoes are being saved for enemy submarines.

In the most probable case, you'll use *OTH* targeting. They're skimmers, after all, and any airplane or satellite can see them or another down-range submarine. You get the coordinates, load them into the weapon control panel, and select the weapon.

Subtalk

OTH stands for "over the horizon."

There are two flavors—one that's encapsulated and one that is launched out a torpedo tube. This tends to waste torpedo rack space, so the forward vertical launch system was installed in the forward ballast tank. With the encapsulated version, you line it up much like a torpedo and shoot it out the tube. The capsule angles upward to the surface. When it pops its nosecone out into the air, a "broach sensor" sees air instead of water, and the nosecone flies off. Now the capsule is a tube that serves as a launch platform for the missile. The first-stage rocket fires, and the missile heads out of the capsule and flies straight up to 3,000 feet.

Had you selected a vertical launch system unit (VLS), things would be slightly different. You would open the tube door and light off a gas generator underneath. The missile is safely protected from the seawater by a membrane cap at the top of the tube. The gas generator is a solid rocket-fuel charge that is ignited over a reservoir of water.

On the Way Up

The rocket fuel makes the water flash to steam, sending a pressure pulse into the bottom of the tube. The missile breaks through the membrane and rises out of the sea engulfed in a steam bubble. As soon as the missile dries off, its first-stage rocket fires and it blasts off to rise, like the tube-launched version, to 3,000 feet.

At the top of the parabolic flight curve, the first-stage rocket fuel is exhausted. Explosive bolts jettison the stage, and it tumbles to earth. The purpose of this pop-up is to windmill the missile's jet engine on the way down from the maneuver. The speed of flight starts turning the compressor, building up pressure in the combustion chamber. It is hoped that before the missile crashes into the sea, the jet engine ignition will be successful. The windmilling compressor raises the temperature in the combustion chamber and, at the right time, fuel is injected and the spark plugs are lit off. Ignition is achieved, building up tremendous temperature and pressure in the turbine inlet. The turbine is small, only big enough to turn the compressor so that the engine is self-sustaining. The remaining energy of the hot gases, after going through the turbine, is converted to the kinetic energy of the nozzle outlet flow. The high momentum of the exhaust propels the missile the remainder of the way to the target.

On the Way Down

Also on the way down, the missile extends midlength winglets for control. The missile is now at a high subsonic speed flying at an altitude of less than 50 feet, using GPS to navigate, confirmed with stellar navigation. Somewhere near the target, the missile may send out a few radar pulses to confirm the location of the target, or it may home in on the radar signal of the target. The weapon then executes a final pop-up maneuver because it can hit the target more accurately from directly above and because the target ship's close-in defenses shoot outward, not upward. The missile penetrates the superstructure of the ship and, a few decks in, detonates the high explosive. Yet another bad day for one of our targets.

But let's say you get the word to take out Badguyville, a city in Ugly Country. You program in the waypoints (go to B street and turn left at the 7-11, and then go to the Hyatt, take the second right, and come down on the Military Intelligence Complex—the north wing of it, third door on the left). This requires a TLAM, for Tomahawk land attack missile. Once the programming is done, the launch is much like an anti-ship launch, except that the navigation on the way in may use topographical features to help it pinpoint the target. You can launch a TLAM from the Med and hit the desired window of the Kremlin.

This brings us to the final Tomahawk variant—the TLAM-N, the nuclear variety. The warhead is small, but, dude, it's a *hydrogen bomb*—what more do you need?

Future Weapons

While our torpedoes are great, shooting a target 40 miles away means an hour wait (a 63-knot torpedo goes that fast only in its terminal run, unless you program it to go out at max speed, but doing that would alert the target and burn fuel). It would be great to have something faster. As luck would have it, a new torpedo is on the horizon. This time, the Russians truly did invent it fist; we simply stole it from them.

This new torpedo has solid rocket fuel and a pointy nosecone. The rocket fuel makes the unit blast down the bearing line to the target, and a vapor bubble starts at the nosecone that grows until the vapor covers the entire missile. At that point the unit is supercavitating—an intense form of cavitating, which we learned about earlier—and speeds up to 300 knots. The blue laser seeker guides it to the target. If all goes well, the kinetic energy of 300 knots of missile and the high explosive make for a bad day for the enemy.

Launching such a unit can be a bear. If the rocket ignites while the unit is in the tube, it will overpressure the tube and rupture it. The hot gas will blow into the torpedo room and

> **Beneath the Surface**
>
> The other future weapon system coming is a submarine-launched antiair missile, or SLAAM, that could fly out of the sail and blow up those pesky P-3 Orion-type marine patrol aircraft. The next time you say "mark on top," think SLAAM. Sure, he "snapped you up" (detected you), but he didn't live to tell the tale.

detonate all the weapons. For some time it was believed that the *Kursk* went down from attempting to launch a supercavitating torpedo.

Firecontrol (or How I Put My Torpedo on the Target)

The submarine uses primarily passive listen-only sonar, so a large part of getting ready to put a weapon on the target is finding out how far away the target is, what direction he's going, and at what speed. This package of data is called the "firecontrol solution." Getting it involves multiple people and millions of dollars in equipment.

The solution to a target can actually be obtained with paper and pencil. Just as the Navy still insists on checking the high-tech navigation systems with a low-tech system, it insists on using low-tech ways of nailing a target, just in case that fancy, overpriced combat control computer becomes inoperable. In fact, good officers of the deck can get a firing solution (a solution just close enough to reality that a torpedo will hit) in their head from periscope observations or sonar readings. The basic idea comes from trigonometry and states that, for a distant object moving perpendicular to the observer, if you know the rate of change of the bearing to the object (how fast the direction to him changes, measured in degrees per minute) and you know his perpendicular speed, then you know the distance to him (range = perpendicular velocity ÷ bearing rate).

> **Secrets of the Deep**
>
> There are only two kinds of ships: submarines and targets. Targets are broken down into two flavors—hostile submarines, called "submerged targets," and surface ships, called "skimmers" (after all, they just skim the surface). Naturally, officers and enlisted personnel who sail on surface warfare ships are politely called "skimmer pukes."

This is the beginning of the determination of range using the Ekelund range calculation. In general, this equation states that the range to a contact is approximately equal to the speed across the line-of-sight of the target divided by the bearing rate (degrees of change of bearing per minute). Officers of the deck are expected to do multiple leg Ekelund range trigonometry in their heads. (This is easier than it sounds because the sin and cosine functions are approximated, and the Ekelund range is meant to be a rough guess.)

The previously mentioned equation is a single-leg Ekelund range. A more refined range comes from a two-leg or three-leg measurement. You measure the target's bearing rate on one "leg" for about two minutes, and then you maneuver the ship. After you collect data on the second leg, you take the change in speed across the line-of-sight and divide by the change in bearing rate to get range. If you don't want to do this in your head, you can use a bearing rate slide ruler. No good junior officer of the deck's wardrobe is complete without it.

You can also determine the contact's heading and speed using a plotting table and speed rulers. With some intelligence from sonar picking up the turncount, a good fire-control party can put a torpedo on a contact without any help from the computers.

That said, the computers are faster and more accurate, but they still require the officers operating them to insert guess ranges and speeds. Without a skillful human in the chain, the computer just displays useless data. The firecontrol computer integrates sonar bearings being fed from the spherical array into smooth FIDUs, or fixed-interval data units, packaging bearing data into 20-second averages. On the dot-stacker display, the computer displays a vertical dot stack of FIDUs that will "stack" if the correct target guess solution is entered. After three legs of target motion analysis (three maneuvers of your own ship across the line of sight), usually only one combination of guess speed and target course will make the unruly Z-shaped dot stack come into a vertical line. When it does, you've got a firing solution.

What if that perfect, refined solution dot stack suddenly veers over on one side? And what if the officer tracking bearing rate notices that the target bearing rate suddenly changes? Or what if the officer plotting the target narrowband frequency vs. time suddenly shifts? Any of these indicates that the target has maneuvered. One of the firecontrol watchstanders then calls, "Possible target zig, Master One," and a team procedure is executed to either confirm or deny the zig. The firecontrol coordinator (the XO) makes the call. If the coordinator believes the target has zigged, he announces, "Confirm target zig!" If the torpedo is being lined up, the captain will call, "Check fire," which aborts the torpedo launch. A new set of TMA maneuvers by the ship to find the target's new solution. The question is, why did he maneuver? Did he detect you? If so, there may be trouble. You may even have to "clear datum" (submariner talk for getting the hell out of Dodge until the situation improves).

Once the solution to the target is nailed down, the XO calls out, "Captain, we have a firing solution." (Usually that statement is said with pride and hunger for the attack—the same tone of voice you might use to say, "Honey, the steaks are ready.")

At that point, it's time to rock and roll.

Navigation, or "Where the Hell Are We?"

This complicated question is usually asked at the navigation plotting table. One answer comes from paper and pencil on the old-fashioned paper chart. No matter how much technology evolves and no matter how many plasma displays can be linked to the GPS system, the U.S. Navy will always keep using the things that won us the War of 1812—a chart, a pencil, a compass, and a chronometer.

If you know where you are at a certain point—say, at Pier 22—you draw a straight line from your previous location in the direction (heading) you've driven. Since distance equals rate multiplied by time, if you know your speed and the time interval, you can calculate the distance down that pencil line. This is called a DR position, for deduced reckoning (shortened to "dead reckoning" by a landlubber nonqual who didn't know where the term came from). Unfortunately, a DR position can be way off due to wind, tides, and, most of all, current.

Therefore, we need to know where we *really* are. Let's skip over 600 years of maritime navigation to show how it's done today. First, you use the Global Positioning System, which is a series of signals broadcast to Earth by navigation satellites to pinpoint your actual location on the Earth's surface to within about 20 to 50 feet. That's good enough to lob an intercontinental ballistic missile and hit the bunker dead center. This position information is called a fix. Frequently the navigator sounds like a heroin junkie as he moans, "I need a *fix*!"

This is one of the reasons for coming to periscope depth. At PD the periscope antenna pulls down the GPS signals from the satellites and the system gives you a fix. But what about the 8 or 10 hours you're down without that fix? The DR position can have too many errors in it; if you're running flank, the "fix error circle" can grow to be 20 or even 30 nautical miles in diameter. And an error circle that big can cause a disaster. A submarine in the Med ran into a submerged mountain one sunny afternoon. She emergency blew to the surface and limped into port with a ruined sonar dome and a ruptured forward main ballast tank. (The new captain was waiting on the pier with the commodore when she arrived at the Italian pier, and the old captain went to command a dusty desk in the basement of ComSubLant.)

So submerged navigation is the critical key. There are two main solutions to this problem. The first is SINS, short for ship's inertial navigation. This unit is a gyroscope on steroids with a lot of bells and whistles. If tended to with care, it will give the navigator a decent fix—but it is still treated as a DR-type position and regarded with some amount of distrust.

The second machine is the secure fathometer, or bottom sounder. Bottom contour (BC) navigation can work wonderfully when the bottom has a lot of features (like over the Mid-Atlantic Ridge). But if the bottom is featureless, the BC fix is useless. When the bottom is flat and sandy, another means of getting that fix is required. And that's why we invented the magnetic field measurement system.

> **Beneath the Surface**
>
> The magnetic field measurement system is still coming out of development, but it relies on variations in the Earth's magnetic field from concentrations of iron that focus magnetic lines of force. A fourth method is in prototype testing—gravitational measurement, which detects minute variations in the Earth's gravitational pull.

The trouble with BC, magnetic navigation, and gravitational measurement is that you need to spend time—*a lot of time*—wandering around taking data and charting the values on a chart, and then publishing the chart, checking the chart, and refining the chart. While this might be a daunting situation for many navies, in the United States it comes free: The ballistic missile submarines, or "boomers," on strategic deterrent patrol, have nothing to do but wander the ocean aimlessly, doing their "hide with pride" thing. (In their determined attempts to "remain undetected" they turn and "clear datum" from fishing trawlers, yachts, merchant vessels, and anything that could "snap them up.") While the boomers are wandering, their equipment is measuring the bottom for BC charts and measuring fluctuations in the Earth's magnetic field for the GM charts.

The bottom line is that a submarine can navigate fairly well without undue exposure in the dangerous atmosphere at periscope depth, while not risking breaking the hull on an underwater mountain.

The Least You Need to Know

- The attack center is on the starboard side of the control room and is where the firecontrol party conducts the main business of the sub—turning targets into shipwrecks.

- Torpedoes have engines and fuel of their own, to propel them to their targets.

- Modern subs also fire missiles that can attack land sites and surface ships from above.

- Firecontrol is the art of making sure your weapon hits your target. It's not to be confused with "firefighting," which is putting out flames.

Chapter 12

Producing the Power

In This Chapter

- ◆ Theory of relativity
- ◆ Neutrons make the screw go round
- ◆ The hot and the cold of the matter
- ◆ Not-so-safe safety tests

In this chapter and the next, we'll be discussing the plant. That's shorthand for the propulsion plant, which is essentially everything aft of the operations compartment, including the reactor plant, the steam plant, and the drive train.

The nuclear-qualified officers and enlisted men who run the plant are known as "nukes." It isn't unusual to find the occasional "No Nukes" bumper sticker rebelliously posted in a berthing space where the "sonar girls" hang out.

Note: Not all forward sailors are sonar girls. The torpedomen are a class unto themselves. When the boat's in a liberty port, the torpedomen are the ones who end up at the local jail and cause the American ambassador to chew out the captain. The international incidents are usually caused when a torpedoman beats up a local biker. If you ever meet a torpedoman, agree with everything he says.

The sonar girls might also be referred to as "nose-coners" (the work in the forward part of the vessel) or just "coners." In general, these personnel may experience a week of watch without breaking a sweat or getting greasy, and have been given the epithet "sonar girls." While machinist mates and torpedomen may be the more blood-and-guts "rates" (work classifications), the ship would be unable to complete a mission without the sonar girls. But let's face facts—three showers a day and cologne are rarely associated with any of the nukes.

But the fundamental difference between nukes and sonar girls is that the sonar girls truly believe the entire submarine was built as a life-support system for their hydrophones and to bring their ears to new and interesting places. The nukes know the truth—that without them, the boat would be nothing but a dead, dark, airless pipe sinking into the deep. The air-conditioning–dwelling sonar girls sometimes treat the grime-stained, sweaty nukes as a rich man does his chauffeur. When the ship makes landfall in a liberty port, the nukes head for the biker bar and the sonar girls traipse over to the museums. (To all you ex–sonar girls reading this, please don't come to my house for revenge. You won't find me—I'll be at the biker bar with the other nukes.)

We've already shown how the forward tactical spaces work. Let's take a look "back aft." Check your thermoluminescent dosimeter and step into "Disneyland" through the hatch at the aft starboard corner of the crew's mess to enter the reactor compartment shielded tunnel.

Here's how it all works.

$E = mc^2$

Albert Einstein proved that there is an equivalence between energy and mass. Before his equation was formulated, two laws of the universe were sacrosanct: One was conservation of mass, that mass could neither be created nor destroyed. The other, the conservation of energy, was similar and stated that energy could neither be created nor destroyed.

Our friend Einstein turned the world on its ear by stating that matter could indeed disappear in a reaction and end up becoming energy. The constant c is the speed of light, a very huge number, so c^2 is even more gigantic. This means that a very small amount of mass can be converted into an enormous amount of energy. Take a single atom of U-235 uranium. If you shoot a slow neutron at its nucleus, the nucleus will split into two smaller nuclei plus either two or three more neutrons. The thing about it is that if you weighed the uranium nucleus and the neutron to start, and then weighed the three neutrons and the small nuclei when you are done, you'd find that the starting mass (the reactants) weighs more than the final mass (the products).

Now where did that mass go? It became 200 meV (mega-electron volts) of energy, in the form of kinetic energy or heat. So, the uranium in the core simply converts its mass into energy. It sounds simple, but wait until you read about the equipment it takes to tame this beast.

Nuclear Reactor

In the reactor compartment is the reactor vessel, which is a large cylinder of steel fabricated (that is, made) of 6-inch-thick magnesium-molybdenum alloy steel. It has a hemispherical bottom head and four nozzles, or pipes, that connect the vessel to piping systems. (A vessel or pressure vessel is a tank that can withstand internal pressure.)

A body flange connects the upper cylinder to the vessel head, which is just the term for its lid. The vessel is clad (lined) with zirconium to minimize corrosion. "Zirc" is much like stainless steel, but it holds up better to radiation.

Problems of Corrosion

Corrosion is extremely bad in a reactor because the particles of iron oxide, or rust, circulate through the core and become extremely radioactive. One of the great things about using water as a *moderator* and *coolant* is that water itself cannot become radioactive.

But the things floating in it can, such as the "wear products" of pump bearings and corrosion. The worst of these is cobalt-60, which has a very long half life (the time for a certain number of radioactive atoms to decay to the point that only half of that number remains).

The Birth of Crud

It is these tiny metal fragments that gave birth to the word *crud*. Crud is actually a technical term for filtered reactor coolant that originated at the Clinch River Facility, where it was dubbed Clinch River Unidentified Deposits—crud, for short. Crud builds up in the reactor coolant over time and becomes extremely radioactive, eventually posing a health hazard outside the shielded reactor compartment. Crud gathers in elbows of the piping system, where the pipe turns a corner. When main coolant pumps are started or shifted, the rapid change in turbulent water flow inside the pipes causes a "crud burst," after which radiation levels peak.

To combat crud, the coolant purification system was installed to filter out crud and purify the reactor water. The good thing is that the ion-exchange resin makes the reactor water ultrapure and crud-free, minimizing radiation in the engineering spaces.

The bad thing is that now you have a gigantically massive amount of radioactive resin in the coolant purification vessel. In the old days, boats would "blow resin" into the sea. Now that the amount of "curies" of radiation discharged are measured, submarines go into dry dock to blow resin to a lead-lined discharge vault. The high-level nuclear waste goes to the Spent Core Facility (SCF) in Idaho Falls.

The Moderator: Slowing the Neutrons

A moderator is a substance that slows the high-energy fast neutrons that result from uranium fissioning by means of molecular collisions, much like the slowing of a billiard ball when it hits other balls. When the neutrons are slow or thermalized, they are capable of causing another fission. Without a moderator to slow the neutrons, the fast neutrons will just leak out of the core. This is one way in which a reactor differs from a nuclear bomb—neutron leakage.

In a reactor, the reaction is controlled through slowing neutrons in each fission generation. But in a bomb, the fissionable material becomes so densely packed that neutron leakage is minimized. The reactions happen even with fast neutrons, and the reaction is a runaway or uncontrollable escalation in power (the bomb explodes).

Reactors can occasionally receive so much reactivity that they can be critical on fast neutrons, also called prompt neutrons. In this case, the reactor has become prompt critical and thus cannot be controlled. For a brief moment in time, it is no different than a nuclear bomb. But instead of a sustained nuclear reaction, the energy of going prompt critical causes the reactor assembly to blow apart—this is called by polite society a "prompt critical rapid disassembly." It scatters radioactive fission products over the landscape and poisons part of the environment, but most likely it won't blast away an entire city—at least, in most cases. Although the laws of probability and the second law of thermodynamics would not favor a core exploding like a bomb, it is still remotely possible.

The water that circulates through the reactor, then to the boilers and the reactor recirc pumps, and back to the reactor is called primary coolant. It is "primary" because it is in the radioactive loop that confines nuclear contamination to the vicinity of the reactor. This is different than "secondary," which is the steam circuit generated by the boilers to keep the engineroom relatively free of radiation. The "coolant" part is a misnomer—it doesn't so much keep the core cool because keeping the core hot at 500°F is its job. It is more accurately a "heat transfer fluid," which carries away heat from the reactor for use in the steam generators. However, it is quicker to say "coolant" than "heat transfer fluid," so the name stuck.

The vessel is fitted with an interior assembly that takes water from the two inlet nozzles and puts the cold incoming water into an inlet plenum to bring incoming flow evenly to the bottom of the vessel. The incoming water is "cold" (after the boilers took energy away from the water stream, it is relatively cold at 460°F, compared to the outgoing water that is 500°F).

As the water flows down the interior wall, it takes away the heat built up from the radiation.

The Limiting Component

The inside surface of a reactor vessel is a limiting component because it absorbs so much radiation that its strength starts to degrade. At the same time, a reaction between water and zirconium at high temperatures forms hydrogen. (This is the reason why a loss of coolant accident will result not only in a steam bubble in the core, but a hydrogen bubble as well.) The hydrogen causes the metal to become *brittle*.

Every time the reactor vessel is heated or cooled, the metal grows from thermal expansion or shrinks from thermal contraction. An expanding pressure vessel will grow, and a contracting one will shrink, which is very stressful for those cracks.

Add that to the fact that the inner surface of the pressure vessel experiences a lot more stress than anywhere else. (Think of a gun barrel—the interior metal of a gun at the instant of firing is under much more stress than the outside metal.)

The inner surface then becomes limiting when you heat or cool the pressure vessel. You don't want it to experience *brittle fracture* and crack into a hundred pieces when you heat it.

The cold water then flows into the inlet colander, which is a dish made of zirconium drilled with a thousand small holes. You could strain pasta with it, except that it's radioactive. This straightens and smoothes the flow in preparation for coming up through the fuel assemblies.

> **Subtalk**
>
> A **brittle** material has high strength but low toughness, meaning that it can't stretch at all. The brittle nature of the interior surface of the vessel means that cracks can form—and where cracks form, the metal can fail suddenly.

> **Secrets of the Deep**
>
> You are an old friend of thermal expansion: Next time the peanut butter lid won't come off the jar, run the lid under scalding water but keep the jar dry. The lid unscrews and comes right off, doesn't it? You just caused the lid to experience thermal expansion, in which it gets bigger at a higher temperature.

Subtalk _____

You are also familiar with **brittle fracture.** Remember when you put Mom's coffee cup in the freezer for fun and then poured hot coffee into it? The cup shattered into a hundred pieces, didn't it? The ceramic of the cup tried to expand on the inside, but the outside was still frozen and small and wouldn't let the inside grow; the inside cracks made the cup fail. A reactor vessel can do that, too, which is why the nukes heat up a reactor from *dead cold iron* very slowly. When the reactor has been shut down for a long time, such as months during a dry dock availability, it could take 30 hours to start it using a heating rate of $\frac{1}{4}$°F per minute.

This is very important because if one of the fuel assemblies is robbed of its share of water flow, it overheats and melts. A *fuel element failure* would result, leaking highly radioactive *fission products* into the coolant and increasing radiation levels in the ship.

Once the water exits the colander, it goes upward, pushed by the pressure of the reactor recirculation pumps through the fuel modules. Each fuel module is a pipe of zirconium, with zirconium plates inside. There are small passages for water to flow past the plates. Inside the zirconium plates are tiny ceramic balls containing the bomb-grade uranium and other ceramic spheres of burnable poison.

Subtalk _____

A **fission product** poison is a nucleus, born when a uranium atom splits or fissions, that absorbs life-giving neutrons. Xenon is one of these. Xenon is undesirable because it vacuums up the neutrons that give the reactor its power. Sometimes the designers intentionally insert poisons into the core, which temporarily absorb neutrons and keep the reactions from being too hot. As the core ages, the burnable poisons decay away, allowing more neutron activity—but that's okay because the uranium atoms are also running out.

The water coolant flows upward through the passages in the fuel module. While the uranium in the fuel is fissioning, it is giving off heat. The coolant absorbs the heat and carries it away. If the coolant water ceases flowing, the fuel module will still give off heat, but the water will start to boil. Steam is terrible at taking away heat, so the zirconium will eventually melt and send all the uranium and the highly radioactive fission products into the environment.

Subtalk

A **fuel element failure,** or FEF, is a serious but minor incident in which fission products (the result of fissions that are less heavy atoms than the original uranium and are highly radioactive) leak out of the fuel plates and into the coolant. The coolant gets much more radioactive, as does the piping systems. An expensive repair may need to be done. The reactor coolant is sampled every day for its level of radioactivity and the composition of the crud, to make sure that no FEFs have occurred.

But if all goes according to plan, the water leaves the top of the fuel module, collects with the water leaving other fuel modules, is mixed in the exit plenum and leaves the vessel about 40°F hotter than when it came in. Although 40°F may not sound like much, remember that the water passes through the fuel in less than a second, and there is a gigantic amount of it. Try raising your entire pool's water temperature by 40°F in one second: It will take one hell of a heater, one the size of a four-story building.

The reactivity of the core, which correlates to its power level and is a measure of how many neutrons are flying through the reactor, depends upon the density of the water coolant/moderator (primary water) and the height out of the core of the control rods.

The Control Rod

A control rod is a bar of material (in the U.S. Navy, the control rods are cruciform in cross-section) that is inserted at a specific level into the core. The rod is made up of a material that is a "black hole" for neutrons and that stops the nuclear reactions by taking away the fission-generating neutrons. In other navies, the control rods are made of boron. In America, they are made of much better stuff: hafnium. Turns out that Admiral Rickover saw the potential of hafnium and cornered the market on it.

Control rods must be pulled out of the core from the top (or pushed into the core from the bottom or side). Reactors typically use gravity to help control rods fall downward into the core during a safety trip, or a scram. A reactor that had to scram using its control rods to go upward into the core using a motor would not "fail safe" because if the rod drive motors failed, the rods would just sit there. A U.S. Navy reactor has a rod drive mechanism that fails safe: To scram (shut down) the reactor, the rod drives intentionally lose power, causing electromagnets to go dead. The electromagnets are in the top of "alligator assemblies" that grip the rods. When they lose power, springs open the alligator jaws so that their grip is broken and the rods—helped by gravity and assisted by a coiled spring—are driven into the core, shutting down the nuclear reactions. The springs are called "scram springs" and are extremely strong. They are also very long. (Don't forget that "scram" comes from the old nuclear pile term for the Safety Control Rod Ax Man, who dropped the control rod by cutting the rope holding it.)

At nuclear prototype school, if a student studying to be a nuke falls asleep at a desk, an instructor will "scram" him by dropping a scram spring on the desk (the spring is a classroom visual aid). The spring loudly boings and bongs and makes a terrible racket, both startling and embarrassing the sleeper. The student quickly learns never to sleep during study time. This is harder than it sounds, since the students work rotating 12-hour shifts and are thus constantly tired.

It Keeps Going and Going and Going ...

How many miles to the core does a sub get? Some reactors are designed as "one-shot" installations, so they last up to 70 years. The reactor fuel that the ship goes to sea with won't run out until the ship is scrapped. But most U.S. reactors built in the last 20 years need to be refueled every 8 to 10 years. A reactor does have a specific life, measured in efph, or effective full-power hours. Think of it as the gas tank gauge for the reactor. Fresh out of the new construction ("newcon") shipyard, the reactor is at BOL, or beginning of life. After operating hard for 10 or 15 years, the reactor is at EOL, or end-of-life.

For example, if a core is built to have 12,000 efph, that means it could run at 100 percent power for 12,000 hours. Or 50 percent power for 24,000 hours, or 25 percent power for 48,000 hours. The power level of the reactor is logged every 10 minutes, partly to calculate how many efph have been burned. As a point of reference, on an extended patrol of 50 days, you may only burn 300 efph. A nuclear submarine would rarely burn more than 500 to 700 efph a year.

In the previous example, the reactor would last 17 years. The efph burnout is so slow because submarines on patrol are typically at low power (about 25 percent) while slowly cruising around, lurking in the sea, and listening for enemy submarines. The only time power rises above 50 percent is when the ship is sprinting to get out of port to get on-station or to transit from one position to another more promising for the hunt.

End-of-Life Cores

End-of-life cores can present tactical problems. Imagine if an ambulance engine failed to start in an emergency. Similarly, an EOL reactor may not be able to be started because of xenon poisoning. Xenon, a fission product resulting from a uranium nucleus splitting in two, is an unpopular result because, of all the possible fission products, it absorbs neutrons that are needed for the production of fissions and power. It is also a bad actor because it is a gas. As the uranium burns up and xenon builds up, its gaseous nature makes fuel elements start to swell. Eventually they can bulge into the water passage, clog water flow, and cause local fuel melting or fuel element failure, raising shipwide radioactivity levels.

The good news is that xenon is "burned" at power by neutrons, accelerating its decay to an innocuous element. The bad news for an EOL reactor is that when the plant is shut down, the levels of xenon in the core prevent it from being restarted because there is not enough reactivity from the uranium remaining to burn up the xenon. The reactor might have been humming along just fine coming into port, even flanking it at 100 percent power, but then the crew shuts down the plant to hot standby. Ten hours later, an emergency deployment order comes in from *ComSubLant* to put to sea immediately and chase a bad guy.

No dice: The core is xenon precluded and can't be started up—you could try, but all you'd do would be to raise all control rods to the top of the core, and the power level would not come out of the intermediate range into the power range. Like an engine cranking but not catching, the reactor just wouldn't start. But wait 24 hours until the xenon decays away on its own, and the reactor would start right up.

Since the post-shutdown levels of xenon depend on preshutdown power levels, an EOL reactor is treated carefully to keep it low in power level the day before shutdown, even if it means idling it at 18 percent power next to the pier for 20 hours after the ship comes into port. In this case, the nukes remain "back aft," sweating in the engineroom "steaming the plant" while the freshly showered sonar girls go skipping down the pier to go shopping.

Subtalk

ComSubLant is the acronym for Commander Submarines Atlantic, the admiral-in-command and the boss of the submarine force on the East Coast. Submarines administratively report to the commodore or squadron commander while in port, but at sea, the ship reports to ComSubLant. When assigned to a task force or carrier battle group, the submarine will "outchop" (leave the command of) ComSubLant and "inchop" the carrier battle group commander.

Hot Standby

Hot standby is the condition of a shutdown reactor (all control rods on the bottom, rod drives unlatched, rod control inverter fuses removed and locked) with main coolant pumps in "one slow/zero" (one loop's main coolant pump on, the other loop's pumps off) and the steam generators (boilers) filled to the top with boiler feed water.

The reactor plant primary coolant water has cooled to between 350°F and 400°F, and the plant hibernates. Reactor power initially decays to the intermediate range at –1 decade per minute; then it comes into the startup range and slowly levels off to a very low "neutron level." Hot standby is used for shutdowns of up to a few weeks, and this is a condition that easily lends itself to a rapid restart (four hours or less), as opposed to a cold wet layup.

This Ain't Hoops: The Cold Wet Layup

Cold wet layup is the condition of shutdown in which the entire plant is cooled to ambient temperature (room temperature to 100°F) so that maintenance can be conducted. The plant goes into cold wet layup if it is going into the dry dock. Startup from cold wet layup may take a long time, perhaps up to 20 or even 30 hours, because the core must be heated very slowly to avoid brittle fracture. Brittle fracture of the reactor vessel can happen much more quickly cold because of the DBTT, or the ductile-to-brittle transition temperature; this can be around 350°F, below which the vessel is no longer ductile, but brittle.

We learned about ductile-to-brittle transition in World War II when we built all those Liberty ships. They tended to crack and break in half when they were in cold water. Another example is when the steel antitheft bar you use on your steering wheel is defeated when the car thief sprays refrigerant on it. When it gets very cold, near 0°F, it is easily shattered with a light tap from a hammer because it transitions from ductile to brittle.

Coolant Loops

The reactor has two loops, or circuits of piping, going from the reactor vessel (the outlet is hot, at 500°F) to the steam generators (boilers), from there to the reactor recirculation pumps, and from there back to the reactor inlet.

Also called "main coolant pumps" by the older, saltier nukes, the reactor recirc pumps push the water through the reactor and the boilers. This takes thousands of horsepower. A main coolant pump is as big as three refrigerators; it is the biggest electricity hog on the ship. This is why it is tough to start the reactor on the batteries—the main coolant pumps will suck the battery dry in no time.

As the reactor power rises, the pumps need to be upshifted to provide more flow to the core. Below 50 percent power, the pumps can run nicely quiet at slow speed. But if control orders up all ahead flank, the pumps need to be shifted to fast speed.

Some pumps can run on reduced frequency, slowing to superslow, which is excellent for noise reduction when straining the sonar ears to snap up a bad guy.

The discussion of tonals previously did not reveal that some of the worst actors when it comes to putting out tonals are the main coolant pumps.

Three pumps are in each loop, for a total of six. At any given time, four are running. When the pumps are lined up to run in slow speed, with two per loop, the pump lineup is said to be in "two slow/two slow." This always sounds funny to the nonqual, like the reactor is just too slow. Sometimes a single pump per loop can be running, such as during a reactor startup. While running in "one slow/one slow," reactor power is extremely limited, and it is vital to get a turbine generator started so you can start the second pump per loop.

Main coolant pump design was difficult because, unlike with Russian systems, Admiral Rickover insisted that the pumps be "no leakage" designs. Most pumps have seals installed to allow the shaft of the impeller (water wheel) to rotate, and the seals can't keep all the water from leaking from the turning metal shaft. A conventional pump would allow primary coolant to leak into the reactor compartment *bilges*, which would lead to extremely high levels of radioactive contamination in the compartment. Rickover demanded that his engineers build a totally enclosed, canned pump that would use primary coolant to circulate around the motor itself. Of course, Rickover was told it could not be done. Rickover had a furious temper tantrum and kept his engineers working nights and weekends until they performed the impossible mission and built the American main coolant pump, which remains an engineering triumph to this day.

> **Subtalk**
>
> **Bilges** are the unused spaces at the keel or bottom of the ship, in the frame bays where leakage water collects. The spaces are dewatered by the drain system and the drain pump. If the drain pump fails, after some time (weeks or months) the ship would be completely flooded from the drop-by-drop leakage of all the seawater systems. The trim pump (used to transfer water between variable-ballast tanks) functions as the drain pump backup in the event of a drain pump failure.

Natural Circulation

The idea behind natural circulation (sometimes called thermal siphon) is that hot water rises and cold water sinks. This makes the water flow upward through the core from the buoyancy of hot water, sink through the boilers, and end up cold back at the bottom of the core.

This takes some serious engineering to make water flow downward through the boilers (you have to lay them on their sides) and to make the water bypass the pumps. But in natural circulation, below about 35 percent power, you don't need main coolant pumps at all. Talk about noise reduction! This is one way the Ohio class boomers and the Seawolfs stay so quiet.

Emergency Cooling

The emergency cooling, or XC, system uses this same principle. If the core can't be cooled by the coolant circulated by main coolant pumps during a shutdown, the XC system is used. The XC system removes the decay heat (8 percent of full-power level) that will otherwise melt fuel in a loss of flow accident.

Here's how it works: One coolant loop reactor vessel outlet nozzle has a pipe that goes to a heat exchanger tank at the same elevation as the core. The pipe goes into the tank to a series of tubes. The tank contains seawater and is a hard tank that is exposed to full seawater pressure. The cold seawater takes up the heat of the hot primary coolant in the heat exchanger tubes, so the primary water in the lower part of the tubes is much colder than the primary water entering the tubes. The cooled primary water sinks and flows to a reactor vessel inlet nozzle and into the core. The cold primary cools the core, heats up, and therefore rises so that it flows out to the XC heat exchanger tank, continually giving up reactor heat to the seawater and the environment.

Similarly, the seawater XC heat exchanger tank is piped so that hot water from the tank flows upward out a hull valve at the top of the hull. Seawater supplying the tank comes from a valve mounted at the bottom of the hull. Hot seawater rises and the flow momentum causes a suction, so cold water flows into the tank from the bottom.

This all sounds very handy, but it can be lethal. If injected into a critical reactor, the ultracold water from the XC system would cause a nasty cold water accident that would destroy the core and that could even cause a prompt critical rapid disassembly (see Chapter 6). This tends to make the Navy want to keep the system valved out, or isolated by valves, so that it would activate only on purpose. Besides, the XC hard tank is a seawater system—what if it floods at test depth, inside the inaccessible reactor compartment? It is safest to shut the seawater valves when the ship is submerged, to prevent a flooding accident from a ruptured XC heat exchanger tank at sea.

But what if the ship is at the pier and all power fails, so there's no main coolant pump running to provide cooling flow through the core, and for some bizarre reason the crew does nothing (from food poisoning, terrorist attack, or another scenario)? The core would overheat in a loss of flow condition and cause reactor damage and a nuclear accident. This tends to make the safest thing an XC system that actuates automatically on loss of flow when the reactor is shut down. So what's the answer? Keep the XC system automatic and risk a nuclear accident, or keep it valved out and risk a different kind of nuclear accident?

The Danger of Safety

That's quite a problem—a safety system that itself could cause a massive accident. The cure would seem worse than the disease. This is a real issue in the nuclear business. After all, in the Three Mile Island accident, the operators shut off the automatic systems that were acting correctly to save the core, and they did it *in the interest of safety!*

And never forget that the worst nuclear accident of all time, Chernobyl, was caused by a *safety test!* The comrade safety engineer insisted that the plant's main coolant pumps be tested in case the plant lost all power from the grid and "went black." The plant's design basis was that the turbine generators, while spinning down from lack of steam, would have enough energy during the coast-down to power the main coolant pumps and keep sufficient flow through the core. But this had never been tested because it was judged too dangerous.

But the safety engineer won the argument, saying that a safety design that is never tested cannot be relied upon. He eventually won his argument, and a test protocol was written to test the turbine coast-down powering the main coolant pumps. At four o'clock in the morning, the plant was intentionally tripped off the grid and "taken black."

The safety engineers were wrong. The main coolant pumps didn't get the energy they needed, so the core—at power—was starved of flow. The result was a steam explosion that blew up the reactor. That resulted in a fire that blew radioactive fission products over the entire continent of Europe and killed dozens—maybe even hundreds—of emergency responders. The accident also has led to thousands of cancer deaths and the permanent evacuation of an entire city that was contaminated by the radiation. (It is believed that the comrade safety engineer himself was killed during the accident.)

Back to the conundrum, the lineup of the XC system. Eventually, the Navy compromised. When the ship is within 50 miles of land, the XC system is *rigged* (submarine term for "lined up") for in-port operation, able to be automatically activated. An automatic valve opens on loss of main coolant pump flow and opens the XC primary water valves. The seawater hull and backup valves are kept open, and the core is protected by emergency cooling flow. Farther than 50 nautical miles from land, the XC system is rigged for at-sea, with the seawater valves shut, the XC hard tank vented, and the automatic XC primary valves isolated and deactivated.

The hot water coming from the reactor flows under the pushing force of the main coolant pumps to the steam generators. These are vertical vessels that are separated into two areas. The primary coolant water flows in an inlet nozzle to a plenum and then up through a tubesheet and into all 1,800 U-tubes of the boiler. The U-tubes look like upside-down U's; the coolant flows up and then down. The primary flows out of the tubes, back through the tubesheet, to the exit plenum at the bottom of the vessel, out the outlet nozzle, and on to the main coolant pumps. On the outside of the tubes and in the top four fifths of the vessel, secondary coolant water (called boiler feedwater) is admitted to the secondary side of the boiler. The hot U-tubes heat the water and make it boil to steam.

The Coolant Loops

The reactor coolant piping has two loops, two circuits of water going from the reactor to the boilers and back. But nuclear engineers speak of a PWR (pressurized water reactor) as having a primary loop and a secondary loop. This comes from the fact that the reactor coolant/moderator primary water never comes into contact with the atmosphere. It circulates, gets hot, and heats a secondary loop of water to become steam. The steam loop is therefore not radioactive, leading to enhanced safety.

This is not true of a BWR, or boiling water reactor: The water boils in the core, and the steam resulting from the boiling goes to the turbines. This is a much more difficult system to deal with because the steam part of the plant is as contaminated and radioactive as the reactor part. Taking apart a steam turbine requires anticontamination procedures. Add to that the fact that BWRs are not inherently stable like PWRs are, and you can see why the Navy chose a PWR.

Staying Stable

"Inherent stability" means that a change in the reactor does not lead to a core "runaway" or "out of control" condition. As an example, take a typical PWR pressurized water reactor steaming at 30 percent power. Now open the throttles to 50 percent power and take more steam out of the boilers. When you do this, the boilers remove thermal energy from the primary coolant, so the primary leaving the boilers is colder. This colder-than-before water flows to the reactor. It is much more dense than the previous reactor inlet water, so suddenly dense water comes into the reactor core. Since the primary water is a coolant and a moderator, and because a moderator is a substance that slows neutrons so they can cause fission while minimizing neutron leakage, the moderator suddenly becomes a better moderator. Suddenly, fewer neutrons leak from the core, adding to the reactor power level; the neutrons are better slowed to make them thermal neutrons, which also raises core power. So, the starting event, opening the throttles or "steam demand," resulted in the core power rising. In other words, reactor power has followed steam demand, and the core is inherently stable.

That's not so with a BWR boiling water reactor. In a BWR, when the throttle is opened, the steam pipe (which is the reactor outlet) pressure goes down, causing suddenly more boiling in the core (more boiling means more steam, so you do initially get more power). But wait—steam is a poor moderator compared to liquid water, so neutrons suddenly start leaking from the core and fewer neutrons are slowed to allow more fissions. So, reactor power actually declines. You asked for more power, and the reactor gave you less! This means you have to intervene with a Rube Goldberg pressurizing valve system to keep things stable.

Now, even worse, what if you ask a BWR for less steam? If you shut the throttle valves, taking less steam because you need less power, the steam pressure out of the reactor goes up, and the bubbles of steam in the reactor collapse. What was steam vapor becomes water, and water is a great moderator. So, reactor power goes up. You asked for less power, and the reactor gave you more! Again, a separate intervention system is required, and the entire setup is less stable. By Admiral Rickover's judgment, it was less safe.

Keeping Water from Boiling: The Pressurizer

You just can't help noticing that we've been talking about 500°F liquid water as if it existed that way in nature. How can that be? Every gallon of water that you know of has this tendency to boil at 212°F. Otherwise, how would you make the pasta? Somehow, the Navy managed to get this water to stay a liquid at that temperature. How did that happen? Part of the answer is that, for water to boil to steam, there needs to be a lot of room: Steam takes up a lot more space than the same amount of liquid. Imagine trying to boil water for the spaghetti, but as an experiment you filled the pot to the very rim and then welded the lid in place. As water temperature rose, there would be no steam because there would be no room for the water molecules to expand away from each other. The water would remain liquid. In fact, you could keep on heating the water to 500°F, but there's just one thing—the water inside the pot would experience a large increase in pressure, from 14.7 psi (atmospheric pressure) to a whopping 1,750 psi.

So, the main coolant system has a tank connected to it by a water pipe (water transmits pressure). The tank is called a pressurizer, and it functions to keep the entire primary system pressurized to that 1,750 psi so that it won't boil. This is done by keeping the pressurizer at a saturation condition, with heaters to raise its temperature to 617°F. The heaters boil the water in the pressurizer and form a steam bubble inside it, where liquid and vapor coexist at 1,750 psi and 617°F, just as vapor and liquid coexist at 212°F at 14.7 psi.

If the pressurizer's heaters fail, the pressure of the primary coolant falls, until eventually the reactor starts to boil water. This is a nuclear accident known as a loss of pressure accident, and it has similar results to a loss of coolant accident.

To combat the possibility of a loss of coolant accident from a leak in a coolant loop, the primary loops have special valves installed close to the reactor vessel. If one of the piping loops springs a leak, the reactor operator shuts the main coolant cutout valves (MCCOVs) from the reactor plant control panel (RPCP) and isolates the loss of coolant. The valves are called gate valves because a large plate is slammed into the piping path by hydraulic action. But instead of using hydraulic oil, the system is designed to use primary coolant itself, coming from the valve operating water flasks (large stainless-steel vessels pressurized by high-pressure air). Another isolation valve can isolate the pressurizer, if needed.

The Least You Need to Know

- The propulsion plant, is essentially everything aft of the operations compartment, including the reactor plant, the steam plant, and the drive train.

- A moderator is a substance that slows the high-energy fast neutrons that result from uranium fissioning by means of molecular collisions, much like the slowing of a billiard ball when it hits other balls.

- Rickover demanded that his engineers build a totally enclosed, canned pump that would use primary coolant to circulate around the motor. It remains an engineering triumph to this day.

- Water in a reactor gets a lot hotter than the boiling point, but it remains liquid because it is pressurized.

Chapter 13

Producing the Power II

In This Chapter

- ◆ How to avoid health risks from radiation
- ◆ Radioactivity
- ◆ How to breathe underwater
- ◆ Flushing

You can avoid the health risks from radiation in three ways: time, distance, and shielding. By time, we mean minimizing the time you are being irradiated. By distance, we mean that a smaller dose of radiation exists at the bow of the ship than in the reactor compartment shielded tunnel. Radiation diminishes rapidly with distance. Finally, shielding is a means of keeping radiation away from your flesh and blood through the use of matter.

Avoiding That Certain Glow: Shielding

One means of shielding from radiation is to use lead. Lead keeps away gamma radiation, which is much like x-rays. Gamma rays are electromagnetic waves that cause tissue damage. Just as cancer patients get radiation sickness from the radiation treatments, gamma radiation from the reactor will give you radiation sickness if you are not shielded from it by lead or another heavy element.

Neutron radiation can be shielded by anything containing hydrogen because a hydrogen atom is a proton with an electron orbiting it. A proton is the same mass as a neutron, and physics shows that an object is best slowed by another object of the same mass. If you want to slow the cue ball, you first try hitting the rim of the heavy table, but that impact with a large mass doesn't slow the cue ball at all. But aim the cue ball at a group of other billiard balls, and after several collisions, the other balls absorb the kinetic energy and the cue ball slows to a stop.

So it is with neutron radiation. You need to use a bunch of protons, and hydrogen is essentially protons. They can be in the form of water, H_2O, or a hydrocarbon such as paraffin, gasoline, or oil.

The most practical shields on a sub are water (the reactor vessel shield tank is a tank of water built around the reactor core that attenuates or lessens neutron radiation) and polyethylene, a form of plastic that can be molded in blocks. The reactor compartment shielded tunnel is lined with about 6 inches of lead and 12 inches of poly.

The forward bulkhead of the reactor compartment is the location of the diesel fuel oil tank, which is both a shield and the place where the fuel oil is stored. The tank is self-compensating: When fuel oil is used, the bottom of the tank is filled with seawater so that the oil always floats on water and so there won't be a loss of shield accident to irradiate the crew.

Nuclear Instruments

Enough about radioactivity. Let's get back to discussing power and how a modern sub creates it. We were up to the steam plant. The steam plant begins in the steam generators, or boilers. Hot primary coolant from the reactor heats boiler feedwater until it boils. Boiler feedwater is high-pressure liquid water at about 180°F and 480 psi. It gets its high pressure from the boiler feed pump, which is a massive multistage axial pump about the size of a refrigerator.

The water is full of chemicals that will prevent corrosion in the boilers. The boiler feedwater comes in contact with the U-tubes full of primary coolant at 500°F and begins to boil.

The flow must rise through passages that change direction suddenly. Although vapor (steam) can do this, the entrained water droplets can't, and the droplets fall back into the boiler. The steam leaving the boiler first goes through the bulkhead (wall) between the reactor compartment and the engineroom, and then immediately goes through an isolation gate valve. On the port side, the valve is called *MS-2*. On the starboard side, it is *MS-1*.

The valve slams the piping shut to isolate a major steam leak. The steam continues to the steam headers, which are just large pipes—one on the port side, one on the starboard side—that make their way to the turbines.

The piping makes a complete circle in the overhead before elbowing down to the turbine. When heated from ambient to 455°F, the pipe grows several inches. Without these "racetracks," the pipe would break off after a few cycles of heating and cooling.

The racetracks join the turbines through valves called throttle valves. One is a manual throttle valve, controlled by an operator. The other is an automatic throttle valve that tries to maintain the turbine at a constant speed. This throttle is called a governor.

Ship Service Turbine Generator (SSTG)

The first turbine in the piping system is the SSTG, for ship service turbine generator. This is a large box of insulated steel enclosing rotor blades that rotate and stator blades that don't. Think of a turbine as a black box that turns the temperature energy of steam (called enthalpy) into mechanical work. It does this using two kinds of stages.

The first is an impulse stage, which is the same kind of thing you'd see in a water wheel. The speed of the flow pushes a bucket passage in the rotor (the rotating part of the turbine), turning the wheel of the turbine.

The second stage is an impulse stage, in which the passage that the steam goes through on the stator (nonmoving part) and the rotor expands as the steam goes through it. This makes the steam give up enthalpy and pressure while increasing its velocity, and this velocity is directed like a rocket engine to push on the rotor. After multiple stages, the turbine exhausts the steam to the main condenser.

Secrets of the Deep

There are two SSTGs: one on the port side and one on the starboard side.

The governor-type throttle valve keeps the turbine spinning at a constant 3,600 RPM, regardless of the load of the generator. The generator is mated to the turbine by the rotor shaft. The generator is a metal box enclosing a nonmoving stator with copper wire windings. Inside the stator, the rotor—from the turbine rotor shaft—rotates. The rotor also has copper wire windings.

The idea is that spinning a wire loop inside a magnetic field generates a current. The stator generates an electromagnet's field. When the rotor spins in it, the moving magnetic field generates electrical current. It takes tremendous torque, or twisting force, to do this, which is the job of the steam turbine part of the assembly. The generator converts mechanical work into electrical power. The combination turbine-generator then converts the thermal energy of steam into electrical energy.

The electricity from the generator is fed to the nonvital buses. A bus is an electrical load center. Examples of nonvital bus loads include these:

- Main feed pumps

- Condensate pumps

- Hydraulic pumps

The nonvital bus is linked to the vital bus by a circuit breaker. The vital bus gets its power from the SSTG when things are going well. But when they aren't and the turbine trips off, the vital bus gets its power from a motor-generator that converts battery DC power to AC power.

Here are some examples of a vital load:

- Slow-speed main coolant pumps

- Main seawater pumps

- The ship's lighting

- The wardroom coffeemaker

Main Engines

The second turbine set in the steam system consists of the port and starboard main engines. These have ahead stages and astern stages. The ahead stages are controlled by the ahead throttle; the astern stages are controlled by the astern throttle.

The stages are similar to the SSTG's stages, with impulse stages and reaction stages. The main engines each spin their shafts, which go into the body of the reduction gear. For all the tremendous power of the main engines (more than 15,000 horse-power each), they are small compared to a diesel engine of the same power. The diesel would be four stories tall, perhaps twice the size of a house, to have this much power, whereas the main engines are the size of a compact car.

This difference in size is partly because steam is extremely efficient. But it also must be noted that the main engines are only part of the overall cycle. Once you add the volume and weight of the reactor compartment, the SSTGs, the main condenser, and all the peripheral equipment, it turns out that a large marine diesel engine takes up much less space than the nuclear equipment.

Main Condenser

The steam exhausted from the main engines and SSTGs is very low in pressure and low in temperature, at least compared to the temperature and pressure at which it enters the turbines (turbine inlet temperature 455°F, pressure 444 psi; turbine exhaust temperature 160°F, pressure 5 psi).

Either the steam must be discarded overboard because it would fill the submarine (this would make the steam plant an open cycle), or it must be returned to the boilers in a closed cycle. An open cycle would make no sense because you would have to make pure water in a gigantic quantity to feed the boilers. As a practical matter, the ship must use a closed cycle and reuse the steam from the turbines. Again, as a practical matter, it makes sense to condense the steam to water and pump the water back to the boilers.

This is a requirement that is for more than practicality. It turns out that the laws of thermodynamics must be satisfied: To convert thermal energy to mechanical work, heat must be transferred from a high temperature and must be rejected at a low temperature. The open cycle would reject heat to the low temperature of the sea. The closed cycle must reject heat also before feeding the turbine exhaust steam back to the boilers.

This is done in the port and starboard main condensers. The condenser is a large horizontal, cylindrical vessel. Seawater is pumped into tubes inside it, while exhaust steam flows outside the tubes. Seawater is usually extremely cold, at about 28°F (the salinity [saltiness] enables it to be colder than the freezing point of fresh water). Even in the tropics, seawater at 70°F is still much colder than exhaust steam at 160°F.

> **Beneath the Surface**
>
> The condensate drips down and collects in a basin at the bottom of the condenser, called the hotwell.

In any case, the steam sees the cold seawater and condenses to water (or condensate). If you take an ice-cold beer out into a steamy humid day, the outside of the can will immediately "sweat," or develop drops of condensation. This is exactly what happens in the main condensers.

Main Seawater System

The main seawater system brings seawater into the hull and backup valves and through 18-inch diameter monel piping to the main seawater pumps. These pumps suck the water from outside the hull and push it through the condenser tubes.

If the plant loses a main seawater pump, the condenser stops working, and eventually the turbine inlet valves trip shut (because if the condenser is lost, there is nowhere for the steam to go).

So, the main seawater system is vital to maintaining propulsion. But a system with piping this big, exposed to seawater pressure, has the capability of flooding the ship and taking it down in a matter of minutes. For this reason, the "chicken switches" in the maneuvering room can slam shut the hull and backup valves in the seawater piping system.

The condensate that gathers in the hotwells of the condensers is pumped from the condenser by the condensate pumps. The pumps are fairly low-horsepower units that merely move the water to the bigger, higher-horsepower main feed pumps.

Main Feed System

The condensate that is pumped forward goes to the suction of the main feed pump, which is a vertical 12-stage axial pump that raises water pressure all the way to boiler pressure at about 450 psi. After moving through the main feed pump, the water is no longer condensate; it is now boiler feedwater.

The feedwater goes to a control valve called a feed-reg valve (short for feedwater-regulating valve) that either opens or shuts to maintain the proper level in the steam generator. This is a fairly big job because if the valve were to go full open, the feed pump would overfill the boilers.

The steam generator water-level control system (SGWLC system, pronounced "squiggle") uses level detectors and flow detectors to position the feed-reg valve correctly.

So, the water from the boilers makes a complete circle—to the turbines, to the condenser, to the hotwell, through the condensate pumps to the main feed pump, through the fed-reg valve, and back to the boiler.

Reduction Gear

The shafts of the main engines turn gears inside the reduction gear. The main engine turbines are efficient at high speeds, but the screw is efficient at low speeds. To mate the two, the reduction gear knocks down the 10,000 RPM level of the main engines at flank to the 200 RPM speed of the screw. The main engine shafts turn small pinion gears that turn a large gear some 15 feet in diameter. This gear is connected to the shaft.

Here's a look to the future: The reduction gear, though an engineering marvel, is too loud. It will be replaced by electric motors. The future main engines will be propulsion turbine generators (PTGs) that will make AC voltage through electrical generators. The current from these generators will be fed to an oil-enclosed AC motor outside the pressure hull that will turn the screw. It will be much quieter and much more efficient.

Secrets of the Deep

The reduction gear hand-hole doors are locked, and only the chief engineer has the key. This prevents flashlights and tools from ruining the gears. It also prevents sabotage: A wrench thrown into the gears will put a ship in dry dock for up to a year.

Clutch

The clutch is no different than the clutch in your car. It is hydraulically controlled and is simply a device that uncouples the shaft from the reduction gear. Once the heavy reduction gear and main engines are separated from the shaft, the remaining drive train is light enough to be turned by the emergency propulsion motor, the EPM. Upon loss of the reactor, the ship can come to periscope depth, snorkel, load the diesel, and feed the power to the emergency propulsion motor, make way, snorkeling and submerged, at about 5 knots.

Thrust Bearing

Many nonquals make the mistake of thinking that the screw pushes the ship through the water. This is not true. The screw pushes on the thrust bearing, which is anchored to the steel of the hull. The thrust bearing is what pushes the ship through the water.

The thrust bearing is one of the limiting components of ship speed. As the ship goes to ahead flank, the hull trembles, probably from the thrust bearing being overloaded.

> ### Secrets of the Deep
>
> The emergency propulsion motor (EPM) is a large motor that is driven from the DC buses. It allows the ship to move through the water even if the reactor has been scrammed. No need to surface to do it—the emergency diesel running on the snorkel can provide all the power required. But it will be a smelly, seasick trip back to port if you can't recover the reactor. The diesel exhaust gets sucked into the snorkel, and soon every crewmember aboard has pounding headaches. Staying at periscope depth for 24 hours a day makes the boat seasick city, thanks to that wonderful cylindrical and unseaworthy hull.

Shaft Seals

The shaft seals surround the 12-inch-diameter shaft where it penetrates the hull and keeps seawater from outside the people tank from coming inside. Sealing off a hull penetration is easy, but sealing off a rotating hull penetration is tough.

The shaft seals do this by generating leakage from inside the hull to the outside of the hull, using auxiliary seawater that is pumped to a higher pressure than the outside pressure.

Electric Plant

The SSTGs power the nonvital buses (a bus is a load center). Circuit breakers connect the port and starboard nonvital buses to the port and starboard vital buses. Circuit breakers connect the nonvital buses to the motor-generators.

The motor-generators simply link the AC side of the electric plant to the DC side with the DC batteries. For the DC battery to supply AC loads, the motor generator at the DC end is a DC motor. The DC motor is connected to a shaft that is connected to an AC generator.

The DC electricity is converted to mechanical work in the motor, and the mechanical work is converted back to electrical energy, but this time to AC electrical energy through the AC generator side. On the DC end are the DC buses, which are connected to the motor-generator breakers and the battery breaker.

Battery

The battery is the submariner's best friend. It keeps him alive when no other electrical source can. It lives under the torpedo room and consists of 100 or so wet cells. While the battery has many lovely qualities, it has a pesky tendency to generate hydrogen when a battery charge is done.

The battery's energy is measured in amp-hours, and its discharge rate in amps depends on the loads. Recovering from a scrammed reactor requires powering up two main coolant pumps, a condensate pump, and a main feed pump. That will suck the battery dead in a matter of less than a half hour. If the restart is not done skillfully, the diesel may have to be used to supplement the battery until the reactor is back.

Secrets of the Deep

Hydrogen generated by a battery charge has been known to sink submarines, as it did the Golf submarine raised by the *Glomar Explorer.*

Evaporator

A submarine is a gigantic consumer of pure water. The reactor plant needs it for small leaks in the system. The steam plant has a larger amount of leaks, as any steam plant does. The ship's ventilation system condenses these steam leaks to water, which collects in the bilges for later dewatering by the drain pump. The boiler makeup water comes from makeup feed tanks, but these tanks will go dry if fresh water is not made to replenish them.

Fresh water is made by the evaporator. Seawater from the auxiliary seawater system is admitted to a basket. Low-pressure auxiliary steam is admitted to the outside of the basket. The seawater boils, and the vapor is taken away from the basket and condensed by an auxiliary seawater system condenser. The pure water is pumped away to the freshwater tanks. The remaining seawater in the basket has very high salinity and is called brine. The system sounds simple, but it breaks down all the time.

When the evaporator goes down, the first thing to go are showers, the second is laundry, and the third is cooking. The crew suffers abjectly when the evaporator is broken. No showers and dirty sheets and sweaty clothes make for an irritating run. The mechanics get the urgent and usually vulgar word from all hands to get the evaporator back online.

Mike's Corner

The ones who complain most vocally about the broken evaporator are the two-shower-a-day sonar girls.

The evaporator is shut off, or secured, during the rig for ultraquiet when the sub is seeking or trailing another sub because all that steaming and boiling is loud.

Refrigeration Plant

A steam plant inside a pipe makes for a hot, humid work environment. Two varieties of refrigeration plants are installed to keep the atmosphere less steamy. This is more for the electronic equipment than for the personnel, but the sonar girls would disagree.

The refrigerant used in one of the plants is an atmospheric contaminant, so life gets miserable when it breaks. Not only is the ship at 130°F inside, but the crew has to wear emergency air breathing masks while fixing it.

Atmospheric Control—How to Breathe Underwater

The first thing you need when you're stuck inside a closed tube underwater is oxygen. You get this from one of two places. First, the oxygen banks have stored oxygen in high-pressure bottles. You crack open the manifold valve, called the bleed valve, to bleed oxygen into the ship. How sweet it is!

The oxygen banks can be loaded from external oxygen trucks when the ship is at the pier. This procedure is a gigantic pain because the piping must be "oxygen clean" so that no microscopic oils, not even the oils from the skin of your fingers, contaminate the inside of the piping spools used to bring oxygen aboard. The procedure is also dangerous. Hydrogen's bad, but so is oxygen. The *Hindenburg* and the *Challenger* blew up from hydrogen, but *Apollo I*'s horrible fatal fire was from oxygen.

In with the Good Air ...

The second way to get your oxygen is from The Bomb, the unofficial name for the oxygen generator. This is a fairly heavy and massive box that takes in distilled water from an ion-exchange resin bed and puts an ultrahigh DC voltage on it. Oxygen collects at one electrode and hydrogen collects at the other, in a process called hydrolysis (and no, this has nothing to do with getting rid of the hair on your girlfriend's legs). Talk about dangerous—The Bomb makes a stoichiometric mix of oxygen and hydrogen, the perfect prelude to a chemical explosion and fire.

The hydrogen is discarded by dissolving it in the auxiliary seawater just before it goes overboard out the hull and backup valves. The oxygen is compressed and put into the oxygen bottles.

... Out with the Bad

So that takes care of oxygen, the stuff you inhale. Now, what about carbon dioxide, the stuff you exhale? Rising levels of carbon dioxide will drop the crew in their boots. As the ship gets farther from port, the flies on board start to slow down until they are moving in slow motion, and you might feel headaches or drowsiness. That's all a part of the carbon dioxide level that's higher than Mother Nature's level.

To get rid of the carbon dioxide, the engineroom has carbon-dioxide scrubbers that use amines in a process that vacuums it right out of the air stream and discards it overboard in the auxiliary seawater system. But the ship smells of amines.

What about carbon monoxide, which gets in thanks to the galley and the diesel? And what about the hydrogen generated by the battery charge? This is where the burners come in. These are devices with tiny wires that glow cherry red from an electrical current. They oxidize at high temperature any carbon monoxide and change it to carbon dioxide.

This is vital because carbon monoxide is a severe poison and will turn you into an idiot in no time (although, with a torpedoman, how do you tell?).

Now, what about the oil from the hydraulic systems and the turbine lube oil systems? Nasty stuff, all those hydrocarbons going airborne and screwing up lungs all over the sub. The precipitators are supposed to take care of this, sucking oily air through filters and electrostatic devices that ionize oil and make it stick to an electrode. Again, these devices are total nonhackers because the ship always smells oily, particularly back aft.

In general, it's not the low-level radiation that gets you on a submarine; it's the lousy atmospheric controls and the stress and lack of sleep. Forty-year-old submariners tend to look like they're 50, and the atmosphere is one of the prime suspects.

Mike's Corner

In this dolphin-wearer's opinion, the burners are slackers and don't do a great job. The atmospheric analyzers always showed carbon monoxide as marginal. The burners are supposed to help with that nasty ozone, but they get poor marks on that score.

Secrets of the Deep

Some odors on a submarine (with showers and laundry secured) can be a terrible thing. So far, nothing will eliminate the stench of your fellow submariner.

Ship Control

Ship control is done using hydraulics, or high-pressure oil. Oil pumps put the high pressure oil into accumulators, which are vessels with pistons in them loaded by air. When there is demand for hydraulic oil to move something, the accumulator gives instant supplies of high-pressure oil. Then the pump kicks on to recharge the accumulator.

Beneath the Surface
Ship control is just power steering on steroids.

The hydraulic oil controls the planes and rudder through huge rams, which are cylinders with pistons in them. Put hydraulic oil at high pressure on one side and air at low pressure on the other, and the high-pressure hydraulic oil will push the piston inside the cylinder. If the piston is connected to the sternplanes, the sternplanes move.

Trim and Drain System

The trim system is a pump and a number of piping runs that connect variable ballast tanks. Ballast water comes into the ship near the center of gravity at the depth-control tanks. The trim system then pumps that water to either the forward variable-ballast tank to tilt the ship on its nose, or the aft variable-ballast tank to tilt the ship nose up. The trim system can pump water out of the depth-control tanks if she's heavy or can allow water in if she's light.

The drain system uses an identical pump to the trim system, except that the drain system takes a suction on the bilges of each space and discharges the bilge water overboard. If you didn't do this once a day or three times a week, the ship would slowly fill with water from seal leaks and pinhole leaks.

If one system gives you trouble, the functioning pump can be valved into the system in trouble. This is called cross-connecting. Trim pump won't start? Line up the drain pump to the trim system and pump away. Drain pump out of order? Just line up the trim pump and drain away.

Hovering

Hovering is used on an attack sub for one thing: to break through arctic ice by doing a vertical surface. Okay, that and to impress people on sailboats. At neutral buoyancy and zero speed, air loads or blows the depth-control tank, and water leaves depth control at the center of gravity. The ship gets light and starts to ascend. At 2 feet per minute, the sail will smash through 1-foot-thick ice. To go back down, just flood depth control and you sink like an express elevator.

The chief of the watch's station at the ballast control panel has a "joystick" and a hovering computer. When you're rigged to hover, push the joystick down to the flood position, and down you go. Raise the stick to the blow position, and you go up.

The boomers use the hovering system to get ready to launch submarine-launched ballistic missiles. You steady on missile firing depth, hover, open a missile door, spin it up, target it, and hit the gas generator switch. Up it goes in a bubble of steam. As soon as it pops out, its rocket motor ignites and it is no longer your problem. One less maintenance mouth to feed.

Food and Cooking

Submarine food is some of the best in the fleet. Eating and movie watching are two submarine pastimes, and they are lethal to the waistline. The frozen stores lockers hold enough food for about 50 to 60 days. The fresh fruit goes fast, but then there's canned goods and steaks. On a long mission, large 12-inch-diameter food cans are loaded onto the passageway decks and plywood is put on top. You have to walk around the ship all hunched over in a crouch until you "eat your way down."

Four meals are served each day:

- Breakfast (omelets)
- Lunch (sliders, the hamburgers so greasy that you don't swallow them because they slide right down)
- Dinner (steak or seafood)
- Midrats (midnight rations: chili, rice, and peanut butter sandwiches)

> **Mike's Corner**
>
> If you were watching your waistline, you might try to cut out meals, but in the close confines of the ship, you smell the food and come running.

Toilets

This is the most important thing for the nonqual to learn. The toilet looks kind of like a regular toilet, except that it's made of stainless steel and has an 8-inch ball valve at the bottom. A small globe valve through a 1-inch pipe fills the bowl with seawater.

You do your business and then stand up and pull the long bar handle of the ball valve. The ball valve opens, connecting the toilet basin with the sanitary tank, and the waste flows down the pipe into the tank. Talk about stink! Then refill the bowl with seawater.

Blowing Sanitary

On the older subs, when the sanitary tank was full, it would be "air loaded" with 700 psi air so that the sewage would leave the ship and be discarded to the ocean. This required that all the heads (bathrooms) have signs posted on them reading:

SECURED—BLOWING SANITARY

If you see that sign, DO NOT FLUSH! If you do, you will get 700 psi solid waste blown in your face. Sometimes, annoying people are set up so that they go in to use the toilet without a sign on it. They open the ball valve and get a faceful.

In one ship, the unpopular chief always opened the ball valve when he was still sitting on the throne. When they "got" him, he opened the ball valve while sitting on the toilet during a sanitary blow. They say it was like a ping pong ball on top of Old Faithful! The high-pressure air had to go somewhere—you couldn't have it go over-board, or you could be detected by the bubbles. So—get this—the air was *vented inboard* and brought into the ship. They used a charcoal filter to make the incoming air less stinky, but the filter was overwhelmed in no time. For some reason, my bunk was always located by the charcoal filter! Phew!

Modern nuke subs have sanitary pumps that are positive-displacement piston pumps that pump the sanitary waste overboard. This is a more complex thing to maintain. (Besides being complex, it ain't pretty!) The pumps also tend to be noisy. One sub's sanitary pump was so loud that the sub could be detected 40 nautical miles away.

Trash Disposal

Trash disposal is no problem. You use the TDU, or trash disposal unit. It's a vertical torpedo tube with the breach door near the galley. You put garbage in the trash com-pactor, which puts the trash into a plastic bag weighted with a 10-pound lead weight and makes it a perfect cylinder. You keep filling the TDU until it's full of compacted garbage. At that point, at the next periscope depth, the muzzle door at the keel is opened, the tube is flushed with auxiliary seawater, and the garbage disappears.

But do not run out of weights. Once you do, you have to keep the garbage aboard. If the run has been so long that you've run out of weights, the frozen stores locker is empty and the garbage can go in there.

Also, be careful not to screw up the interlocks on the TDU. It is operated by cooks, and if you happen to open the breach door and the muzzle door at the same time, you'll have a 10-inch-diameter hole in the people tank. And the muzzle valve could get jammed open with a stuck weight. That could be very bad news!

The Least You Need to Know

- Primary coolant circulates through the reactor, gets hot, and makes steam in the boilers.

- The steam turns the turbines that make electricity and power the shaft and the screw.

- Be careful of The Bomb—it helps you breathe but is not friendly.

- Never flush when the ship is blowing sanitary. The smell won't leave for weeks!

Part 4

Operating a Nuclear Submarine

While the equipment of a nuclear submarine is intricate, the operation of that equipment is an even greater challenge to the newcomer.

A nuclear submarine is comparable in complexity to the space shuttle. Operating the space shuttle requires years of training for some of the brightest engineers and scientists in the United States—astronauts. Similarly, while the submarine's equipment may take years to master, becoming a master at nuclear submarine operation takes more than a decade.

Nuclear submarine commanding officers have typically been on three or four sea tours submerged, each tour lasting three or more years. So, in a book like this, all I can do is scratch the surface. But, since there's a whole lot of surface to scratch, let's get started. Here's Sub Driving 101.

Chapter 14

Rules Written in Blood

In This Chapter

- ◆ Rigging ship
- ◆ Collision at sea will ruin your entire day
- ◆ Staying dry
- ◆ Remaining undetected
- ◆ Polite company on deck

Everything you do on a nuclear submarine starts and ends with a procedure. Much like in aviation, where there are checklists for any action, submarines' procedures are "written in blood" by the people who did this before you and learned the hard way. This chapter is a short checklist of checklists, to make sure you don't forget anything while commanding your own nuclear submarine.

The Rigs

Up forward, where the torpedomen and sonar girls live, the Submarine Standard Operating Procedures (SSOP, or SOP for short) manual is the Bible. Back aft, where the nukes preside, the Reactor Plant Manual far outranks the Bible—as far as can be seen, it also outranks U.S. Navy Regulations.

As part of the SOP, each operation has a "rig." A rig is a seagoing term for a lineup per checklist. Here are some of the rigs normally done onboard.

Rig Ship for Collision

This involves ensuring the watertight integrity of each compartment. All compartment bulkhead watertight hatches are shut and dogged. An S latching mechanism with a lever keeps them shut "on the latch" so that a hatch can be easily and quickly opened, but in this rig you must "dog the hatch" by spinning the operator wheel in the center of the 600-pound steel hatch. This extends bananas of steel or "dogs" to grip the hatch seating surface and lock the hatch in place.

All ventilation dampers are shut (the dampers are watertight inside steel ventilation ducts that are also pressure bulkheads). The fan room is shut down and isolated. All hull openings are shut (on the surface, the bridge access hatch is shut, and the weapons shipping hatch or escape trunk upper hatches are shut).

In the event of collision, the ship will be at its most watertight.

Rig Ship for Flooding

This is the same as rigging for collision, as far as procedural actions are concerned, but the focus of the crew is on combating a flooding condition. This includes the engineering officer of the watch back aft at his chicken switch panel and the chief of the watch at the ballast control panel's emergency main ballast tank blow switches.

Rig Ship for Fire

This is the same as rigging for collision, with the same procedural steps, except that the fire hoses in the affected space are deployed for use on the fire. Emergency air breathing masks (EABs) are donned, and an oxygen breathing apparatus (OBA) is worn by a designated individual in the space. An OBA is a small chemical oxygen generator that fills rubber breathing bladders and serves as a portable EAB (invented before the Scott air pack, which is essentially a small SCUBA system).

Rig Ship for Surface

The bridge access hatch is opened, the clamshells are pulled down, grating is put over the hatchway, the bridge communication box is installed, the compass alidade is brought up and connected, the windshield is installed, the flag mast is rigged, the running lights are rigged out, and the officer of the deck's watch is shifted to the bridge.

The ship then "surface ventilates": Air is drawn in through the bridge access hatches and circulated to all spaces by the fan room, and atmospheric controls are rigged. (The scrubbers, oxygen bleed, and the Bomb are secured—shut down—but the precipitators and burners are kept running.)

The main ballast tank vent operators are locked with padlocks so that they cannot function and inadvertently flood a main ballast tank.

Rig Ship for In-Port

This is done after the rig for surface. The deck cleats are rigged out and locked in preparation for coming alongside the pier. The ship's "lines" (ropes used to tie the ship to the pier) are pulled out of the line lockers and coiled on the deck.

Once the ship is *fast* to the pier, the main ballast tank vents have gasketed vent covers bolted onto them because the vents leak slightly.

Subtalk

Fast is an oddball nautical term. When you are "fast to the pier" or doing a "fast cruise," you are going 0 knots—that is, you are standing still.

At a point 50 nautical miles from land inbound, the ship rigs emergency cooling (XC) for in-port operation. This "valves in" (lines up) the seawater heat exchanger tank. It also opens isolation valves that will actuate the XC system automatically. This will occur if the reactor loses all main coolant pump flow.

Rig Ship for Dive

This rig is usually done in stages. At first, the interior of the ship is rigged. This unlocks the main ballast tank vent operators so they will function when called on to vent the main ballast tanks. Certain valves (the escape trunk and bridge access trunk vent and drain valves, the inboard and outboard induction and diesel exhaust valves, and others) are shut. The high-pressure air banks must be at a minimum pressure (and, hence, air content) level as well.

The next stage is rigging the deck for dive. The lines are put into the line lockers, which are then shut and locked. The deck cleats are rotated flush into the hull and are bolted. All hatches except the bridge access hatch are shut and dogged, with trunk vents and drains shut. The chief of the watch in control is notified by the last man down that the deck is rigged for dive, that the last man is down, and that the hatch is shut.

The next stage is to rig the ventilation and atmospheric control systems. The carbon dioxide scrubbers are started up, the Bomb is turned on, and the oxygen bleed is established. The carbon monoxide/hydrogen burners and precipitators should already be running.

Any air compressors that are running are secured. The fan room is already blowing air throughout the boat, but its suction is switched from the outside air through the bridge hatch to the normal inside suction. To execute this part of the rig, the chief of the watch announces on the 1MC, "Secure surface ventilation, recirculate!" (This is pronounced, "REEEEEE-circulate.")

The final stage is rigging the bridge for dive. The officer of the deck watch is shifted to control, and the bridge equipment is taken below. The clamshells are faired into the top of the sail, and the access trunk hatches are shut and dogged.

All rigs for dive must be done by two people. A submarine qualified enlisted watch-stander or chief usually performs the rig, and a submarine qualified commissioned officer checks the rig. (Remember, this procedure is "written in blood," so somewhere along the line, someone got into trouble with reporting a rig that was not correctly done.)

> **Beneath the Surface**
>
> The rig for deep submergence does not apply during battle stations.

Once the rig for dive is complete, the ship is ready to be submerged.

Rig Ship for Deep Submergence

At the shallower of either 600 feet keel depth or half of test depth, the ship rigs for deep submergence. In this rig, all watertight hatches are shut and dogged, and watch-standers man every deck of every compartment with sound-powered phone headsets on, ready to report the status of any leakage or flooding.

Rig Ship for Patrol Quiet

Once submerged, the ship runs the pumps that the latest exterior sound survey shows to be the quietest. All hands are reminded to be cautious of maintenance activities (and to be careful not to drop tools), not to slam hatches, and not to tap on anything metal. Caution must be used in lifting weights in the torpedo room; the weights are gently placed on mats on the deck and are not dropped. Stereos may be played, but not at a loud volume.

Rig Ship for Ultraquiet

The rig for ultraquiet is different in each ship, according to the captain's preferences. Usually this rig modifies the rig for patrol quiet (which selects the pumps that are running).

Main coolant pumps are switched to slow or superslow speeds—or, if natural circulation is possible, the pumps are switched off. Fans are switched to slow speed. The evaporator is secured. All use of potable water by the crew is minimized—showers and laundry are secured.

All maintenance is then secured. The galley is secured except for preparation of cold meals (cold cuts, bread, peanut butter, etc.). The overhead lights may be rigged for red (white lights turned off, red lamps turned on), to remind all hands of the rig for ultraquiet. In some ships, one side of the engine-room is shut down (an SSTG, a main engine, a main condenser, and that side's main seawater pump and condensate pump), although this is tactically risky.

This rig is used when the ship is trailing a hostile submarine to minimize the levels of radiated ship noise.

Secrets of the Deep

During rig for ultraquiet, all hands not on watch are required to be in their bunks, and all activities such as card playing, movie watching, and exercising are prohibited.

Rig Ship for Female Visitors

Nudity is secured. Not that there is much—you might see the occasional sonar girl heading for his third hotel shower of the day, wrapped in a towel from his armpits to his knees. Crew must wear complete uniforms rather than skivvies (underwear). Heavy-duty cursing is secured. Loud shouting is secured.

A ship may occasionally be rigged for female visitors while rigged for dive: During a dependents' cruise, mothers, girlfriends, and sisters are allowed aboard while the ship does a quick sortie and dives to no deeper than 400 feet, perhaps doing some "angles and dangles" (maneuvers that intentionally dive to a 30 degree down angle and rise to a 30 degree up angle).

Mike's Corner

Come to think of it, the rig for female visitors is the same as the rig for visiting admirals.

The Least You Need to Know

- On a sub, the rules are written in blood. Each rule is there for a reason, usually in response to someone screwing up years ago.

- As part of Standard Operating Procedure, each operation has a rig, or checklist, of things that must be done.

- Tiptoe during the rig for ultraquiet and secure that stereo. If you're off watch, hit the rack and read a book. There's a bad guy out there—don't tip him off.

- No nudity is allowed when females (or admirals) are aboard.

Starting a Nuclear Reactor

In This Chapter

- Normal and fast recovery
- The who-to-fear department: the XO
- Call him "Eng"
- Divorcing from the shore

Reactor startups come in two flavors: normal and fast recovery. The fast recovery startup restarts the reactor after a scram, sort of like restarting the car after getting gas. All temperatures are near-normal, and the machine is used to being operated—so, in a way, a fast recovery is easy. It takes significant skill and practice to perform one, but it is procedurally less complex than normal startup.

Normal startup is the procedure used to start the plant after a prolonged shutdown. It is governed by Reactor Plant Manual Operating Procedure 5 (OP-5) and Operating Instruction 27 (OI-27). OP-5 is somewhat general in nature and discusses why things are done a certain way. It still has the force and effect of law, at least within the Submarine Force, and violation of any of its requirements will lead to disqualification or worse.

OI-27 is a valve-by-valve checklist that goes into extreme detail. Although it is over 30 pages long, reactor plant operators know it so well that they can quote at length from it. One senior submarine officer knew OI-27 so well that he had a junior officer open the procedure and call off a paragraph—he quoted from it, and for every error the wardroom got one bottle of beer. He could do this for an hour, and while there would be enough beer for a small party, it was astonishing how few mistakes he made.

By-the-Book Normal Reactor Startup

So how do you start a nuclear reactor? First, open your eyes when you are shaken awake by the duty chief. It is 1:45 A.M. Your face is in a puddle of drool on the wardroom table, where you faded out a half hour ago, after working on the prestart checklist all day. You stand on your feet, tuck in your khaki shirt, and retie your boondockers (naval combat boots). Then you put 2 teaspoons of coffee grounds into a cup and stir it up in "bug juice," the sugary Navy-issue Kool-Aid equivalent. Then you fill the cup back up with fresh coffee from the pot and slurp it down before walking back aft into the engineering spaces.

Mike's Corner

Normal reactor startup is just not right unless done in the wee hours of the night. If all goes well, by 0600 (or 6:00 A.M.) when the chief engineer comes in, the ship will be divorcing from shorepower.

Subtalk

The **commodore** is the commander of the submarine squadron and the captain's boss. This is true only in port, since at sea the captain reports only to a senior admiral, such as ComSubLant, or the commander of a battle group.

Your relief will take over at 0700, in time for officers' call with the XO. Maneuvering watch will be set at 0730, at which point you'll climb to the sail and take the OOD watch and drive her out for the op. By the time you see your rack, the ship will be submerged and it will be after evening meal.

XO Does Not Mean Hugs and Kisses

The XO, or executive officer, is second-in-command of the submarine. He does all the "heavy lifting" for the captain, allowing the captain to step back and think tactically and review the situation. All of the duties you would think are the captain's are really done by the XO. The captain hangs out in his stateroom in deep thought while the XO fights the fires. The captain comes in at 10 A.M., has lunch with the officers, and then leaves for golf with the *commodore*.

Meanwhile, the XO is in early and flies through a foot-tall stack of paperwork, and is five ass-chewings into the day by the time officers' call commences at 0700. At officers' call, all the department heads (chief engineer, navigator, weapons officer, and supply officer) and the division officers (junior officers who report to the department heads) sit at the wardroom table and go through the XO's list. If you worked for central casting and had to send in someone for the XO's role, you would think of the meanest man you know but imbue him with a father figure's authority.

On one ship of the force, the XO was hated and feared. Officers complained bitterly about him. The last day of his XO tour, in a foreign port in the middle of an intense op, with his relief on board and his car waiting, the officers were all holding back tears.

Observing this as a young midshipman, I asked one of the officers what was going on. "You hated the XO," I said.

"He was a second father to me," the lieutenant sniffed, as he pushed me out of the way. You'll never forget your first love, and you'll never forget your first XO.

Secrets of the Deep

The XO runs the ship and is the busiest man aboard, often working until late in the night or extremely early in the morning. If you need the impossible done, the XO's your man. If you become selected for XO, get a good vacation in first. For the next three years you will barely do anything but work and sleep—and the latter is not guaranteed. Oh, and make sure your wife is the independent type who'd just as soon have you out of her hair at sea someplace.

In the Submarine Force, the XO is a jack of all trades. As a senior nuke, he probably had a chief engineer tour before becoming XO, so he's more experienced than the chief engineer. He tends to keep the eng (chief engineer) hopping, making sure all the reactor paperwork is perfect. He has his own staff to run the administration of the ship, and every junior officer "dotted line" reports to the XO on anything the XO wants or needs. Every memo on its way to the captain is "chopped" (seen by and commented on) by the XO.

Prewatch Tour

Back to the reactor: You find the duty chief and ask him to pass the word on the 1MC to station section three watches aft, and to send the messenger around to the bunks of the watchsection to get everyone aft for the startup.

As you walk into the engineering spaces, you have begun your "prewatch tour." You practically live back aft, so anything out of the ordinary is immediately apparent. One of the things you do is make sure the watchstanders are alert. They've all taken their stations, all of them bleary-eyed, wrinkled, and unshaven. For a moment, a feeling of pure affection for the nukes of this crew overwhelms you. What heart these young-sters have, up in the middle of the night to start a reactor with no complaining, all of them calm professionals.

As you walk the nooks and crannies of the plant, down into the bowels of engineroom lower level at the refrigeration plant, you are reminded of a line from Hemingway that one of the junior officers loves to misquote: "I went below to see how things were. Things were bad." You smile to yourself as you climb the ladder to engineroom upper level and huddle up with the engineering watch supervisor and the ERUL (engineroom upper level) watch.

The engineering watch supervisor, or EWS, is the Robin to your Batman, a chief who is a highly qualified nuke. He could run the watchsection without you, but he probably wouldn't want to. You stand between the SSTGs and talk about the startup and the status of the plant. The EWS replies that everything is *nominal* and ready for the startup. You tell him to see you in the maneuvering room in five minutes.

You go to the door of maneuvering, the nuclear control room. It is a sacred place, not unlike the high priests' chamber of a temple. People do not raise their voices in ma-neuvering. No one enters without the permission of the ranking nuke inside, unless they are the chief engineer (eng), the XO, the captain, or the EOOW himself.

Eng *Is* His Name

The *eng* (pronounced "ennnnj") is the universal Navy nickname for the chief engineer, or engineer, for short. Officers have gone for their whole three-year engineer tour without anyone calling them any-thing but "eng."

It is sometimes thought that people have forgotten the eng's real name. If you call him at home and his wife answers, you still ask for "the eng." She under-stands. It wouldn't surprise you if his kids called him that. On some ships, where the eng is particularly bothersome, he may instead be called "feng," short for "the F-word eng."

> **Mike's Corner**
>
> The eng is the ranking nuke aboard, and he is all powerful, a deity aboard the ship. This is why, when he gets chewed out at officers' call by the XO, it is like watching God the Father chewing out Jesus Christ. And if the XO is like a celestial being pulling the puppet strings on a deity, the captain is unbelievably powerful.

The Engineering Officer of the Watch

The EOOW is the engineering officer of the watch. He is the eng's representative running the reactor plant. When the reactor and steam plant are shut down, the officer nuke on duty is the engineering duty officer, or EDO. When watches are stationed to start up the plant or when the reactor is already critical, the EOOW is stationed and his watch occurs back aft. At no time will the EOOW leave the engineering spaces.

The EOOW is ultimately responsible for reactor safety and ship safety back aft. Of all he does, the EOOW's duty during flooding is one of the most important because skillfully operating the chicken switches could save the ship from a *Thresher* disaster.

> **Beneath the Surface**
>
> The EOOW must have someone relieve him of the watch if he needs to have a bowel movement. That's because although the aft spaces are equipped with urinals, they have no commodes.

Entering Maneuvering

The door to maneuvering has a chain at waist level. You open the chain but don't come in until you announce, "Entering maneuvering."

Your favorite reactor operator (RO) acknowledges: "Entering, aye." He holds his palm in the air, his eyes on the reactor plant control panel (RPCP). You slap him five and stand behind the RPCP and scan the gauges. Wordlessly he hands his log clipboard over his shoulder. You read the trends of the temperatures and pressures and power readings. After years of doing this, you can read the log like the expression on your girlfriend's face. The status of the reactor plant is *nominal*.

On Being Nominal

When something is nominal, it means two things:

- There is a clearly defined range of expected and safe values for this measurement.

- The current value of the measurement is within that range. This is the same as being in spec (within specified range or in specification).

Being nominal is *not* the same as being *normal—nothing* on a submarine is normal. After all, what normal people would weld themselves into a steel pipe with 120 other sweating guys and go hundreds of feet underwater for months on end, living in the immediate vicinity of nuclear weapons and nuclear fuel? Nope, nominal is as close as things get to being normal on a submarine.

At this point, it's time to review the steam plant control panel (SPCP) gauges to the left of the RPCP. You scan that log and nod at the throttleman. On the right of the RPCP is the EPCP, or electric plant control panel. The electrical operator (EO) looks sleepy, so you punch him in the head and call for coffee. Naturally, he's grateful. Again, you scan the panel and read the EO's logs. The plant, both inside and outside maneuvering, is nominal. You go over to the EOOW seat, an elevated bar stool with a chair back near a bookshelf/table. Above the table is a large piping schematic of the plant. Black grease-pencil marks valves that are open or shut by procedure. Red marks are danger-tagged valves, usually tagged shut. You review the danger tags and the EOOW log. Next is the estimated critical position, or ECP.

> **Beneath the Surface**
>
> More about being nominal: For example, you could ask the question, "How's your girlfriend?" The answer might well be, "She's nominal." That means that she's within the range of expectations, but it also implies that she is not necessarily on the good side of that range. In theory, a girlfriend can be anything from wonderfully sweet to demonically evil, so anything in between is in spec or nominal. If the value is on the good side of the range, the answer might be different.

Estimated Critical Position

Estimated critical position (ECP) is a calculation done of the amount of negative reactivity the core has due to xenon fission product poisoning in it from the last shutdown. You go into charts that show core life (the number of effective full-power hours, or efph, already burned), the number of hours since shutdown, and the preshutdown "power history." All of that correlates to an amount of xenon remaining in the core. You also take the temperature of the reactor into consideration. The charts give you a position (inches withdrawal from bottom of core) of the *controlling rod group* to pull to the point that the reactor is critical. If the core is not critical within a few inches of the ECP, the OI-27 procedure requires you do certain things, such as recheck the ECP or the nuclear instruments. If the nuclear instruments are malfunctioning and you keep pulling control rods, you could take the core to prompt criticality (see Chapter 6 for more about nuclear accidents).

> **Subtalk**
>
> An **inverter** is an electrical device that, like a big rheostat, uses resisters to lower a DC voltage. By doing so, it creates a stair-step wave function of voltage to make an AC current. This converts DC to AC. For a reactor control inverter that uses three-phase AC power, the inverter "freezes" the AC wave at a particular point.

The controlling rod group is a number of control rods that are linked together on an *inverter.* For example, the outer ring of control rods would be group III. The middle ring would be group II, and the central six control rods would form group I.

At a certain stage of core life, you begin by pulling group III to the top. You leave group II on the bottom and pull out group I until criticality; you "control on group I rods," meaning that core temperature is controlled on group I. Later on in core life, group II and III would switch positions, with II on the top and III on the bottom. This evenly burns up the fuel in the core.

Phoning the Eng at Home

You check the ECP and sign it off. If the eng were on board, he would sign it, too. In some cases, the eng would want the ECP faxed to his house, but since you are an engineer-qualified junior officer, all he wants you to do is call him and tell him about it. You check your watch. The Rolex Submariner says it is 0215. You grab the landline phone and dial the eng's home number. You report the ECP, and the sleepy eng tells you he recommends starting the reactor.

The phone by your head whoops. "Eee-ow," you say, the pronunciation for EOOW.

"Duty officer," the voice says. It's your roommate and stateroom-mate, Keith, who gets sloppy drunk in liberty ports but is as buttoned down as an admiral otherwise, and in fact, is expected to achieve flag rank someday. "Time to call the captain. You got a recommendation?"

"Engineer recommends starting the reactor. Section three watches are manned aft. Request to start the reactor."

"Request to start the reactor, aye." He repeats it all back formally. "Wait one."

"Wait one, aye."

Keith may be your roommate onboard and ashore, and you know what he's thinking before he does, but you still go through all the formalities.

Reviewing the Procedure

While you're waiting, you review the procedure. The operating instructions are in a 5-inch-thick binder. The paper itself is an engineering marvel, made of the same filmy plastic Tyvek stuff that FedEx uses for its large envelopes. You open the binder to OI-27 and scan a few paragraphs. The words are as familiar to you as a dog-eared section of the Bible is to a minister.

The phone whoops again. "Eee-ow."

"Duty officer. Start the reactor."

"Start the reactor, aye," you say and hang up.

You pull the 2MC microphone out of its cradle in the overhead, click the button, and listen as your voice, like the voice of God, booms through the engineering spaces. The volume is cranked up to be heard over the scream of the turbines, and your voice sounds even louder because the ship is quiet as a tomb with everything shut down. "Engineering watch supervisor, come to maneuvering."

You stand up and pull off the chain around your neck where the reactor safety key is kept. With it, you unlock a drawer below the bottom shelf of the bookcase. Inside are three fuses, each the size of a flashlight. You relock the drawer and put the key back around your neck. The EWS stands at the chain at the door by the throttleman.

"Request to enter maneuvering."

"Enter maneuvering." You hand the EWS the fuses and address him formally. "Engineering watch supervisor, place fuses in inverter cabinets alpha, bravo, and charlie, and shut scram breakers."

"Place fuses in A, B, and C, and shut scram breakers, aye." He disappears forward for a few minutes. You make an entry in the EOOW log and then look up as the EWS returns. "Request to enter."

"Enter maneuvering."

"Sir, fuses placed in inverters alpha, bravo, and charlie. Scram breakers alpha, bravo, and charlie are shut."

"Very well, Chief, thank you and have a good startup."

The chief whacks the reactor operator on the head. "Watch this guy, sir. No screw-ups on my watch."

The RO utters an expletive without taking his eyes off the RPCP. You take station, standing behind the RO where you can see the entire panel. You make another entry in the EOOW log: *Commencing normal reactor startup.*

"Reactor operator, conduct normal reactor startup."

"Conduct normal reactor startup, aye."

You grab the 2MC microphone and announce, "Commencing normal reactor startup."

Starting the Pumps

The RO stands and grabs a main coolant pump starter on the port side. "Starting main coolant pump four in slow speed." He pulls up on the T-switch, and the pump starts. The indicating lights come up, and the pressure indicators on the panel jump. "Starting main coolant pump three in slow speed." He starts another pump. There are now two pumps running in slow speed in each coolant loop, up from the previous configuration of one pump per loop. "Running two slow/two slow pumps, sir."

"Very well."

"Latching group III rods," the RO announces. He moves a selector switch marked Inverter to the C position. Then he pushes the pistol grip of the rod control switch at the center of the lower sloping section (it's right in the center of a little reactor plastic shape) from the twelve o'clock position to the nine o'clock position. At the same time, he pulls the pistol grip out of the panel about 2 inches. "Applying latch voltage to inverter charlie."

You look at the latch voltage display. Latch voltage doubles as latch current from inverter charlie flows to the alligator assemblies of the control rod drive mechanisms for group III rods. Previously, the alligator assemblies were open, but when latch voltage was applied by pulling out on the rod switch, the electromagnets in each alligator assembly energized and the assemblies all clamped down on the threaded section of the rod bars. To make sure the alligator thread engages the rod thread, the RO drives the rods in. Rods are already at the bottom, but by doing this he turns the alligator assemblies until they engage the threading.

"Group III rods latched."

"Very well."

"Withdrawing group III rods to top of core," he announces. He stands up and rotates the pistol grip to the right.

You won't go critical on group III unless something is very wrong, but you watch the panel like a hawk.

"Group III rod bottom lights out," the RO says.

The outer ring of rod bottom lights winks out as the rods come off the bottom of the core.

Mike's Corner

It takes quite a bit of strength to pull out rods, but none at all to push them in. This is deliberate: Admiral Rickover wanted the RO to know when he was increasing reactor power. During a long startup, the RO's hands shake as he pulls the rods. The rod control lever always returns to the "hold," or neutral, position when the RO's hands are not on it.

The digital counter climbs as the rod group comes higher, reeling off until the group climbs to 20 inches, then 30, then 35, until the rod group is to the top. Meanwhile, you watch the neutron level deep in the startup range and the startup rate meter. Nothing much happens to either gauge. If you had been shut down for a long time, with the neutron level so low that it is essentially unreadable (in the fiduciary range), you would have had to conduct a miserable "pull and wait" startup. Instead of pulling the rods out of the core, the RO would pull out for 3 seconds and you'd wait for 57 while watching the power level. Then you'd repeat this for the next five hours until the power level came back on the scale of the meter.

The RO lets go of the rod lever with the group at the top of the core. "Latching group II," the RO says. He switches the inverter switch to position B and moves the switch to the nine o'clock position while pulling it out of the console. "Applying latch voltage to group II. Group II rods latched."

"Very well." Group II will remain at the bottom of the core, but it is latched so that in case of shock, the rods won't jump up and cause a power spike.

"Latching group I." He moves the inverter switch to position A and repeats the latch procedure. "Pulling group I to criticality."

You sharpen your gaze on the neutron level and startup rate.

"Group I rod bottom lights out."

First Wiggle of the Startup Rate Needle

As the group I rods come out of the core, the startup rate needle budges off the 0 indication to +.2 decades per minute The RO keeps pulling until the needle shows 1 decade per minute and then lets go of the lever. The startup rate decays to 0. He pulls again, and startup rate slowly climbs to 1 decade per minute. The neutron-level needle slowly moves upward, unwinding around the dial, every few minutes changing by a decade (going from 10^{-9} to 10^{-8}, then 10^{-7} and upward). Finally, when at a 1 decade per minute startup rate, the RO puts the rod control switch to neutral. The startup rate decays to a nonzero level, steady at +.3 decades per minute.

"The reactor is critical," he announces, making a notation in his log sheet. The ECP predicted that this would happen at 24.0 inches. The actual position is 23.7. Not bad.

You pick up the 1MC microphone, near the 2MC. This one announces to the entire ship.

"The reactor," you pause for dramatic effect, "is critical!" Another log entry, and the startup continues.

"Pulling group I to the power range," the RO says. He grabs the rod control switch again and takes her to a startup rate of +1 decade per minute The neutron level climbs slowly to the top of the startup range. The intermediate-range needle also starts to climb, the two ranges intersecting for 2 decades. "Source range channel selector switch to startup rate scram cutout," he says as he rotates a large switch on the panel.

"Very well," you acknowledge. At this point, the startup range nuclear instrument is de-energized by the source range channel selector switch. If the delicate neutron detector were energized much longer, the bombardment of neutrons would make it fail. At this point, there is no automatic scram coming from the startup range meter. Protection is now provided by the level of the startup rate meter for the intermediate range. If it goes to +9 decades per minute, the reactor will scram.

Beneath the Surface
Until the main coolant temperature is in the green band, the heatup rate will be no more than 5°F per minute. Since starting temperature is relatively warm at 360°F, we can heat this up fast. If it were low, we would be limited to a degree per minute, and the startup would take much longer.

Now the core is reactive enough that the RO can pull rods to a +1.5 decade per minute startup rate. When he lets go, the startup rate decays to 1.0 decades per minute. She's waking up by herself now, and you just watch as minute by minute the reactor comes humming out of the lower level of the intermediate range. At the top of the intermediate level is the power range. In the power range, the core has the ability to raise coolant temperature.

Near the top of the intermediate range, the startup rate declines on its own to zero. The reactor operator pulls out for a few seconds (this is called "shimming out") and watches the panel.

Subtalk

The T_{AVE} is the average of main coolant temperature entering the core and leaving the core. If T_{IN} = 460°F and T_{OUT} = 500°F, then the T_{AVE} = 480°F. The T_{AVE} must always be in the **green band,** which is from 475°F to 485°F. All studies of reactor safety begin with the assumption that T_{AVE} is in the green band. If you operate outside, the warranty is off. When the T_{AVE} comes out of the green band, the reactor operator **shims** or **bumps** rods in or out to lower or raise the T_{AVE}. (In the power range, reactor power follows steam demand. The throttleman determines reactor power by how much he opens the throttles; all the control rods do is supply excess power to the core to change the T_{AVE}).

"Reactor is in the power range," he calls. You repeat the announcement on the 2MC. "Heating up main coolant to the green band," he announces.

Now that the core is in the power range, raising the control rods raises reactor power, which heats up the coolant. Average coolant temperature, or T_{AVE} (pronounced "Tee-av"), is currently 360°F.

"Establishing five degree per minute heatup rate," he says, putting a graph on top of his log clipboard.

Heating Up the Core

For the next 30 minutes, the RO heats up the core. The T_{AVE} needle slowly climbs. The power-level meter shows between 0 and 5 percent as he heats up.

"T_{AVE} is in the green band, sir," he reports.

"Very well." You pick up the 2MC. "Engineering Watch Supervisor, come to maneuvering."

The EWS requests to enter, and you wave him in. The two of you glance at the RPCP. Then you tell him to start the steam plant: "Engineering watch supervisor, equalize around and open main steam one and two. Bring steam into the engineroom, warm up the main steam headers, pull a vacuum on port and starboard main condensers, start port and starboard SSTGs, and warm up port and starboard main engines."

For once the EWS does not repeat back the order exactly. This exception to the rule is a tradition: "Suck two, spin four, aye."

He disappears to go up forward. While you wait, you know that he and the engineroom upper-level watch are opening valves that will allow steam from the boilers to go around the big bulkhead stop valves, MS-1 and MS-2. This will lower the differential pressure (DP) across the valves and make them easier to open. When the DP is less than 50 psi, the EWS and ERUL will start cranking MS-1 and MS-2 open, which takes a good five minutes each.

"MS-2 indicates open," the RO says. A light on his panel has changed from a bar to an O. After a few more minutes, he announces that MS-1 is open.

The noise begins. The steam header begins to warm up, and the water inside it from condensation is blown out by steam pressure. That roaring noise you hear is the EWS and ERUL "blowing down" the steam traps, which are devices that keep condensate—water drops—out of the steam headers. After 10 minutes of blowing down the headers, the EWS goes below to help the ERLL watch take a vacuum to the condensers. They start the port and starboard main seawater pumps, get the condensers cool, and then use steam pressure from the auxiliary steam system to suck down the condensers to a vacuum. The condensation of steam to liquid causes the vacuum: Steam takes up a lot of volume and liquid a lot less, so the shrinking of the condensation process makes the condensers a vacuum. But the cycle starts with a lot of air in the pipes, and air will not condense. The air ejectors are devices with venturi tubes, and steam is blown through the venturis to cause low pressure, which sucks the air out of the condenser and puts it into the engineroom. The air ejectors are what would make the engineroom radioactive if you were using a boiling water reactor or if you had a primary-to-secondary leak.

Soon the EWS is back in engineroom upper level, and he begins to spin the port SSTG. You can hear the turbine start to roll. At first it rumbles. Then it growls, moans, and screams like a jet, the noise rising to a screech and finally a howl until the pitch comes up to a shrill whistle.

The EWS appears at the door. "Port TG on the governor and ready for loading."

Shifting the Electric Plant

It's time to shift the electric plant. "Electrical operator," you say, "shift the electric plant to a half-power lineup on the port TG." The electrical operator acknowledges and then lines up his synchroscope to the port SSTG breaker. He will monitor voltage and frequency on the SSTG side of the breaker against the nonvital bus side, which is supplied by shorepower. The two buses must be synchronized. This means that the AC current that rises and falls must be at the same point of the cycle on each side of the breaker. A meter compares the frequencies of the AC power on either side, and the needle rotates slowly in the "fast" direction; the frequency is higher on the SSTG end so that when it suddenly takes load, it slows slightly. When the needle gets to the twelve o-clock position, the EO rotates his breaker control switch and the SSTG breaker shuts. He uses a voltage dial to "take load" on the SSTG and unload shorepower.

"The electric plant is in a half-power lineup on the port SSTG," he reports.

You announce it on the 2MC. The EWS has disappeared to the lower level to start a main feed pump. The steam generator levels have been dropping since he opened MS-1 and MS-2. You hear the pump start, and steam generator water-level indications on the steam plant control panel rise back up to the normal level.

Beneath the Surface

The cables are too heavy to remove by hand. It takes a crane to get them off the hull.

Soon the EWS starts the starboard turbine and reports it ready for loading. After similar actions at the electric plant control panel (EPCP), the EO reports that the plant is in a normal full-power lineup.

You order the EO to open the shorepower breaker.

"Engineering watch supervisor," you order, "remove the shorepower cables." He and an electrician climb into the access hatch for shorepower and disconnect the heavy cable connectors. When he's done, you dial up the duty officer and report the ship divorced from shore power. Then you request permission to spin the shaft as necessary to keep the main engines warm. He gives permission.

Cracking Open the Throttles

The EWS starts the main engine turbines and turns control of them over to the throttleman. For the next eight hours, the throttleman will crack open the throttles every few minutes to keep the main engines warm. Since the clutch is engaged, this spins the shaft and turns the screw a half turn, but this is acceptable because it won't put much stress on the lines holding the ship to the pier.

You're done. The reactor is now at about 18 percent power with T_{AVE} in the green band at 480°F. Nothing to do now but wait for your relief to take over from you so you can go to officers' call and then to the bridge to drive her out. You yawn and take a cup of coffee from the engineroom upper level watch.

The Least You Need to Know

- The executive officer (XO) is the busiest person on a sub.
- The Chief Engineer (Eng) is in charge of the nuke reactor.
- Being nominal is *not* the same as being *normal—nothing* on a submarine is normal.
- The EOOW is ultimately responsible for reactor safety and ship safety back aft.
- Removing the shore power cables is the last step before the ship is completely divorced from shore power—and on its own.

Chapter 16

Getting Underway

In This Chapter

- ◆ Divorcing from the shore
- ◆ Ship control: driving the ship
- ◆ Telling time
- ◆ Periscope depth

It's after officers' call, and the duty officer has stationed the maneuvering watch. You relieve him of the duty and then climb to the top of the bridge access trunk to the bridge to station yourself as the officer of the deck, the OOD.

Behind you, in a cubbyhole, is the lookout. You check to make sure that he's alert and has binoculars. The phonetalker joins you on the bridge. He plugs in his sound-powered headset and tests the circuit. All orders to control are made in parallel over the sound-powered circuits in case the bridge box breaks down.

Checking the Bridge

You check the bridge to make sure it's rigged. The windshield is installed and the communication box is mounted. You test the circuits, and they're working. The chart is in the satchel, as is the flashlight and the bullhorn. The compass alidade is connected—a gyro compass mounted behind the windshield with little sighting viewports so you can look down a compass bearing. You strap on a pair of binoculars and adjust them to your eyes. It's a bright, sunny morning with excellent visibility. The running lights are rigged out. You look down at the deck. The deck crew are singling up the lines. Previously, the lines went from the bollard on the pier to the deck cleat on the ship and back to the pier bollard. Now the lines only go from the *bollards* to the *cleats*.

> **Subtalk**
>
> A **cleat** is a two-horned projection from a ship's deck around which is wrapped a "line" (the rope that holds the ship to the pier, but never call it a "rope"). A **bollard** is a large chunk of metal poured into the concrete of the pier. It looks like a light bulb made of iron, but it's about 4 feet tall. Some bollards have horizontal cylindrical posts coming out each side. They are used to secure a ship to the pier.

You review the chart and the current and tide table. The chart has the navigator's track laid out. You study the turning points and the landmarks. Since you are departing Norfolk, it should be easy. You've conned the ship out of here more than 20 times. But complacency is the mariner's enemy, so you study the chart yet again.

The bridgebox rasps with the executive officer's voice: "Bridge, XO, maneuvering watches are manned."

"XO, Bridge, aye."

A voice calls out below you: "Captain to the bridge."

Enter the Captain

"Aye, sir, come on up." You lift the grating and the captain climbs up. (His nickname is *El Jefe*, like a South American dictator, but don't call him that in his presence.)

"Good morning, sir," you snap.

"Morning, Mr. Smith. What's the status?" He climbs up to the top of the sail, where stainless-steel rails frame an area called the "flying bridge."

You take a deep breath and make your report: "Sir, we are answering bells on both main engines with main coolant pumps in two slow/two slow, the electric plant is in a normal full-power lineup, the ship is divorced from shorepower, and the cables are removed. We're spinning the shaft as necessary to keep the main engines warm. Maneuvering watch is stationed. Navigator's visual fix is in and agrees with SINS and the GPS Navsat fix. The subnote is on board, and we have Squadron's permission to get underway. The security swim is complete with no discrepancies; all ballast tank vent covers have been removed. The ship is rigged for dive, with the exception of the bridge, the deck, and the ventilation lineup, which is in surface ventilate mode. Lines are singled up, the pier linehandlers are stationed, and the pier crane is standing by to remove the gangway. The radar is secured, but the Raytheon commercial radar is mounted and ready to rotate and radiate."

> **Beneath the Surface**
>
> You use the Raytheon instead of the ship's radar because the radar uniquely identifies the ship as a Navy warship in general and a Navy submarine in particular.

The captain nods. "Remove the gangway and rotate and radiate on the Raytheon," he orders.

You acknowledge him and pick up the bullhorn. "On deck," you call to the chief of the boat, who is also the auxiliaryman chief or head "A-ganger." "Take off the brow!"

A few moments later, the diesel engine of the pier crane roars as it removes the gangway from the deck. It's almost time.

"Bridge, Navigator," the bridgebox booms, "request to rotate and radiate on the Raytheon."

"Navigator, Bridge, aye, wait," you reply. "Captain?"

"Rotate and radiate the Raytheon."

"Aye, sir. Navigator, Bridge, rotate and radiate." You look at the captain. "Sir, request permission to get underway."

"Off'sa'deck," the captain orders, "get underway."

Taking In All Lines

"Get underway, aye." You pick up the bullhorn and yell down to the chief of the boat: "On deck, take in all lines."

The linehandlers pull in the lines from the pier crew. When the last line comes over, you reach into a cubbyhole below the windshield and to the right of the bridgebox and grab the handle of the 150 psi air horn. You pull the lever toward you, and a blasting foghorn as loud as a 747 sounds over the water of the basin. You give it a full eight seconds while you look aft at the lookout and mouth the words "Shift colors!" He's already on it, up on the flying bridge beside the captain hoisting the Stars and Stripes on a temporary flagmast.

Your complete attention is focused on the ship's movement in the channel to avoid collision or running aground. The navigator below is taking fixes and plotting them on the chart. Based on the ship's speed and time-to-turn, he will be "marking the turn point" as you approach a place on the track where the intended course changes.

At first you order up all ahead one third, 4 knots, so that there is no bow wave while the deck gang puts the lines in the line lockers and rotates the cleats into the hull. Once the deck is rigged for dive, the captain will allow you to speed up to standard (14 knots) or full (18 knots).

Your available ship control options include the following orders (speeds indicated are on the surface):

- All Stop
- Back one third
- Back two thirds
- Back full
- All ahead one third (about 4 knots)
- All ahead two thirds (8 knots)
- All ahead standard (12 knots)
- All ahead full (16 knots)
- All ahead flank (20 knots)
- Rudder amidships
- Right 5 degrees rudder
- Right 10 degrees rudder
- Right full rudder
- Corresponding left rudder orders
- Steady course or steer course XXX (000 to 359)

While that seems like a short list, it's good enough to get you anywhere you want to go.

Keeping an Eye on Inbound Shipping

The contact coordinator is sharing the periscopes and radar plot with the navigator to watch inbound shipping. He makes a report: "Bridge, contact, new visual contact Victor Seven bearing one one zero, inbound merchant tanker, range 15,000 yards, course two seven zero. He's in the inbound traffic separation scheme."

"Very well," you acknowledge. Then you repeat the information to the captain while searching on that bearing with the alidade and then your binoculars.

After following the navigator's turns, you steam into the outbound traffic-separation scheme. The captain orders a speed increase to flank. The wind and the bow wave roar in your ears, and 30,000 shaft horsepower shakes the deck as the ship steams toward the dive point.

Submerging

The captain indicates what time he'd like to be submerged, either by verbal order (transcribed to the status board) or in his *night orders.*

Submergence in a nonemergency is done at the 100-fathom curve, where the ocean depth is 600 feet deep at the continental shelf. If the ship is submerged in shallower water, it is conducting littoral operations.

At the 100-fathom curve, the captain expects that the ship will be completely rigged for dive, that a navigational fix is onboard that agrees with the SINS and DR positions, and that the secure fathometer is functional.

> **Subtalk**
>
> The captain's **night orders** are a logbook of his intentions for the officer of the deck for the evening watch (1800 to 2400) and midwatch (0000 to 0600). They include tactical thoughts, navigation orders, when to contact him, when the OOD is expected to come to periscope depth, and other miscellaneous things.

How to Tell Time Underwater

The chronometer (clock) is a 24-hour clock and counts off the watches. The chronometer is usually set to Greenwich Mean Time or Zulu Time (although how annoying is it to set the clock to the same time as Big Ben?).

During the Cold War, great work was done analyzing when to attack the Russians. Since they are on Moscow time, if you hit them at 3:00 A.M. Moscow time, you're bound to get the least capable officer of the deck in the command post (the Russian term for the control room). Likewise, if you are attacking the Chinese, hit them at 0300 Beijing time. The watches start at midnight (0000, pronounced zero zero zero zero). The first watch, or midwatch, goes from 0000 to 0600 (zero six hundred).

Secrets of the Deep

Don't say "hours" after the time—that's Army talk.

The morning watch goes from 0600 to 1200. The afternoon watch, as you'd expect, is from 1200 to 1800. The evening watch extends from 1800 to 2400.

Taking Her Down

Assuming that you are the OOD, at the dive point minus one minute, you give your report to the captain: "Sir, ship is rigged for dive, sounding is one zero zero fathoms, and we are one minute to the dive point. Request permission to submerge the ship to one five zero feet and attain a one third trim."

The captain replies, "At the dive point, submerge the ship to one five zero feet and attain a one third trim." Or he may say, "Dive the ship" or simply "Take her down."

At the dive point, the navigator or his navigation electronics technician calls, "Mark the dive point!"

You order the diving officer, "Diving Officer, submerge the ship to one five zero feet and obtain a one third trim."

The diving officer takes command of the ship's speed during the evolution. He orders the helmsman to ring up all ahead one third.

Secrets of the Deep

You always make an engine order as "all ahead one third," even if your ship has only one screw.

OODs who abbreviate this to "ahead one third" in the interest of logic risk being flamed on by the captain.

The diving officer orders the chief of the watch at the ballast control panel (BCP) to sound the diving alarm and announce "Dive, dive," and then open the forward group's main ballast tank vents.

The chief of the watch announces on the 1MC "Dive, dive," and then hits the diving alarm lever. The chief of the watch announces "Dive, dive" again. He reaches up to the right vertical panel of the BCP and flips up the toggle for the forward group's main ballast tank vents.

You "train" (turn the view of) the periscope to examine the bow, putting the view angle downward. This is done to check that the forward main ballast tanks are venting correctly. You should see geysers blasting upward from the bow if all is going well. You call out, "Venting forward."

The diving officer makes the order to the chief of the watch to open the aft main ballast tank vents. You train the scope aft and down. You witness those vents opening and call, "Venting aft."

> **Beneath the Surface**
>
> The diving alarm sounds a bit computer-generated as it sounds its OOOOOOO-GAAAAAAAH. On some ships, the captain may have stolen a WWII submarine's diving alarm and rigged it to the 1MC, making it somewhat more macho.

Eventually, the ship sinks deeper into the sea. The diving officer calls out the depth. You do a surface search for close surface contacts and then train the scope aft again. When the waves cover the aft deck, you call, "Deck's awash." The diving officer continues to call out depth until you are at the depth where the top of the sail submerges. Then he calls, "Sail under." You are now essentially invisible to surface traffic, so you do another low-power surface search.

The waves come closer to your view. When the waves wash over the periscope, you call, "Scope's awash." When you see the underside of the waves, you call, "Scope's under." You take a moment to do a circle search with the view trained upward at the waves, and then you train the scope to the bow, click up the periscope grips, and reach into the overhead. A steel ring about the size of a bicycle tire surrounds the upper optic module of the periscope. You reach for it and rotate it clockwise. You hear the whoosh of hydraulics, and the optics module disappears into the periscope well. You call, "Lowering number two scope."

By now the angle of the deck is about 5 degrees to 10 degrees down. You watch the diving officer as he orders the planesmen to pull out at depth 150 feet. At this point, he obtains a one third trim.

If he's confident, he'll orders all ahead one third and orders the planesmen to zero their planes. The ship may tip nose-up or nose-down, and it may sink or rise. Depending on ship behavior, the diving officer will flood or pump from the depth-control tank to get the ship neutral overall, and then pump from the depth-control tank to forward or aft variable ballast to keep the ship in balance.

> **Mike's Corner**
>
> A good diving officer will take up to 20 minutes to take her down. He may order all stop to allow the ship to coast down and observe the depth behavior. Eventually, he'll bring the ship back to all ahead one third, and he'll report that the ship has a satisfactory trim.

You report the trim condition to the captain and request to go deep and "chase PIM." (PIM is the point of intended motion, or the moving dot in the sea where the ship is scheduled to be—"where the brass expect your ass." Skimmer pukes call this the "track.")

The captain gives his permission, and you order the ship deep and to her best speed to chase PIM and listen for the particular enemy that you perceive as a threat.

Coming to Periscope Depth

If you've been deep for some time, away from the hassles of the surface, there are some things you're missing.

For one, the "fix error circle" has been growing. Remember, the Ship's Inertial Navigation System (SINS) is an overgrown gyroscope, and it provides only a guess of the ship's actual position. An error begins to set in the longer SINS has been from a "fix," or a comparison to the actual ship's position. It is recommended to get a fix for SINS at least every 24 hours, but it's even better to "settle SINS" by getting a fix every 8 hours.

The supply officer wants to eject garbage from the TDU (trash disposal unit), which is done at shallow depths for safety reasons.

The engineer wants to "blow down" his steam generators every week or so, and that is done at shallow depths to avoid seawater leaking back into the boilers. A steam generator blowdown is simply opening a series of valves that dump steam generator water to the sea. It is done as a bottom blow or a surface blow, depending on what chemicals in the boiler are out of spec. This is a noisy evolution, so don't do it near a hostile submarine.

Finally, the communications officer will be annoyed if you don't catch the submarine broadcast every eight hours. A missed message is a black mark against the captain. If something urgent is going down, you'll be summoned to periscope depth by an ELF transmission).

So, as the officer of the deck, you need to know how to come to periscope depth (PD) safely and rapidly. While this is easy in mid-Atlantic away from the shipping lanes, it is intensely difficult in the Strait of Gibraltar, where there are more than a hundred surface ship contacts. The idea of safely coming to PD is avoiding surface ships.

The first step is to call the captain and obtain his permission to come shallow in preparation for coming to periscope depth. You let him know what you're planning to do up there, how long it will take, and what effect it will have on PIM. If PIM is moving at

20 knots, an extended time at PD at 6 knots will kill your transit plans. (You can't go fast at PD—it would rip off the periscope and would put up a rooster tail mast wake. You might as well just wave your arms and say, "Hey, skimmers, here I am—come get me!") Usually the captain will concur with your recommendation and order you shallow.

Don't forget this step: Call the sonar supervisor and tell him you're planning on coming shallow in preparation to coming to PD. You'll be taking the ship above "layer depth," and all his acoustics will be going to hell. In addition, you'll need the maximum alertness of the sonar supervisor and his boys to keep you safe from collision as you approach the surface.

You pick up the microphone to the sonar circuit and say, "Sonar, Conn, coming shallow in preparation to coming to periscope depth."

"Conn, Sonar aye," the speaker replies.

"Diving Officer," you order, "make your depth one five zero feet!"

He acknowledges: "Make my depth one five zero feet, aye." He then orders the planesmen: "Helm, ten degree rise on the bowplanes, Sternplanesman, five degree up bubble." The helmsman/bowplanesman pulls up until he gets a 10 degree up angle on the bowplanes, and the sternplanesman pulls up until the ship's angle is 5 degrees up. The ship climbs out of the deep (best listening depth) to 150 feet keel depth. The diving officer calls out the depth every 50 feet.

"One five zero feet, sir," he says when he's arrived.

You pick up the microphone to sonar and say, "Sonar, Conn, one five zero feet, report all contacts."

"Conn, Sonar aye." There will be a delay as the sonarmen scan all broadband bearings seeking surface ship targets. Whatever they had when you were deep may no longer be audible because of the layer effect.

Secrets of the Deep

The top 200 feet of the ocean are stirred by the waves and warmed by the sun to between 70°F and 50°F. Sound characteristics depend heavily on ocean temperature. Below 200 feet, the sun is unable to warm the water, and wave effects leave this deep volume of the sea alone. Consequently, below 200 feet the water is cold, no more than 28°F (the salinity allows water to be colder than the freezing point of freshwater).

It will take sonar about one minute to make their report. While you wait, you turn your sonar repeater screen to the broadband passive spherical array. You can see the bright stripes, mostly vertical, that mark the bearings where there are surface ships. You're about to execute a maneuver to observe the bearing behavior of the surface contacts.

> **Secrets of the Deep**
>
> At 200 feet or so, there is a sharp and immediate temperature change in the ocean water from the warm layer to the deep cold. This depth, which can be anywhere from 100 feet to 250 feet, is called the layer depth. Below the layer, sound bounces off the layer and stays deep. Above the layer, sound exhibits a "sound channel effect" and bounces in the narrow volume between surface and layer. If you are deeper than the layer, odds are good that you can't hear what's overhead because sound waves reflect off the layer. If you are shallower, you can't hear things that are deep.

"Conn, Sonar, hold one sonar contact, Sierra Five Seven, merchant vessel bearing zero one zero, bearing rate left point five degrees per minute."

"Sonar, Conn, aye." You are on course east, 090, so the contact at 010 (on your left) is drifting left—always a good sign. Now it's time to do TMA, target motion analysis, to see what its range is.

"Sonar, Conn, maneuvering to two seven zero." You address the helmsman: "Helm, left ten degrees rudder, steady course two seven zero."

It will take the ship about a minute to make the turn at your slow speed of all ahead two thirds.

"Steady course two seven zero, sir," the helmsman reports when he's on course west.

"Very well. Sonar, Conn, steady course west, report all contacts." Part of what you are doing is "checking your *baffles.*"

"Conn, Sonar, search complete in the previously baffled area. Continue to hold only Sierra Five Seven, bearing zero one two, bearing rate right zero point six degrees per minute."

"Sonar, Conn, aye."

Subtalk

Baffles refer to the cone behind the ship's screw, where the passive broadband spherical array cannot hear because of the location of the sphere. Even if the sphere could listen astern of the submarine, it would be useless because of the noise of the machinery aft. For this reason, the ship is turned in order to give the sphere the ability to hear in the baffled area.

The towed array can be used to penetrate the baffles and hear aft. Other sensors are being considered to look astern at the baffles, but until they are operational, there continues to be a blind spot aft of the ship.

Doing the Math

You pull out your bearing rate slide rule—or, even better, you calculate the range in your head. The range (by the Ekelund range calculation) is approximately equal to the change in speed across the line of sight divided by the change in bearing rate. Your initial speed of 8 knots was done at 80 degrees to the line of sight, so your speed across the line of sight is $8 \times (\sin(80)) = 8 \times (.984) = 7.9$ knots, which corresponds to a bearing rate of 0.5 degrees per minute (dpm). On the second "leg," the speed across the line of sight was 8 knots at 102 degrees to the line of sight, or $8 \times \sin(102) = 8 \times (.978) = 7.8$ knots, which corresponds to a bearing rate of 0.6 dpm. Therefore, range is equal to $(7.9 - (-7.8)) / (0.5 - (-.6)) = (7.9 + 7.8) / (.5 + .6) = 15.7 / 1.1 = 14.3$ nautical miles = 28,600 yards.

Anything outside of 20,000 yards is not a threat.

You may have done this calculation in your head like this:

Leg 1: ~8 knots across the LOS (since $\sin(90) \sim 1$), .5 dpm

Leg 2: ~8 knots across the LOS, .6 dpm

Range = $(8 + 8) / (.5 + .6) \sim 16/1 = 16$ miles = 32,000 yards

So, the mental range is 32,000 yards, the bearing slide rule range is 28,000 yards, and (since you "stacked dots" on the contact on the fire-control computer) the fire-control range is 26,000 yards. (The firecontrol computer "smoothes" the data using FIDUs, or fixed-interval data units, which is more accurate than sonar's guess of bearing rate.)

The contact is not a problem.

Now try doing this with 34 contacts in the Strait of Gibraltar. The firecontrol system will help. Having a junior officer of the deck (JOOD) stationed to assist with contact solutions will also help. But in the end, select a course for the ship that ...

◆ Will not put you into shoal water.

◆ Has the feature that all contacts on the right are drawing right, and all contacts on the left are drawing left.

In this case, the risk of collision is minimal.

Now you call the captain on the phone. He answers in his stateroom: *"Very well."*

Subtalk

"**Very well**" (pronounced "vwell") is an officer's response to a report or recommendation. If the chief of the watch says, "Recommend commencing MBT blow," saying "Very well" does *not* mean, "Okay, do it." It only means, "I hear you." The French might say, "Well received." Our zoomie friends (a zoomie, of course, is a member of the U.S. Air Force) might say, "Roger."

"Captain, Off'sa'deck, sir. Ship is at one five zero feet, course west, hold one sonar contact, Sierra Five Seven, range 28,000 yards, bearing zero one three and drawing right. Request permission to come to periscope depth and conduct evolutions (whatever you discussed before)."

"Very well, OOD, come to periscope depth and conduct evolutions."

You acknowledge and order the diving officer to take her up: "Dive, make your depth six six feet! Helm, all ahead one third."

The diving officer orders the bowplanes to 5 degree rise and orders the sternplanes to establish a 5 degree up bubble and approach periscope depth.

You call out, "Lookaround, number two scope!"

This is the prompt for the ship control party to call out data to avoid breaking off the periscope.

"Speed six knots!" the helmsman says.

"Depth one two zero feet, sir," the diving officer reports.

If the speed is less than 9 knots, you can raise the scope without fear of it breaking off in the slipstream of the water flow around the hull. But beware—any speed over 4 knots makes a rooster tail wake that could lead to your being detected. (Nonqual, what is the number one order in the captain's standing orders? Answer: "Remain undetected.")

"Very well," you say. "Up scope."

Note: Never say "Aye, aye" to your spouse—it gives the hint that you think they are giving you *rudder orders*. Rudder orders are the orders that the conning officer (the officer of the deck or the captain) gives to the helmsman.

The helmsman's job is to maintain the course given or place the rudder at the specific rudder angle given, not to think about where the ship is going. For that reason, when an admiral or headquarters (or your wife) is directing you at the "task level" or micromanaging you, the offender is giving you rudder orders.

Secrets of the Deep

Never say "Up periscope." It sounds like a cheap U-boat movie. Always say, "Up scope." Similarly, declare "Scope's breaking," "Scope's clear," "Scope's awash," "Scope's under," or "Lowering number two scope." Everyone in the control room knows it's a periscope, so why waste two syllables?

Naval officers hate rudder orders. If the XO is on your case and you feel lucky, after he issues a string of orders, you can just say, "Rudder orders" and he will know that you mean, "Back the hell off, I know my job."

A good XO will chuckle and then reissue the orders. A bad one may confine you to quarters, or put you in hack.

Beneath the Surface

There is a vast difference between "Yes, sir" and "Aye, aye, sir." The uttering of "Aye, aye" is in response to a direct order and means, "I understand your order and will comply with same." Our zoomie buddies would say "Roger, wilco" (at least, they used to before that made it into the cartoons and sounded stupid). "Yes, sir" is sometimes inappropriately substituted for "Aye, aye" in a nautical setting, and will result in the abuser being called a nonqual. Ouch. "Yes, sir" simply indicates that the answer to a question of information is the affirmative. For example: "Is the sounding correct?" "Yes, sir." "Take her down." "Aye, aye, sir."

Rising from the Well

You reach into the overhead to the steel hydraulic control ring that circles the periscope upper hull penetration. You push it to the right so that it turns about 10 degrees counterclockwise. The hydraulic system should thump, and the periscope will start to come out of the periscope well at about 2 feet per second. The optics module emerges, and you crouch down to put your eye to the eyepiece while the unit is still rising. As soon as the periscope grips come out of the well fairing at your toes, you snap them down. A good officer of the deck can get three or four seconds of periscope viewing while the unit is still rising from the well.

Train the view far upward with the left grip (rotate it like you're revving up a motor-cycle). The right grip should be set to low power. This side is also like a motorcycle throttle—rotate it toward you for high power or away from you for low power. When the view is trained up as far as it can go, the center of the reticle is at 70 degrees from the horizontal, so the edge of your vision is directly overhead. Spin the scope rapidly around through half a dozen circles.

This is a dangerous time for the ship, since you are completely vulnerable to being hit by a surface ship, and the tremendous momentum of a high-tonnage surface ship can rip the hull open like a screwdriver puncturing a soda can. The control room is as quiet as a funeral. Everyone is waiting for the word from you that all is safe above you. The slightest sound you make is pounced on.

The view during the day is amazing. You can see the underside of the waves from a hundred feet down. They roll far overhead in ripples, looking silvery like a wrinkled mirror. Slowly they get closer. As you come up, you are looking for dark shapes blocking the view of the waves—the underside of a ship hull. While you look up, you concentrate in the ahead direction. After a few circles, you train the view slightly flat-ter until you can see farther from the hull. As you get shallower, keep flattening the view and listen to the diving officer as he calls out the depth.

At night, the view depends on the moon and starlight. On a clear, moonlit night, the surface above is surprisingly bright.

Night Vision

Going to PD at night safely depends on the conning officer keeping his vision night-adapted. There are three ways to do this:

- Wear wraparound red glasses.

- Wear red goggles, the old-fashioned motorcycle type.

- Wear a black eye patch over one eye. (You'll look like a pirate, but if you're sneaking up on a surface battle group, it's appropriate.)

Before you go shallow to 150 feet, you "rig control for red," which turns off the white fluorescent lights and turns on red ones. Before you begin the ascent to PD, you "rig control for black": You turn off all the lights and shut a heavy black curtain around the conn (periscope platform) to keep out the stray light of the instrument panels (all lit in red, except, for some reason, the firecontrol displays, which are inex-plicably green—some defense contractor didn't read the specifications).

A good submariner teaches his children to "rig control for black" before going to sleep. Before turning on the car's dome light at night, always announce, "Rig control for white"—a sure way to annoy your spouse.

On an overcast night with no moon, things are much darker, but you can still tell the difference between the sea and dark shape. Fortunately, sonar is straining to hear "near field" sounds with hydrophones mounted on the sail. If there are no ship hulls in sight, at a depth of 90 to 80 feet, you can call out, "No shapes or shadows." The ship control party will relax slightly. If you do see something, say only, "Emergency deep!" The crew will remain quiet as you continue the ascent—even though you called "No shapes or shadows," you may have missed a close contact, and your mistake will become evident as soon as the periscope penetrates the surface.

The diving officer may be having some trouble at this point. The ship's trim (closeness to neutral buoyancy and fore-aft balance) was estimated and calculated, but things have changed since the last PD. The water temperature and salinity may be different, which greatly affects the ship's buoyancy. Also, the evaporator is a demon, bringing water aboard the ship and making pure water out of seawater and sending it to the makeup feed tanks for reactor fresh water tanks; this makes the ship heavy aft, or it could be sending to the potable water tanks, which makes the ship heavy forward. Or, if the evaporator was secured, you may have used up potable water (it ends up in the sanitary tank after passing through the crew) and the sanitary tank may have been pumped, or the drain system may have been used to pump bilges dry. The ship could be off by several tons. Every few hours, the diving officer "enters a compensation" by flooding seawater to or pumping seawater from depth control tanks. If he's good, you come smoothly to PD. If he's not, you "hang up" with the periscope wet. This is the time to shout at the diving officer. Use profanity—vulgarity conveys a wealth of meaning. Practice using the "F-word" three times in the sentence, "Diving Officer, get us up!"

Breaking and Clearing of the Scope

Assuming that the diving officer can maintain decent depth control, the waves grow closer to the view until the periscope begins to form a wave as it tries to penetrate the surface. The view goes white with foam.

You call, "Scope's breaking." If the diving officer continues to "hang you up," you can scream at him.

As soon as the scope clears, you announce, "Scope's clear." Again the control room personnel await your next word. You perform three fast circles, one each second, looking for close hulls and lights. If things are good, you say, "No close contacts!" Then you do a low power search. You've made it.

If you see anything, shout "Emergency deep!" Don't forget to lower the periscope as fast as you can: A collision could rip off the periscope and open an 8-inch hole in the hull.

The Least You Need to Know

- ◆ While getting underway, your complete attention is focused on the ship's movement in the channel, to prevent her from running aground or colliding with another ship.

- ◆ Clocks on U.S. subs are usually set to Greenwich Mean Time, known by the U.S. military as Zulu Time.

- ◆ At night, through the periscope, the view depends on the moon and starlight.

- ◆ The water temperature and salinity greatly affect the ship's buoyancy.

Chapter 17

Reacting to an Emergency

In This Chapter

- ◆ Being seen at night
- ◆ Emergency deep
- ◆ Multitasking
- ◆ Fast recovery

So you've broken through "the layer" and ascended to periscope depth. You're wheeling around the periscope optics module like a square dancer whirling his partner after drinking a pot of coffee. Either you see an ominous shadow in the scope before you penetrated the surface, or as soon as the scope cleared you see a close contact, a hull looming over your view. Or, if at night, you see the running lights of a close surface ship.

Running Lights

Running lights, by the way, are lit by ships after twilight and shut off at sunrise. Usually they consist of a red "sector light" on the port side with the light shining red from straight ahead to the after port quarter, about a 120 degree visual sector. On the starboard side, the running light is green and also shines from straight ahead to the after starboard quarter. The stern of the ship has a white "all-around" light that shines 360 degrees. At night, if you see a red light on your right and a white light to the right of the red, that means the ship has an angle on the bow between port 000 degrees and port 120 degrees.

The red has significance because that ship has the right-of-way. If you see a green light on the left and a white light further to the left, the ship has an angle on the bow between starboard 000 degrees and starboard 120 degrees. The green also has significance because that means *you* have the right-of-way (the other ship sees *your* red running light). If you see a red light on the left or a green light on the right, no problem—the contact is "beyond closest point of approach (CPA) and opening." That means he'll get further away without a risk of collision.

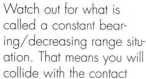

Secrets of the Deep

Watch out for what is called a constant bearing/decreasing range situation. That means you will collide with the contact because he is getting closer without his bearing drifting right or left of you. He's coming straight for you. Turn the ship *immediately* and notify the captain.

How Could This Miserable Situation Happen?

So your field of view has a bow on surface ship within a few ship lengths. The thought flashes through your mind—as your life passes before your eyes—how could this miserable situation happen? You're about to get run over by a surface ship. Why didn't sonar hear it? Why couldn't you get a good Ekelund range to it? The answer will disappoint you: The most dangerous ship in the sea, a supertanker, with its 100- or 150-foot-deep keel fully loaded, is so chock full of oil that the sounds of the engines and screws are muffled. An oil supertanker (or VLCC, for very large crude container) is quieter than a sailboat *when it is coming straight at you.* Submariners *hate* supertankers.

Mike's Corner

The last time I lived through a real emergency deep, it was in the middle of the night. The close contact was a fishing trawler, less than a ship length away. How did we miss that one? Sometimes fishing trawlers shut down their engines and drift, perhaps to attract the fish. Instead, they almost ended up catching a very large HY-80 fish.

Back to your worst nightmare in the periscope view: Odds are, your heart will race, your throat will close, your eyes will open wide—all the signs of panic—because if you don't act in the next half second, you are going down.

Hopefully you find your voice and shout, "Emergency deep!" If not, perhaps you can croak out, "Oh my God!" or the equivalent. It doesn't really matter—anything you say with any level of voice emotion other than a perfectly calm announcement of "No close contacts" will result in the control room crew taking immediate action to save the ship.

Reacting to the Emergency

Let's assume that you manage to shout out "Emergency deep." The first thing you have to do is push away the periscope optics module and snap up the grips. You then reach into the overhead above the module and grab the control ring and push it right or clockwise. A judgment call needs to be made—if you feel a collision, stop the periscope-lowering operation: If the pole of the scope is ripped off by the hull of a surface ship, by continuing to lower the scope you may uncork the hole of the periscope penetration and flood the ship through an 8-inch hole. As the periscope comes down, you turn to face the control room crew. Adrenaline has flooded your system, so in annoyance you see that everyone is moving in ultraslow motion.

The diving officer acts first. He calls out, "Emergency deep, aye," in a clear enough voice that everyone hears him and takes action—in case your croaked call at the periscope wasn't heard by all. Next he orders, "All ahead full!"

> **Secrets of the Deep**
>
> Just as the diving officer controls the ship's speed during diving, he also controls it during an emergency deep.

The helmsman pushes his bowplanes to 10 degrees dive—you would think he would shove them to a more drastic angle, but, remember, you are going only about 4 knots. With a down angle of 20 degrees or 30 degrees, the bowplanes would just act like big speed brakes and slow the ship. Plus, a drastic down angle could kill you by lifting the stern out of the water and drying off the screw—which would mean no thrust to get you deep. While he pushes the bowplanes down to 10 degrees, he rings up all ahead full on the engine order telegraph.

The diving officer supervises the helmsman and makes the order to put 10 degrees down on the bowplanes even as the helmsman is doing it. He looks over at the stern-planesman and orders a down angle on the ship of 10 degrees—again an attempt to get the ship down while avoiding the screw coming out of the water.

Multitasking

The chief of the watch is also busy. He's multitasking as well, with one hand on the joystick of the hovering system on the sloping port lap section of the ballast control panel, pushing the stick to the "flood" position so that the depth control tank will fill with several tons of seawater, in an attempt to make the ship suddenly heavy to get deep fast. With his other hand, he has grabbed the 1MC microphone and shouted, "Emergency deep, emergency deep!" In the rig for patrol quiet, he also sounds the general alarm and gives the order to rig ship for collision. In the rig for ultraquiet, instead of using the general alarm and the 1MC, the word is passed over the sound-powered phones. In the rig for ultraquiet, a stealthy emergency deep is essential. Odds are, the risk of collision came in the first place from the hostile ship you were trailing—no sense alerting him that you are there by sounding the bonging general alarm and passing word on the noisy 1MC system.

The ship takes a fairly rapid down angle, reacting to the screw's acceleration to ahead full and the weight in the depth control tank.

The diving officer calls out the depth. "Seventy feet, eighty feet, ninety feet, sir." About then, the captain runs into the control room, wearing only his boxers and T-shirt. He squints at you and shouts, "What the hell's going on?"

"Depth one hundred feet, sir," the diving officer calls. "One two zero, one three zero, pulling out. Helm, zero your planes; Sternplanes, zero bubble."

The chief of the watch pipes up, "Securing flooding to depth control."

"Depth one five zero feet, sir. Helm, all ahead two thirds."

"Sonar, Conn," you shout irritably into the 8MC microphone. "What the hell was that up there?"

Mike's Corner

If the recriminations come instead of the shock of a collision, then you've survived without a scratch. The captain will be furious. He'll probably have you relieved so that you can come to his stateroom for an ass-chewing along with the sonar supervisor. The XO will scowl at you with his arms crossed as you explain why you didn't hear what happened. Three watches from now all will be forgotten and you'll be "steaming as before."

Reactor Scram, Snorkeling, and Fast Recovery Startup

One of the games the captain likes to play is to see if he can sneak aft without anyone noticing. If he can creep into the engineroom without the nukes knowing, he can hit the reactor scram switch at the RCP cabinet forward of maneuvering and shut down the plant, as a test of how alert the nukes are. Immediately, all hell breaks loose.

Your first sign of a reactor scram is the blaring siren sounding in the maneuvering room, an ambulance in your face.

"Reactor scram," the reactor operator announces as he silences the alarm. "Oh, hell," you think. A flashing light (the "annunciator") on his panel flashes GROUP SCRAM if the one controlling rod group has dropped to the bottom, or FULL SCRAM if all three rod groups are driven to the core bottom (much more rare). The controlling rod group's rod bottom lights flash on, and the RO announces, "Group I rod bottom lights." Meanwhile, the group elevation digital counter resets by spinning from the rod group's previous height down to zero.

Meanwhile, the throttleman, who had his throttles wide open at ahead flank, spins them shut (clockwise), and the screw windmills to a near stop. The ship is now without power and is coasting down. The throttleman puts the needle of the engine order telegraph to all stop. The needle controlled by the control room rolls to all stop in acknowledgement.

Since you were at flank, the reactor operator quickly stands and downshifts the reactor recirculation pumps from two fast/two fast (two pumps in each loop at fast speed) to one slow/one slow. If he's good, he can do this in about a second. Reactor power goes sinking into the intermediate range at $-\frac{1}{3}$ decade per minute. The RO's voice is sad as he announces that power is dropping out of the intermediate range into the startup range—it's like the patient's heartbeat went from fluttering to a dead stop. "Reactor power in the startup range, sir. Taking source range channel selector switch to startup range, switching low-pressure cutout switch to low-pressure cutout."

Secrets of the Deep

When the XO says, "Let's reset the counter" or "Let's zero the counter," he means to forget whatever was discussed or what happened before and consider a new argument. Alternately, it means, "Adjust your attitude right now, Mister." This phrase is used predominantly by senior nuke officers because it tends to irritate the rest of the crew. If the XO is unpopular, there will be a nuke electrician in engineroom upper level doing his famous imitation of the XO, saying, "Mr. Jones, now let's just zero the counter on that one."

The reactor temperature goes screaming downward, which is a very bad thing. The throttleman's speed on shutting the throttle to stop taking energy from the boilers is critical. Now that the throttle is shut, only the ship service turbine generators (SSTGs) are taking energy from the boilers. Fortunately, the electrical operator just tripped the nonvital buses. (These are load centers, and they're not really "nonvital." Just as your arm is important to you but is less important to your survival than your heart, the nonvital buses can be dropped in a crisis without killing the ship.)

Reactor Scram

The engineering officer of the watch makes sure all these actions happen, and he simultaneously announces on the 1MC shipwide circuit, "Reactor scram." As the nonvital buses trip, the SSTGs come off the line and their inlet throttles are shut by engineroom upper level. The steam system is now buttoned up. The main seawater system pumps are downshifted or stopped to conserve power, and the power-hogging main feed pump is secured.

At the announcement of the scram, the 7MC speaker blares out the officer of the deck's reply: "Reactor scram, Maneuvering, Conn, aye." If there is a tactical emergency (such as a scram just before an emergency deep) the OOD will call for power even though the plant is scrammed. This robs steam energy from the boilers and dangerously lowers reactor temperature, but it gives the conn power for a short time. But usually, the OOD will concur with the throttles being shut.

Control announces on the 1MC, "Rig ship for reduced electrical." All through the ship, nonvital electrical loads are shut down. The fan room turns off (immediately after the EO opens the SSTG breakers), and the ventilation system's absence is immediately felt. Since the air conditioners went down at the SSTG breaker opening, the engineroom temperature climbs as high as 120°F or 130°F, and your armpits melt and sweat rolls into your eyes.

So, now you've buttoned up the reactor plant and kept it safe. The OOD has seen to the ship's safety, although you're expecting a call from him any second. The thing to do now is determine the cause of the scram. Until you do, you can't start back up. The ship has no power or propulsion, so you're at a fork in the road. If you can get power back in five minutes, you'll use the emergency propulsion motor for bare steerageway, about 4 knots, on the battery. If the reactor has a problem, the OOD will come up and snorkel on the diesel until you rope down the problem.

The speaker box clicks as the OOD in the control room gets ready to talk on the 7MC circuit. Up forward, the OOD has lost all propulsion power, so he is using the coast-down speed of the ship to "plane up" to a shallower depth, usually 150 feet. This prepares the submarine to come to periscope depth if the reactor will be down more than a few minutes.

"Maneuvering, Conn," your stateroom-mate says formally, "report the status of return of propulsion."

By now either the XO or the captain or the engineer have shown up wearing red baseball caps (so you know it's a drill), or they've shown up with frowns on their faces (and you know it's not). The reactor controls officer (RCA) and the reactor controls chief petty officer arrive at the door to maneuvering and request to enter.

"Sir, the cause of the scram was a drill for training," they may say. If that's the case, you can start back up. "Recommend commencing fast recovery startup," they'll say, and you're almost there. Or they may say that it's a drill but that the cause of the scram is unknown.

"We Are Troubleshooting"

Today, they tell you, "Sir, the scram was inserted by the captain for training. Cause of the scram is simulated to be unknown. We are troubleshooting. Recommend snorkeling."

You nod and put your mouth to the 7MC microphone. "Conn, Maneuvering, scram is a drill, cause simulated to be unknown, recommend snorkeling on the EPM."

"Very well, shift propulsion to the EPM," the OOD says and hangs up. The announcement comes over the 1MC, "Prepare to snorkel!"

The engineering watch supervisor arrives at the door. "Enter maneuvering," you say. Then you say formally, "Engineering Watch Supervisor, shift propulsion to the emergency propulsion motor."

"Shift propulsion to the EPM, EWS aye," he says. He runs aft to the reduction gear and farther aft to the clutch. Using a hydraulic operating valve, he disengages the clutch so that the drive train is broken between the reduction gear with its main engines and the EPM/shaft. He returns to maneuvering and makes the report that propulsion is on the EPM, and you report the same to the OOD in control.

Up forward, if you are the OOD, you are taking all actions required before coming to periscope depth, except with the knowledge that there is minimal power. You clear baffles at 150 feet and tell the sonar supervisor that you're about to come up and that he should report all contacts.

Back in maneuvering, the captain (wearing his red ball cap, so he's "not really there"—yeah, right) is asked to pick up the JA phone. It's the OOD, asking permission to come to PD. The captain says, "Come to periscope depth and snorkel," and then hangs up. The deck angles up as the engine order telegraph dings to all ahead one third. The throttleman is on sound-powered phones to the EPM back aft, where an electrician is operating the EPM speed adjuster. He says, "EPM, Maneuvering, ahead one third."

The EPM operator moves the speed adjuster to full voltage and the EPM begins to turn. At 30 RPM, he reports to the throttleman, "Ahead one third."

The trouble is, the remaining loads and the EPM are draining the battery like crazy. The EO shakes his head and says, "Four hundred amp hours remaining on the battery. That's twenty minutes, sir, maybe less."

"Very well," you acknowledge.

Up forward, the OOD is sweating as he brings the sub to PD with only 4 knots of speed. It's taking forever, and the risk of collision is severe—if there's an emergency deep, you can't crank it up to full with the clutch disengaged.

Finally, the OOD gets the scope dried off and orders the chief of the watch to raise the snorkel. The control room auxiliary mechanics drain the induction manifold and open the outboard and inboard induction valves. The snorkel head valve is tested and watched through the periscope as it opens and shuts. On the OOD's order to commence snorkeling, the word is passed on the 1MC by the chief of the watch, "Commence snorkeling!"

Mike's Corner

The sound of the emergency diesel coming to speed is perhaps the sweetest sound a submariner can hear.

Down the auxiliary machinery space, the A-ganger blows out the exhaust headers with 700 psi air, opens the exhaust inboard and outboard valves, and rolls the diesel on the same 700 psi air. The next sound is the throaty roar of the emergency diesel as it cranks up to full speed. It can be heard all through the forward spaces.

You can't put the ship's electrical loads on a cold diesel, though. It has to warm up for a few minutes. Back aft, you tap your foot as the electrical operator shakes his head like a surgeon over a dying patient. "Ten more minutes on the battery sir."

"Dammit," you mutter, the sweat rolling down your forehead into your eyes, your armpits soaked. All you can do is review the fast recovery startup procedure while waiting—or perhaps bug the RCA for a status report. But during a drill, he'll be surrounded by drill monitors and not very chatty. Besides, as soon as he has fixed the problem, you'll be the first to know.

Finally, the word comes from the diesel room: "Maneuvering, Diesel, the diesel is warm!"

"Electrical operator, parallel the diesel!" you order the EO.

A Tricky Maneuver

This one's tricky: The diesel isn't a smooth, fast-spinning turbine; it's a 12-cylinder lurching beast, and it speeds up and slows down and is a bear to parallel. But if the EO gets it right, he can get the breaker shut the first try. If things don't go well, the breaker trips from being out of phase and has to be reset at the motor control center before trying again. If things are really bad, a poor breaker shutting could stall the diesel.

But this time the gods smile, the diesel breaker shuts, and you order the EO, "Shift to a half-power lineup on the diesel."

He loads the diesel generator, picking up all vital and nonvital loads on it. Just as things calm down, with the ship snorkeling on the diesel and the plant finally under control, the RCA and the reactor controls chief re-enter maneuvering.

"Cause of the scram was a drill inserted for training," they say. "Recommend fast recovery startup."

You smile—soon the air conditioning will be back and the captain, XO, and feng (code for f***ing engineer) will be out of your kingdom.

"Very well." On the 7MC, you say, "Conn, Maneuvering, cause of scram was a drill. Request to conduct fast recovery startup."

Secrets of the Deep

On some ships, the captain requires the OOD to ask captain's permission to conduct fast recovery startup. On others, the captain considers it an immediate action. Assuming that your ship is the latter, the OOD can say, "Conduct fast recovery."

"Engineering Watch Supervisor," your voice booms on the 2MC, "come to maneuvering." When he shows up, you say, "Engineering Watch Supervisor, reset group one scram breakers and conduct a fast recovery startup." He acknowledges and disappears. In seconds, he's back, reporting the scram breakers shut.

"Reactor Operator," you say, "conduct fast recovery startup."

"Conduct fast recovery, aye," he says. "Starting main coolant pumps three and four." He starts the reactor recirc pumps that were off before, switching the plant back to two slow/two slow. "Latching group one rods." He takes the rod control switch to the nine o'clock position and drives in the rods while pulling the switch vertically out of the panel. After 30 seconds, he releases the switch and rotates it to the three o'clock position and says, "Pulling group one rods to criticality at five decades per minute."

Unlike the wimpy normal reactor startup at one decade per minute, reactor power now comes roaring out of the startup range and into the intermediate range at 5.0 decades per minute—which means that the neutron level multiplies by 10 times every 12 seconds.

Beneath the Surface

The emergency reactor startup is no namby-pamby slow/gentle/safe restart—a civilian reactor operator watching this would faint dead away. In fact, it is considered so dangerous that it is done only if the ship is greater than 50 miles from land.

"Group I rod bottom lights are out," the RO announces. "Source channel selector switch to source range startup rate scram cutout. Low-pressure cutout switch to normal."

Reactor power is flying out of the intermediate range. It won't be long now.

"Lowering startup rate to plus one decade per minute," the RO says as power reaches the top of the intermediate range. "The reactor is in the power range." The needle of the power range meter budges off zero to about 3 percent. "T_{AVE} is 423 degrees, sir. Heating the reactor at five degrees per minute."

"Very well." The RO is using excess power to heat the primary coolant. He graphs the heatup rate, bumping rods in and out as required to heat up at 5 degrees per minute. You glance at your watch. If T_{AVE} is in the green band at 475 degrees, that's 10 minutes of starting up.

Finally, the T_{AVE} needle comes into the green band. "Sir, T_{AVE} is in the green band!"

"Start the Engineroom!"

"Engineering Watch Supervisor," you order on the 2MC, "start the engineroom!"

First the EWS zips to engineroom lower level and restarts the main seawater system. Then he uses steam to the air ejectors to take a vacuum on the main condensers. He runs up to engineroom upper level, where the ERUL watch is blowing down the moisture out of the steam headers. The next task is to start the ship service turbine generator.

The beautiful sound of an SSTG spinning up to power comes next as the EWS cranks her up. Soon it's screaming behind you as it whines to full speed.

"Request to enter," the EWS says. "Port turbine generator is at 3,600 RPM, on the governor and ready for loading!"

"Electrical Operator," you command, "shift the electric plant to a half-power lineup on the port SSTG."

The EO parallels in the port turbine generator and picks up the electrical loads on it while unloading the diesel. Finally he trips the diesel breaker. "Half-power lineup on the port TG, cooling the diesel," he says.

"The electric plant's in a half-power lineup," you announce on the 1MC. That's the EWS's signal to start a main feed pump. (With the diesel, he may have started it before—the trick is do a fast recovery without the diesel when you draw down the boilers and, at the very last minute, with an SSTG online, start a main feed pump.)

"Secure from the rig for reduced electrical," the 1MC announcement comes from control.

Return of the AC

Mercifully, the air conditioning turns back on, and cool, dry air blows over your sweat-soaked coveralls. Ah, God, that feels good! The starboard turbine roars to life, and the EO shifts to a full-power lineup. For the next 20 minutes the diesel will cool. The sweating EWS shows up at the door. "Request to enter. Both main engines are warm; recommend shifting propulsion."

"Thank you, Chief," you say. "You are the man." You pick up the 7MC mike and say, "Conn, Maneuvering, recommend shifting propulsion to the main engines."

"Maneuvering, Conn, shift propulsion to the main engines."

"Conn, Maneuvering, shift propulsion to the main engines, aye, request all stop."

The engine order telegraph dings to all stop.

"EWS, shift propulsion to the mains," you order. The EWS waves a salute and disappears. In 20 seconds, he's back.

"Propulsion is shifted to the mains."

"Conn, Maneuvering," you announce on the 7MC with a flourish, "propulsion is shifted to the main engines, ready to answer all bells, answering all stop."

"Maneuvering, Conn aye."

The engine order telegraph rings up ahead one third. The throttleman opens the throttles and cranks the screw to 30 RPM as he answers the bell on the telegraph.

"Control, Diesel," the phonetalker from the diesel room says, "diesel is cool, recommend securing snorkeling."

The word comes on the 1MC: "Secure snorkeling. Reeeee-circulate!"

Sweet Talk from the Engineer

The diesel crashes to a halt. In the diesel room, the operator shuts the inboard and outboard exhaust valves. In control, the watchstanders shut the inboard and outboard induction valves. The snorkel mast comes down, and the deck tilts as the officer of the deck takes her deep.

The engine order telegraph dings to all ahead standard, and the throttleman opens the throttles to 120 RPM. The depth indicator shows you're down to 450 feet.

The scram drill is over. The engineer snarls, "I guess that was just *barely sat*."

"Thanks, Slopehead," you smile.

"That's 'Slopehead, sir' to you, A-hole."

"Get out of here, Feng, Sir."

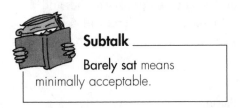

Subtalk

Barely sat means minimally acceptable.

He shuts the chain to maneuvering and disappears forward. You put your hands behind your head and your feet on the EOOW desk, a grin on your face. You haven't heard a compliment like that from the engineer in years.

The Least You Need to Know

◆ Running lights allow ships to be seen at night.

◆ Memorizing and executing step-by-step reactions to emergencies (*immediate actions*) allow submariners to do the right thing even when they're on the verge of panic.

◆ During a sub emergency, each crewmember often has to do more than one thing at once.

◆ A fast recovery startup is so dangerous that it can't be done less than 50 miles from shore.

Chapter 18

A Day in the Life of a Modern Submarine and Her Crew

In This Chapter

◆ At sea

◆ In port

◆ Staying submerged

◆ Shipboard organization

◆ Submarine careers

So, you wonder, what is it really like living and working aboard a nuclear submarine? Let's take a look. The ship's schedule and rhythm are vastly different depending on whether the ship is at sea or in port.

At Sea

At sea, the ship's clock is set to Zulu Time (Greenwich Mean Time). This usually starts the "jet lag" feeling submariners feel constantly. The feeling lingers because the watches are six hours long, and most watchsections are one-in-three. This means that your watch schedule would start rotating around the 24-hour clock with an 18-hour schedule:

Morning watch	0600–1200 (noon)	On watch
Afternoon	1200–1800	Off watch, division duties
Evening watch	1800–2400	Off watch, sleep
Midwatch	0000–0600	On watch
Afternoon	1200–1800	Off watch, division duties
Evening watch	1800–2400	Off watch, sleep
Morning watch	0600–1200	On watch

Notice how your sleep cycle keeps rotating around the clock? This assumes that you have time to sleep. The morning and afternoon watches are filled with drills during transit. It is not unusual for you to skip sleep to respond to watches and fight division problems. At one point on the *Hammerhead*, I went 72 hours without sleep.

Secrets of the Deep

Here's an example of a hit: "*Deficiency:* the engineering officer of the watch *failed* to order the throttles shut immediately." If one has had enough hits, he may reply to the XO, "I'll take that hit," which means, "Fine, the criticism is valid, but I'd like to see anyone else aboard do better, including you, XO." Executive officers don't take kindly to someone saying he'll take a hit.

Casualty Drills

The 0600 watch relief goes down and the offgoing watchsection has breakfast. After the galley and crew's mess are cleaned up, the briefing is called for the morning watch's drills. The XO or chief of the boat brief a fire drill or reactor scram or flooding.

The drill monitors, with their red ball caps, move out into the spaces, and soon all hell breaks loose. Hours later, the drill monitors meet again in the crew's mess or wardroom and grade the drill.

The watchstanders may be called in to get a report card on their drills. This is called a critique. Comments given about mistakes made during the drills are called hits.

Training

Training may be conducted in the crew's mess or wardroom. If the ship is deploying to hostile waters, much of the training will be "recognition drills." In this training, periscope photos of enemy surface combatants and submarines are shown on the screen, and the officers identify them. The captain may go around the room and make the officers take turns. He may time how long it takes to identify 10 targets.

However the training may be conducted, every officer aboard can identify the bad guys with a tenth of a second glimpse from the periscope angle.

Other training may center on drill performance and casualty recovery. The enlisted personnel attend daily "school of the boat" sessions to learn the submarine's systems. Officers are given daily tactical training to get qualified and to refresh those already wearing dolphins. The navigator may hold a lecture on restricted waters piloting. The XO may give training on the Mark 48 torpedo. The captain may give training on the duties of the approach officer during a battle stations attack.

> **Beneath the Surface**
>
> Training attendees are expected to participate and speak up. There is no sitting in the back of the room doodling on notebook paper. And never show up unprepared for training. The XO is watching.

War Patrol ("In Trail")

Ah, there's nothing like being on a war patrol, in trail of a bad guy. The ship is rigged for modified ultraquiet (ultraquiet with the evaporator running and hot meals served). That means that when the crew is off watch, all hands are required to be in their bunks.

There is no heavy maintenance, and even preventive maintenance is secured. The equipment loves being in trail because it runs "at steady state," with no startups or shutdowns and at a constant temperature, just the way NavSea designed it.

The only off-watch activities are doing reconstruction for the patrol report. Reconstruction is putting together "chartlets" (cartoon charts depicting the dance of their own ship and the trailed submarine) and a narrative of what the bad guy did during the watch.

> **Mike's Corner**
>
> Reconstruction can generate heated debate: "He turned left here, did a loop-the-loop Crazy Ivan, and then headed south." "Bulls***, sir, he turned right, did a circle baffle clear and went southwest." "Did not!" "Did too!" It can be like kindergarten. Since no one is allowed to sleep until unanimous agreement is reached, eventually the watch is reconstructed—in ink—and the watchsection retires for a between-watch nap, uninterrupted by drills.

Field Day (Janitorial Ops)

Don't think that field day is the fun you had in school. Field day means that every man heads to his spaces with a sponge in hand for a deep cleaning. The XO may order your division into the depths of engineroom lower level to degrease the bilges.

You go into the bilges with a white T-shirt and skivvies. You come out blacker than a coal miner. Thank God it lasts only six hours. And you thought you joined the Navy to do something glamorous ....

Repairs

Emergent repairs are conducted at sea for any equipment vital to the mission—or, even more important, crew creature comforts. The evaporator, air-conditioning equipment, washing machine, or VCR will be worked on around the clock until they are repaired.

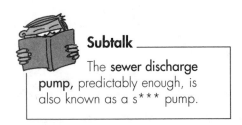

Subtalk

The **sewer discharge pump,** predictably enough, is also known as a s*** pump.

This can turn into an occupation based on stubborn equipment. And then there's the glamour factor—just try spending four watches tearing apart and putting back together a *sewer discharge pump.*

This does not make for a great day at sea. But it is preferable to the engineer or captain riding your case because the gear isn't functional.

In Port

Finally you've returned from an arduous deployment or NATO run or northern run, and you are tossing over the lines back at home port. Think this is the fun part? By the time you have a week tied up at Norfolk Naval Station, you'll be begging to go back to sea.

Repairs, Repairs, Repairs

At sea you generated the OOC (out of commission) log and the OOS (out of service) list. Now it's time to attack the problems with all that nonperforming equipment. Get your spare parts, your tech manual, and your test gear from the tender ship, and go to work. The division chief petty officer, the division officer, the department head, the XO, and the captain will be keenly interested in the status of all progress.

If things are serious, the Intermediate Maintenance Facility (IMF) may be called. This is a fancy name for the tender tied up at the end of your pier and the repair forces aboard her. The IMF mobilizes mechanics, spare parts, tools, machine shops, and squadron-level expertise to fix the boat. If that doesn't do the trick, it's time for the shipyard.

Navy Paperwork

There's no joy quite like Navy paperwork. The radio messages are composed of bureaucratic drivel and calls for reports and more reports. The XO makes an in-port living of getting the officers and chiefs to fill out the damned reports. If any future or current CNOs are reading this book, this area needs to be fixed pronto.

More Training

You thought at-sea training was intense? Wait until you have to interrupt your day for in-port training. It lasts twice as long and makes the day seem endless.

Admirals and Other Annoyances

Then there's the inevitable admiral's visit. You field day every day for a week and then shrug casually when the admiral comments about how clean the ship looks, as if she looks that sparkling every day. "A good officer," one captain said, "is like a duck. He's going like hell at the business end, but above the water he looks cool and collected."

That's the approach to an admiral's visit. If asked why something is not right, respond with, "Why, sir, we planned that very carefully. [Insert suitable lie here]" It translates to, "Oh, dammit, I didn't want you to see that." Of course, everyone plays the game that they can fool the admiral. Admirals usually know better—they've been there themselves. That's how they got to be admirals.

Mike's Corner

Don't forget to rig ship for female visitors before the admiral arrives, even if it's a guy admiral. It won't do to have crewmembers walking to the showers buck naked when a three-star is going down the passageway.

The Shipyard

So the tender IMF facility can't fix the boat? Time to pull into the shipyard and rest that weary keel on the dry-dock blocks. It's miserable, with all those "yardbirds" wandering around touching your equipment. It's even sadder if you're going into overhaul and the yardbirds bring by "ripouts"—paperwork that turns a system or piece of equipment over to the shipyard to pull it out of the boat to work on it.

Soon holes are being torched in the hull so the yardbirds can take out turbine casings and pumps. In an overhaul, only the reactor plant and engineering spaces stay recognizable. The forward end of the boat is stripped down to deckplates and hull hoop frames. The crew moves into a barge office, where the business of "ship's force" is done. You'll want to get out of the shipyard as soon as possible.

Staying Submerged for Months

Imagine that you're on an 8-week NATO run, a 12-week northern run (this usually involves the Barents Sea, the marginal ice zone or MIZ, and/or the polar icecap), or a 6-month Med run. What's it like being down so long?

The ship's endurance is limited only by the crew. On a long run, you may load large cans of food (12 inches in diameter and 12 inches tall) with plywood on top. You walk on top of the cans, hunched over, and during the "op" you eat your way down to the deckplates.

The fresh vegetables and milk go in the first week. After that, it's canned or freeze-dried food. A typical evening meal might be steak and potatoes with gravy and string beans, with ice cream and pie for dessert, and, of course, fresh Navy coffee. Lunch could be fried seafood, cold cuts, fried chicken, or burgers ("sliders"). Breakfast is always omelets or eggs with bacon and toast. Midnight rations include peanut butter and jelly over white bread, chili, and rice or soup. It's all fattening, and it's all great.

So make sure you lift weights in the torpedo room and run in place between the main engines. There may be a treadmill in the torpedo room, but there will be a line. If you serve on a boomer, you can run laps in Sherwood Forest (missile compartment upper level).

Mike's Corner

I found that something happens to your dreams when you're under for a while. It could be the food or the atmospheric controls (or lack of controls) or the sustained lack of a visual horizon—or perhaps the stress or the lack of sleep. Whatever the cause, your dreams will seem like the part in *The Wizard of Oz* when it becomes full color. Wild, colorful images fill your dreams. People you've long forgotten come back to you while you sleep. I've never had dreams like the ones I had on the *Pargo* and the *Hammerhead*.

And speaking of weirdness at sea, some very strange things have happened to me at depth. For example, there I was submerged 453 feet beneath the surface; it was Day 53 of a submerged record Med run. I was shaving in the officers' head. I heard female voices in the passageway behind me. I turned so fast that I hurt my neck. There was no one there. When I turned back, I heard them again. They were *not* the voices of my friends pulling a prank—they were unmistakably women in their early 20s, giggling and talking. I clamped my eyes shut. One of the women said my name. I turned, and the female voices kept on. I opened my eyes and their chatter stopped.

This happened every time I took a shower after Day 53. I was afraid to tell anyone until finally, at midrats, after watch, it was just the damage control assistant and me. I looked at him sheepishly and confessed to hearing things. I told him the whole story. His expression was one of relief. "You, too? I thought I was the only one going crazy." Then the navigator and XO said they had been hearing things as well. Either the ship was haunted or we were seeing a natural psychological barrier to being submerged for too long.

On that same run we trailed a Soviet Victor for 40 days and 40 nights. We were out so long that we ran out of food, except for soup and coffee and juice. For the first time, talk in the control room and maneuvering room stopped being about beautiful women. The men talked about Wendy's and Pizza Hut and Burger King and lobsters with drawn butter and a sizzling T-bone steak.

Shipboard Organization

The ship's organization begins with the captain, who commands the ship and the crew and is responsible for the mission. Here's who's who below the captain:

Executive Officer (XO): Second in command. Runs the administration department with the chief yeoman and the chief medical officer. Is responsible for the ship's records and correspondence. Has dotted-line responsibility for all the ship's officers. Battle station: fire-control coordinator.

The Department Heads

Navigator (Operations Officer and sometimes also the Weapons Officer—when combined, he may be called the Tactical Systems Officer) (Nav): Usually third in command, which gives him the collateral duty of Senior Watch Officer (makes up the watch, quarter, and station bill). Is responsible to the captain for the ship's navigation and to the XO for administrative duties. Runs the quartermaster division, which keeps the ship's position. The communications officer and electronics material officer (usually the same guy) report to the navigator. Battle station: geo plot.

Engineer (Eng): Busiest man aboard. May outrank the navigator to be the third in command. The engineer runs the engineering plant and reports to the captain. The following officers are under the engineer's command: the main propulsion assistant and mechanical division officer (MPA), the reactor controls assistant (RCA), the chemistry and radiation controls officer (CRA), the electrical officer, and the damage control assistant. Battle station: in the maneuvering room as engineering officer of the watch.

Supply Officer (Suppo or "Pork Chop"): Responsible to the captain for the ship's spare parts load, food loadout, and the cooks division. A good supply officer is a thief with a criminal record just clean enough to allow him to serve in the armed forces. When a critical spare part is needed before deployment, it comes in on a flatbed truck at two in the morning—and it is marked with the name of someone else's ship. Don't ask the suppo about it. When you need a single switch to replace the bad one on the washing machine, the good suppo buys a completely new $100,000 washing machine, rips out the switch to put in the one inside the ship, and leaves the carcass of the new machine on the pier. If you are lucky enough to have a good suppo, the ship is in constant trouble with squadron but always has the best steaks and coffee and never lacks for a spare part. The supply officer may not have a battle station because he may not have the tactical smarts to put a weapon on a target.

Weapons Officer (Weps): In charge of the ship's weapons, the firecontrol system, the torpedo room equipment and the sonar division, and the firecontrol division and the torpedomen. The sonar officer, torpedo officer, and first lieutenant report to weps. Battle station: weapon control officer.

The Division Officers

MPA (Main Propulsion Assistant and Machinery Division Officer): Reports to the engineer. The MPA is usually the "bull lieutenant" or most senior junior officer aboard. He runs the machinery division back aft and helps the engineer with the other division officers. Usually the MPA is engineer-qualified, so he can man the senior supervisory watch in the shipyard and stand in for the engineer. Battle station: pos one or pos two.

Electrical officer (EO): Reports to the engineer. The electrical officer reports to the engineer and runs the electrical division. Electricians are perhaps the smartest personnel aboard and are consequently difficult to manage. A good electrical officer is a diplomat. Battle station: time-bearing plot or geo plot.

CRA (Chemistry and Radiation Controls Officer): Reports to the engineer. The CRA is responsible for the reactor and steam plant's chemistry. This may sound mundane, but the CRA is one of the busiest junior officers aboard. Battle station: time-freq plot or time-bearing plot.

RCA (Reactor Controls Assistant): Reports to the engineer. The RCA runs the reactor control technicians, the group of reactor operators responsible for the electronics that control the reactor. These are sharp cookies, so the RCA job is cake until the moment of reactor scram, when he needs to be adept at troubleshooting and repairing electronic gear in a crisis. Battle station: geo plot.

DCA (Damage Control Assistant): Reports to the engineer. The DCA runs the auxiliary mechanics (the "A-gangers") and the internal communications technicians ("IC-men"). He owns the diesel and the comms circuits and is supposed to have detailed knowledge of how to help the ship survive casualties. Battle station: pos one or pos two.

Communications Officer (Communicator or Commo): Reports to the navigator. The communicator runs the radiomen and ESM technicians. He is required to have special qualifications to write messages in a crisis and handle nuclear weapon release communications. Battle station: time-bearing or geo plot.

Sonar Officer: Reports to the weapons officer. Sonar is in charge of those unruly sonar girls and their migraine headache of an equipment list. Battle station: officer of the deck.

Torpedo Officer: Reports to the weapons officer. The torpedo officer is in charge of the torpedomen, a division with a lot of heart and even more muscle. Don't mess with the torpedo officer, or large men with tattoos will come calling. Battle station: in the torpedo room.

First Lieutenant (1LT): Reports to the weapons officer. Is in charge of the deck equipment and linehandlers. The name is misleading; the job can be done by the most junior officer or a midshipman.

The Leading Chiefs

You've heard it before: The chiefs do the real work on the submarine and get none of the credit (since the credit goes to the "O-gangers," or officers). Much of this is true. The chiefs do much of the heavy lifting of running the submarine because the junior officers are typically too green to pick up the reins with any confidence. The junior officers who have been aboard two years pull their own weight, but if not for the chiefs, the other officers would be lost.

The chiefs command their division, starting from the leading petty officers down to the lowest seamen. They evaluate their men and put them up for medals and awards. They supervise their spaces and fix their equipment. They order spare parts and squirrel them away so that they can be found in a crisis. They are capable of communicating with the lowest nonquals and the captain himself. But the biggest duty of any chief is training his division officer.

Watches and Watchstanding

The at-sea watchsection consists of the following forward watchstanders:

OOD (Officer of the Deck): In tactical command of the submarine, responsible to the captain for the position and motion and employment of the ship and its weapons. The OOD has the deck (the command of the ship's equipment) and the conn (the command of the ship's course, speed, depth, and sensor and weapon employment).

JOOD (Junior Officer of the Deck): In a nontactical situation, the JOOD is the OOD-under-instruction, taking the conn in order to learn the position of OOD. In a tactical situation, the JOOD is an OOD-qualified officer who assists with prosecuting the target and advises and assists the OOD.

Diving Officer: Responsible for the ship's depth. This can get difficult in a casualty and may affect ship safety.

Chief of the Watch: Operates the ballast control panel and commands the watchsection under the OOD.

Helmsman: Operates the outboard control yoke at the ship control panel that operates the rudder and bowplanes. He is responsible under the OOD for maintaining or changing the ship's course, and under the diving officer for the angle of the bowplanes.

Sternplanesman: Operates the inboard control yoke at the ship control panel that operates the sternplanes. He is responsible under the diving officer for the ship's angle (bubble).

FTOW (Fire Control Technician of the Watch): Responsible for obtaining fire-control solutions to contacts and for the operation of the firecontrol equipment.

Messenger of the Watch: The legs of the forward watchsection. He wakes up people or notifies them that the OOD demands their presence in control, or he checks the status of things.

Auxiliaryman (A-ganger) of the Watch: Stands ready to operate the diesel. He controls potable tanks and the depth control and drain system.

The watchsection consists of the following aft watchstanders:

EOOW (Engineering Officer of the Watch): Commands the reactor plant and all reactor plant operations. Responsible to the OOD for maintaining propulsion and answering all bells.

RO (Reactor Operator): Operates the reactor through the reactor plant control panel (RPCP).

EO (Electrical Operator): Operates the electric plant through the electric plant control panel (EPCP).

Throttleman: Operates the steam plant through the steam plant control panel (SPCP), particularly the throttles that control the main engines. Answers the engine order telegraph and coordinates with the RO and EOOW to answer the bell.

EWS (Engineering Watch Supervisor): Responsible to the EOOW for commanding the engineering watchsection outside the maneuvering room.

ERUL (Engineroom Upper Level Watch): Responsible to the EWS for operating the ship service turbine generators, the main engines, and the steam plant.

ERML (Engineroom Middle Level Watch): Responsible to the EWS for operating the engineroom freshwater system, air-conditioning systems, and other ERML equipment.

ERLL (Engineroom Lower Level Watch): Responsible to the EWS for operating the main condensers and main and auxiliary seawater systems.

Submarine Careers

So you want to stop being a nonqual air-breather and instead become a submariner?

There are two ways to the deep. One is to be an enlisted sailor and attend the enlisted schools required as prerequisites to being a submariner. The second is to be an officer, either through Annapolis or Naval ROTC (Reserve Officer Training Corps), both college programs graduate personnel who can be commissioned officers. A third officer accession route is through OCS, a three-month program that turns college graduates into officers in a boot-camp type environment. Other programs funnel qualified enlisted personnel into officer accession programs.

"Nukes," either officers or enlisted men, must attend the Nuclear Power School, a six-month theoretical series of courses. Then the Nuclear Prototype School puts graduates of NPS into a six-month operator training course of an actual nuclear power plant.

For nukes and non-nukes, all hands must attend three months of Submarine School, which acquaints nonquals with submarine systems. The officers learn the art of approach-and-attack. All students learn submarine escape and damage control.

After Submarine School, officers and enlisted personnel are sent to their first submarine to get qualified. For enlisted personnel, this can take six months. For an officer, it takes upward of a year. After earning dolphins, the submariner can proudly go where no nonqual can—to test depth and beyond.

Welcome aboard, and take her down!

The Least You Need to Know

- Soon after submerging, submariners begin to suffer a "jet lag" type of malady.

- Unless a submarine is actually at war, much of the activities involve drills and exercises.

- There are two ways to the deep: as an enlisted sailor or as an officer.

Part 5

Subs at War

The great majority of research and development that has gone into the modern submarine has been prompted by the underwater ship's value as a military weapon. Submarines were invented in the first place to attack enemy surface ships.

If submarine developers had been pushed along by scientific research only, today's subs would be far more primitive than they are. But modern submarines are instruments of combat and intelligence-gathering, and as such are finely honed machines meant to stealthily deliver death.

First we will go where the action is and look at "fast-attack" submarines, both those that are in use today and those that are in development for use in future conflicts. Then we'll look at America's submarine-launched ballistic missiles, which of course come in both nuclear and non-nuclear varieties.

Chapter 19

Nuclear "Fast Attack"

In This Chapter

- ◆ Sixty-two L.A. subs
- ◆ The importance of HY-100 steel
- ◆ The Virginia class sub of the future
- ◆ The latest in eyes and ears
- ◆ Submersibles and the bottom of the sea

You already know a great deal about the Los Angeles class of sub from the tour you took of the USS *Hampton* in Chapters 1 and 2.

Backbone of the Nuke Fleet

The Los Angeles class is the backbone of the U.S. Navy's nuclear-powered attack submarine fleet. These subs hunt enemy submarines and surface ships, launch cruise-missile strikes on land-based targets, and gather intelligence.

Beneath the Surface

Los Angeles class specifications:

➤ Displacement: 6,900 tons (submerged)

➤ Length: 360 feet

➤ Hull diameter: 33 feet

➤ Draft: 32 feet

➤ Speed: 25+ knots official statements; 35–39 knots actual

➤ Diving depth: 800+ feet official statements; 1,300 feet actual

➤ Weapons: Mark 48 antisubmarine torpedoes, Tomahawk cruise missiles

➤ Complement: 16 officers, 130 enlisted crew members

The Los Angeles class includes 62 submarines. The style of sub was upgraded after the first 39 were built, so the last 23 submarines are known as "improved 688s." The 688Is are improved in that they have the Vertical Launch System (VLS) to launch cruise missiles from the forward ballast tanks, and the improved battle control (fire control) systems to launch weapons and track targets.

The major difference between the original L.A. class subs and the improved version is that the latter are equipped with the BSY-1 combat systems. The improved subs also have retractable bow planes (replacing sail-mounted fairwater planes) and hardened sails to break through ice during Arctic operations.

Secrets of the Deep

The first 12 Los Angeles class submarines were named after the areas in the United States represented by the congressmen who supported the building of the subs. It was Admiral Rickover's way of saying thank you.

One thing has remained constant throughout the L.A. class's existence: You don't have to be aboard one for long before you realize that this vessel has one and only one purpose: It was built to make war. These are attack submarines, designed to hunt down and destroy a target. In submarine-speak, it's said that the sub *prosecutes* the target.

Seawolf Class

Seawolf-class submarines are a pure product of the Cold War. They were specifically designed to operate, without any help from supporting ships, against the Soviet Union's best submarines and most dangerous surface threats. The first of the class, the USS *Seawolf*, was commissioned on July 19, 1997, at Electric Boat Shipyard.

Secrets of the Deep

Seawolf class specifications:

➤ Builders: General Dynamics Electric Boat Division

➤ Power plant: One S6W reactor, one shaft with 52,000 SHP with pump-jet propulsor, Improved Performance Machinery Program Phase II, one secondary propulsion submerged motor

➤ Length: 353 feet (107.6 meters)

➤ Draft: 35 feet (10.67 meters)

➤ Beam: 40 feet (12.2 meters)

➤ Displacement: 7,460 tons surface displacement; 9,137 tons submerged displacement

➤ Official speed: 25+ knots

➤ Actual speed: 40+ knots maximum submerged speed; 20 knots tactical ("silent") speed

➤ Official operating depth: "Greater than 800 feet" (official statement); 1,000 feet (actual)

➤ Armament: Eight 660mm torpedo tubes, 50 Tomahawk cruise missiles or 50 Harpoon antiship missiles or 50 Mark 48 ADCAP torpedoes or up to 100 mines

➤ Crew: 12 officers; 121 enlisted

The *Seawolf*'s mission was to beat Soviet subs to the punch, to destroy Soviet submarines that were armed with nuclear missiles before they could fire those weapons at cities in the United States. With its communications, surveillance, and warning capabilities, it is also prepared to provide off-shore support for a land battle.

Cold (War) Down There

Since the former Soviet Union, a communist state and the enemy of the United States during the 45 years following World War II, was the focus of the Seawolf class sub, the ship was designed to function (no, thrive) under the polar ice cap.

To make it function well under ice, the sub has a strengthened sail. The sub also has a two-deck torpedo room so that it can fire at two different targets simultaneously. This is also the fastest American submarine, beating the tactical speed of the USS *Los Angeles* by more than 5 knots.

Beneath the Surface

Seawolf class subs have twice as many torpedo tubes as Los Angeles class submarines.

Quiet Down Below

Much effort went into keeping the *Seawolf* quiet and giving her a state-of-the-art ability to hear. The idea was that, when stalking Soviet subs, the *Seawolf* could hear but not be heard. The sound-reduction efforts were effective.

The Seawolf class sub is 10 times quieter than the improved Los Angeles class subs (such as the *Hampton*, which you toured in Chapters 1 and 2) and a whopping 70 times quieter than the original Los Angeles class subs.

The Seawolf type sub is a stealth ship that can sneak up on an enemy and, if necessary, put an army of "combat swimmers" into the water. The sub also has a special silo for launching an invasion of swimmers. Another new feature of the Seawolf class is a *dry-deck shelter*, known as the DDS.

New Steel

The Seawolf class subs were the first in the United States' fast-attack arsenal to be constructed of a new stronger and tougher form of steel. The hulls were made completely of HY-100 steel, built to withstand tremendous pressure. (Previous submarines had been made of HY-80 steel.)

The new form of steel made its debut back in the 1960s on U.S. Navy deep-diving submersibles like the *Sea Cliff* and the *Turtle*. Also beating the Seawolf class submarines to the punch when it comes to using HY-100 steel in its hull was a submarine designed in the Netherlands called the *Moray*. The stronger steel enabled the Dutch sub to dive to 360 meters.

A Superior Sub

The Seawolf program began in the mid-1980s. Not knowing that the Cold War was about to end without a shot being fired, the *Seawolf* was designed to be the world's superior submarine well into the twenty-first century.

It was designed to accommodate state-of-the-art weapons. It was built to be flexible so that when weapons systems were upgraded, the submarine could be easily upgraded as well. This was not just true of the submarine's ability to make war. Its communication, sensor, and propulsion systems were also designed not just to be the best, but to stay that way for a while.

The *Seawolf* underwent sea trials in 1996 and exceeded all expectations. The submarine and its crew made their debuts at the same time. Among the things tested were the sub's ability to submerge, run at speed, and run quietly.

Expensive Units

The contest was not even close. Seawolf class subs were to be the most expensive ever built. Projections back in the mid-1980s held that the total program would produce 12 submarines at a cost approaching $4 billion per sub, up from the $350 million to $500 million per 688 (cost-per-unit varies depending on how you amortize the development cost per unit—otherwise, the cost of the ship is merely time and materials, but do you count the man-hours of the new construction crew?).

Then the Cold War ended, and the necessity of Seawolf subs seemed diminished. In President George H. W. Bush's State of the Union Address in 1992, he proposed the rescission of $2.8 billion dollars originally destined for the Seawolf program. By 1995, it was agreed that there would not be 12 Seawolf subs, but rather 3. The third and final of these, the USS *Jimmy Carter*, was commissioned in December 2001. That final boat will undergo an upgrade that is expected to be completed in 2004.

Virginia Class

Despite the fact that the Seawolf class had been designed to be *the* submarine in the world well into the twenty-first century, the truth was that the Seawolf was too large and too expensive. Plans were put in motion to replace the Seawolf class subs with a newer, smaller, cheaper submarine.

The Virginia class attack submarine is the future of submarines. It is designed to perform at world-superior levels both at great depths under the sea and in *littoral operations*. It was decided that four of these would be built.

The first and third Virginia class submarines will be built by The Electric Boat Division of General Dynamics in Connecticut. The first was laid down in 1999. The *Virginia* (SSN-774) is scheduled to be commissioned in 2006. The third sub in the class, the USS *Hawaii* (SSN-776), is scheduled to be commissioned in 2008.

Subtalk

Littoral operations are those that a submarine undertakes in shallow water.

Newport News Shipbuilding will construct the second submarine, the USS *Texas* (SSN-775), which is scheduled to be commissioned in 2007, and the fourth submarine in the series, the USS *North Carolina* (SSN-777), which should be commissioned in 2009. Thirty of the Virginia class submarines are scheduled to be built, but as we have seen, these numbers have a way of changing over the years.

Designed by Computer

Using sophisticated software known as CAD/CAE (computer aided design and engineering) simulation systems, the designers who are making the Virginia class submarines—the design-and-build teams and engineering teams—are using computers every step of the way.

Looking at the specifications for the Virginia class sub, you'll note that it is considerably smaller than the Seawolf subs. The new sub displaces 7,300 tons when submerged, compared to 9,137 tons displaced by the Seawolf when submerged.

Secrets of the Deep

Virginia class specifications

➤ Length of hull: 377 feet

➤ Beam: 34 feet

➤ Displacement: 7,300 tons submerged

➤ Top speed: 38 knots when submerged

The hull structure and its structurally integrated enclosures are designed so that everything can be easily repaired, replaced, and upgraded—that is, easily accessible for standard tools.

Many of the compartments aboard the submarines will be assembled separately in a modular fashion and then, in one piece, will be snapped into place. For example, the submarine's command center will be installed as a single unit. It will be attached ("snapped on") to cushioned mounting points, which are part of the submarine's "modular isolated deck structures."

Ultramodern

The submarine will have a state-of-the-art feel. There will be few switches or buttons; equipment and systems will be activated through a single touch of a "touch spot" on a computer screen—much like those that many of us are familiar with on the screens of ATMs.

Those who have practiced for their career in submarines by playing video games will be rewarded on the Virginia class sub. On this ship, the steering and driving control mechanism is a two-axis, four-button joystick.

The Virginia class will not be significantly quieter than the Seawolf class, but it will be just as quiet. That means that it will still be 10 times quieter than the submarine you toured at the beginning of the book; it also is quieter than any Russian submarine.

> **Beneath the Surface**
>
> The new U.S. subs will remain the quietest in the world because of a new design in the propulsion system that features acoustically kind isolated deck features (no rattling) and a new anechoic (sound-absorbing) coating.

The C3I System

C3I means Command, Control, Communication, and Intelligence. The C3I system for the Virginia class submarines is being designed by Lockheed Martin Naval Electronics & Surveillance Systems–Undersea Systems (NE&SS–Undersea Systems) of Manassas, Virginia.

All the Virginia class systems—weapon control, sensors, countermeasures, and navigation systems—are integrated into one system that can be operated from one computer, the so-called Q-70 Color Common Display Console.

Weapons Systems

The Virginia-class submarine can launch rockets vertically—that is, straight up. In fact, it can launch 16 missiles simultaneously. The missiles are called Tomahawk missiles or SLCMs, for submarine-launched cruise missiles.

Like old-fashioned submarines, the Virginia-class subs will also be able to launch fire torpedoes horizontally. The submarines will be equipped with 12 vertical missile launch tubes and four 533-mm torpedo tubes. They also have the capacity to fire up to 26 Mk 48 ADCAP Mod 6 torpedoes and Sub Harpoon antiship missiles from their 21-inch torpedo tubes.

Baby Sub in the Pouch

Virginia class subs will have what is to be called the AN/WLY-1 acoustic countermeasures system, which will be able to listen for and locate potential enemy subs. The acoustic countermeasure system is being developed by Northrop Grumman.

Also, mounted on one of the ship masts will be a state-of-the-art electronic support measures system. Known as the AN/BLQ-10, this is being developed by Lockheed Martin Integrated Systems.

Incorporated into the hull of the Virginia class subs will be an integral lock-out/lock-in chamber. The chamber will hold a minisubmarine and will be used to launch attacks from Navy Sea Air Land (SEAL) teams. It can also be used for Marine reconnaissance units that may be working on counterterrorism or localized conflict operations.

> **Beneath the Surface**
>
> Remember periscopes? They will be a thing of the past. The Virginia class submarines will no longer have periscopes. Instead, they will have Kollmorgen AN/BVS-1 Photonic Masts, with attached sensors such as LLTV (low-light TV), a thermal imager, and a laser range-finder. With photonics, no periscope pole penetrates the hull. This allows the control room to be located in the wider, roomier middle level.

The Virginia class subs will have futuristic three-dimensional high-frequency sonar sensors for use in littoral waters (it's an improved under-ice sonar). The main sonar suite will know what is above, below, and to the sides of it, no matter where it is or how fast it is going.

The propulsion system for the Virginia class submarine will consist of a General Electric Pressurized Water Nuclear Reactor S9G, two turbine engines with one shaft, and a pump-jet propulsor. The S9G is a natural convection design that does not require main coolant pumps until it goes faster than 50 percent power.

Submersibles

That is the "gouge" (a collection of information even a professor could understand) on combatant submarines. But what about submersibles? Is a submarine the same thing as a submersible?

Submersibles are not at all the same as submarines, nor are they simply minisubmarines. Submersibles are designed to go into very deep waters. Because of this, they are never designed to be very agile. They usually, but not always, rely on cables or tethers to a surface ship for power or signal communications. They are built to withstand the crushing pressure of the depths of the deepest parts of the ocean. They tend to be rounder and squatter than their submarine counterparts. Finally, submersibles have small crews—usually just one or two men.

Submersibles investigated the *Thresher* sinking site, the *Scorpion* site, and numerous Russian submarine wrecks. You remember *Alvin* and the remote eyeball, *Jason*, that went down to the *Titanic*? That equipment was funded by the Navy. Why? To dive to Russian sub wrecks, in order to grab stray weapon pieces, but primarily to get the remote camera and manipulator arms into the hull itself—avoiding the costs of another Project Jennifer (the operation of the *Glomar Explorer* to raise the Soviet Golf submarine, complete with nuclear warheads and code safes).

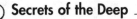

Secrets of the Deep

Submersibles have been extremely useful. Back in 1966, a submersible was used to retrieve an atom bomb that had been lost at sea when a B-52 crashed.

At one point, the Office of Naval Research (ONR) had a top-secret project to have MIT/Woods Hole engineers interview prison inmates to determine how safes are cracked, in the hopes of programming a robot arm to crack Russian safes in the interior of Russian sub wrecks. Once you get the Russian code books, you can translate all those old, undecrypted messages you've saved and can put together the intelligence puzzle. In addition, Russian safes held top-secret Russian war plans. Did the project work? Let me ask you—did the United States win the Cold War?

Beneath the Surface

Submersibles are valuable tools when laying cable or pipeline at the bottom of the ocean. They are also useful in placing phone-tapping equipment on submerged phone lines, as off the coast of Russia during the Cold War. The United States had Russia wired for sound during the latter part of the Cold War, and it got to the point that we had nearly "real time" communications interception and decryption. If you can read your neighbor's mail, you pretty much know what he's up to. To hell with the thought that it is ungentlemanly—it works.

Deep Quest

The United States built the appropriately named submersible *Deep Quest*, which launched in June 1967. It was 12 meters long and displaced 5 tons when on the surface. It could move at a maximum speed of 4½ knots using two reversible-thrust motors.

Deep Quest was built out of double spheres—one for the crew and one for the motors—with a common fairing around both. It could go as deep as 8,000 feet.

Military subs have difficulty going one quarter that deep. The submersible could absorb pressure equivalent to 7 tons psi.

Jacques Cousteau

A few years before that, in 1963, a submersible was built in France by the Westinghouse Electric Corporation and the OFRS, a company owned by the French deep-sea explorer Jacques Cousteau, who later became an American TV star with his appearances in documentary TV specials.

The ship, called the *Deepstar 4000*, carried many different types of scientific equipment for researching the ocean's bottom. *Deepstar 4000* could operate 3,300 feet beneath the surface, and it discovered many new ecosystems and species.

The ship was 17 feet, 9 inches long; 11 feet, 6 inches wide; and 6 feet, 6 inches wide. It ran on two fixed reversible 5-horsepower motors and had a maximum speed of 3 knots.

The Least You Need to Know

- The Los Angeles class is the backbone of the U.S. Navy's nuclear-powered attack submarine fleet.

- The Seawolf class subs were the first in the United States' fast-attack arsenal to be made completely of HY-100 steel.

- The Virginia class of attack submarines is the future of submarines.

- The Virginia class will have futuristic improved sensors.

- Submersibles are designed to go into very deep waters; because of this, they are never designed to be very agile.

Chapter 20

Submarine Missile Systems

In This Chapter

- ◆ Rockets don't kill people—people kill people
- ◆ Firing missiles from a sub
- ◆ Arming to destroy the world
- ◆ Scaling down

Ever since World War II, when the Nazis rained missiles down upon England, rocket science has been used to make war. Since submarines were also predominantly tools of war, it was inevitable that submarine science and rocket science would one day—well, if not merge, then certainly join forces.

In this chapter, we look at the missile systems that were put in place to combat the Soviet Union during the Cold War—or, to put it more precisely, to keep from combating them. We also look at the missile systems that are in place today to help protect freedom.

Fire Arrows

Rockets, which are usually referred to today as missiles when they contain a warhead, probably got their start as fireworks used in celebrations. In fact, it didn't take long before rockets evolved into weapons. Known as "fire arrows," they were used in China by the Mongols in the thirteenth century. Rockets as weapons are even an instrumental part of our American history. Remember the "rocket's red glare" from our national anthem? Those were British "Congreve" rockets, launched at Ft. McHenry in Baltimore.

And what do we do on our Independence Day, also known as the Fourth of July? We set off rockets, that's what. Rockets went on to be used as life-saving and signal devices, but they weren't really effective as weapons until World War II.

Types of Fuel

How do missiles work? Missiles produce the hot, expanding gases that thrust them forward by burning two ingredients in their combustion chambers: a fuel and an oxidizer. Jet engines combine their fuel with oxygen in the air to produce combustion. The expanding hot gases at the jet turbine exhaust nozzle create thrust to propel the jet. Missiles that must function in the upper atmosphere and in the vacuum of space carry not only fuel, but an oxidizer as well—usually oxygen or an oxygen-containing chemical.

Two basic types of missiles exist, distinguished by the form of the fuel and oxidizer used. Some missiles—and today's fireworks—use a form of gunpowder, a solid material, as fuel. These solid-fuel missiles have the advantage of being storable; their disadvantage is that, once started, they cannot be shut down.

> **Beneath the Surface**
>
> Submarines that run on nuclear power and are armed with ballistic missiles are designated SSBNs (submersible ship ballistic nuclear), as opposed to an SSN (submersible ship nuclear). They are also called FBMs, for fleet ballistic missile submarines. The Submarine Force calls them "boomers," for obvious reasons.

Liquid-fuel missiles carry their fuel and oxidizer in liquid form. The liquids are "cryogenic," meaning that they are at very low temperatures. They can be shut down and restarted by controlling the flow of propellants through valves and pumps. Solid-fuel missiles are ignited by a small powder charge that sends a flame shooting down a hollow tube at the rocket's core. The heat ignites the solid propellant and sends exhaust gases racing out the nozzle.

Newton's Law

Just as Newton would have predicted, the hot gases released by the fire in a missile's combustion chamber push outward and flow out the nozzle at the rocket's end. This pushes the rocket in the opposite direction. According to Newton, each force produces an equal and opposite reaction. The action is the ejection of expanding high-velocity gases. The reaction is the force in the opposite direction. Imagine being on a skating rink and tossing lead weights north—the reaction would propel you south. This is "thrust."

Missiles work because the thrust they produce is greater than the weight of the rocket, the force exerted on it by gravity. It follows that the lighter the missile is, the less energy it takes to push it. That's why most modern missiles are built in what are called stages. In other words, a series of missiles are stacked on top of one another.

The bottom missile—the first stage—ignites first, of course. When the first stage is out of fuel, it is jettisoned—that is, cut loose—from the rest. The rocket immediately above that one then ignites. With the weight of the lower stage gone, the spacecraft is lighter and more efficient.

As you can see, a rocket is never heavier than when it is first launched. The second stage does not have to worry about dragging upward the weight of the first stage's engines and empty fuel tanks. When the second stage runs out of fuel, in turn, it is jettisoned and the third stage takes over. This process continues until only the "payload" is left. In the case of submarine-launched ballistic missiles, that payload is either a bomb or a decoy (sent to confuse radars or antiballistic missile defenses).

SLBMs: Submarine-Launched Ballistic Missiles

The fact that today's war submarines fire missiles is an extension of the Cold War and the arms race that had both the United States and the Soviet Union trying to develop an intercontinental ballistic missile, a rocket with a warhead on it that could launch from one country and strike with acceptable accuracy on the other side of the world inside the enemy country.

In fact, the first missiles to be used on subs were adapted from the rockets that were being tested in the dessert and at Cape Canaveral. In 1955, the secretary of defense established a Joint Army-Navy Ballistic Missile Committee to adapt the Jupiter missile—a liquid-fuel missile—for use on Navy vessels.

The Army would be responsible for the adaptation of the missile, while the Navy would develop a launching system that could operate aboard a ship. Working on the project on the Army end was rocket scientist Wehrner von Braun, who had developed the V-2 rocket weapon for Germany during World War II.

Switching to a Solid Propellant

The goal of the program was to have a rocket system ready for ships in 1960 and for submarines in 1965. Even as work on the adaptation of the Jupiter rocket was proceeding, experts were thinking that a solid-fuel rocket would be better for ship and sub launches. The Navy's reason was that "the solid propellant would alleviate the serious hazards and difficult logistics, handling, and storage problems associated with liquids." By May 1956, Lockheed was recommending that the Jupiter be converted into a solid-fuel missile.

> **Beneath the Surface**
>
> Optimism was built into the plans for a sub missile system. It was assumed that because the first actual usage of the weapon being designed was seven years away, a rocket should be built to launch not a 1958 warhead, but rather a 1965 warhead. Designers believed that the newer warhead would be considerably lighter.

As the design progressed, the Jupiter missile underwent a name change. By the end of 1956, the missile being designed for the Navy was named the Polaris. About this time, it was decided that the Polaris would be developed for ships and subs simultaneously rather than for ships first and then for subs five years later. No longer was an Army missile being adapted for Navy use; a completely new missile system was to be designed.

Since many of the missile system's subsystems had to be designed simultaneously by the Lockheed Corporation, communication among the various divisions of production was essential. The technical branches in the designing organization's included Launcher, Missile, Fire Control and Guidance, Ship Installation, Navigation, and Operations and Test.

> **Secrets of the Deep**
>
> The intention was always to put nuclear warheads on submarine-based ballistic missiles. The thinking was that this would deter the Soviet Union from striking first in a nuclear war. If the Soviets thought they could obliterate the United States' ability to retaliate with a first strike, they would now know that all warhead-carrying subs would have to be eliminated as well in a first strike. That was an impossibility, given the technology of the time.

The Polaris Takes a Bow

The Polaris missile made its first successful test flight from Cape Canaveral, Florida, on January 7, 1960. The nuclear warhead that it would carry was developed by Lawrence Livermore National Laboratory, by a team headed by Harold Brown starting in 1957.

In July 1960, the nuclear warheads that would fit the Polaris were ready. In November 1960, the Polaris was launched from a submarine (the USS *George Washington*, the first-fleet ballistic missile submarine) for the first time. The submarine could carry 16 Polaris missiles.

The Polaris was the only missile fired from American submarines until 1972, when it began to be replaced by the Trident I missile. For a time during the 1950s, the British attempted to develop their own SLBM. It was to be called the Skybolt, but it didn't work very well. By 1963, the United States agreed to supply Polaris missiles to submarines of the Royal Navy. The British subs that were capable of firing the Polaris missiles were known as the Resolution Class Ballistic Missile Submarines. The Polaris A3 missiles had a range of 2,559 nautical miles, which qualified it as an intercontinental ballistic missile, a missile that could be fired from one continent and make a very big crater on another.

> **Beneath the Surface**
>
> Between 1960 and 1966, 40 Polaris missiles were test-launched from U.S. subs.

The Poseidon Adventure

The Poseidon was a two-stage solid fuel rocket that began to replace the Polaris on U.S. submarines in 1972. The new missiles were a big improvement. They could propel much heavier (multiple) warheads, and they could strike targets with much greater accuracy.

The Poseidon missile weighed 32 tons. It, like the Polaris, was made by Lockheed in the United States. It was 34 feet long and had a diameter of 6 feet, 2 inches. Its range was 2,156 to 2,803 nautical miles, depending on the weight of the warhead it was pushing.

Trident

The third type of sub-launched missile developed in the United States, this one also by Lockheed, was the Trident I that was first flight-tested in 1977. It first became operational in 1979. The Trident I missile weighed 35 tons. It was 34 feet, 1 inch in length and had a diameter of 6 feet, 2 inches.

In 1989, the Trident I missiles began to be replaced by Trident II missiles. Trident II missiles also replaced their forefathers, the Blue Steel missiles, on Vanguard-class submarines of the Royal Navy.

> **Beneath the Surface**
>
> The Trident missiles were first installed on Benjamin Franklin class and Lafayette class submarines.

A Trident missile is launched from the USS Henry L. Stimson *in 1985.*

The Blue Steel missile, which lacked intercontinental capabilities, began development in Great Britain in 1954 and was operational from 1964 to 1969. It was 35 feet long, had a wingspan of 13 feet, weighed 7½ tons, and had a range of about 150 miles. It was a medium-range ballistic missile. So, when these were used by the Royal Navy with Tridents purchased from the United States, it was a big upgrade in capability.

Secrets of the Deep

Specifications for the Trident I:

- ◆ Built by: Lockheed Martin Missiles and Space, Sunnyvale, California
- ◆ Power: Three-stage solid-propellant rocket
- ◆ Length: 34 feet
- ◆ Weight: 73,000 pounds
- ◆ Diameter: 6 feet, 2 inches
- ◆ Range: 4,600 statute miles
- ◆ Guidance system: Inertial
- ◆ Warhead: Nuclear multiple
- ◆ First deployed: 1979

A Three-Stager

The Trident II, which was a big improvement over the Trident I, has three stages and burns solid fuel. It is inertially guided and has a range of more than 4,600 statute miles. That's more than 2,000 nautical miles more in range than the original Polaris missiles. There wasn't a place on Earth that couldn't be targeted in minutes by one of America's nuclear attack submarines.

The Trident II could carry a lot more payload than the Trident I because it was made of graphite epoxy, which was a lighter, stronger, and harder material than had been previously used.

Secrets of the Deep

Specifications for the Trident II:

- Built by: Lockheed
- Power: Three-stage solid-propellant rocket
- Length: 44 feet
- Weight: 130,000 pounds
- Diameter: 6 feet, 11 inches
- Range: 4,600+ statute miles
- Guidance system: Inertial
- Warhead: Nuclear multiple
- First deployed: 1990
- Cost per submarine: $30.9 million

The missile had more range than its predecessors because of a new aerodynamic shape. It had an aerospike at its tip, which telescoped outward and reduced drag by approximately half. When the missile was launched, steam pressure from a gas generator was used to push it out of the launch tubes. A gas generator is essentially a charge of solid rocket fuel pointed to a reservoir of distilled water. When the solid rocket fuel ignites, the reservoir immediately "flashes" to steam and, like exploding gunpowder in a gun barrel, propels the missile out of the missile tube. The steam from the gas generator charge "blankets" the missile on the way out of the water so that water never touches the missile.

When the rocket emerges into the air, its upward velocity decays to zero as gravity pulls it to Earth. A "zero gee" sensor and a "broach" sensor tell the missile-guidance computer that it is safe to ignite the solid rocket propellant, and the engine comes to full thrust. The missile continues upward in its initial trajectory. Two minutes later, the first and second stages have burned themselves out and the third stage is firing. By this time, the missile is traveling more than 3½ miles per second.

Deployment of Ballistic Missiles and PALs

Ballistic missile deployment was debated and discussed at length before these missiles' initial at-sea appearance. The U.S. Air Force and U.S. Army were worried about the same scenario that Stanley Kubric made famous in the movie *Dr. Strangelove, or, How I Learned to Stop Worrying and Love the Bomb*. In the movie's premise, a crazed base commander sends his B-52 wing to Russia without authorization in a strategic attack as a first strike. This was more than Hollywood fiction—there were true worries that nuclear warheads could be deployed without authorization and would start a global thermonuclear war. This, in essence, would be a suicide bomber blowing up the world.

Beneath the Surface

A little-known fact is that during the Cuban Missile Crisis, an American destroyer was dropping grenade-sized depth charges on a Soviet submarine in an effort to turn it back to Russia. The stressed-out Soviet submarine commander ordered his nuclear-tipped torpedoes armed and was ready to launch them. A nuclear detonation at sea would have caused a nuclear escalation that could have proved disastrous. The Russian skipper was talked out of this mad and unauthorized course of action, but from the stories of his crew, it was a near miss.

To prevent unauthorized uses of nuclear weapons, Army and Air Force nukes had PALs, or preventive action interlock devices. A PAL would render a nuclear bomb, missile, or projectile completely inert unless a code unknown to the military unit were transmitted to the warhead by an outside command-and-control unit. This would prevent a renegade senior commander from launching on a whim.

The Army and Air Force insisted that SLBMs have PALs. The Navy argued against them, insisting that a radio signal to unlock the weapons would be senseless in a submarine scenario. The winning element of the debate was the second strike theory: The United States might come under an all-out nuclear strike by the Soviet Union to cripple all command-and-control, and the retaliatory force of the "boomers" would be useless because there would be no one to send out the PAL codes.

The Navy won the day: There are no PALs on submarine-launched ballistic missiles. The ship's captain is authorized to launch the missiles. Hollywood made this the subject of another movie, *Crimson Tide*.

Part of the force of the nuclear triad (Air Force strategic bombers, Air Force silo missiles, and Navy SLBMs) is the enemy's realization that the Navy can strike at any time, without command and control. Somehow the Russians needed to be informed that the Navy missiles had no PALs, in a way they would believe, so that they would fear the submarine missiles and would be deterred from a first strike.

The Russians were reluctant to believe official statements of the U.S. government, and they believed that the American media was as tainted as their own. The only way to get the Russians to believe that the Navy could strike on its own, without external command-and-control, was to feed them information from a spy.

Students of espionage have long known the technique of using a compromised agent to feed the enemy information that is desired for him to have. Both the Walker spy ring and the Aldrich Ames cases were allowed to linger on by the U.S. intelligence agencies in order to feed information to the Russians so that they would believe it. One of the morsels of intelligence sent over to Moscow was Contingency 12.

Contingency 12

Contingency 12 is part of the "war plan." The war plan is the document that tells each unit what it does when "the balloon goes up" (all-out nuclear war commences). Part of the war plan for FBMs (boomers) is that if a missile submarine commander becomes convinced that the United States has fallen victim to a surprise nuclear strike, he is fully authorized to retaliate on his own, *with no orders from the Pentagon or White House.* For example, if a boomer's continuous radio broadcast from shore stops, the captain orders the ship to PD. If at PD there is no tactical radio signals, no television signals, and no civilian radio signals, the captain may reasonably believe that the United States has come under nuclear attack. If so, he consults the war plan for his ship. In some cases, the war plan calls for him to launch the entire battery at preselected Russian targets. In others, it orders him to become a "Strangelovian" doomsday device and remain undetected for one, two, or even three months after the war; when the enemy believes it to be safe to come out of the bunker, the belated U.S. nuclear assault rains down on his head.

Of course, this is useless unless the enemy knows it. After the Walker spy ring was done doing business, Moscow knew the frightening reality. And it acted to bring the Cold War to a quick end. With no trailing of the U.S. boomers, the Russians could not win a first strike.

Antiship Missiles

During the 1967 Six-Day War, a missile fired by the United Arab Republic sank an Israeli destroyer. This success led the United States—McDonnell Douglas, in particular—to begin development of an antiship missile.

The missile was the Harpoon, a product so good that it has been used (in a series of upgraded forms) ever since. It is a flexible missile that can be launched from ships, airplanes, or submarines. About five of these could take out an aircraft carrier.

The Harpoon weighs 1,498 pounds. It is 15 feet, 2 inches long and has a $13\frac{1}{2}$-inch diameter. It can carry a 500-pound warhead and has a range of 86 nautical miles.

Tomahawk

First deployed in 1974, Tomahawk missiles, made by General Dynamics, are remarkably versatile. They are submarine-launched cruise missiles and can carry a nuclear warhead, although conventional warheads can also be used. They can also be fired from the normal torpedo tube of a Los Angeles class submarine in the encapsulated version. The Tomahawk has been preferentially fired from vertical launch tubes since the appearance of the 688I class submarine. However, 688Is may load up with encapsulated Tomahawks in addition to the VLS versions for a massive land assault, or if detailed to attack a large surface battle group that is not escorted by a submarine asset.

The Tomahawks are just shy of 21 feet long and are 21 inches in diameter. They have a range of 1,347 nautical miles and are used both by the U.S. and Royal navies.

The Least You Need to Know

◆ Missiles produce the hot gases that thrust them forward by burning two ingredients in their combustion chambers: a fuel and an oxidizer.

◆ The first missile to be launched by a sub was called the Polaris.

◆ The Poseidon, a two-stage solid fuel rocket, began to replace the Polaris on U.S. submarines in 1972.

◆ Trident and Tomahawk missiles have followed.

Part 6

The History of Submarines

In this final section, we'll look back to the early days of submarines. The first subs, created to carry out attacks in times of war, had just as much chance of killing their crews as they did of sinking an enemy ship.

We'll give credit to the men who share the title of "Father of the Submarine": Simon Lake and John Holland. And we won't leave out the contributions of Jules Verne, who envisioned the modern submarine with unprecedented clarity in his nineteenth-century science fiction.

From there, on our journey through time, we'll look at the submarines of World War I and World War II, and the technological achievements that led right up to the dawn of the nuclear age.

Chapter 21

Pre–Twentieth-Century Submarines

In This Chapter

- The beginning of submarine warfare
- The *Hunley* jinx
- *Holland:* The submarine's dad
- Verne: From science fiction to science

The submarine was first conceived by the great inventor and artist Leonardo da Vinci in the fifteenth century, long before anyone built one. The next published reference to submarines came in 1580. The book *Invention or Devices*, by William Bourne, contained the passage, "It is possible to make a Ship or Boate that may goe under the water unto the bottome, and so to come up again at your pleasure." Bourne never built a model for his principle, and his early attempts to alter buoyancy—"let water in/pump water out"—did not work.

Halley's Diving Bell

English astronomer Edmund Halley—the same fellow after whom the comet is named—was the first to build an underwater container in which work could be done. He built a wooden container in which men could salvage sunken ships in a dry environment.

That container was lowered to the ocean's bottom on a rope. Because it was shaped like a bell, it became known as Halley's Diving Bell. The most innovative thing about the bell was the way in which it replenished its air supply.

According to submarine historian Brayton Harris, the air system worked "with weighted barrels of air, sent down from the surface":

> There was a vent hole in the bottom of each; the air inside the barrel would be compressed and forced out through a hose in the top, which was led into the diving bell. A valve released stale air from the top of the bell as fresh air flowed in from the barrel.

First Attack Sub: The *Turtle*

The first submarine to attack another vessel in warfare was the *Turtle*, which was built by David Bushnell in 1775, just in time for it to participate in the American Revolution. The *Turtle* was the first practical submarine ever built. It could go underwater, stay underwater while a man functioned inside it, and move from one place to another. It was also the first sub ever built for war.

The sub was called the *Turtle* because it was egg-shaped and resembled two turtle shells pressed together. It was built to withstand the increased water pressure at depth. The driver breathed through brass tubes, which were attached to scuba tubes that stuck up above the surface of the water.

Secrets of the Deep _____

Specifications for the *Turtle:*

- ◆ Nation: United States
- ◆ Launch: 1775
- ◆ Crew: One
- ◆ Displacement on surface: 2 tons
- ◆ Displacement submerged: 2 tons
- ◆ Height: 6 feet
- ◆ Width: 4 feet, 6 inches
- ◆ Armament: One 150-pound bomb
- ◆ Power: Hand crank

Float valves kept water from pouring into the breathing tubes if water placed over their tops. Foot-operated valves allowed water into and pumped water out of the hulls so that the buoyancy of the vessel could be altered.

Handles inside the craft were attached to oars on the outside. Moving the handles one way propelled the craft forward, and moving the handles the other way caused the *Turtle* to back up.

The Colonial Army used the *Turtle* to attack British ships that were docked in New York Harbor. The idea was to have the *Turtle* dropped off at the mouth of the harbor and allow the tide and the craft's own propulsion system to move it into attacking distance.

The *Turtle*'s weapon was a 150-pound keg of dynamite. The plan was to use a drill to attach the bomb to the hull of an enemy ship. The bomb would be on a clock, the timer for which would be started when the *Turtle* pulled away from the enemy ship.

The pilot on the night of the mission was Sgt. Ezra Lee, the first submarine warrior. The first ship he chose as a target got off easy because Lee's drill wouldn't dent the hull; he had apparently chosen a spot where there was a bolt or iron casing.

Lee ejected the bomb as he made his escape, with at least one boat in pursuit. When it exploded an hour later, a huge geyser of water rose up out of the harbor. But no ship was damaged.

A few nights later, Lee made a second attempt to use the *Turtle* in anger, but this time the vessel was spotted and had to retreat before its bomb could be attached.

Soon thereafter, the British sunk the American boat that had been carrying the *Turtle*. The *Turtle* was salvaged but was never used for warfare again. The world would have to wait 80 years, until the Civil War, for the return of submarine warfare.

The CSS *H. L. Hunley*

The first submarine to ever sink an enemy vessel, several generations after the *Turtle*'s first attempt, was the CSS *H. L. Hunley*—but there is a hitch to that ship's claim to fame. The truth is, the *Hunley* killed many more of its own crew than it ever killed of the enemy.

On the night of February 17, 1864, the Confederacy's Lt. George E. Dixon and a six-man crew set sail in the *Hunley* in the waters of Charleston Harbor to attack the Union ships that had formed a blockade in the harbor to prevent the South from getting supplies through.

The Peripatetic Coffin

Built on a shoal at the entrance to the harbor stood Fort Sumter, the key to the harbor's defense because it protected the city of Charleston, South Carolina. The fort had been built by the Federalists but had been captured by the South in the battle that had started the Civil War. On this still, calm night, Fort Sumter and the harbor were lit by a three-quarter moon. This was the night that the *Hunley* earned its nickname: the Peripatetic Coffin.

Horace L. Hunley

The concept for the *Hunley* came in 1861, from two New Orleans engineers named James McClintock and Baxter Watson. The money to build the submarine had been supplied by a group of private investors. Top among that group was the man after whom the ship was named, Horace L. Hunley.

Born in Tennessee and raised in New Orleans, Hunley was a Tulane University graduate, businessman, lawyer, and customs official. Hunley described himself as a man "of high ideals and profound devotion to the Southern cause." He proved it—and with more than money. But that came later.

Prototypes

A submarine prototype, the *Pioneer*, was built and successfully tested, only to be scuttled on the eve of Vice Adm. David Glasgow Farragut's capture of New Orleans. McClintock, Watson, and Hunley went to Mobile, Alabama, where the military commander there, Major General Dabney H. Maury, offered assistance to the submarine project.

Two of Maury's engineers, Lt. George E. Dixon and Lt. William A. Alexander, joined the effort. A second submarine, similar to the *Pioneer*, was built. However, this ship sank in a squall during testing.

Fatal Flaw: The Bulkheads

Undaunted, Maury's engineers built a new model: the *Hunley*. At the Park and Lyons workshop in Mobile, a cylindrical steam boiler was cut in half lengthwise. The ends were removed, and bulkheads coming nearly to the top were inserted. This turned out to be the craft's fatal flaw: The bulkheads were not flush with the overhead.

Tapered wedges were added at bow and stern, doubling as ballast tanks. The tanks were flooded by valves on the bulkheads and emptied by hand pumps. The *Hunley* was 35 feet long, with a 4-foot beam. Two manholes provided access for a nine-man crew.

One crewman, in the bow, piloted the vessel. The others hand-turned the propeller crank. Glass panes in the manhole coamings (a raised frame for waterproofing) provided an outside view. Submerged, reckoning was done by compass, by the light of a candle whose guttering would also warn of a failing air supply. Top speed was 2 to 3 knots in calm waters.

Tragic Testing

Only with its testing did the *Hunley* begin to give harbingers of the nightmare she was to become. In the rough waters of Mobile Bay, the *Hunley* sank, killing a nine-man crew.

It was thought that perhaps she would have better luck in calmer water, so the next test was in Charleston Bay, which fit the stillwater bill. To get to Charleston Bay, the *Hunley* was loaded on two railroad flat cars. The submarine arrived in Charleston on August 15, 1863. General P. G. T. Beauregard, that city's military commander, put the *Hunley*'s new crew under the command of Lt. John Payne.

On August 29, the *Hunley* was put into the water and somehow became entangled in the lines of a steamer ship. The sub foundered and sank. Eight more men died in the incident. Lieutenant Payne was the only survivor.

But a war was going on, and no one was about to give up. More tests were ordered, and these were completed successfully. But after the test, tragedy again struck. The *Hunley* was moored to another ship that unaccountably shifted position, swamping the sub. Once again, eight men died and Lieutenant Payne was the only survivor.

Subtalk

H. L. Hunley specifications:

- ◆ Nation: Confederacy
- ◆ Launched: 1863
- ◆ Crew: Nine
- ◆ Displacement: 2 tons on the surface
- ◆ Armament: One spar torpedo (bomb at the end of a stick)
- ◆ Power: Hand crank
- ◆ Top speed: $2^1/_2$ knots on the surface.

One More Try

After that incident, General Beauregard began to think that the sub might be cursed and was ready to scrap the entire project. But he was talked out of it by the inventor McClintock, who convinced the general to give the *Hunley* one more try.

A new crew was assigned, all men from the Mobile works. The new crew included Horace Hunley. The new crew didn't last any longer than the previous ones had. Although the briefest test was scheduled with a maximum chance for success, the sub sank anyway on October 15, 1863. This time, its own namesake was among the dead.

41-Day Bombardment

As the *Hunley* lay on the bottom, Union gunners pressed the siege. Charleston was bombarded day and night. The attack lasted for 41 consecutive days. Fort Sumter was reduced to rubble. Only its northeast wall was left standing. But somehow the Confederate defenders held on. Their defense continued, and the North was not allowed to take control of the harbor.

Still, the situation was desperate, and Beauregard had no choice but to allow lieutenants Dixon and Alexander to raise the *Hunley* for one more try.

Here is Beauregard's eyewitness account of that raising:

> The spectacle was indescribably ghastly; the unfortunate men were contorted into all kinds of horrible attitudes; some clutching candles, evidently endeavoring to force open the manholes; others lying in the bottom tightly gripped together, and the blackened faces of all presented the expression of their despair and agony.

Reconstructing the accident, it was believed that the pilot, Hunley, had put the boat in a steep dive, failing to shut the seacock (flood valve) on the forward ballast tank.

The forward ballast tank had filled with water, eventually spilling over that fatal open area at the top of the bulkhead, into the hold. The candle went out; the valve handle fell off and was lost on the floor. In darkness, the crew drowned.

Last Mission

Yet—and this is perhaps the most amazing thing about the entire story—volunteers were once again found to man the *Hunley*'s new crew. For this mission, a spar was installed at the front of the ship with a torpedo at the end. Back then, a torpedo was simply a bomb used in a marine environment.

The torpedo was a copper case filled with 90 pounds of powder. On February 17, 1864, at 8:45 P.M., the *Hunley* closed on the Union's sloop-of-war, the *Housatonic*. A shuddering blast sent both warship and sub to the bottom.

The *Housatonic* lost five men. The *Hunley* and all her crew were lost. In her jinxed career, the *Hunley* had killed 5 of the enemy and 33 of her own crewman. The numbers were not good, but one thing could not be denied: The era of submarine warfare had begun.

Secrets of the Deep

When the wreckage of the *Hunley* was finally found, the skeletal remains of eight of her crew were found, still in their seats.

The CSS *David:* Semisubmersible Torpedo Launch

Unlike the CSS *H. L. Hunley* and the USS *Alligator*, which were *divers*, the CSS *David*, a vessel of the Confederate navy during the U.S. Civil War, was a "semisubmersible torpedo launch," also known as a "snorkel submarine."

The snorkel sub *David* was developed and built as part of an effort to break through the Union blockades at Charleston Harbor and other key port cities that were preventing the South from getting fresh supplies to its troops.

Subtalk

A **diver** is a boat that can remain fully submersed for an extended period of time.

The blockades were known as Lincoln's Anaconda Plan. The ships that kept out the supplies had wooden hulls, which would be vulnerable to the attack of the torpedo boats.

The first *David* was constructed during the mid-1860s and became a prototype for future torpedo boats. Eventually, 20 of the boats were built, and all were referred to as *David*. The sub was propelled by a steam-condensing engine and a screw propeller. The helmsman's deck and boiler were about 10 feet above the surface of the water. The first *David* capsized on its first test, drowning several of its crew members. The cause was either water turbulence or heavy winds.

Secrets of the Deep

CSS *David* specifications:

- Length: 54 feet
- Interior diameter: 5.5 feet
- Height to top of funnel: 10.67 feet
- Crew: Captain and three men
- Explosive charge: 134 lbs. of black powder

The key to the boat's attack was a long "torpedo spar" that protruded from the bow. The spar was actually a log with a copper casing at the end. The log was attached to the bow with a guide line so that the torpedo could be detached from inside the ship. Between 60 and 150 pounds of gunpowder fit inside the copper casing at the end of the log.

The canister was built thick so that it could withstand heavy rusting and pitting. The torpedo was put into the enemy vessel by ramming it with the spar, thus detonating the torpedo canister. The theory was that there would be enough gunpowder in the canister to blow a large hole in the enemy's hull and sink the ship.

Designers were positive that this would work against wooden-hulled ships, but they were less certain of the effectiveness of the torpedo spar against the new Monitor ironclads, with iron hulls, that were being built by the North. Because the hulls of the new ironclads were so far beneath the surface of the water, the Confederated coastal guns had been ineffective in stopping them.

> **Beneath the Surface**
>
> Because the *David* boats capsized so frequently and death and injury were so common among the crews, it became increasingly difficult as the war went along to find volunteers who were willing to serve on one of the *David* subs.

Attack on the USS *New Ironsides*

During the autumn of 1863, after the boat had been tested successfully by a new crew, plans were made for the first *David* to attack the northern iron-hulled ship known as the USS *New Ironsides*. The new commander was Lt. William Glassell.

The *New Ironsides*, aware that it could be the subject of a sneak attack, made itself hard to find by anchoring in a different spot each evening. But the *David* found her. Here is what one crew member of the *David* wrote about that first encounter with the *New Ironsides*:

> When within 50 yards of her we were hailed, which was answered by a shot from a double-barreled gun in the hands of Lieutenant Glassell. In two minutes we struck the ship (we were going at full speed) under the starboard quarter, about 15 feet from her sternpost, exploding our torpedo about six and a half feet from her bottom. The enemy fired rapidly with small arms, riddling the vessel but doing us no harm. The column of water thrown up was so great that it recoiled from our frail bark in such forces as to put the fires out and lead us to suppose that the little vessel would sink. The engine was reversed for backing, but the shock occasioned by the jar had been so great as to throw the iron ballast among the machinery, which prevented its working. During this delay the

vessel, owing to the tide and wind, hung under the quarter of the *Ironsides*, the fire upon us being kept up the whole time.

Finding ourselves in this critical position and believing our vessel to be in a sinking condition, we concluded that the only mean of saving our lives was to jump overboard, trusting that we would be picked up by the boats of the enemy. Lieutenant Glassell and the fireman (James Sullivan) swam off in the direction of the enemy's vessels, each being provided with a life preserver, and were not seen afterwards. The pilot stuck to the vessel, and I being overboard at the time and finding that no quarter would be shown, as we had called out that we surrendered, I concluded that it was best to make one more effort to save the vessel. Accordingly, I returned to her and rebuilt my fires; after some little delay got up steam enough to move the machinery. The pilot then took the wheel and we steamed up channel, passing once more through the fleet and within three feet of the *Monitor*, being subjected the whole time to one continuous fire of small arms ....

The only casualty of the battle was Acting Master Howard of the *New Ironsides*, who was killed by a shotgun blast fired by Lieutenant Glassell. The USS *New Ironsides* suffered structural damage. Although the ship was not destroyed, the attack created "shock waves" to the Union naval command under Admiral Dahlgren.

The Admiral's Dispatch

On October 7, 1863, in response to the news of the attack on the *New Ironsides*, Admiral Dahlgren (of the North) sent a dispatch from the U.S. Flagship *Philadelphia*, marked "confidential," to Union Secretary of the Navy Gideon Wells. The dispatch read:

> My Dear Sir: ... Among the many inventions with which I have been familiar, I have seen none which have acted so perfectly at first trial.

> The secrecy, rapidity of movement, control of direction, and precise explosion indicate, I think, the introduction of the torpedo element as a means of certain warfare. It can be ignored no longer. If 60 pounds of powder, why not 600 pounds?

The admiral continued to lobby for the development and construction of torpedo boats to be used by the Union navy. He wrote on October 17, 1963, "Last night an object, believed to be a torpedo boat, was seen by our picket boat .... It is evident that the enemy plans to prosecute this mode of warfare, and I therefore urge reprisals in kind."

When the U.S. Navy was slow to respond to the admiral's requests, he changed his plan a bit. Now he began to urge that the North develop weapons to counter the South's torpedo boats. This time he got action. Spars of log booms were floated near the anchorage of Union ships, acting as an obstacle for torpedo boats.

A Practical Defense

A proposal by Chief Engineer Henry Mason of the USS *Pasaic* turned out to be one of the most practical defenses against the Southern torpedo boats. Mason wrote a letter on January 8, 1864, to Lt. Commander E. Simpson, in which he described his invention:

> In compliance with your request, I herewith enclose a hasty sketch of the torpedo guard which I proposed to you last night. The light iron outriggers a are hinged at b and can be raised by pendant blocks, and falls over the stanchion c. Rope or wire netting can be used on these outriggers, as shown by the black diagonal lines in the side view, but I believe the simplest and most effective guard is horizontal courses of iron wire, secured to the outriggers only ....

Attack on the USS *Memphis*

On March 6, 1864, the CSS *David* attacked the USS *Memphis* on the North Edisto River. A month later, the Confederate torpedo boat attacked the USS *Wabash* in Charleston Harbor.

Although construction on the additional 20 *David* boats began in 1864, the first *David* is the only one that saw action.

Robert Whitehead Invents the "Automobile Torpedo"

From the time it was invented in 1866 until the dawn of the atomic age, the *automobile torpedo* was the most deadly and feared naval weapon. More than 25 million tons of shipping were sunk by torpedoes.

The man who invented the torpedo was a British man named Robert Whitehead. Whitehead (1828–1905) was born near Bolton, Lancaster, in the United Kingdom, in 1823. He came from a family of engineers and took up the family vocation. As a boy, Whitehead served his apprenticeship with the engineering company Omerods of Manchester. At the tender age of 12, Whitehead left Omerods to seek his fame and fortune.

Back in those days, good English engineers were rare, and he knew he would be able to find a good job. After working as a teenager for a time in a shipyard in Toulon, he secured the good job he had been looking for—as a consultant engineer in Milan.

As a young adult, Whitehead was an inventor with many patents to his name. Unfortunately, these were turbulent times in Europe, with frequent wars and boundary changes. Whitehead sometimes found himself possessing patents in countries that no longer existed. After moving to Austria during the 1850s, Whitehead produced the first screw propeller and cylindrical marine boiler to be built in that country.

> **Subtalk**
>
> The **automobile torpedo** has nothing to do with cars. The automobile, the kind that you drive into the gas station, did not yet exist. The word *automobile*, in this sense, simply means that the torpedo could move on its own.

Der Kustenbrander

In 1864, Whitehead took a job as manager of a major engineering company based in Fiume near Trieste, in Austria, doing work for the Austrian navy. While working there, he was approached by an Austrian navy captain, Giovanni de Luppis, who wanted to build an unmanned, self-propelled surface boat packed with explosives that could be directed at blockading warships.

The floating bomb would be called the *Der Kustenbrander* (Coastal Fire Ship). De Luppis and Whitehead did not have creative chemistry together and failed to produce a functional weapon, so their partnership broke up.

Alone Again, Naturally

Alone again, Whitehead decided to pursue the concept of a self-propelled unmanned vessel containing explosives. Of course, this was the seed for the idea that would lead to the automobile torpedo—and a profound and permanent change in naval warfare.

The first decision Whitehead made was to produce a weapon that would strike an enemy ship and blow a hole into its hull below the waterline. For obvious reasons, enemy ships would sink quicker if they were attacked lower. When Whitehead's final invention was perfected, it was the automobile torpedo.

Although more than a lifetime passed between the invention of the automobile torpedo and World War II, the essential components in the weapon remained the same.

Secrets of the Deep

Whitehead was honored in many countries of the world for his invention, but strangely, he never received much respect in his native land. This lack of respect even stretched into the post–World War II years. During the 1950s, a superb collection of torpedoes were put on display at the Torpedo Experimental Establishment at HMS *Vernon*. Despite the collectors' efforts, the British navy decided to scrap the collection.

The British began to purchase automobile torpedoes in bulk for the first time in 1871. The torpedoes were tested at Weymouth and Portland. The British government purchased the manufacturing rights for the weapon from the Whitehead Torpedo Company, Fiume, Austria, in 1871. In 1895, the Whitehead Company set up its first manufacturing site outside Austria, in Wyke Regis, near Weymouth. Because so many of the early torpedoes were exploded in testing, there are several types for which no examples have survived.

John P. Holland: Father of the Modern Submarine

Born in 1841, in Liscannor, County Clare, Ireland, John P. Holland conducted some of his first scientific experiments when employed with the Christian Brothers in Limerick. Holland was trying to build the first "aeroplane." He had an obsession with both sea and air travel.

He left that firm at the age of 32, however, because of ill health and moved to Cork, where he began to work seriously on a submarine design that he had been tinkering with in his head since he was 18.

Holland believed that submarines would dominate naval warfare of the future because they would be able to sneak up on ironclad ships and fire upon them broadside from close range.

Supporting the Fenian Movement

In 1873, three years after Jules Verne's *20,000 Leagues Under the Sea* was published, Holland moved to Boston, Massachusetts, to join his mother and two brothers who had emigrated there years before. Holland worked for a time in an engineering firm and then taught for six years at St. John's Catholic School in Paterson, New Jersey.

He completed a design for a functioning submersible warship for the U.S. Navy, but it was rejected—insulted, in fact—as "a fantastic scheme of a civilian landsman." So

Holland looked elsewhere for a client. He went on to build a small sub to attack a British ship in support of the Fenian Movement (an Irish organization dedicated to overthrowing British control in Ireland), a cause that was near and dear to the heart of Holland's brother, Michael.

The sub would hold three men. It would be transported across the sea aboard a harmless-looking merchant ship. When the merchant ship was close to the British ship, the sub would be placed surreptitiously into the water so that it could make its attack.

Holland Number One

Holland's first submarine, the *Holland Number One*, was built in Paterson in 1877. It was 14 feet long and powered by a 4-horsepower engine. It held only one man. Holland hauled the craft to the nearby Passaic River to test it out.

A large crowd, including the Fenian clients, gathered to watch as the sub was placed in the water—and promptly sank to the bottom because someone had forgotten to screw in two screw plugs. A second attempt the following day went much better, and the Fenians gave Holland the money to develop a larger sub that would be "suitable for war." In fact, Holland now had the money to quit teaching and dedicate all of his time to the development of submarines.

Holland scuttled his *Number One* in the Passaic after removing the parts he could reuse. Years later, the vessel was retrieved and is now preserved in a Paterson museum.

The Fenian Ram

The warship that Holland built to attack the British ship was called the *Fenian Ram*. It was constructed at the Delamater Iron Works, New York. Launched in May 1881, the sub was 31 feet long. It was driven by a 15-horsepower engine and had a top speed of 9 miles per hour over water and 7 miles per hour under water.

The sub displaced 19 tons and was armed with an underwater canon fired by compressed air. Before the *Fenian Ram* could be used in warfare, however, the Fenians backed out of the deal. They refused to pay Holland, and Holland refused to deliver the sub.

Proving that it was nothing personal when it came to the British, Holland offered his sub design to the British years later. At the dawn of the twentieth century, the British launched their own submarine, designed by Holland.

Contracts and Condescension

As the years went by, the U.S. Navy began to take Holland more seriously—a little. Holland eventually won an open competition for the best sub design and earned a contract with the U.S. Navy. Thus, in 1896, the John Holland Torpedo Boat Company was set up with Charles A. Morris as chief engineer.

The trouble was, whatever had prompted the Navy to refuse to take Holland seriously in the first place carried over: Even though the Navy gave Holland a contract to design a submarine, they were determined to keep an extremely close eye on him; they apparently considered him a "gifted amateur."

As it turned out, the changes that the Navy experts insisted upon made the submarine too cumbersome to be functional. Holland said that the sub had been "overengineered," and development was abandoned in 1900.

Number Six

Holland's sixth craft, *Holland Number Six*, which was developed independently of the Navy, was his largest and most successful. It was 53 feet long, and its power plant was a 45-horsepower gas engine. It carried a crew of 15 and had a torpedo tube in the bow.

Number Six went for its first test run in New York Harbor in 1898, and all went well. The secretary of the navy, Theodore Roosevelt, recommended this craft to the Navy. The Navy eventually purchased the sub—although for only about half of what it had cost to design and build—and the first submarine in the U.S. Navy was commissioned the USS *Holland* on October 12, 1900.

In addition to selling submarines to the British, Holland supplied a sub to the Japanese in 1904 for use against the Russians. Holland received the Rising Sun from the Emperor of Japan for his contribution to the Japanese naval victory. Holland died in 1914.

First Electric Motor

In the late nineteenth century, England and France considered each other potential enemies and so tried to pump up their navies to protect themselves against the other. In 1887, the French built the *Goubet* (GOO-bay) *I*, which is remembered as the first submarine to run on an electric motor. The *Goubet I* held a crew of two. It was 16½ feet long and displaced 1.6 tons on the surface (1.8 submerged).

Two years later, the *Goubet II* was launched. It was larger, at 26 feet long, but it still held only a crew of two. The second version, like the first, ran on an electric motor, in this case a 4-horsepower Siemens electric road car engine. It had a range of 20 nautical miles when running at full speed (6 knots on the surface).

Jules Verne's Version

One of the most famous submarines of the nineteenth century was fictional. It was the *Nautilus*, invented by science-fiction writer Jules Verne. The make-believe submarine appeared in several of his works.

Jules Verne's *Nautilus* was 229$\frac{1}{2}$ feet long and 26 feet wide. Its hull was cigar-shaped, cylindrical with tapered ends. The propeller had four blades, was 20 feet in diameter, and had a pitch of 24$\frac{1}{2}$ feet. While running on the surface, only 10 percent of the sub was visible.

The platform had inclined sides. The wheelhouse had a 20 square foot interior and four windows, and was forward. To withstand the pressure of the depths, the windows were a foot thick. But they went all the way around so that the captain had a 360-degree view. Also forward was a 24$\frac{1}{2}$-foot air reservoir.

At the aft of the sub was a spotlight. The hull was built with overlapping metallic plates so that its surface resembled the scales on a fish. The captain's cabin was 16.3 feet long. The first mate's cabin was only 8.2 feet long.

Just because the captain and crew are living underwater does not mean that the finer things of life must be ignored in Verne's fantasy world. There was a room in the center of the sub that was a luxurious 32.7 feet long, 19.6 feet wide, and 16.3 feet high. It served as a combination drawing room, salon, and museum. This is where Captain Nemo played the pipe organ. The museum consisted of a priceless art collection and a voluminous collection of marine specimens. Down the hall was a library with 12,000 volumes.

Speaking of unnecessary things, Verne's sub had a decorative fountain made out of a big shell. You don't find too many of those on real subs. The captain also had a 16.3 foot-long dining room that was "exquisitely furnished."

At the center of the sub was the staircase that led to the platform. Also in the middle somewhere was the airlock, which allowed divers to exit and re-enter the sub. Moving toward the front of the sub was a 6.5-foot cabin, a 9.9-foot galley, a couple of storerooms, a 16.3-foot berth room (where the crew slept), and the engineroom, which was the largest space on the sub, a full 60.6 feet long. The engineroom was divided into two sections, one to generate electricity and the other to operate the sub's machinery.

The Least You Need to Know

◆ English astronomer Edmund Halley was the first to build an underwater container in which work could be done.

◆ The first submarine to attack another vessel in warfare was the *Turtle*, which was built by David Bushnell in 1775.

◆ The first submarine to ever sink an enemy vessel was the CSS *H. L. Hunley*—but the *Hunley* killed many more of its own crew than it ever killed of the enemy.

◆ The snorkel sub *David* was developed and built as part of an effort to break through the Union blockades at Charleston Harbor.

◆ One of the most famous submarines of the nineteenth century was fictional. It was the *Nautilus*, invented by science-fiction writer Jules Verne.

Early Twentieth-Century Submarines

In This Chapter

- ◆ From fiction to fact
- ◆ Early British subs
- ◆ World War I scorecard
- ◆ Defending against the U-boat

The man who took Jules Verne's ideas from the realm of science fiction into the real world was Simon Lake. According to Lake's biographer, Herbert Corey, "Perhaps no man in the past century has had as much to do with the shape of history as Simon Lake. That statement is intended as a query rather than as a statement of fact. It may be debatable, but it is also defendable."

Simon Lake's Theory of Negative Buoyancy

Lake was educated in the High School of Toms River, New Jersey; the Clinton Liberal Institute, in Fort Plain, New York; and the Mechanical

Beneath the Surface

In 1918, Simon Lake published a book entitled *The Submarine in War and Peace*.

Secrets of the Deep

The *Argonaut* specifications:

- Launched: 1897 (rebuilt 1899)
- Crew: Five
- Displacement: 60 tons when submerged
- Length: 36 feet
- Beam: 9 feet
- Armament: None
- Engine: Gasoline
- Range: Unknown
- Top speed surface: 5 knots
- Top speed submerged: 5 knots
- Longest trip: 1,725 nautical miles

Course at Franklin Institute, Philadelphia. He entered his father's foundry and machine shop in New Jersey in 1883 and later became his partner.

Lake invented a steering gear, a dredge, and other vessel appliances many of which were built and were chiefly used by fishing and oyster vessels in the Chesapeake and Delaware bays.

Inspired by the works of Verne, Lake designed and submitted submarine plans to the Navy in 1892. Lake built his first experimental submarine in 1894, called *The Argonaut, Jr.*

The sub was successfully demonstrated at Atlantic Highlands, New Jersey. In 1895, Lake formed the Lake Submarine Company of New Jersey. The company built the *Argonaut*, and the craft functioned so well that Lake received a letter of congratulations from Verne himself.

The company went on to build numerous submarines for the United States and foreign countries. Lake served as president and general manager until 1916, and then he acted as vice president and consulting engineer. Among the innovations credited to Lake are even-keel hydroplanes, ballast tanks, divers' compartment, periscope, and twin-hull design.

Lake was awarded more than 200 patents in his life and today is one of the men considered The Father of the Modern Submarine.

Steam on the Surface, Electricity Below

The French submarine *Espadon* (Swordfish), launched in September 1901, was another one of the first French subs. Despite the fact that it was only 106 feet long, it held a crew of 30. It was armed with four 450mm torpedoes, traveled 9.75 knots on the surface and 8 knots when submerged, and displaced 157 tons on the surface and 213 tons when submerged. This was an experimental sub and actually ran under a number of configurations during its 18-year life.

The most interesting thing about the sub was that it ran, at least on the surface, on steam power. When on the surface, it ran on a single-screw triple-expansion steam engine. When the sub dove, it switched its power source to an electric motor.

Earlier in the year, the French had built the submarine *Farfadet*, which was built for a little over the equivalent of $50,000 and ran on single-screw electric motors both on the surface and submerged. *Farfadet* came to a bad end when she dove before anyone remembered to close the conning tower hatch. She sank on July 6, 1905, killing 11 of her 25 crew in the process. Four years later, the submarine had a second life when she was raised and recommissioned as the *Follet*, which served until 1913.

The ABCs of British Subs

The first submarines designed in England were the A1 and A-class subs, which launched on July 1902. The first British subs, launched the previous year, had been designed by Holland. The ships, which held a crew of 11, were closely based on Holland's design as well.

Secrets of the Deep

A1 specifications:
- Launch: July 1902
- Crew: 11
- Length: 100 feet
- Width: 10 feet, 2 inches
- Top speed surface: 9.5 knots
- Top speed submerged: 6 knots
- Power: 160-horsepower gasoline engine, and one 126-horsepower electric motor
- Range: 320 nautical miles
- Armament: Two 18-inch torpedo tubes
- Constructed by: Vickers
- Displacement surface: 191 tons
- Displacement submerged: 270 tons

The *A1* had an improved conning tower from the Holland-designed ships. For the first time, British subs could run on the surface even when the seas were choppy. Thirteen A-series subs were built. The last few served in World War I. *A7* and her crew were lost when she dove and struck bottom near Whitesand Bay.

B-Class Subs

Great Britain's A-class subs were followed by, of course, B-class submarines. The B1 sub was launched in October 1904 and held a crew of 16. Some of the A-class subs still had not yet been constructed when the B-class program was begun.

Secrets of the Deep

B1 specifications:

- ◆ Launch: October 1904
- ◆ Crew: 16
- ◆ Length: 135 feet
- ◆ Width: 13 feet, 6 inches
- ◆ Height: 9 feet, 10 inches
- ◆ Top speed surface: 13 knots
- ◆ Top speed submerged: 7 knots
- ◆ Power: One electric motor, one single-screw gasoline engine
- ◆ Range: 1,500 nautical miles
- ◆ Armament: Two 18-inch torpedo tubes
- ◆ Displacement surface: 280 tons
- ◆ Displacement submerged: 314 tons

They handled better when submerged than the A-class subs had, and the surface performance was improved because of a higher superstructure atop the hull. Still, the subs did not present a pleasant—or a particularly safe—work environment.

The ships stunk of gasoline and oil. Because there were so many petroleum fumes in the air, each spark meant that there was a chance of explosion. And there were lots of sparks because of the 1904-quality electrical wiring. Other countries, including France, had been experimenting with steam and electricity as alternatives to the dangerous gas engine. In Italy, an internal blaze in a sub that ran on gas led to a ban on gas engines on subs from 1908 on.

Beneath the Surface

The first Victory Cross for the Royal navy during World War I was presented to the commander of a B-class sub.

Baby, Let Me Take You on a C-Class

While the B-class subs made men mad, there was a marked improvement in the C-class subs, which made their debut in 1906. Four years later, in 1910, there were 37

C-class subs in service. These could travel 12 knots on the surface and 7½ knots when submerged.

Submarines traveled to Asia for the first time in 1910, when three C-class subs were towed to Hong Kong by a sloop so they could join the China Squadron. Four C-class sub were sent into World War I but were scuttled in the Baltic Sea so that they would not fall into enemy hands.

D-Class

D-class subs debuted in 1908. They were bigger (163 feet by 20½ feet by 10.4 feet) and stronger, and, unlike their predecessors, they could send and receive wireless messages. During World War I, eight D-class subs offered protection to vessels ferrying troops from England to France across the English Channel.

The new subs were not only larger on the outside—they were larger on the inside as well. There was room for a crew of 25. The D-class subs displaced 483 tons on the surface and 595 tons when submerged.

E-Class: British War-Time Sub

The E-class submarines, 55 of which were built between 1913 and 1916, were the state-of-the-art British submarines during World War I. These subs were mass-produced because of war needs. At one time, 13 shipyards were building E-class subs simultaneously.

The most famous E-class sub was *E11*, which sank the enemy Turkish battleship *Hairredin Barbarossa* in the Dardanelles area. Of the 55 E-class subs that were built, 22 were lost during the war.

Naturally, the E-class subs were better prepared to make war than their ancestors in the British alphabet soup. These subs contained five 18-inch torpedo tubes and one 12-pounder gun. The subs were now large enough for a crew of 30. They displaced 667 tons when on the surface and 807 tons when submerged.

E-class subs were 181 feet long; 22 feet, 8 inches wide; and 12 feet, 6 inches high. The power plant consisted of two twin-shaft diesel engines and two electric motors. Top speed on the surface was 14 knots; submerged, it was 9 knots. The subs also had superior range and could travel far from base in pursuit of the enemy.

> **Beneath the Surface**
>
> A milestone of sorts took place on November 5, 1915. That was the day when one submarine first sank another submarine. The *E20*, which was hunting German U-boats in the Sea of Marmar, was sunk by the German sub *UB14*.

The F-Class Gets an F in Class

The F-class subs were built in 1912. They were 142 feet long and held a crew of 35. The tragic *F4* sub, however, was lost on March 25, 1915, during a short trial run off Honolulu. She had broken apart at a depth of 300 feet, a depth that had previously caused this class no problems. Because of the loss, the other F-class subs were withdrawn from service and re-engineered.

The *F4* was a record-setter even after she was lost. Five months after she sank, she was found and pulled to the surface. A deep-sea diving record was set in the process.

Although the British submarines did improve during the course of World War I, they did not do so as rapidly as might have been possible if, as they say, the left hand had known what the right hand was doing.

The men who were learning about submarine combat on the fly were the first experts in submarine combat. And they were the ones who should have been making recommendations about the changes for future generations of British subs. But the men who were designing the new subs often made their decisions without any practical knowledge of what it was like to fight in a war while submerged beneath the sea.

The Great War

World War I began in late June 1914. The principal navies involved at first were Great Britain and Germany, both of which had strong navies that featured submarines. When the war started, Germany lined up its navy and prepared for all-out war.

A row of destroyers (surface ships) were on the surface, while behind, forming a second line just behind the first, were German submarines. These were known as U-boats. But the British did not take the bait and did not send its entire navy for a showdown.

Britain refused to allow the Germans to determine how the war was fought. And so the submarine war started more slowly. Here are a few of the major incidents in the early days of the Great War featuring submarines:

- **September 5, 1914:** The *U-21* (the twenty-first U-boat built) sank the British cruiser *Pathfinder* with one torpedo. The *Pathfinder* went under three minutes after it was hit.

- **September 12, 1914:** The British sub *E.9* (the ninth E-class sub built) sank the German light cruiser *Hela* with two torpedoes.

- **September 22, 1914:** The *U-9* sank three British cruisers in under 90 minutes. The ships sunk were named *Aboukir, Hogue,* and *Cressy.*

- **October 17, 1914:** In the first sinking of one sub by another in this war, the *U-27* sank the *E.3*.

So Much for Experts

Again, as hostilities started, both England and Germany thought of their military submarines only in terms of attacking military targets on the enemy's side. And they didn't give the sub much credit, either.

The sub had never been an efficiently effective tool in warfare, and many thought it never would. But, as it turned out, the German U-boats were a major factor in the upcoming war and were used to its best advantage against civilian ships. Near the end of the first year of the war, Germany decided to shift the focus of U-boat attacks from British warships to British merchant ships. Germany would wage submarine warfare against Britain's ability to do business.

Here's the scoreboard for the first year of the war when it comes to submarine fighting:

- Germany sank seven warships and 10 merchant ships. Britain lost four submarines.

- The British sank two warships. Germany lost five U-boats.

U Stands for *Unterseebooten*

The *U-1* was built in 1906. By the end of World War I, the *U-166* had been completed. The first had twin kerosene engines producing 400 horsepower. The electric motors used when submerged produced equal power. The sub was 139 feet long and carried a crew of 22. This boat was used mostly for training.

By the end of the war, the new U-boats being produced carried a crew of 39 and were 235 feet long. They traveled very fast on the surface of the water (16.2 knots), and they were known to attack on the surface. The firepower of the U-boats grew steadily from the start to the finish of the war.

Numbers *U-81* through *U-92* and above were capable of carrying 10 torpedoes on a cruise of more than 7,500 miles. Those numbered 93 and above were larger and had 16 torpedo tubes, but a range of only 3,800 miles.

May 1915: Sinking of the *Lusitania*

The most famous ship to be sunk by a submarine was the RMS *Lusitania*, which was a luxury liner known for its speed. It could get across the Atlantic Ocean faster than any other ship. The *Lusitania* was 785 feet long and displaced 40,000 tons.

The *Lusitania*—and her nearly identical ship the *Mauretania*—were driven by huge marine steam turbines and driven by four props. That power enabled the *Lusitania* to travel faster than 25 knots. The ship was large enough to hold 2,000 passengers and 850 crew.

The *Lusitania*, the oldest of the twins, was launched on June 6, 1906, and christened before 20,000 spectators. At first her hull vibrated violently when she went at top speed. Correcting the problem took more than a month and necessitated the removal of more than 140 second-class cabins.

On September 7, 1907, the *Lusitania* set out on its maiden voyage across the Atlantic. Unlike the *Titanic*, which sank on its maiden voyage, the *Lusitania* completed 201 successful crossings of the Atlantic before disaster struck.

Her final journey began in the rain from New York Harbor on Saturday, May 1, 1915. With World War I in progress, there was concern even before the trip began about German submarines in the Atlantic. But the British felt that the *Lusitania* was too fast to be successfully attacked.

The *Lusitania* was not as fast as it had once been, however. Because of the war, there were not enough sailors to supply the ship with a full crew, so only 19 of the 25 boilers could be fired up. This slowed the craft and added hours to the trip.

Rendezvous with a U-Boat

As the ship left New York City, on board were 1,959 people, 159 of them American citizens and 123 children. The orchestra played "Tipperary" followed by "The Star Spangled Banner." As this was happening, the German U-boat *U-20* was on its way out of the port of Emden, looking to disrupt British shipping out of the port cities of Liverpool and Bristol.

On May 4, the *Lusitania* was already halfway across the Atlantic. The German U-boat *U-20* was off the Irish coast. The sub was busy even before the *Lusitania* came on the scene. On May 5, the sub fired upon and sank a schooner. That night it fired upon but missed a Norwegian cargo boat. Following the attacks, the sub was running low on diesel fuel. It had only three torpedoes left.

The German submarine did further damage the next day. On May 6, it sank two more British ships, the *Candidate* and the *Centurion*, each with one shot. In the early morning hours of May 7, the sub was sitting in wait off the coast of Ireland. Commander Turner of the *Lusitania* was warned by the British Admiralty that U-boats were in action along the Irish coast.

One Torpedo Left

Thirty miles off shore now, the *Lusitania* encountered thick fog and was forced to slow down. By sunrise, the commander had slowed the ocean liner to 15 knots. Once more he was warned by the British Admiralty that there was U-boat activity in the area.

At quarter to two that afternoon the lookout on the *Lusitania* reported seeing a periscope. But after further observation, it was decided that the lookout was mistaken. The captain of *U-20* watched the approaching ship and, realizing that it was the *Lusitania*, could not believe his good fortune. At 2:12 P.M., the U-boat fired her one remaining torpedo. The lookout on the *Lusitania* immediately spotted the trail of bubbles in the water being left by the torpedo and sounded the alarm.

A Violent Explosion

But there was no time for the slowed *Lusitania* to take evasive action. The torpedo struck its hull broadside, and the explosion shook the ship violently. The captain, reacting to the alarm when the explosion occurred, now tried to save the ship by grounding it on the beach.

Communications on the ship were disrupted. The intercom was not working. Confusion reigned. A distress call was sent out stating that the *Lusitania* was listing. There was an attempt to place people in lifeboats and lower them into the water, but the ocean liner was still traveling at 18 knots, even with a hole in its hull, and the lifeboats either broke up as they hit the water, broke against the side of the ship because of the listing, or were sucked into the props. However it was happening, everyone who tried to go over the side in a lifeboat ended up in Davy Jones's locker. The lifeboat idea was quickly abandoned.

Distress signals continued to go out. When the main generator on the ship went out, the signals continued to be broadcast using emergency battery power. Ships nearby changed course and began to head for the stricken liner.

Only a few minutes had passed since the explosion, but Commander Turner found that he was having trouble controlling the ship. He managed to get it pointed toward the shore, however. Then the *Lusitania* rolled onto her side, causing a panic. Some passengers jumped into the water.

Beneath the Surface

Commander Turner survived the sinking of his ship, the *Lusitania*, by submarine attack. He was given another command, the *Invernia*. One year later, it, too, was sunk by torpedo. Turner once again survived, but 50 of his crew did not.

Many of these details are known to us today because they were observed through the periscope of the very sub that had sunk the *Lusitania*. The submariners watched until the ship rolled over and then turned around and escaped. Within a half-hour of the attack, the *Lusitania* had slipped under the sea. Many who jumped into the sea were rescued, including Commander Turner, but the death toll was a horrible 1,198. That included 785 passengers, mostly Americans.

Within two years, the United States joined Great Britain in fighting the Germans, and her boys didn't come back until it was over.

How German U-boats Drew the United States into the War

By 1915, the United States could tell that the remainder of this war, as well as future wars, would feature submarines as a key factor. That year U.S. Secretary of the Navy Josephus Daniels wrote: "One of the imperative needs of the Navy, in my judgment, is machinery and facilities for utilizing the natural inventive genius of Americans to meet the new conditions of warfare. We are confronted with a new and terrible engine of warfare in the submarine."

In 1916, the U-boats were doing more damage than ever to British merchant shipping, and they were an increasingly bothersome (and deadly) presence to U.S. shipping as well. That year, U-boats sank an average of 80,000 tons of British shipping per month.

In April 1916, the United States officially informed Germany that it was fed up with the U-boat attacks:

> Unless the Imperial Government should now immediately declare and effect an abandonment of its present methods of submarine warfare against passenger and freight-carrying vessels, the Government of the United States can have no choice but to sever diplomatic relations with the German Empire altogether.

Three months later, however, a German statement made it clear that the Germans felt justified in using the U-boat in any way they chose:

> If we are finally to be bled to death, we must make full use of the U-boat as a means of war, so as to grip England's vital nerve. A victorious end to the war within a reasonable time can only be achieved through the defeat of British economic life—that is, by using the U-boats against British trade.

Late that summer, German U-boats further irritated the United States by sending the *U-53* to a spot off Newport, Rhode Island, just in international waters, where it surfaced and allowed itself to be seen. It then headed back to Germany, sinking five merchant ships—one Dutch, one Norwegian, and three British—on the way.

> **Beneath the Surface**
>
> By 1917, German U-boats were sinking 300,000 tons of British shipping a month. That was the peak, however. Merchant ships began to organize themselves into armed convoys.

In March 1917, three U.S. merchant ships were sunk by U-boats. By the end of 1917, we were over there, and we weren't coming back until the war ended.

Development of the Depth Charge

Surface ships could be easily frustrated by submarines during World War I. The submarine could sit directly below a surface ship, and the surface ship couldn't do anything about it. The ship had no way to attack downward. And so the depth charge was developed.

The depth charge was a bomb that could be dropped off the side of a ship. It sank toward the bottom, exploding only when it reached a predetermined depth. The charge could be set to go off when it reached the depth of the target. The first U-boat to be sunk by a depth charge was the *U-68* on March 22, 1916.

The depth charge continued to be used as an antisubmarine weapon through World War II, but it was never a very efficient one. As it turned out, it was not as easy to drop a bomb on a submarine as it might have seemed, and correctly determining the depth of the target was less than an exact science in those days.

Tests later found that a depth charge had to explode very close to a submarine to be effective. If it went off within 14 feet of the sub, it probably was a kill. If it exploded between 14 and 28 feet, it might disable a sub. But if the depth charge exploded 60 feet from the sub, the submarine might be undamaged—although more than one crewmember would need to change his underwear.

> **Beneath the Surface**
>
> The Germans referred to depth charges as water bombs.

The War Comes to Us

Many today think that World War I was a war fought far, far from the United States. It was fought, after all, "Over There," as the song says. But as we have already seen, the war came very close to North America during the years up to 1917. In 1918, the submarine war came right into U.S. waters and did damage.

The culprit was the *U-151*, which sailed 11,000 miles to the Chesapeake and Delaware bays. While there, the U-boat laid mines, telegraph wires, and sank ships—27 ships, in fact, counting those that were sunk by the mines that the *U-151* laid. Six of the later U-boats, known as U-cruisers, worked off the U.S. coast during the war. Although, with the exception of the *U-151*, they didn't cause much fuss, they did prove that it was possible for a submarine to function on a mission for a lengthy period of time while many thousands of miles from home.

> **Secrets of the Deep**
>
> Many submarines have what are called signal ejectors, which are small torpedo tubes for launching flares, decoy torpedoes, or other diversionary items.

By the summer of 1918, the war was all but over, but the U-boat captains never let up. The armistice was finally signed on November 11, 1918. Two days earlier, a German sub sank the British battleship *Britannia*.

The Least You Need to Know

- Simon Lake was the father of the submarine, doing in reality what Jules Verne had done in fiction. Lake's sub was called the *Argonaut*.

- The first British submarines were in classes lettered A through F, each a bit more sophisticated than the one before. These were the subs used by the British during World War I.

- The submarine used by the Germans during World War I was known as the U-boat. It became a major factor in the war when it declared all-out war on British (and sometimes American) merchant shipping.

- U-boats sank ships in the Chesapeake and Delaware bays during World War I.

Chapter 23

Between the Wars

In This Chapter

- ◆ Becoming effective in war
- ◆ Building the *Surcouf*
- ◆ Losing the "submersible battleship"
- ◆ The *Squalus* disaster

Wartime brings about technological advances. It's a corollary of "Necessity is the mother of invention." Like other technologies, submarine technology continued to advance between the world wars, so the subs that began World War II were far more advanced than those that finished World War I. Here is a quick look at some of those advancements.

The United States Launches the S-boats, 1918

Although all of the major manufacturers of submarines based their products on the designs of the "fathers" of subs, Simon Lake and John Holland, by the end of World War I the U.S. subs were far behind those of the Europeans. And America was determined to catch up.

The results of that determination were the S-boats. The new subs were larger and more durable. They had increased range and, because they could carry and fire more torpedoes, they were far more dangerous to the enemy. Two designs were used for the building of the S-boats, one by Lake and one by Holland. The Holland design was determined to be superior, and only one sub (S-2) was built to the Lake design.

Secrets of the Deep

The S-boats were built at several locations: Bethlehem Steel at Quincy and San Francisco, the Portsmouth Navy Yard and Bridgeport, Connecticut.

The new subs could travel between $14\frac{1}{2}$ and 15 knots, although their performance was always treated as a disappointment by the Navy. Fifty-one of them were built in all between 1918 and 1924. They could dive to 200 feet and had a range of 5,000 miles.

The S-boats were the best subs the United States had between the wars, but there were frequent troubles:

◆ Four sank due to internal systems problems.

◆ Two were rammed and sank.

In December 1927, a Coast Guard cutter off the coast of Massachusetts accidentally rammed the *S-4*. Forty sailors died, and the tragedy led to safety improvements. (See the following section "The Momsen Lung.") Six S-boats were still in use at the beginning of World War II. All six either were under repair or were being used for training when Pearl Harbor was attacked.

Sonar

One of the developments in sub technology was an increased usefulness of active *sonar*. (Although, as I've previously pointed out, the effectiveness of sonar is usually exaggerated in fiction.) Here's how active sonar works:

The active sonar hydrophone transmits a sound when an electrical impulse is sent to a piezoelectric material that vibrates when subjected to a time-varying electrical current. The hydrophone vibrations send a sound wave into the water, and the wave propagates outward in a spherical wave. When that sound strikes an object and bounces back (echoes), the sonar measures the time from transmission to reception, divides the time in half, and determines how far way the object is by multiplying the half-time interval by the speed of sound in water. Radar is similar to active sonar, except that it is used in the air.

Subtalk

Sonar stands for sound navigation and ranging—despite the fact that it does nothing for navigation. Apparently *sonar* has a better ring to it than *sor*.

Secrets of the Deep

The sound waves used in active sonar are in the range of human hearing. You can hear the ship's transmission of a sonar pulse and the incoming sonar of another sub—or, God forbid—torpedo. When the USS *Hammerhead* lingered at a Soviet anchorage off Tripoli, Libya, we hovered directly under the Soviet nuclear battleship *Kirov,* which continuously transmitted sonar in rising and falling sonar pulses. However, we were so close that the *Kirov*'s sonar computer rejected the return as being from the surrounding sea. The loud sonar transmissions went on for days on end and caused crew fatigue.

Sonar was invented by French physicist Paul Langevin (1872–1946) during World War I, allowing submerged submarines to be detected from above for the first time. In addition, Langevin worked with Pierre Curie and was noted for his work on the molecular structure of gases and for his theory of magnetism. Langevin was imprisoned by the Nazis after the occupation of France; he was later released and managed to escape to Switzerland. After the war, he returned to Paris.

The Momsen Lung

Following the tragic sinking of the *S-4* in December 1927, an effort was made to come up with a device that would enable submariners to breathe in cases of emergency. In 1929–32, Charles Bowers Momsen developed a submarine escape breathing apparatus that came to be known as the Momsen Lung.

Beneath the Surface

Charles Bowers Momsen was born in Flushing, Long Island, New York, on June 21, 1896. He attended the U.S. Naval Academy and graduated with the Class of 1920 in June 1919. After his initial service in battleships, he was trained as a submarine officer and commanded three submarines from 1923 to 1927. Following those commands, Momsen was assigned to the Bureau of Construction and Repair. He died on May 25, 1967, as a vice admiral.

The Momsen Lung, which hung around the neck and was strapped around the waist, is an oblong rubber bag that recycles exhaled air. The device held a canister of soda lime that removed poisonous carbon dioxide from exhaled air. It then replenished the air with oxygen. Two tubes led from the bag to a mouthpiece: one to inhale oxygen and the other to exhale carbon dioxide.

Besides helping the submariner breathe, the device allowed a slow rise to the surface, thus avoiding "the bends."

603,000 Tons and What Do You Get?

As we've seen, the submarine had already proven itself as an effective weapon of war during World War I. Fewer than 50 German U-boats sank an incredible 603,000 tons of allied merchant shipping in February 1917 alone.

The staggering toll of destruction caused many Allied admirals to reconsider the view of the submarine. Almost all the top navy officials in the Allied camp started the war with the opinion that the battle fleet, with its dreadnoughts and cruisers, was the ruler of the sea. They viewed the submarine as little more than a useful reconnaissance tool for the fleet.

Beneath the Surface

In 1927, the United States launched the only submarine it had ever designed specifically to lay mines. It was called the *Argonaut* and displaced 4,145 tons when submerged. The sub was still around at the beginning of World War II. It was stationed off Midway during the Pearl Harbor attack in 1941. The *Argonaut* saw action in August 1942 when it dropped off and picked up the Second Raider Battalion after it had attacked enemy installations in the Gilbert Islands. On January 10, 1943, the *Argonaut*, with a crew of 89, failed to return from an operation off Lae in the Pacific.

Much of this view was caused by the limitations of these early submarines. At the start of World War I, submarines had short range and slow speed, and carried a small number of torpedoes.

Secrets of the Deep

After the staggering losses of early 1917, the Allies instituted the convoy system to reduce their merchant shipping losses. They dedicated destroyers and aircraft to seeking out and hunting down the German U-boats. These measures barely managed to stop the submarines.

A Force to Be Reckoned With

However, rapid advances in submarine design, coupled with the performance of the German submarines in their unrestricted submarine warfare campaign, convinced the naval hierarchy of the Allied nations that the submarine was a formidable offensive force.

After the war, the Treaty of Versailles specifically forbade the Germans from building submarines. At the Washington Naval Conference in 1922, Great

Britain attempted to have submarines banned totally as weapons of war. However, the measure did not pass. Many nations saw the submarine as an equalizer in naval power. While nations such as France, Italy, or Japan could never build fleets as large as Great Britain or America, they could build submarines, which were an inexpensive way to attack either the enemy battle fleet or merchant shipping.

French Take Lessons to Heart

Between the wars, the French, in particular, took the lessons of the U-boat to heart. Although they had a sizeable navy, it was inferior to the British and Americans. The French realized that if they came into conflict with either nation, they would have to find a way to disperse their opposition's numerical advantage.

The French navy had long advocated the theory of *Guerre de Course*, or commerce raiding, as a means of equalizing the naval balance. A few well-armed cruisers set loose on the oceans of the world could terrorize merchant shipping in the four corners of the globe.

The enemy would have to send squadrons of war ships to chase down the raiders, thus depleting its strength and allowing the French navy to gain local superiority whenever and wherever it chose.

However, building cruisers was expensive, and their number was limited by the Washington Naval Conference. If the French used their cruisers as commerce raiders, they would have too few to use with their main battle fleet.

If the French kept all their cruisers with the battle fleet, there would not be any ships for commerce raiding. The problem seemed unsolvable until advancements in submarine design allowed the construction of bigger and longer range submarines.

A New Class of Ship

Naval architects were capable of building submarines of 2,000 tons or greater by the mid-1920s. The French navy studied the new capabilities and realized that if it could combine the best qualities of the submarine and the commerce raider, it could create an entirely new class of ship.

The new class, which the French christened the Cruiser Submarine, mated the large-caliber guns of a cruiser to a submarine hull. The effect was to create a commerce raider that could destroy enemy ships with gunfire or torpedoes.

Once the enemy ship was destroyed, the cruiser submarine could disappear below the waves to reappear for another attack when the opportunity presented itself. Such a ship would drive the enemy's navy crazy. The enemy would be unable to locate the ship when it was submerged, and its powerful guns and torpedoes would make it a potent adversary when it chose to fight.

Cruiser Sub Specifications

The French government was impressed with the possibilities and asked the navy to draw up the specifications for the new ship. The proposal was finished in 1929 and represented both a substantial departure from submarine design and an impressive warship.

The new cruiser submarine was 393.7 feet long and 29.5 feet wide, and it drew 23 feet of water under the bow. Fully loaded, the ship displaced 2,880 tons. The ship was powered by diesel motors that provided 7,600 horsepower and gave it a top speed of 18 knots on the surface and 10 knots submerged. The ship was provisioned for a patrol of 10,000 miles.

The offensive punch was provided by two 8-inch guns mounted in a power-operated turret on the forward portion of the ship. The ship was also equipped with four 21-inch torpedo tubes in the bow and four twin-trainable torpedo tubes located on deck. Twenty-two torpedoes were carried on patrol. The ship also carried two 37mm anti-aircraft guns that could be used to combat merchant ships.

How to Aim the Guns

In order to use the 8-inch guns effectively, the cruiser submarine needed some way to determine the fall of the shells. On a normal cruiser or battleship, spotting was done by a gunnery officer sitting in a fire direction center located high on the ship's superstructure.

Subtalk

A Marcel Bensson MB 35 Passe Partout was a single-engine, single-seat spotter aircraft.

The low silhouette of the submarine made this solution impractical, and the submarine was provided with a *Marcel Bensson MB 35 Passe Partout*.

In order to store the aircraft when not in use, the aircraft could be disassembled and stored in a hangar located aft of the bridge.

A Varied Crew

The new submarine was operated by a crew of 207 officers and men, which included a variety of naval ratings not normally found on a submarine. Gunnery officers, pilots, and aircraft maintenance personnel were assigned to the crew.

The plans for the new ship were quickly approved even though they approached the limits of the Naval Treaty for the size of a submarine. The ship was allocated to the 1926 building program for funding, and the Cherbourg Navy Yard was commissioned to build the new ship.

> **Secrets of the Deep**
>
> In addition, space was provided on the French sub to hold 40 prisoners. Under international law, the crews of merchant ships were to be taken off before their ship was sunk, so space was provided to care for these men.

Two Years in the Building

The keel was laid in December 1927. Because of the ship's size and complexity, it took almost two years to complete. However, the naval engineers were able to overcome all of the countless problems associated with building such heavy armaments on a submarine and ensuring that it would work after being repeatedly submerged for several hours. The ship was christened the *Surcouf* and was officially launched on October 18, 1929.

During the next few months, the ship underwent extensive tests. The submarine was tested for handling and seagoing characteristics. Diving trials were conducted to determine the submarine's capabilities underwater.

The main battery was fired and the accuracy was tested. Torpedo attacks were undertaken, and the air crew practiced assembling and disassembling the Marcel Bensson MB 35 Passe Partout spotting aircraft.

> **Beneath the Surface**
>
> The first cruiser sub was called the *Surcouf*, after the famous French pirate Robert Surcouf.

Many Problems

As can be expected, the novel design and complicated features caused many problems. The 8-inch gun turret seals did not work well and had to be replaced. The weight of the gun turret also made the submarine difficult to trim when underwater.

All of these problems and many others were identified and fixed. However, the sea trials confirmed that the concept of the cruiser submarine was sound and that the *Surcouf* was ready for action.

The ship was officially commissioned into the French navy in 1933 and after its entry into the fleet, it visited many ports to show off its unique design and weaponry. It amazed all the civilian and military personnel who saw it.

Largest Sub in the World

The ship's size made it the largest submarine in the world at the time, and its huge guns left no doubt as to its purpose. Even as the ship made its ports of call, improvements were in the works.

A second spotting aircraft was delivered in 1935. The Marcel Bensson Company had gone bankrupt, and the firm of ANF-les Mureaux completed the second aircraft under the designation MB-411. Trials were conducted with the new aircraft, and the single-seat configuration was found wanting.

The pilot had enough problems just flying the aircraft without trying to adjust the fall of the *Surcouf*'s 8-inch shells. ANF-les Mureaux was quick to find the solution. The aircraft was reconfigured to a tandem-seat aircraft that could carry the pilot and a spotter. The arrangement worked very well, and the MB-411 was soon brought on board the submarine in place of the MB-35.

Surcouf in World War II

When World War II erupted, the *Surcouf* was ready to take to the high seas in search of ships. However, the war was against Germany, not England or the United States.

The Germans had only a small merchant marine, and their warships were effectively bottled up in their harbors by the British fleet. There was little for the submarine to do in the early part of the war, and it was sent on patrols in the Atlantic in the hope that it would catch one of the few remaining German merchant ships. However, the cruiser submarine did not account for any enemy ships.

When France was overrun in May 1940, the *Surcouf*, along with several other ships of the French navy, sailed from their ports to England to continue the fight. The crews did not know what fate awaited them in England, but they were certain that they did not want to let their ships fall into the hands of the hated Nazis. The ships and their crew were immediately interned when they sailed into Plymouth. Neither the crews nor the governments of France or England knew what to do with the ships.

Operation Catapult

While the politicians tried to decide the fate of the ships, the British navy launched Operation Catapult on July 3, 1940, fearing that the ships might be returned to Nazi control. The operation was designed to seize or sink any French ships that had escaped from metropolitan France. British warships in the Mediterranean attacked French ships in French colonies, while armed British boarding parties seized French ships in English ports.

When the British sailors approached the *Surcouf* and demanded its surrender, the French submariners refused and fought to protect their ship. One French sailor was shot and killed, and at least one British sailor was injured in the ensuing fight. However, defending the submarine in an unfriendly harbor was beyond the capacity of the crew, and they were soon overwhelmed and taken off the boat. The boat was taken over by the Free French and continued its service to the Allied cause.

In December 1941, the *Surcouf* was sent as part of a large Free French task force to occupy the French islands of St. Pierre and Miquedon off Newfoundland. The governor of the islands was loyal to Vichy France, and the Allies did not like having a potential enemy base so close to the Atlantic shipping routes. The attack was carried out without any problems, and the Free French naval forces took the islands without firing a shot.

Finding a New Role

After the attack, the Allies searched for a new mission for the *Surcouf*. There was some discussion in the British Admiralty about using the cruiser submarine as a convoy escort, but the idea was quickly abandoned.

While the *Surcouf* would have made an excellent escort, the fact that it was a submarine would have surely caused problems. Allied aircraft and escorts shot at submarines first and asked questions later.

It would have been difficult to tell the *Surcouf* from a German U-boat at a distance or in bad weather, and the naval authorities decided to send the boat to the Pacific instead. In the vast reaches of the Pacific, the submarine's powerful armament and long range would make it ideal for attacking Japanese merchant or warships as they moved among the islands of their far-flung empire.

Refitting

Before the submarine went to the Pacific, it had to be overhauled and refitted. The best place to accomplish this task was in the United States, and the Philadelphia Navy yard was selected for the refitting.

The Free French sailors were excited about their new mission and being given the opportunity to fight for France. However, before the submarine left England, three British officers came aboard and took command. Henceforth, the submarine fought as the HMS *Surcouf*.

The refit was completed in January 1942, and the original three British officers that brought the submarine to America were replaced with Lt. R. J. G. Burner, leading signalman Harold F. Warner, and telegraphist Bernard Gough. These three Englishmen plus the French crew took the *Surcouf* to the Pacific and battled the Japanese.

Canal Duty

The ship underwent sea trials and, after passing all the tests satisfactorily, set sail for the Panama Canal in February. The transit through the Atlantic and the Caribbean should not have been difficult, but the *Surcouf* never arrived at the Panama Canal.

The 6,762-ton American cargo ship SS *Thompson Lykes* reported a collision with an unknown ship during the evening of February 18, 1942. The collision occurred off Christobal near Panama. U.S. naval authorities noted that the area of the collision corresponded to the anticipated position of the *Surcouf* at the time.

Only one member of the American cargo ship reported seeing anything of the ship they collided with, and he reported seeing the bow of a submarine. It is quite likely that the SS *Thompson Lykes* rammed and sank the French cruiser submarine *Surcouf* on that February evening.

The loss of the *Surcouf* ended a unique chapter in naval history. The one-of-a-kind, "submersible battleship," as some called the *Surcouf*, met its end without ever sinking a ship or firing its guns at an enemy.

Rescue of the *Squalus*

The most daring and successful rescue mission involving a stricken submarine had to be the rescue of the USS *Squalus* (SS-192) in 1939. The *Squalus*'s problems started on May 23 when she suffered a catastrophic valve failure. The failure occurred during a test dive early in the morning near Portsmouth, New Hampshire, off the Isle of Shoals.

Because of the valve failure, the submarine partially flooded and came to rest with its keel on the bottom in approximately 240 feet of water. Thirty-two sailors and one civilian survived the flooding; they had crowded themselves into the forward section.

The rescue attempt began on May 24. The USS *Falcon,* parked above the *Squalus,* lowered a submersible called the McCann Rescue Chamber. The chamber was repeatedly lowered to the submarine, and crewmen were hauled upward one by one. All 33 survivors were rescued.

The Least You Need to Know

- ◆ Naval architects were capable of building submarines of 2,000 tons or greater by the mid-1920s.

- ◆ S-boats made up the U.S. fleet of subs between the world wars.

- ◆ The *Surcouf* was officially commissioned into the French navy in 1933 and was then the largest sub in the world.

- ◆ The most daring and successful rescue mission involving a stricken submarine was the rescue of the USS *Squalus* (SS-192) in 1939.

Chapter 24

Submarines of World War II

In This Chapter

- ◆ Biggest war ever
- ◆ U-boats in the Atlantic
- ◆ I-boats in the Pacific
- ◆ Three classes of U.S. subs

During the late 1930s and early 1940s, the world erupted into what was—and hopefully will remain—the largest and deadliest war in history. Germany, Italy, and Japan took on the rest of the world, and for a while they had us on the retreat.

But once the United States got into it at the end of 1941, following the attack on Pearl Harbor, the tide turned quickly and the evil threat was vanquished in four horrible years.

In this war, more than any other, the submarine played a large role. As they had done during World War I, German U-boats still patrolled the Atlantic. And now, Japanese subs were found in the Pacific.

Japanese Midget Subs at Pearl Harbor

Submarines were a part of the war in the Pacific, too, starting immediately with the Japanese attack on Pearl Harbor, the attack that brought the United States into the war. The Japanese used five midget submarines in the attack.

> ### Beneath the Surface
>
> Three of the midgets have been salvaged, two in the weeks following the Pearl Harbor attack and a third in 1960. Two of the subs are on exhibit in Fredericksburg, Texas, and a third is on display in Eta Jima, Japan. The other two midget subs are unaccounted for.

Those subs had been brought into the battle area by larger Japanese submarines and then put into the water near Pearl Harbor on the night before the attack. One of the midget submarines was spotted just before dawn and was fired upon by the USS *Ward*.

This is considered the first action of the Pearl Harbor attack and, therefore, of the Pacific War. Unfortunately, it was not seen as an indication of a larger attack to follow, and this harbinger of the U.S. Navy's worst day went unheeded.

> ### Beneath the Surface
>
> The occupant of the midget sub that drifted ashore in Hawaii three days after the Pearl Harbor attack became the first Japanese POW captured by the United States in World War II.

Later in the day, with the attack underway, one of the midget subs managed to make it into Pearl Harbor, and there it was fired upon and sunk by the USS *Monaghan*. Another midget missed the harbor and drifted onto the east coast of Oahu three days after the battle.

Midgets Deadly Down Under

The midget subs were not finished, either. On May 31, 1942, they showed up again, this time in Sydney Harbor, off the Australian coast. One of the midgets was caught in a net that had been stretched across the harbor. She blew herself up rather than be captured.

> ### Beneath the Surface
>
> The Japanese midget submarine that is on display in Sydney is actually a composite of the two midgets that made it into Sydney Harbor; only half of each survived.

One sub managed to get into the harbor and fired upon the cruiser USS *Chicago*. The torpedo missed its target but struck an Australian barracks ship, killing 21. The midget that did all the damage got away. A third midget sub made it into the harbor briefly but hit a depth charge and was destroyed.

U-boats in the Atlantic

As far as the big subs went, the biggest menace in the Atlantic remained the German U-boat, several generations superior to the ones that had attacked British merchant shipping during the last war. Those attacks had been lessened by using guarded convoys of ships. That method was not as effective in the early 1940s, however. Now there were many more U-boats than there had been, and they attacked the Allied convoys in packs. One convoy near Greenland in 1941, had 24 percent of its ships sunk by German submarines.

Secrets of the Deep

Specifications for *U-2511*: German sub:

- ◆ Launch: 1944
- ◆ Crew: 57
- ◆ Displacement surface: 1,621 tons
- ◆ Displacement submerged: 2,067 tons
- ◆ Length: 251 feet, 8 inches
- ◆ Width: 26 feet, 3 inches
- ◆ Height: 20 feet, 4 inches
- ◆ Armament: Six 21-inch torpedo tubes, four 30-mm antiaircraft guns
- ◆ Top speed surface: 15.5 knots
- ◆ Top speed submerged: 16 knots

As soon as the United States declared war on Germany, U-boats moved into the waters off the North American coast and began to sink every ship they could find. Here's the scorecard:

- ◆ **January 1942:** 23 ships sank
- ◆ **February 1942:** 31 ships sank
- ◆ **March 1942:** 48 ships sank

That was just the number of ships sank off the North American east coast. Around the world, 273 ships were sunk by submarines during March 1942.

Yank Subs Spread Thin

On the other hand, the United States had only 111 submarines in its entire fleet as the war began. Of course, that soon changed. But when the Japanese attacked Pearl Harbor, the U.S. Navy had 60 subs in the Atlantic and 51 in the Pacific—and those were split into two groups, one in Hawaii and the other in the Philippines.

Needless to say, not all of them were new. When the Japanese attacked the Philippines within hours of the Pearl Harbor attack, the United States had 28 subs in the waters off those islands. But the submarines were not used to good advantage. They attacked 45 off-shore Japanese ships and fired a total of 96 torpedoes. They sank a total of three Japanese ships. One U.S. sub was lost, scuttled after it was attacked by a Japanese plane, and the others retreated to Australia.

> **Secrets of the Deep**
>
> According to the U.S. Navy's Report of Gunnery Exercises for 1940–41, "It is bad practice ... to conduct an attack at periscope depth when aircraft are known to be in the vicinity."

> **Beneath the Surface**
>
> The U.S. subs did have their successes. In 1942, 180 Japanese ships were sunk by U.S. subs. Three quarters of a million tons of Japanese ship and supplies were sent to the bottom. The truth was, however, neither the German nor the Japanese military ever considered U.S. submarines a major threat. They were far more concerned with battleships and aircraft carriers.

If U.S. submarines were at a premium, so were combat-experienced submarine commanders. The truth was, the United States didn't have any. All of them were learning as they went, and some were learning more quickly than others. Many were careerists who had adjusted well to the bureaucracy of peace time but who knew nothing of combat leadership. Three out of 10 submarine commanders were relieved of their duties during the first year of America's participation in World War II.

Another problem that U.S. subs had during the first half of the war was there were never enough torpedoes. U.S. factories were producing only two torpedoes a day when the war started. It was still less than 10 per day by the end of 1942. Those torpedoes that were available might not work. Many torpedo attacks became disasters from malfunctioning torpedo detonators.

Planes Can't Stop Them

In the Atlantic, the Allies tried to combat the U-boat menace with aircraft that dropped bombs and torpedoes into the water—but this at first was not terribly effective. The bombs sometimes exploded when they hit the water. Even if they didn't, there was no way to predetermine in which direction they would go after they hit the water.

In two and a half years of trying this, only three U-boats were sunk. The Allies' ability to combat subs with planes steadily improved, however. Improvements in radar and the quality of depth charges helped.

The U-boats were impossible to attack when they were in port because the Germans had constructed "bomb-proof submarine shelters." The roofs on these shelters were made of 16-foot-thick concrete.

The U-boat threat on military and merchant shipping in the Atlantic was rendered nil for a time in 1941–42 when the Allies broke the Axis codes and could tell where the U-boats were by following their communications. The convoys simply were instructed to go where they ain't. After a time, however, the Germans came up with new codes, and the subs' locations were again a mystery.

Beneath the Surface
In a bizarre tale, in August 1941, a German U-boat was captured by British aircraft. The *U-570* surfaced and surrendered as RAF bombs fell into the waters around it. The submarine was hauled to England and converted into a British submarine. It spent the rest of the war as the *Graph*.

Sinking of the *Laconia*

A German submarine commander at the helm of the *U-156* unintentionally caused a big controversy when, on September 12, 1942, he ordered torpedoes to be fired at the armed troopship the *Laconia*. The attack was successful, and the *Laconia* went down.

Eight hundred Allied servicemen were on board. At first it appeared to be a major victory for the U-boat. Then someone heard cries for help in Italian. Oops! The ship had also contained 1,800 Italian prisoners of war, who were supposed to be on the Germans' side. And even worse from a public relations point of view, it was later learned that there had been 80 women and children aboard.

Beneath the Surface
The Germans put out a call to enemy ships and said that, if they wanted to join in the rescue effort, they would not fire upon them. But all Allied ships thought it was a trap and did not respond. In fact, while towing a string of lifeboats behind it, the *U-156* was attacked by a U.S. B-24 bomber.

Not everyone on the *Lanconia* died, fortunately. The *U-156* came to the rescue and managed to save 193 lives. Other Axis ships came as well.

"Is This a Self-Service Station?"

In order to run regular missions on both sides of the Atlantic, the Germans devised a method whereby they could lengthen the time a U-boat could be out without returning to a base. The Germans built refueling stations in the middle of the ocean, called *milchküe*.

Subtalk

Milchküe means "milk cow."

It turned out that these gas stations were not the greatest idea, however. They were very easy to spot, and Allied subs could wait until several ships were being refueled at once to maximize the effectiveness of an attack. Nine of the milk cows had been built and put in place in 1943, but by June of that year, all but two of them had been destroyed.

That doesn't mean it was all going the Allies' way, however. One hundred Allied ships were sunk by German U-boats during March 1943. But that was about the peak. The tide in the war was turning.

Allied air power was beginning to rule the war. By May 1943, the number of Allied ships that were being sunk by U-boats had been cut in half, while the number of U-boats destroyed leaped. A full quarter of all of Germany's U-boats had now been sunk, and that percentage was growing larger each month.

By the second half of 1943, U-boats had been recalled and were not a factor for the rest of the war. By D-Day, only 35 U-boats were available to take on the more than 1,500 ships of the Allied invasion at Normandy.

Secrets of the Deep

In May 1943, the Allies debuted a new antisubmarine weapon called the airborne homing torpedo—or, more commonly, "Wandering Annie" or "Fido." The weapon homed in on the sound of an enemy sub's propeller. This was an improvement over the first acoustic torpedo that had been invented earlier by Germany. These torpedoes, called T5, were designed to go after whatever was causing the loudest noise in its vicinity. The loudest noise, however, all too often turned out to be made by the U-boat that was firing the torpedo. Big mistake.

Subs Off the West Coast

In 1942, the Japanese began sending submarines into the waters off California. For a time, the subs stalked supply ships heading for Hawaii. Nine Japanese I-boats were sent the first time, but they managed no attacks on U.S. ships. However, they did manage to be spotted, so the United States knew they were there. The Japanese submarines' intrusion into U.S. waters had a psychological effect on the U.S. public, making the people of California feel vulnerable to Japanese attack.

A second and third try were more successful. Three cargo ships were sunk off the West Coast by I-boats in 1942. Causing the most fear, however, was the fact that the North American mainland was shelled on two occasions by Japanese submarines. One June 7, 1942, a radio station on the shore of Vancouver, Canada, was fired upon. Thirteen days later, a shell went off on the shore of Astoria, Oregon.

Although terrorism might have been the best results from I-boat activities off the American West Coast, those same Japanese subs were having a major impact on the Japanese invasion of the Dutch West Indies. Japanese subs sank 40 cargo ships while losing only two I-boats.

Secrets of the Deep

Specifications for *I-201*: Japanese sub:

- ◆ Launch: 1944
- ◆ Crew: 100
- ◆ Displacement surface: 1,291 tons
- ◆ Displacement submerged: 1,450 tons
- ◆ Length: 259 feet, 2 inches
- ◆ Width: 19 feet
- ◆ Height: 17 feet, 9 inches
- ◆ Armament: Four 21-inch torpedo tubes
- ◆ Top speed surface: 15.7 knots
- ◆ Top speed submerged: 19 knots

The Longest Torpedo

The record for the longest distance traveled by a torpedo fired from a submarine before striking a ship that it subsequently sank is 12 miles. The incident occurred on September 13, 1942, when Japanese sub *I-19* fired six torpedoes at the U.S. aircraft carrier *Wasp*. Three of the torpedoes struck the *Wasp* and sank her.

Of the three torpedoes that missed, two found a target. One struck the battleship *North Carolina* and caused enough damage to send that ship back home for repairs. The other traveled an amazing 12 miles and sank the destroyer *O'Brien!*

Pestering the Island Hoppers

As the war in the Pacific progressed and the Americans island-hopped their way across the Pacific toward Japan—taking back land held by the Japanese and building airports for bomber planes—many I-boats moved to the front lines. The I-boats were not nearly as effective against the U.S. Navy's invasion force as they had been against cargo ships.

The Japanese were the only force during World War II to have a submarine that came with an airplane perched on top of it. The plane, which could land in the water, was taken near a target atop the submarine—which, of course, had to travel on the surface. The sub could submerge only when the plane was in the air. These were boats in the I-400 class.

In June 1944, 21 Japanese submarines tried to help defeat the U.S. invasion of the island of Saipan. Fourteen of those 21 were sunk; the others fled, and no damage to Allied ships was incurred. Now the I-boats were taking it a lot more than dishing it out, and this was the way it remained as Japanese forces continued to retreat toward the mainland, increasingly desperate.

Gato, Balao, and Tench Classes

By 1943, the United States had three main classes of submarines involved in the war: the Gato, Balao, and Tench. Gato boats were very large. The first ones were too easily visible from great distances while running on the surface, so subsequent models had much smaller fairwaters.

The early Balaos had an operating depth that was deemed too shallow. That had been increased to 400 feet by 1943. The first Tench class subs did not have adequate range, so later models had what was once an external main ballast tank converted into a fuel storage tank.

Secrets of the Deep

Specifications for the *Drum*, a Gato class sub:

- Launch: May 12, 1941
- Crew: 80
- Displacement surface: 1,825 tons
- Displacement submerged: 2,410 tons
- Length: 311 feet, 9 inches
- Width: 27 feet, 3 inches
- Height: 15 feet, 3 inches
- Top speed surface: 20 knots
- Top speed submerged: 10 knots

One of the big improvements in U.S. subs during the war was the time it took them to dive: It took about 50 seconds for a U.S. sub to submerge when the war started, but that time was down to 40 seconds by 1944, and 30 seconds by 1945, at war's end. That 20-second difference is huge when people are shooting at you.

As the war began to go the Allies' way, the need for new subs decreased. By mid-1943, the United States was producing only seven new subs per month, and all production on subs stopped by the end of that year. The effort formerly put into building subs was shifted to building landing craft for sea-to-land invasions.

The United States may have had a total of 51 subs in the Pacific when the war began, but that number was up to 140 by mid-1944. Six hundred Japanese ships were sunk by U.S. submarines in 1944. By that same time, because of attrition, the Japanese had only 26 subs left.

Secrets of the Deep

Specifications for the *Diablo*, a Tench class sub:

- ◆ Launch: November 30, 1944
- ◆ Crew: 85
- ◆ Displacement on surface: 1,860 tons
- ◆ Displacement submerged: 2,420 tons
- ◆ Length: 307 feet
- ◆ Width: 27 feet, 3 inches
- ◆ Height: 15 feet, 3 inches
- ◆ Armament: Ten 21-inch torpedo tubes, two 150mm guns
- ◆ Range: 12,152 nautical miles at 10 knots
- ◆ Top speed surface: 20 knots
- ◆ Top speed submerged: 10 knots

Suicide Subs

New submarines being built in Japan were very different from those that had come before. As desperation grew, the Japanese High Command came up with the underwater equivalent of the kamikaze, the suicide pilot. Japan began to produce suicide subs, called *kaiten.*

The kaiten were actually torpedoes with a human pilot. A 24-inch Type 93 surface-ship torpedo called the Long Lance was adapted to make the minisub. The kaiten could travel up to 40 knots and had enough fuel to go for five hours.

Subtalk

Kaiten is Japanese for "revolution."

The suicide subs attacked for the first time in November 1944, launched by I-boats—but they were never as effective against the U.S. Navy as the kamikaze planes were. During that first attack, they sank some ships at anchor in Ulithi Atoll. In January 1945, 32 kaiten attacked and sank one tanker and one landing ship, and damaged two transport boats. Not only did the Japanese lose all 32 minisubs (of course), but two of the I-boats they had been launched from were sunk as well.

The kaiten made appearances at the battles of Iwo Jima and Okinawa at the end of the Pacific War, but again with minimal effect. We later learned that the Germans were designing their own suicide subs as well in 1945. They were never put into operation, but 286 were built. These were two-man, two-torpedo midgets that could dive to 165 feet and had a range of up to 60 miles.

The End of the War

U-boats continued to do damage to British shipping, their old forte, right up until Germany's surrender. A U-boat sank two small British steamers, while another sank a Norwegian minesweeper, both on May 7, 1945, the last sub action of the European war.

When the war in Europe ended, Germany's largest sub (the *U-234*) was on its way to Japan. It was intercepted in the middle of the Atlantic and surrendered. Found on board were examples of German technology that the Japanese would have found useful. There was a state-of-the-art electric torpedo, two disassembled but complete fighter planes, and, most troubling of all, 550 kilograms of uranium packed into lead boxes. Sounds like it was a very good thing that the war against Germany ended when it did.

The Least You Need to Know

- Submarines were more effective during the first half of the war, before Allied air power and radar turned the tide.

- Airplanes were not particularly effective against submarines at the beginning of the war, but techniques improved as hostilities continued.

- As was true in World War I, subs in this war were more effective against merchant shipping than against military targets.

- As the war neared an end, Germany planned and Japan used suicide submarines.

Glossary

1MC   Shipwide public address system.

2JV   Engineering spaces sound-powered phone circuit.

2MC   Public address system for the engineering spaces.

4MC   Emergency public address system. The submarine's 911 circuit.

7MC   Ship control intercom circuit.

8MC   Sonar/conn intercom.

ACR   AntiCircular Run. A torpedo interlock that prevents the weapon from acquiring on the firing ship ("own ship"). When the torpedo turns more than 160 degrees from the approach course to the target, the onboard gyro sends a signal to the central processor to shut down the unit. It then sinks.

active sonar   The determination of a contact's bearing and range by pinging a sound pulse into the ocean and listening for the reflection of the ping from the target. Generally not used by submarines, since it gives away the ship's position.

aft   The back of a sub; "aft of" means further back than.

anechoic coating   A thick foam coating attached to the outside of the hulls of some submarines. It absorbs incoming active sonar pulses without reflecting them back, while damping out internal noises before they can get outside the ship. Analogous to stealth radar absorptive material on a stealth aircraft.

angles and dangles   Test in which a submarine takes a rapid down angle and then a rapid up angle to see if everything aboard is stowed for sea.

ASH   Anti–Self-Homing. A torpedo interlock that measures the distance from the firing ship. If the torpedo comes back toward the firing ship at 80 percent of the return trip, the ASH interlock will shut down the unit. It will flood and sink.

baffles   A "cone of silence" astern of most submarines where sonar reception is hindered by engines, turbines, screws, and other mechanical equipment located in the aft end of the submarine.

ballast tank   Tank that is used solely to hold seawater ballast, weight that allows a ship to sink or, when blown, allows a ship to be light enough to surface.

ballistic   1. To travel by a path guided only by gravitation and velocity rather than propulsion. A ballistic missile is one that has an initial rocket guidance that, when the engine shuts down, simply "falls" the rest of the way to the target on a ballistic trajectory. 2. Condition of the ship's engineer when he sees how dirty the engineroom has become.

battleshort   A condition in which the nuclear reactor's safety interlocks are removed. Used only in a severe emergency or in battle, when an accidental reactor shutdown is more dangerous to the ship due to loss of propulsion than the potential risk of a reactor meltdown. Only the captain can order battleshort.

beam   Width of a ship at its widest point.

bearing   Direction to a contact, expressed in degrees of an angle. A contact to the north is at 000, to the east is at 090, and so on.

blow   Process of blowing high-pressure air into the main ballast tanks, forcing out the water.

Blue/Gold crew   A two-crew ship (such as a boomer) has one crew at sea operating the ship while the other crew is at home resting and training. During a refit or "upkeep," both crews work together. Then the off-going crew goes home and the oncoming crew takes the boat back to sea.

blue nose   Title given to those who have crossed the Arctic Circle.

Bomb   Nickname for the oxygen generator, since it makes oxygen from electrolysis of seawater, in which oxygen and hydrogen are in close proximity and can cause a "rapid unintentional energy release" (polite term for an explosion).

boomers   American slang for strategic missile submarines, a.k.a. FMBs (fleet ballistic-missile submarines) or SSBNs (submersible ship nuclear ballistic).

bottom bounce   Description of sonar waves that have been sent to the ocean bottom and have bounced back. A bottom bounce contact is one that is received by the ship's sonar gear after the incoming signal has arrived via bouncing on the sea floor.

breech door   A torpedo tube's inner door.

bridge   Small space at the top of the submarine's sail used for the officer of the deck to conn the submarine. The height allows the best view of the surroundings of the ship.

bridge access trunk   Tunnel from the interior of the submarine to the bridge.

broadband   Noise containing all frequencies and white noise, such as heard in radio static, rainfall, or a waterfall. Broadband detection range is high for surface ships, which are noisy, and low for submarines (less than 5 miles) due to the submarines' quiet designs.

bubblehead   Derogatory slang for a submariner, used by Airdales (aviators) and skimmer pukes (surface warfare sailors).

buoyancy   A force that acts in the opposite direction as gravity upon objects that are less dense than their surroundings. Buoyant forces are caused by unbalanced pressure effects on the surfaces of a submerged object, and the pressure forces are caused by gravity pulling down the liquid of submergence.

cavitation   Steam (water vapor) bubbles generated on the low-pressure side of a screw blade. At depth, the bubbles migrate into the wake and experience static pressure of the deep and collapse, emitting a screaming noise. This is a dead giveaway that a submarine is accelerating. Surface ships always cavitate, since the water pressure is insufficient to keep bubbles from forming on the low-pressure side of a prop blade.

chicken switches   Hydraulic control levers that, when operated, direct hydraulic oil to the hydraulically operated ball valves at the hull penetrations for a seawater-piping system.

clamshells   The steel or fiberglass hinged plates that cover the top of the bridge cockpit when rigged for dive and that are opened when rigged for surface. When they are shut, the top of the sail is completely smooth.

clear datum   Tactical euphemism meaning to run away.

C.O.   Commanding Officer. Official title of the captain of a Navy ship.

CommSat   Communications satellite in a geosynchronous orbit that sends and relays Navy radio traffic.

conn   1. The periscope stand in the control room where the officer of the deck controls the ship's motion. 2. The duty of controlling the ship's motion, as in, "The captain has the conn."

conning tower   No longer exists on modern nuclear subs. On diesel boats, the conning tower was a space inside the fin from which the periscope was manned, allowing a shorter periscope. Also the term for the fin itself, now called the sail.

contact   Another ship, detected by visual means, sonar, or radar. A contact may be hostile or friendly.

control room   1. A submarine's nerve center that includes the ship control consoles, firecontrol consoles, periscopes, and navigation equipment. Russians call this the command post. 2. Nickname for author Michael DiMercurio's office, in operations middle level of the house.

course   The direction that a ship is going measured in true compass degrees. North is 000, east is 090, and so on.

critical   The point at which a nuclear reactor's fission rate is constant without an external source of neutrons. The chain reaction keeps fissions continuing using only neutrons from fissions.

delayed neutrons   Fission neutrons that, while born as fast neutrons with high kinetic energy and a low probability of causing another fission, are slowed by the moderator to become thermal neutrons. They are called "thermal" because they have only the kinetic energy that they would have based solely on their temperature. Thermal neutrons have a high probability of causing a new fission. If you want to have continuing fission reactions, you need to slow the fast neutrons with a moderator so that the thermal neutrons can cause the next fission. In low-leakage cores, the reactor becomes closer to being critical on prompt neutrons. A nuclear bomb is essentially a low-leakage core that goes critical on prompt neutrons.

Delta   Name of a class of Russian boomers. Also means "difference," as in "delta bearing rate" signifying the change in bearing rate over two legs.

depth charge   A gift dropped from a surface ship that detonates at a particular depth. Cheating skimmers may put rocket engines on depth charges and shoot them at you from a distance.

depth control   Ability to control a ship's depth within a narrow control band. Done either manually, with a computer, or with the hovering system (when stopped). Particularly vital at periscope depth because failure to maintain depth control may cause the sail to become exposed (broached), giving away the ship's position, or keeps the periscope wet, risking collision with a surface ship.

Dialex   Electrically powered phone circuit between officers' staterooms, control, maneuvering, the torpedo room, the engineering spaces, and the auxiliary spaces. Used for unofficial communications.

direct path   A sound wave being received by sonar that does not arrive by bottom bounce, surface bounce, or layer bounce, but by an almost straight line from the contact.

dogs   One answer to "What animals go to sea with submarines?" Banana-shape pieces of metal that act as clasps to keep a hatch shut.

dolphins   Second answer to "What animals go to sea with submarines?" Pin worn above the left pocket of qualified submariners' uniforms. Qualification typically takes a grueling year. Enlisted men wear silver dolphins, and officers wear gold. Also a general logo for the Submarine Force.

Doppler effect   Effect responsible for train whistles sounding shrill when approaching and low pitched when receding. When a moving platform emits sound waves, the waves are compressed in the direction of platform velocity and are rarefied (spread out) in the opposite direction of velocity. The compression of the waves raises their frequency, yielding a higher note. This also applies to a ping or pulse reflected off a moving platform. The return pulse is up-shifted or down-shifted, depending on the contact's motion toward or away from the hydrophone.

draft   The depth of water that a ship draws, especially when loaded.

dry-deck shelter   Used to store and launch a swimmer-delivery vehicle as well as combat swimmers.

Echo   Name of one of the first generation of Russian nuclear submarines. Also a return ping from a contact hit with active sonar.

electronics countermeasures   Detection of threats and targets using the electromagnetic spectrum. Detection of radio signals and radars yields valuable intelligence in the target environment. Also called ESM for electronic signal measures.

electronics countermeasures cubicle   Small room where the ESM equipment is operated.

EMBT blow   Emergency Main Ballast Tank Blow.

emergency blow   Blowing the water out of the main ballast tanks using ultra–high-pressure air. This empties ballast tanks in seconds, lightening the ship and allowing it to get to the surface in an emergency such as flooding.

Eng   Chief Engineer, pronounced with a soft *g*.

EO   Electrical Operator. Enlisted nuclear-qualified watchstander who mans the electric plant control panel (EPCP) and reports to the EOOW.

EOOW   Engineering Officer of the Watch. Nuclear-qualified officer who runs the nuclear power plant. Responsible to the OOD for propulsion and propulsion plant damage control.

EPM   Emergency propulsion motor. A large DC motor aft in the engineroom, capable of turning the shaft to achieve 3 knots using battery power alone. The EPM is an electricity hog and will exhaust the battery in a matter of 15 or 20 minutes.

escape trunk   A spherical airlock used on American nuclear submarines. The device can be used to make an emergency exit from a sub sunk in shallow water. Principally used for divers to lock in or lock out.

Ethan Allen   First class of U.S. boomers to fire Polaris missiles.

EWS   Engineering Watch Supervisor. A chief who is a roving supervisory watchstander in the engineering spaces. Reports to the EOOW.

Exocet   French antiship cruise missile.

fairwater   Refers to horizontal planes mounted on the sail, which have given way to bowplanes. The term is derived from the potential flow in fluid mechanics, which states that a few meters above the hull the flow field will be unaffected by the fluid boundary layer caused by friction at the hull. Hence, this area is "fair water."

fast attack   Navy term to describe the Albacore hull surface-of-revolution nuclear submarines, as opposed to the old-fashioned Skate class or the *Nautilus*-type boats that looked like Guppy diesel submarines but had nuclear reactors shoehorned into them. Fast-attack submarines can travel at or above battle-group transit speeds and can thus intercept a fast-transiting surface force, which in the days of the Cold War was a major issue. However, the moniker is shortened; the actual title should be "fast attack never come back," based on the crazy operational tempo in which SSNs go out and stay out on their missions, thereby pissing off dozens of Navy wives.

fast neutrons   Neutrons with high energy born from uranium fission. Also called prompt neutrons because they exist immediately after a fission of a uranium nucleus, which results in two lower-mass nuclei and several fast neutrons. Usually fast neutrons will just leak out of the core unless they are slowed by a moderator.

fathom   Unit of depth equal to 6 feet.

fathometer   Bottom-sounding sonar that directs an active sonar pulse down to the ocean bottom and measures the time for the pulse to reflect back—and, hence, measures the distance to the bottom. The pulse is a high-frequency, short-duration pulse that is considered secure because it attenuates quickly and is hard to detect.

fin   British term for the sail on a sub.

final bearing and shoot   Order by the captain to shoot a torpedo after he takes one last periscope observation of a surface target.

firecontrol party   A team of people whose task is to connect a weapon and a target. This includes sonar operators, the captain, the XO, the OOD, the JOOD, Pos One, Pos Two, Pos Three, the weapon control panel operator, and manual plotters (geographic, time bearing, and time frequency).

firecontrol system   A computer system that accepts input from the periscope, sonar, and radar (radar input comes only when the ship is on the surface) to determine the fire-control solution. The system also programs, fires, steers, and monitors torpedoes and cruise missiles. Synonymous with battle-control system.

firecontrol target solution   A contact's range, bearing, course, and speed, which is a great mystery when using passive sonar. Determining the solution requires maneuvering the ship and doing calculations on the target's bearing rate. Can be obtained manually or by using the computer.

firing point procedures   An order by the captain to the firecontrol party to tell them to prepare to fire the weapon, done during a deliberate approach when the solution is refined (as opposed to a snapshot). The solution is locked into the weapon, and the ship is put into a firing attitude.

fix   A ship's position. Determined by visual triangulation or radar when close to land on the surface ("piloting"), or by GPS NavSat, bottom-contour sonar, or gravitational measurement when submerged.

flank speed   Maximum speed of a U.S. submarine. Requires fast speed reactor main coolant pumps and 100 percent reactor power.

flash   The highest priority of a radio message. Receipt required within minutes or seconds.

forced circulation   Forced flow of water coolant through a reactor using pumps instead of natural circulation.

forward   The front of a submarine; "forward of" means further forward than.

geographic plot   1. A manual plot saved from World War II submarine days, using the plot table to deduce a firecontrol solution. Works well on unsuspecting targets traveling in a straight line Target zigs require experts on this plot. The plot is useless in a melee situation. 2. A mode of display of the firecontrol system showing a God's eye view of the sea with the own ship at the center and the other contacts and their solutions surrounding it.

Gertrude   Term that dates back to World War II for any equipment that provides underwater communications. Now called "UQC," or underwater telephone (see UQC).

goat locker   The chief petty officer's quarters.

Harpoon   Antiship cruise missile.

head   Marine term for the bathroom.

helm   The control yoke (steering wheel) that turns the ship's rudder. Also short for helmsman.

horizontal salvo   Multiple torpedoes shot toward the target with slightly different bearings, to increase the chances of a hit.

hot racking   When the number of crew members exceeds the number of racks, the lowest-ranking enlisted men are forced to "hot rack": One watchstander occupies the rack while the other is on watch, and the rack never gets a chance to cool off.

hovering system   A depth-control computer system that keeps the ship in one point underwater. Used by boomers when launching missiles. Used by fast-attack submarines to establish a desired vertical speed (depth rate) to vertical surface through polar ice.

hull   The pressure-tight shell of a submarine, also known casually as the people tank. For single-hulled ships, such as American vessels, this shell is steel. For double-hulled Russians, it could be either steel or titanium. Other navies use steel.

hull array   One of the sonar hydrophone element assemblies (arrays) of the BQQ-10 sonar suite, consisting of multiple hydrophones placed against the skin of the hull over about one third of the ship's length. Used mostly as a backup to the spherical array because the hull array's sensitivity is reduced by own-ship noise generated inside the hull.

HUMINT   Human intelligence, gained by foreign agents or American intelligence officers.

hydrophones   An underwater microphone or earphone, depending on its use. A hydrophone is a piezoelectric material that deforms when subjected to an electrical current. In active sonar, the electrical current comes from the sonar suite to generate vibrations to cause a sound pulse or ping. In passive sonar, incoming sound waves force the material to vibrate, generating an electrical current that is analyzed by the sonar suite's computer and displayed in the sonar room and in the control room.

intermediate range   Nuclear power level between the source range and the power range. In the intermediate range, the neutron level is high enough to sustain a chain reaction but not enough to change coolant temperature or generate steam.

JA   Sound-powered phone circuit between control, maneuvering, and the captain's stateroom.

JOOD   Junior Officer of the Deck, an assistant to the OOD. When in transit, the JOOD is usually an unqualified officer in a training position, is given the conn, and is supervised by the OOD. In trail or on patrol, the JOOD is a submarine-qualified OOD standing a watch to assist the OOD in prosecuting the target, which is usually a hostile submarine.

ladder   A marine ladder is a very steep staircase. On a submarine, it could be a steep staircase or an actual ladder. The former are in the forward spaces; the latter are in the engineering spaces.

layer, layer depth   The top 100 to 250 feet of the ocean, stirred by waves and heated by the sun, is warm; deeper there is little motion and little heating. The warm water forms a layer over the deep cold. Often the transition is an immediate one, going from 28 degrees when deep to 60 degrees shallow. This channels sound near the surface and allows a submarine to hide when deep. It also makes an approach to periscope depth hazardous because sonar may not be able to hear close contacts until the ship is above the layer.

leg   The straight-line travel of a submarine during passive sonar target motion analysis (TMA) between maneuvers. During a leg, the crew attempts to establish a steady bearing rate to the target and establish speed across the line of sight to the target. Two legs determine a firecontrol solution. Three legs confirm the solution. Four legs indicate that the captain is afraid to shoot. A large sign at Prospective Commanding Officer School reads, "You don't need another goddamned leg!"

line of sight   1. The firecontrol diagram's main branch, which shows the bearing to the target, the target at the top, and the own ship at the bottom. 2. A mode of the firecontrol system used to simplify matters for the captain or to set up for a snapshot, in which the target is depicted as a rowboat at the top of the display and the own ship is another rowboat at the bottom of the display, so that the headings of both ships are easily seen. 3. Description of the travel of UHF, EHF, and VHF radio waves, which do not bend. If you can see the other platform, you can talk to him. If he's over the horizon, though, you are out of luck unless you are using a relay satellite.

list   Tilt of a ship to the side.

littoral operations   A submarine operation in water shallower than 100 fathoms, usually requiring the use of the secure three-dimensional high-frequency (under-ice) sonar system and a lot of balls. In the Barents Sea, the Russians think nothing of dropping live ammunition on a suspected intruder, so don't get caught. (Want to know what happens if you do? Read *Attack of the Seawolf*, by Michael DiMercurio.)

locking in/locking out   Entering or leaving a submerged submarine through the escape trunk (airlock).

lookaround   1. A periscope observation. 2. A warning by the OOD or captain to the ship control party that the periscope is about to be raised. The diving officer and helmsman report the ship's speed and depth as a reminder, since high speeds can rip off the periscope and flood the ship through the periscope hole.

lose the bubble   To cave in under pressure. When you say, "I've got the bubble," you mean that everything is under control. The term comes from the old-fashioned liquid-filled inclinometers that used a bubble in a water-filled tube, much like a level in the garage. When the diving officer "has the bubble," he has the ship's depth control well in hand. When he has lost the bubble, depth control is lost and the ship either broaches or penetrates a deeper depth limit.

MAD   Magnetic Anomaly Detector. A detector flown on an aircraft that measures changes in the Earth's magnetic field that could be caused by the hull of a submarine.

main ballast tank   Tank that is used solely to hold seawater ballast, weight that allows a ship to sink or, when blown, that allows a ship to be light enough to surface.

main engines (propulsion turbines)   The large turbines that extract thermal energy from steam and convert it to mechanical energy to turn the screw.

main steam valves one and two (MS-1 and -2) Large gate valves on the port and starboard main steam headers, at the forward bulkhead of the aft compartment. These can isolate the main steam system in the event of a major steam leak.

maneuvering The nuclear control room, located in the aft compartment upper level. Smaller than most walk-in closets, it contains the EPCP, the RPCP, the SPCP, and temperature-monitoring panels (1TM and 2TM).

maneuvering watch The watch stations manned when a ship gets underway in restricted waters.

mark on top Term used to note that a hostile aircraft is flying directly over the submarine. Generally means that the submarine has been detected by the aircraft and will be under attack almost immediately. Usually followed by an expletive, as in, "P-3 mark on top, dammit."

master 1. The designation of a contact with a "master number" to coordinate multiple sources of information. Sonar contacts are numbered with a Sierra number, such as Sierra One Five, the fifteenth sonar contact of the day. Visual contacts are numbered with victor numbers, such as victor seven, the seventh visual contact of the day. Radar contacts are similarly given Romeo numbers. To avoid confusion, the OOD will "designate" a particular contact of interest with a master number, such as master one. If master one is being approached with the intent of shooting him, he may be given a target number. Some ships don't elevate master numbers to target numbers, but they simply shoot at the master contact. 2. What you call a master chief petty officer. They love it, particularly when the XO gives them an order, as in, "Master, assemble the crew on the pier." It doesn't sound like an order; it sounds more like talking to a genie.

melee A situation in submarine vs. submarine warfare in which both subs have detected each other and are trying to attack each other. In some cases, they are both maneuvering to try to perform passive sonar TMA on the other sub, which makes a mess because TMA assumes that the target is on a constant course with a constant speed. In the case of a melee, one philosophy is to "go active" using active sonar. The other guy already knows you are there, so stealth is useless. (This does not work if there are multiple hostile contacts, such as when you are in the other guy's back yard, and your active sonar may tip off other hostile combatants.) When you go active, you get a quick firing solution so that you can hit him with one shot. A second philosophy is to clear datum, run away, and then come back with stealth on your side. A third philosophy resembles the Western shootout, in which you execute a snapshot salvo to see if you can fill the water with weapons to either scare the opposition or kill him with a lucky shot.

moderator A substance that slows fast neutrons to make them thermal neutrons, which will enable them to cause another fission reaction. The means of slowing the fast neutrons is by making them experience collisions with other nuclei, just as a cue ball in a billiards game is slowed by collisions with other billiard balls. The best moderator is water because it is rich in hydrogen, which is essentially a proton, and a proton has the same weight as a neutron. Other hydrocarbons, such as paraffin and diesel oil, work because the high concentration of hydrogen slows the neutrons. Graphite (carbon) is sometimes used, although the higher molecular weight of the carbon neutron makes it a less effective moderator, and more neutrons will leak from the core.

MPA   1. Main Propulsion Assistant. Usually the "bull" lieutenant on board, who is the most expert junior officer assigned to the ship and who runs the machinery division. 2. Maritime patrol aircraft, such as the P-3 Orion, that cruise at low altitude at low velocity looking for submarines with sonobuoys and magnetic anomaly detection, and then drop torpedoes from the air to kill subs.

muzzle door   The outer door of a torpedo tube.

narrowband processor   A computer filter that screens out all noise except a single frequency. Much like the tuner on a radio.

natural circulation   Water flow through a reactor caused only by the heat of the core. Hot water rises and cold water sinks because of buoyancy. Eliminates the need for noisy main coolant pumps, allowing quieter operation.

negative buoyancy   State that causes an object to sink in water, indicating that the object has greater density than the liquid around it.

NESTOR secure voice   A UHF radiotelephone communication system that encrypts a voice signal before transmission and decrypts it after reception. Can be transmitted to the satellite and beamed worldwide. Fast, secure means of communication.

neutral buoyancy   When an submerged object is equally dense as the water around it, it is said to have achieved neutral buoyancy—it will neither rise nor sink.

NMCC   National Military Command Center. A nerve center in the Pentagon where orders originate for fighting a war. Seasoned officers scoff at the idea that the NMCC would survive the first hour of an all-out nuclear war, which is why there are airborne command posts and deep bunkers.

nukes   1. Nuclear weapons. 2. Nuclear-trained officers or enlisted personnel.

Old Man   The captain. Also known as "El Jefe" (but don't ever call him that to his face). Also known as "Skipper" (you can call him that in lighter moments, but in a tight situation, he's always just "Captain").

OOD   Officer of the Deck. Officer in tactical command of the ship, a sort of acting captain. Directs the motion of the ship, giving rudder, speed, and depth orders. Responsible for the ship's navigation, operation of the ship's equipment, and employment of the ship's weapons. Usually has the deck and the conn. Needs the captain's permission to do certain operations, such as going to periscope depth, starting up the reactor, transmitting active sonar, transmitting radio messages, or launching a weapon. Done best while smoking a cigar and telling sea stories.

op   Operation or mission.

op area   A specific ocean area devoted to a particular exercise or operation. Some op areas are permanent, and some are established only for that op.

OpRep 3 Pinnacle   Name of a message that is sent with flash priority to the White House and the NMCC, telling of a dire emergency requiring immediate action, such as an incoming nuclear attack.

overhead   Nautical term for the ceiling.

own ship   The submarine you are in.

own ship's unit   The torpedo launched by your own ship. Your torpedo is a "unit" or "the weapon." The bad guy's torpedo is a "torpedo." *See* torpedo in the water.

passive sonar   Most common mode of employment of submarine sonar systems. Sonar system is used only to listen, not to ping out active beams (since active pings give away a covert submarine's presence). Use of passive sonar makes it difficult to determine a contact's range, course, and speed (solution). TMA, or target motion analysis, is used to obtain a parallax solution when using passive sonar.

patrol quiet   Ship system's lineup to ensure maximum quiet while allowing normal creature comforts such as cooking, movie watching, and taking hotel showers for sonar girls. Maintenance of equipment is allowed with permission if it will not involve tools banging on the hull. Noisy operations, such as steam generator blowdowns, reactor coolant discharge, and TDU operations, are permitted only with the captain's permission.

PCO   Prospective Commanding Officer. The man who will relieve the present captain and become the future captain. Also Prospective Commanding Officer School, a boondoggle for PCOs in which they play in the attack center simulators and board SSNs and try to shoot each other with exercise torpedoes (PCO ops).

PCO waltz   Occurs often during PCO ops when both submarines have detected each other and are attempting TMA on each other simultaneously. *See* melee.

PD   Periscope Depth. An operation in which a ship comes shallow enough to see with the periscope. Certain operations, such as executing a steam generator blowdown, shooting trash from the TDU, and blowing sanitary, can be done only at PD, by decree of the Submarine Standard Operating Procedures manual. Other things may be done only at PD not by decree, but by the laws of physics—these include radio reception of satellite broadcasts, reception of the GPS NavSat, and ESM operations. Being at PD slows the ship, since speeds higher than 8 or 9 knots can rip off the periscope. Being at PD is dangerous because surface ships can get close without being detected by sonar.

pig boat   U.S. submarine during World War II.

ping   An active sonar pulse.

plank owner   Original new construction crew of a ship under construction.

Polaris   First-generation submarine-launched ballistic missile.

poopy suit   Underway uniform, usually cotton coveralls, worn by American sub-mariners. The term's origin is unknown, but it probably refers to showers and laundry service frequently being curtailed when rigged for ultraquiet or when the evaporator is broken, causing the coveralls to stink. A submariner's ideal poopy suit would be Dr. Dentons, with built-in slippers and a flap in the back for going to the bathroom.

port   Left as you look forward.

Pos One   Farthest forward console of the firecontrol system, and the battle-station officer who mans this console. Usually set up to the dot stacker mode with the captain or XO's guess solution to the contact, or shows the geographic display for a God's eye view of the sea.

Pos Three   Farthest aft firecontrol system console. Usually set up to show the geo plot or God's eye view of the sea.

Pos Two   Firecontrol console aft of Pos One. Usually set up to the line-of-sight mode so that the Pos Two officer can generate his own independent firecontrol solution under the XO's supervision.

Poseidon   Name of a second-generation American SLBM.

power range   Nuclear power level above the intermediate range. In the power range, steam can be produced by the reactor for propulsion.

prompt critical   A reactor that is critical on prompt neutrons alone, which no longer needs the effects of the moderator to slow prompt neutrons to become thermal neutrons. The time between generations of fissions in prompt criticality is a millionth of the time between generations of fissions in normal criticality. Hence, prompt critical reactors are difficult to control; the control system would need to have nanosecond reaction time. Therefore, a prompt critical condition is essentially a runaway, out-of-control reactor. In other words, if you possess a prompt-critical reactor, you essentially own a nuclear weapon that is detonating. Run!

prompt critical rapid disassembly   The disappointing condition in which a nuclear reactor has so much reactivity in it that its chain reaction can be sustained on prompt neu-trons alone. This means that it is highly supercritical and its power level will escalate severely to the point that the coolant will be unable to accept the high levels of thermal energy transfer from the core. The result is that the coolant "flashes" from liquid to vapor, with consequent rapid pressure rise. The pressure rises much higher than the mechanical strength of the core and piping systems, and the system rapidly comes apart (disassembles). This description is by definition an "explosion," but nuclear engineers hate that word because the media keeps trying to say that nuclear reactors can explode like nuclear weapons; the *disassembly* term is used instead. Most civilian nuclear reactors cannot achieve a prompt critical rapid disassembly and would merely melt down, but naval reactors with their bomb-grade uranium can go prompt critical. The disassembly would be a simple steam explosion 999 times out of 1,000, but there is a small chance that a naval reactor undergoing a prompt critical condition could experience a nuclear weapon type of detonation, although it would be many orders of magnitude weaker than a Hiroshima bomb. A Russian submarine being refueled on the Kamchatka Peninsula experienced a prompt critical rapid disassembly that blew enough radiation into the environment that it required the permanent abandonment of a 6-mile stretch of land and the refueling pier.

prompt neutrons   Neutrons with high energy born immediately after uranium nucleus fission, resulting in two lower-mass nuclei and several fast neutrons. Also called fast neutrons because of their high kinetic energy. Usually prompt neutrons will just leak out of the core unless they are slowed by a moderator.

propulsor   Sophisticated screw that uses ducting and multistage water turbine blades for propulsion instead of a conventional screw, similar to a water jet. It is extremely quiet and nearly impossible to cavitate. The propulsor's disadvantage is its slow response and acceleration due to relatively low thrust compared to conventional screws.

PSA   Post-shakedown (dry dock) availability, or maintenance period following sea trials.

quartermaster   Enlisted navigation technician.

range   Distance to a contact.

reactor compartment   Compartment housing the reactor, pressurizer, steam generators, and reactor main coolant pumps. Access forward and aft is through a shielded tunnel, since anyone inside the compartment when the reactor is critical would be dead within a minute from the intense radiation.

reactor main coolant pumps   Also called reactor recirc pumps. Large pumps (500 horsepower each) that force main coolant water through the reactor and then to the steam generators. There are three in each of the two loops. A special design allows for zero leakage.

reactor plant control panel (RPCP)   Control panel in the maneuvering room where the reactor operator controls the reactor.

reduction gear   The mechanism that converts the high RPM of the two main engines to the slow RPM of the screw. This solves the problem of how to let the main engines rotate at their most efficient high speed and let the screw rotate at its most efficient low speed. However, it creates the problem of radiated noise. Reduction gears are being replaced by electrical drive, in which the main engines will drive generators that will power a main motor.

rem   Roentgen Equivalent Man. A unit of radiation dosage that takes into account tissue damage due to neutron radiation. It is convenient since it allows gamma, alpha, and neutron radiation to be measured with the same units. A dose of 1,000 rem will kill half the population exposed to the radiation. The yearly dose for submarine personnel is restricted to less than 25 millirem.

rig for black   Submarine term meaning "turn off the lights."

rig for dive   A detailed valve and switch lineup done in preparation to dive. Initially done by a dolphin-wearing enlisted man and checked by a dolphin-wearing officer.

rig for patrol quiet   Ship systems lineup to maximize ship quieting while allowing normal evolutions such as cooking, equipment maintenance, cleaning, and exercise.

rig for ultraquiet   Ship systems lineup done in a tactical situation such as trailing or wartime patrol. The quietest equipment is operating, and cooking, showering, doing laundry, and watching movies are curtailed.

rig for white   Means "turn on the lights."

RO   Reactor operator. Nuclear-trained enlisted man who mans the reactor plant control panel and reports to the EOOW.

RPG   Rocket-propelled grenade or rocket-propelled depth charge. Used by a skimmer and constitutes cheating.

run   An at-sea period, such as an op. Example: northern run (deployment to the Barents Sea in the close vicinity of our Russian friends), NATO run (playing with friendly ships of our allies), Med run (a trip to the Mediterranean), and WestPac run (trip to the western Pacific, usually to the close vicinity of our Russian friends).

run-to-enable   Initial torpedo run that takes it away from its own ship. During the run-to-enable, the warhead is not armed and the sonar is shut down. After run-to-enable, the weapon activates the sonar system (either active or passive, depending on the selection) and executes its search pattern.

sail   The fin sticking out of the top of the hull that houses masts and antennae and periscopes, with the bridge at the top for conning the sub on the surface. So named because they are smooth fins with square profiles when viewed from the side.

scram   An emergency shutdown (trip) of a nuclear reactor, done by driving control rods to the bottom of the core using springs. The term is left over from the 1940s, when the primitive lab reactors had a control rod hanging by a rope. An emergency trip was initiated by the Safety Control Rod Ax Man (SCRAM).

scrubber   Carbon dioxide scrubber. Atmospheric control equipment that rids the ship of carbon dioxide (from breathing and the diesel emergency generator) by blowing it over an amine bed.

sea hag   That lovely and friendly woman in the bar who, by the light of the morning, is revealed to be … not quite your type. POW escape and evade tactics may be called for. Prepare for the crew to taunt you about this for the rest of the run, including posting cartoons of her in the crew's mess.

sea trials   Post-construction shakedown cruise of a ship.

SEAL   Navy Sea/Air/Land commando.

section tracking party   A firecontrol party stationed to man the plots and firecontrol system when tracking a hostile contact for extended periods. Modified battle stations.

senior   What you call a senior chief petty officer. Make sure there is respect in your voice.

shield   A substance that lowers the levels of radiation, including lead (for gamma and alpha radiation), water, oil, polyethylene, polyurethane, and other hydrocarbons such as paraffin (for neutron radiation).

ship control panel (SCP)   The console where the ship's depth, course, and speed are controlled. It resembles a 747 cockpit, with the helmsman on the left, the sternplanesman on the right, and the diving officer behind and between them.

ship control party   The watchstanders manning the ship control panel, including the sternplanesman, the helmsman, the diving officer, and the chief of the watch.

shoot on generated bearing   Captain's order to shoot a torpedo based on the firecontrol solution's estimate of where a target should be, not on the last actual bearing from sonar. When ordered, the firecontrol party locks in the firecontrol solution to the target. When the torpedo reports back, the captain is given one last chance to say either "Shoot" or "Check fire."

Sierra   Name of the third generation of Russian nuclear subs, known for their titanium hulls and high price tags.

signal ejector   A small torpedo tube used to eject flares, communication buoys, and countermeasures. The flares are for exercises against skimmers to indicate, "I got you, I got you, you're dead, skimmer puke!" The communication buoys are called SLOT buoys for submarine-launched one-way transmitter, which can transmit long after the boat has cleared datum to allow a transmission without compromising stealth. The countermeasures are devices built to confuse incoming torpedoes.

SINS   Ship's inertial navigation system.

SITREP   Situation report, a high-priority radio message to a high-level commander reporting the status of a contact or enemy.

Skipjack   Name of the first American nuclear submarine class to have a teardrop-shape hull. Extraordinarily fast but extraordinarily cramped.

skimmer or skimmer puke   Surface warfare sailor.

SLAAM   Submarine-launched antiair missile. Launched from the sail to home in on MPA, marine patrol aircraft.

snapshot   A quick-reaction torpedo shot, usually done when fired upon first or in a situation in which battle stations are not yet manned. Tactic learned from the Russians, who perfected it.

snorkel   A mast designed to bring air into the submarine so that the air-breathing diesel generator can use it for combustion when the reactor is scrammed.

solution   A contact's range, course, and speed. This is a mystery when using passive sonar. Determining the solution requires maneuvering the own ship and doing calculations on the target's bearing rate. The solution can be obtained manually or with the fire-control computer.

sonar   A method or device for detecting and locating objects underwater by means of passively received sound waves from the object or by active pings sent out to be reflected by the objects.

sonar girls   Nickname for forward, non-nuclear crewmembers. *See also* nukes.

sonobuoys   Small objects dropped from maritime patrol aircraft that float on the surface and listen to the ocean below, and then transmit the information gained back up to the aircraft. This gives an aircraft sonar capability.

source range   The lowest range of reactor power, in which the neutrons formed from uranium 235 fission are at a similar level of the neutron source, a neutron-emitter substance intentionally inserted into the system.

spec-op   Special operation, usually classified top secret codeword (higher than top secret) that risks the ship and crew to do something extremely hairy. An example is sailing to within a hundred feet of a Russian shipyard pier in the White Sea. If that doesn't strike you, imagine a Russian submarine submerged in the deep channel off Port Baltimore far up the Chesapeake Bay.

spec-war   Special warfare. Commando operations.

spherical array   A sphere in the nosecone of a submarine that is fitted with transducers over most of its surface that can to hear in all directions except the baffles. This is useful since it tells not only the bearing to an incoming noise, but also its D/E (deflection/elevation). The D/E can give clues that the sound is relayed via bottom bounce or surface bounce, or even that a close contact is deeper or shallower than the own ship.

spin up   To start the gyro and computer system of a weapon in preparation for launch.

spook   A spy, either from Naval Intelligence, the CIA, the National Security Agency, or a nameless U.S. Navy organization, that sends riders onboard to gather electronic intelligence when the ship is on a spec-op.

squiggle   Steam-generator water level control system (SGWLC).

SSN   A fast-attack submarine (submersible ship nuclear). Most submariners agree that it actually means Saturdays, Sundays, and Nights.

SSTGs   Ship service turbine generators. The two turbines aft that turn the ship's electrical generators and provide AC power.

starboard   To the right as you face the bow, or forward.

steam leak, major   When one of the large steam pipes ruptures in the engineroom. The result is rapid cooking of engineering crew unless the leak is isolated by shutting MS-1 or MS-2 valves. Steam leaks are also dangerous because they will overpower the reactor, potentially causing a prompt critical rapid disassembly.

steam plant control panel (SPCP)   Console in the maneuvering room that monitors the steam plan and includes the actuators to control the valves admitting steam to the ahead or astern propulsion turbines. These steering wheel–shape actuators are called throttles.

sternplanes   Horizontal control surfaces mounted at the tail that control the ship's angle and that are moved by high-pressure hydraulic oil (much like a car's power steering).

sternplanesman   Enlisted watchstander who sits in the left seat of the ship control panel and controls the position of the sternplanes. While it sounds like a dull job, this guy can kill you in 10 seconds if he panics in a casualty and puts the planes in the wrong position.

target   1. When a contact with a master number is selected for destruction by the captain before firing point procedures, the contact becomes a target. 2. There are only two types of ships: submarines and targets. All you skimmer pukes out there may as well be wearing a bull's eye on your uniforms. 3. Lovely single girl at the officers club—or better yet, at the nukes' biker bar.

Target Motion Analysis (TMA)   Determination of target's solution by maneuvering the own ship across the line of sight using passive sonar. The own ship does maneuvers to generate speed first on one side of the line of sight and then on the other. Several maneuvers or legs will yield a preliminary target solution, one good enough to get a torpedo hit (a firing solution).

target zig   *See* zig.

thermoluminescent dosimeter   Small capsule worn on the belt that records an individual's radiation dose while that individual is onboard, whether the plant is operating or shut down. While a TLD is assigned to you, it must go where you go; don't leave it in your bunk when you go home, or it will continue to measure the radiation dose as if you are aboard.

throttleman   Nuclear-trained enlisted watchstander who monitors the steam plant control panel and operates the throttles to respond to the control room's call for speed on the engine order telegraph.

throttles   Wheel-shape actuators that control the valves that admit steam to the main engine steam chests. When you open the throttles, the poppet valves come off their seats, more steam flows, the turbines speed up, the reduction gear speeds up, the shaft speeds up, the screw speeds up, and more thrust is generated by the screw. The screw then pushes harder on the screw blades, the higher thrust force pushes harder on the screw, and the force is transferred to the shaft and then to the thrust bearing. This transfers the force to the hull, and the ship experiences a higher thrust. From Newton's laws, force is equal to the first derivative of momentum, or F = d(mv) / dt, and with constant mass this becomes F = ma, where F is force, m is mass, and a is acceleration. So an increased force from the higher thrust on the constant mass of the ship causes an acceleration. The ship accelerates until the level of fluid friction builds up to counter the higher level of force on the hull, and this happens at a higher ship velocity. The ship's velocity levels off at a higher level. Meanwhile, since more steam flowed, more boiler feedwater flows to the steam generators, which become colder, so the main coolant return to the reactor is colder and denser. This makes it a better moderator, so fewer neutrons leak from the core; more fissions occur, so reactor power goes up. The net result of opening the throttles is that the ship speeds up and reactor power rises to a new level. If the throttles are opened too quickly, it results in cavitation and the anger of the OOD and captain. If the throttles are opened too far, the reactor will overpower and experience a power-to-flow scram, which will result in the loss of propulsion; this will greatly anger the OOD, engineer, XO, and captain, and you will be disqualified.

tonal   A pure sound at a fixed frequency, like a bell tone from a musical instrument.

torpedo   A weapon that travels on its own propulsion with the intent of causing major damage to another ship or destroying that ship. Originally called the automobile torpedo because the old definition of torpedo was "marine bomb."

torpedo in the water   Term for the detection of an enemy's torpedo directed toward the own ship, which must be evaded. Immediate actions for a torpedo in the water include these: 1. The OOD orders all ahead flank/cavitate, orders a depth of test depth with a flat angle, and orders right/left 10 degrees rudder to steady on a course to put the torpedo in the edge of the closest baffle (so that sonar can still hear it, but it is substantially behind you). 2. The chief of the watch announces on the 1MC, "Torpedo in the water!" and sounds the general alarm (*BONG BONG BONG*), which automatically mans battle stations. 3. The OOD and firecontrol technician of the watch set up the firecontrol system for a snapshot from the most prepared torpedo tube, with the snapshot torpedo being preset to run down the bearing line of the incoming torpedo in an immediate run-to-enable active or passive search. 4. The OOD announces "Snapshot tube one" (or the correct tube number) on the 1MC. 5. The OOD launches the snapshot. No permission from the captain is required, although he'll be in control by the time step 1 is complete. 6. The incoming torpedo is monitored by sonar. Sonar listens for sounds of the launching ship and, if possible, the OOD determines a better solution to the launching ship using active sonar (the firing ship obviously already knows you're there, so stealth is out the window) and the OOD either steers the first-launched snapshot or shoots another one with the refined solution. 7. The OOD keeps pumping out snapshots—why die with a full torpedo room? 8. When the incoming torpedo gets close and it becomes clear that you are going to die with your boots on, cease worrying. You're a submariner and have already spent time in hell, so you're going to the other place.

transient   A noise that is made by a contact from a temporary condition. For example, someone drops a wrench or slams a hatch or starts a pump.

trim   1. Distribution of weight (seawater variable ballast) to keep the ship level and at a neutral buoyancy. 2. The tilt of the ship either forward or aft.

turbine   A mechanical rotating device with blades that converts the pressure energy, velocity energy, and internal (temperature) energy of a fluid (steam or combustion gases) into mechanical energy. Usually connected to an electrical generator, although in a jet engine or a turbocharger it is connected to a compressor.

ultraquiet   Ship systems lineup done in a tactical situation, such as during a trailing op or in wartime. The quietest equipment is operating, and cooking, showering, doing laundry, and watching movies are curtailed.

unit   A torpedo launched by the own ship.

UQC   Underwater telephone, a misleading term because it is nothing like a telephone. A microphone on the conn is patched into the BQQ-10's spherical array's active hydrophones, which broadcast the voice signal. Similarly, a voice transmission can be received and patched to a conn speaker.

Vertical Launch System (VLS)   Missile launch system on improved Los Angeles class submarines, enabling them to vertically launch cruise missiles and giving the torpedo room more rack space for torpedoes.

vertical salvo   Multiple torpedoes launched with different search depths (one above the layer, one below), to increase the chances of a hit.

vertical surface   The use of the hovering system to bring the ship up vertically to the surface. Afterward, a low-pressure blow is conducted to fill the ballast tanks.

wardroom   1. Officers' mess room. Used also as a conference room, briefing room, reconstruction room, junior officers' office, movie-screening room, and lounge. 2. The group of officers assigned to a ship.

warshot   A weapon that is intended to sink an enemy ship as opposed to an exercise shot.

watch, watchstation   A six-hour shift during which a group of men at their specific stations operate the ship. A watchstation is an individual's assignment during the watch.

watchsection   A collection of watchstanders who run the submarine for a six-hour shift.

waterfall display   The display of the broadband sonar system, with sound data "falling" down the screen with time on the vertical part and bearing on the horizontal part of the screen. A distant contact appears as a bright vertical stripe on the screen. The display is divided into the three horizontal displays: The top is the long time plot with a vertical width of 60 minutes, the middle displays 10 minutes, and the bottom displays 1 to 2 minutes.

watertight door   A very heavy sealed door in the watertight bulkhead between compartments.

weapon control console   Aft console of the firecontrol system, used to line up and program weapons and tubes.

XO   Executive officer. Second in command of the submarine, reporting to the captain for the administrative functions of the ship. At battle stations, the XO is the firecontrol coordinator and is responsible for the target solution.

zig   A contact's maneuver, either a turn, a speed change, or both. Messes up a passive sonar firecontrol solution, requiring the ship to do more TMA to get a new solution. In some cases, a zig can indicate counterdetection (that the contact has detected the own ship) or may be an indication that the contact is doing TMA on its own ship. *See* melee.

Zulu Time   Greenwich Mean Time.

Appendix B

Bibliography

Abbazia, Patrick. *Mr. Roosevelt's Navy: The Private War of the U.S. Atlantic Fleet, 1939–42*. Annapolis, Maryland: Naval Institute Press, 1975.

Alden, John D. *The Fleet Submarine in the U.S. Navy: A Design and Construction History*. Annapolis, Maryland: Naval Institute Press, 1979.

Anderson, Frank J. *Submarines, Submariners, Submarining: A Checklist*. Hamden, Connecticut: Shoestring Press, 1963.

Bagnasco, Erminio. *Submarines of World War II*. Annapolis, Maryland: Naval Institute Press, 1977.

Baker, A.D., editor. *Combat Fleets of the World*. Annapolis, Maryland: Naval Institute Press, 1993.

Blair, Clay. *Hitler's U-Boat War*. New York: Random House, 1998.

———.*Silent Victory: The U.S. Submarine War Against Japan*. Philadelphia: J. B. Lippincott Company, 1975.

Boyd, Carl, and Akihiko Yoshida. *The Japanese Submarine Force and World War II*. Annapolis, Maryland: Naval Institute Press, 1995.

Boyne, Walter J. *Clash of Titans*. New York: Simon and Schuster, 1995.

Compton-Hall, Richard. *Submarines and the War at Sea 1914–18*. London: Macmillan, 1991.

Crane, Jonathan. *Submarine*. London: British Broadcasting Corporation, 1984.

Cremer, Peter. *U-Boat Commander*. Annapolis, Maryland: Naval Institute Press, 1984.

Daniel, Donald C. *Anti-Submarine Warfare and Superpower Strategic Stability*. Chicago: University of Illinois Press, 1986.

Davies, Roy. *Nautilus: The Story of Man Under the Sea*. Annapolis, Maryland: Naval Institute Press, 1995.

DiMercurio, Michael. *Voyage of the Devilfish*. New York: Penguin Putnam, 1992.

———.*Attack of the Seawolf*. New York: Penguin Putnam, 1993.

———.*Barracuda Final Bearing*. New York: Penguin Putnam, 1996.

———.*Phoenix Sub Zero*. New York: Penguin Putnam, 1995.

———.*Piranha Firing Point*. New York: Penguin Putnam, 1998.

———.*Terminal Run*. New York: Penguin Putnam, 2002.

———.*Threat Vector*. New York: Penguin Putnam, 2000.

Frieden, David R., editor. *Principles of Naval Weapon Systems*. Annapolis, Maryland: Naval Institute Press, 1985.

Friedman, Norman. *Submarine Design and Development*. Annapolis, Maryland: Naval Institute Press, 1984.

———.*U.S. Submarines Since 1945*. Annapolis, Maryland: Naval Institute Press, 1994.

———.*U.S. Submarines Through 1945*. Annapolis, Maryland: Naval Institute Press, 1994.

Galantin, I. J. *Submarine Admiral*. Urbana, Illinois: University of Illinois Press, 1995.

Gray, Edwin. *A Damned Un-English Weapon: The Story of British Submarine Warfare 1914–18*. London: Seeley, Service and Company, Limited, 1972.

Hardin, Terri. "Birth of the Nautilus." *Military Technical Journal*. December 1995, pp. 67–71.

Harris, Brayton. *The Navy Times Book of Submarines: A Political, Social, and Military History.* New York: Berkley Books, 1997.

Hoyt, Edwin P. *Bowfin: The True Story of the Fabled Fleet Submarine in World War II.* Short Hills, New Jersey: Burford Books, 1983.

———.*The U-Boat Wars.* New York: Cooper Square Press, 2002.

———.*U-Boats: A Pictorial History.* New York: McGraw-Hill, 1987.

Jackson, Robert. *Submarines of the World: 300 of the World's Greatest Submarines.* New York: Friedman/Fairfax Publishers, 2000.

Jacobs, David. "The CSS Hunley: Coffin Ship." *Military Technical Journal.* June 1996, pp. 74–75.

Kaufman, Yogi, and Steve Kaufman. *Silent Chase.* Annapolis, Maryland: Naval Institute Press, 1989.

Krahn, S. "The Loss of USS Thresher (SSN 593): Lessons for the Development, Implementation, and Use of Standards." Defense Nuclear Facilities Safety Board Presentation, undated.

Kramer, A. W. *Nuclear Propulsion for Merchant Ships.* Washington, D.C.: U.S. Government Printing Office, 1962.

———.*The U-Boat Wars.* New York: Cooper Square Press, 2002.

———.*U-Boats: A Pictorial History.* New York: McGraw-Hill, 1987.

Lake, Simon. *The Submarine in War and Peace.* Philadelphia: J. B. Lippincott Company, 1918.

Lipscomb, F. W. *Historic Submarines.* New York: Praeger Publishers, 1969.

Morris, Richard Knowles. *John P. Holland: 1841–1914: Inventor of the Modern Submarine.* Annapolis, Maryland: Naval Institute Press, 1966.

Newman, Marc. "The CSS David: Confederate Torpedo Boat." *Military Technical Journal.* June 1997, pp. 54–55.

———."The Turtle: First Military Submarine." *Military Technical Journal.* October 1996, pp. 70–73.

Parsons, William Barclay. *Robert Fulton and the Submarine.* New York: Columbia University Press, 1922.

Perry, Milton F. *Infernal Machines: The Story of Confederate Submarine and Mine Warfare.* Baton Rouge, Louisiana: Louisiana State University Press, 1965.

Polmar, Norman, and Thomas Allen. *Rickover.* New York: Simon and Schuster, 1982.

Polmar, Norman, and Jurrien Noot. *Submarines of the Russian and Soviet Navies.* Annapolis, Maryland: Naval Institute Press, 1991.

Rockwell, Theodore. *The Rickover Effect.* Annapolis, Maryland: Naval Institute Press, 1992.

Smith, Gaddis. *Britain's Clandestine Submarines, 1914–15.* New Haven, Connecticut: Yale University Press, 1964.

Stern, Robert C. *Type VII U-Boats.* Annapolis, Maryland: Naval Institute Press, 1991.

———.*U-Boats in Action.* Carrolton, Texas: Squadron/Signal Publications, 1977.

Sweeney, James B. *A Pictorial History of Oceanographic Submersibles.* New York: Crown Publishers, 1970.

Tarrant, V. E. *The U-Boat Offensive, 1914–15.* London: Arms and Armour Press, 1989.

Terreaine, John. *Business in Great Waters: The U-Boat Wars, 1916–1945.* London: Leo Cooper, 1989.

Tyler, Patrick. *Running Critical.* New York: Harper and Row, 1986.

Urick, Robert J. *Principles of Underwater Sound.* New York: McGraw-Hill, 1983.

Index

X-Y-Z

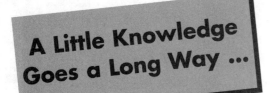
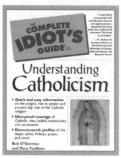

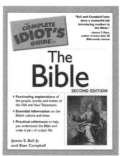

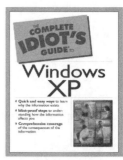